MORALITY TRULY CHRISTIAN, TRULY AFRICAN

MORALITY
TRULY CHRISTIAN,
TRULY AFRICAN

*Foundational, Methodological,
and Theological Considerations*

Paulinus Ikechukwu Odozor, C.S.Sp.

University of Notre Dame Press
Notre Dame, Indiana

Manufactured in the United States of America

The Press gratefully acknowledges the support of the institute for Scholarship in the Liberal Arts, University of Notre Dame, in the publication of this book.

Library of Congress Cataloging-in-Publication Data

Odozor, Paulinus Ikechukwu, author.
  Morality truly Christian, truly African : foundational, methodological, and theological considerations / Paulinus Ikechukwu Odozor, C.S.Sp.
    pages   cm
  Includes bibliographical references and index.
  ISBN 978-0-268-03738-3 (pbk. : alk. paper) —
  ISBN 0-268-03738-8 (pbk. : alk. paper)
  1. Christian ethics—Africa.   2. Afrocentrism—Religious aspects—Christianity.   3. Christianity and culture—Africa.   I. Title.
  BJ1201.O36   2014
  241'.0426—dc23
                                                    2014033016

∞ *The paper in this book meets the guidelines for permanence and durability of the Committee on Production Guidelines for Book Longevity of the Council on Library Resources.*

To my teachers both in the classroom and on the path of life

John Cardinal O. Onaiyekan

Bela Somfai, S.J.

Joseph Boyle, Ph.D.

Elochukwu E. Uzukwu, C.S.Sp.; James C. Okoye, C.S.Sp.

Innocent C. Ekwem, M.D.; Alexander U. Ekechukwu, C.S.Sp.

Michael O. Onwuemelie, C.S.Sp.; Luke N. Mbefo, C.S.Sp.

John C. Cavadini, Ph.D.

Bishop Mathew Hassan Kukah

Bishop Augustine T. Ukwuoma

Livinus N. Odozor, Ph.D.; Bernadette A. Anwuluorah, I.H.M.

Jude C. Ogbenna, C.S.Sp.; Elizabeth (Odozor) Agwu

In Eternal Gratitude

And to my sisters

Anna A. Ebighi

Oluchi S. Aneke

In Memoriam

CONTENTS

PART THREE
Foundations of an African Christian Theological Ethics

ACKNOWLEDGMENTS

Writing a book is always a long-term collaborative venture involving many people, whose efforts vary from the clearly noticeable to the unobtrusive. This book is no exception. From my student days as a seminarian, when the first seeds of this book were sown, to the present, my worldview has been immensely enriched by association with many people. In a painful act of selection, I have listed a few on my dedication page. That list deserves to be pages long, and here again I must mention only a few more who have helped me in one way or another toward the success of the present enterprise.

Many other friends and family members deserve mention and acknowledgment for their help in various ways: Cajetan Odozor; Ekwutosi Odozor; my nieces Chioma Odozor, Ezinwanne Odozor, Edo Odozor, and Uyimeabasi Udoh; and my nephews Kufre Udoh and Uzodimma Odozor. I wish to thank and acknowledge the following friends in a special way for their help in various forms: Obiageli ("Oby") Nzenwa; Nkechi Azie; Fabian Udoh; Francesca Udoh; Nyrée McDonald; Sr. Stella Ihejeto, H.H.C.J.; Dorin ("Onyinye") and Fitzpatrick Nwachukwu; Ichie Francis Amakwe; and Natalie Achonwa. Special thanks to my classmates and friends, Archbishop Fortunatus Nwachukwu, papal nuncio to Nicaragua, and Bishop Godfrey I. Onah, bishop of Nsukka, Nigeria, with whom I have shared some of the views in this book since our days together as students at Bigard Memorial Seminary, Enugu, Nigeria.

Within the University of Notre Dame and outside it, I have had great friends and colleagues. John Cavadini encouraged me at every step of the process to articulate more clearly the subject matter of this book and to seek external funding for the final phase of its writing from the Association of Theological Schools (ATS). Timothy Matovina guided me through the intricate process of applying for external grants, leading to my successfully securing an ATS/Faculty Lilly Fellowship in 2011–12. David Clairmont has been there for me all the time. Dave is not only a valued friend but an indispensable intellectual "sparring partner." Perhaps more to him than anyone else, I owe the conception and execution of this project in its present form. He read everything I threw his way and, as is usual with him, managed to make sense out of even my most inchoate and incoherent thoughts. John, Tim, David, and Jerry McKenny all read the draft of this work in its entirety and offered very helpful suggestions, as did David O'Connor, who read chapter 8 and helped me avoid some egregious philosophical errors. I thank them all. My friend and sister, Nwando Achebe, professor of history at Michigan State University, also read portions of this book and offered me very valuable corrections, especially with the bibliography and issues related to gender in Africa.

A number of my students here at Notre Dame have been part of the making of this book in various ways over the years: Frs. Mark Enemali, C.S.Sp.; Leonce Rambau, C.S.Sp.; Mathias Alonyenu, C.S.Sp.; David Lyimo Eliaona, C.S.C.; Ebenezer Akesseh; Sr. Patricia Idoko, O.P.; and Sr. Reginald Anibueze, D.D.L. My graduate assistant for 2013–14, Alison Fitchett-Clemenhaga, offered tremendous assistance in many ways in the production of this book; she read and critiqued parts of it, and was immensely helpful with collecting and ensuring the accuracy of the references.

I have already alluded to the ATS/Faculty Lilly Fellowship I received from the Association of Theological Schools in Canada and the United States during the 2011–12 school year. Thanks to this grant, I was allowed a year of research leave by the University of Notre Dame. This leave was spent at Trinity Hall among my confreres at Duquesne University of the Holy Ghost in Pittsburgh. The year I spent there was one of my happiest and most productive years in recent times. I was welcomed to Duquesne and to Trinity Hall with the kind of hospitality only Spiritans can give one of their own. My thanks go to the then provincial superior of the Holy Ghost Congregation, USA (now the superior general of the congregation), Fr. John Fogarty, C.S.Sp.; and to the various members of Trinity Hall: Frs. Sean M. Hogan,

C.S.Sp.; Sean P. Kealy, C.S.Sp.; Raymond French, C.S.Sp.; Peter Osuji, C.S.Sp.; Elochukwu Uzukwu, C.S.Sp.; Naos McCool, C.S.Sp.; Bernard Kelly, C.S.Sp.; James McCloskey, C.S.Sp.; John Sawicki, C.S.Sp.; and the Spiritan priest students at the university: Frs. Chike Anyigbo, C.S.Sp.; Emmanuel Ahua, C.S.Sp.; Lazarus Langbir, C.S.Sp.; Isidore Nkwocha, C.S.Sp. The Spiritan community simply let me be and encouraged me in whatever way necessary to do my work. In fact, without the year at Duquesne this work might still be no more than a set of ideas in my head. Thanks, Sean Hogan, for being a very kind and hospitable community superior.

Members of the Theology Department at Duquesne offered me great support and encouragement for which I am most grateful. Special thanks go to George Worgul and to Sr. Agatha Ozah, H.H.C.J., professor of musicology at Duquesne, for all their valuable help during my stay at the university.

My Spiritan confreres on the other side of the Atlantic in Nigeria were also very supportive and crucial in the production of this book. I am blessed with so many bright younger brothers in my Spiritan community in Nigeria. Many of them now teach at Spiritan International School of Theology, where I also served as president of the governing council for nine years (2005–14). My frequent visits to SIST over the years have provided me enjoyable and stimulating opportunities for very happy and serious intellectual engagements with many of these brothers: Frs. Bede Ukwuije, C.S.Sp., from whom I have learned so much about the need for and about ways of rethinking the God problem in African theology; Bonaventure Ugwu, C.S.Sp., whose work on the Holy Spirit is charting potentially new courses on the way we think about and relate to the Third Person of the Blessed Trinity; and Charles Ebelebe, C.S.Sp., whose insights on mission and particularly Spiritan mission in Africa have been a source of new understandings for me. Other members of the SIST faculty have also been helpful in the writing of this book: the rector, Fr. Jude Ogbenna, C.S.Sp.; Sr. Sylvia Nwachukwu, D.D.L.; Fr. Ernest Ezeogu, C.S.Sp.; and Fr. Gregory Olikenyi, C.S.Sp.

As usual, the folks at the University of Notre Dame Press have been most helpful. This is my fourth book with the university press, but the publishing of each one has been a new experience for me. The thoroughgoing professionalism and intellectual rigor I have had the privilege of experiencing at this press is undoubtedly of the best kind possible. I acknowledge with gratitude the help of the interim managing director of the press, Harv Humphrey; the acquisitions editor, Charles Van Hof; the managing editor, Rebecca DeBoer; the production and design manager, Wendy McMillen; and the sales manager, Ann Bromley. A special word of thanks to Margo Shearman, my manuscript editor. Margo worked on my last book on the renewal of moral theology. Her work on that book was as good as it can get; so, I was delighted that she agreed to work on this book. As usual, she has made me sound much better than I could have.

Several portions of this book have appeared previously in articles published in *Theological Studies, Bulletin of Ecumenical Theology,* and *The Nigerian Journal of Theology.* They are used here gratefully with permission.

INTRODUCTION

In 1976 Walbert Bühlmann, Capuchin missionary to Tanzania and for many years professor of missiology in Freiburg, published a book, *The Coming of the Third Church*, in which he declared that we were in the middle of a process of change, "as a result of which the Church, at home in the Western world for almost 2000 years, will, in a short time, have shifted its center of gravity into the Third World, where its adherents will be much more numerous."[1] By whatever indices one chooses to gauge it, the third church is here. Consider this: Latin America alone is home to nearly half of the world's Catholic population. And the Catholic Church in Africa is growing at an annual rate of over 3 percent. With church growth has come a flowering in vocations to the religious life and the priesthood. Today, the largest seminaries in the Christian world are in Africa. Many African churches have become missionary churches as well, with missionaries all over the world. From Europe to the United States, from Oceania to various parts of Africa, African Protestant church workers are crisscrossing the globe, founding new churches. The same applies to the African Catholic Church, whose members—religious and priests from various communities and dioceses in Africa—have fanned out into the entire world on mission.

Andrew F. Walls, the great Scottish missiologist, once noted that "the theological sector has not yet come to terms with the fundamental shift in the center of gravity of the Christian world whereby the Southern continents have become the heartlands of the Christian faith." Walls further contends that even where this shift is recognized as a fact, the implication that this requires something like "a Copernican revolution in theological discourse, is not recognized, and would certainly not be welcome."[2] The reality, however, is that "conditions in the various parts of the Third Church (or third world) are taking Christian theology into new areas of life where Western theology has no answers, because it has no questions."[3] Theologians from the first and second churches often seem to consider issues that are raised in and by the third church as quaint. Usually these issues are considered an "African thing" or an "Asian thing" or a "Latin American thing." This situation needs to change as the world becomes more and more "a single place" and as the church is faced with more evidence of its catholicity.

The good news is that some change has started to take place on this front. The recent global biennial conferences (2008, 2010, 2012) of Catholic moral theologians and ethicists (under the banner of Catholic Theological Ethics in the World Church), initiated by James Keenan, S.J., and organized and sustained by an international planning committee, attest already to substantive theological contributions both to specific regional questions and to the church at large. This global movement is a laudable effort to bring Catholic moral theologians and ethicists to a shared conversation and a deeper awareness of one another's questions.

AIM

As the title of this book suggests, we are engaged in this project with the linking of several conversations: African tradition in its various aspects, both religious and secular; African Christian theology; fundamental moral theology; and religious ethics (that is, an ethics broadly religious and cultural). Each of those conversations has a history, and so to link them means to give an account of how those histories have intersected in the past, why they are intersecting now in a special way, what the nature of their present intersections is, and why we should care about it and advance it. The book does this by posing and an-

A|V: The center has shifted (pp 1-2)

swering two compelling questions: (1) Given the largely Eurocentric nature of Catholic moral theology thus far in the history of the church, what will it take to invest the rest of the church, especially the theological community, through sustained intellectual attention and solidarity, in the history and moral challenges of the church in other parts of the world, in this case Africa? (2) What is to be gained, for the whole church, were this to happen in a deep and lasting way?

To put it another way, *Morality Truly Christian, Truly African: Foundational, Methodological, and Theological Considerations* seriously and, in the main, critically seeks to interrogate key foundational issues in elaborating a moral theology that adequately meets neuralgic issues in the African context in all its complexity and diversity. These issues include: (1) the meaning and function of tradition and culture, with emphasis on the ongoing encounters and contacts between Africans and Europeans from the fifteenth through the twenty-first centuries; (2) the encounter of African Traditional Religion and Christianity, with its missionary impulse; (3) the post–Vatican II permission, better, encouragement to inculturate the faith; (4) the relation (read: accountability) of "new" theologies to theology's history *as* Catholic theology (vis-à-vis Thomas Aquinas or Augustine or Ambrose or the Clements); (5) the impact of political divisiveness in a shifting global political situation; and so on. Authentic ethical living is complex and compound, complex given all that human living entails, from the smallest decisions about food purchases (whether made in an outdoor market or in an air-conditioned supermarket) or voting (stuffing and stealing ballot boxes or counting and allotting ambiguous ballots to one candidate or another) or whom to marry and whether to marry. And as Richard McCormick remarked a long time ago, no one theologian or any other scholar has the competence, wisdom, or time to attempt to offer or even dare to attempt to provide answers to all the challenges that life is throwing at us these days. This is to say that the days of the moral manuals are definitely over, and for good. My hope is that theologizing in such an open way, as I try to do here in this book, will help to bring the church and the entire theological community into conversation about Christian ethics (moral theology) in the African context so that what goes on in that part of the Christian community will be of interest to all as a "Christian theological thing," and not just as an "African thing." I believe that what goes on in the current African church and theology should be of great interest to the theological community elsewhere, given the potential of this emerging church and its current and growing impact on the rest of the church.

Here at the University of Notre Dame I have for a number of years led a doctoral seminar on African Christian theologies. During this period I have been struck by the need for a theologically comprehensive treatment of the section of Catholic moral theology which is often referred to as fundamental moral theology. African and the other parts of the "third church" have long been beneficiaries of theological insights from the older churches of the West. Today, people look to Africa for what it can offer the Christian world, for it does indeed have plenty to offer. However, Africa's "goods" must also meet the test to which other "goods" from everywhere else have been subjected in order to make sure that they meet the demands of the gospel. The purpose of this book then is to show how we can do moral theology today, taking into account both the received Christian theological tradition and the African tradition(s) of morality, and by so doing contribute to the necessary engagement with African Christianity from the point of view of theological ethical discourse.

PLAN OF WORK

This book is concerned with the nature and bases of a Christian ethical discourse that is at once Christian and African. In its three parts, it is concerned strictly with the foundational aspects of moral theology/Christian theological ethics. The first part consists of chapter 1, in which I try to establish the subject matter of the book, provide a brief history of the development of African theology, and identify some of the important interlocutors and issues that will be addressed in the rest of the book. In part two, the second, third, and fourth chapters deal with the question of tradition, the response of African theologians to African tradition, and the Christian responses to the reality of non-Christian religions, all in that order. African theology is being done in a context where there is a living and thriving primal religion. This, as Kwame Bediako would point out, is a different situation from the reality of current Western Christian theology. Also, African tradition is closely bound to African religion in such a way that anyone who opens his or her mouth to speak about one finds himself or herself in the territory of the other. It is thus necessary to address both aspects of this reality as we try to understand the matrix of African theology and the preoccupation of African theologians. The presence of Christianity in Africa in a context where African Traditional Religion is pervasive and the interest of Christianity in seeking converts from this context raises questions both about the African primal religions and about Christianity itself and its claims. This issue is addressed in chapter 4 of the book.

In part three, chapters 5, 6, 7, and 8 build on the previous four chapters as they try to provide the foundational bases for engaging in an ethical discourse that is both Christian and African. In chapter 5 we digest the contributions of Bénézet Bujo to the search for foundations for African moral theology; while in chapter 6 we discuss the role God, or the idea of God, plays as the basis for moral discourse both in general and with particular reference to Africa. Chapter 7 is a discussion of the human person both as subject and moral actor in Christian ethics in Africa. In chapter 8 we take up the subject of moral reasoning in an African Christian theological ethics. The ninth and final chapter is a case study showing how the African church has tried to inculturate moral discourse on the continent. Here we take up the question implied in all our discussions so far of how individuals and the church can engage in ethical discourse and action in the African context. This chapter discusses how, through the Second African Synod and the postsynodal exhortation from this synod, the church has tried to identify some of the more significant moral concerns on the African continent and what its suggestions are concerning what moral actions are to be taken. Thus, although this book is primarily a project in fundamental ethics, its interest and scope go beyond the narrow confines of normative ethics in that its claims and assertions are based on extensive research into and discussions of some carefully chosen practical questions from the African world.

b: 2nd African Synod
post synodal
A: Fundamental ethics

The Nature of African Theology

Chapter One

AFRICAN CHRISTIAN THEOLOGY

UNDERSTANDING AFRICAN THEOLOGY

Theology and Culture

If theologians are in agreement about anything, it is that theology can and does benefit from its location within cultures. Considered as the reflection "on the experience of a particular Christian community in relation to what God has done, is doing and will do,"[1] with Jesus as its reference point, Christian theology, for instance, is further subjected to the interpretive nuances emanating from its contemporary component cultures, including Africa. An African Christian theology therefore arises out of the need for African Christians to make sense of or to grow in understanding of the Christian faith that they have inherited *as* Africans, a faith that they share with many other people around the world. The emphasis here on African theology is deliberate, for even though African theology is theology in every other sense, it is a type of theology whose task is additionally "to translate the one faith of Jesus Christ to suit the tongue, style, genius, and character of African peoples."[2] In Desmond Tutu's view, theology must necessarily be bound by the limitations of those who are theologizing—ethnic, temporal, and cultural, and personality limitations.[3] Every theology therefore

1- How do African Catholic Christians make sense out of the world they meet from a theological perspective.

9

bears the restricting mark of the cultural context in which it is produced, since it is contextual and "the product not only of the religion
it investigates and expounds but also of the cultural ideals and norms
that set its problems and direct its solutions."[4] One would thus agree
with Edward Schillebeeckx that since every theology is conditioned by
its time and situation, it is therefore, despite its deepest intentions, "in
fact 'regionalized,' even if it was not aware of that before." Where
such a theology is "imported" from somewhere else, it is "a colonial-
ist undertaking, even if it could not have been experienced as such to
begin with."[5] African theology is contextual theology. So is Thomistic
theology; so is American theology; and so is European theology; and
so forth. To fail to see that "all theologies have contexts, interests, relationships of power, special concerns," or to pretend otherwise, "is
to be blind indeed."[6]

African Theology as Contextual Theology

The acknowledgment of the contextual nature of theology is important
also because it marks an important shift in theological thinking. This
shift has three important characteristics: (1) new questions for which
there are no ready traditional answers; (2) old answers being charged
upon cultures and regions with new questions; and (3) the emergence
of a new kind of Christian identity apart from much of the traditional
theological reflection of historical Christianity. The theology emerging out of this new identity has particular sensitivity to three areas:
context, procedure, and history.[7] In Robert Schreiter's terms, African
theology is local theology in that it arises from the dynamic interaction of gospel, church, and culture: the gospel raising questions about
the community context, its quality, praxis, worship, and other forms of
action; the church raising questions about the relationship of the local
church to the other churches; gospel and church finding themselves in
interaction within culture.[8] What makes African theology unique therefore is the content and the context of its preoccupation, although, we
should note, it is not bound solely by its content or context, because as
a Christian theological enterprise it shares concerns and sources with
other types of theologies as well.

Some African scholars have sometimes tended to regard African
theology as just a response to the need to present a "purer" form of

the Christian faith to Africans. Thus, one often hears remarks like the following from Onuorah Nzekwu, a Nigerian writer, which sound a warning about the syncretism that characterizes belief in Africa today: "Even though Christianity claims many millions of converts . . . it can only boast of millions of hybrids, who are neither Christians nor traditional worshipers, . . . who belong to no particular faith, only claiming to be one or the other when it suits their purpose."[9] What Nzekwu says here has been echoed by several other observers of the African religious scene—which suggests therefore the need for a deepening of the faith on the continent. Peter K. Sarpong, former Catholic archbishop of Kumasi Ghana, once pointed out that "many so-called Christians have no hesitation in going to the juju man or the fetish priest when it is considered expedient. Newfound churches are thriving on the memberships of the mainline churches. Some members of the latter abandon their mother churches; others retain their membership while they adopt a new church, and see no contradiction in that action."[10] Sarpong's and Nzekwu's views indicate that in the minds of many African Christians there is a war for turf going on in the African religious landscape. In this view theology becomes a means to ensure Christian victory in this battle. In the minds of some the way to win this war is to snuff out "the enemy": African Traditional Religion. Some African writers claim that the missionary effort at implanting the faith in Africa was precisely engaged in this approach, based on a number of assumptions. First there was the presumption that Africans were savages, from whom nothing good could be expected. Although the Christian missionary effort in Africa did not originate the idea of Africans as savages—in fact, the idea originated with atheistic and agnostic anthropologists and other social scientists in the West—it has been argued that acceptance by missionaries of the general European presumption of African "savagery" and "primitivism" had more far-reaching significance than was perceived. Secondly, therefore, "importation of Christianity as understood in European terms was seen as the mighty lever without which other means were of no avail to effect the elevation of the native mind and the civilization of Africa." Africans could become "civilized" only if they became like their European mentors in culture. And the only way to make this happen was "to produce as near replicas as possible of European models of Christian life and conduct—in effect black Europeans."[11]

This is profound. Cf. footnote.

Cf. DuBois 'Souls of Black Folk'.

In view of this socio-historical context, African theology is for many theologians both a rebellion and a quest. As a rebellion, it is a fight against the negative characterization of the African reality, people, and history by outsiders, religious and secular. This rebellion has resulted in a massive shift of emphasis among African theologians to the study and re-evaluation of Africa's cultural, religious, and historical past and has subsequently led a group of African theologians to set about demonstrating "that the African religious experience and heritage were not illusory and that they should have formed the vehicle for conveying the Gospel verities to Africa and that many of Africa's religious insights had real affinity with those of the Bible. In many respects, the African was much more on the wavelength of the Bible than the Occidental ever was."[12] This is the basis of the theology of inculturation that will occupy us quite a bit in this book. However, one must also immediately note that this preoccupation of African Christian theology, laudable as it is, has sometimes also tended to make it appear more like an apologia for African Traditional Religion—with serious consequences, such as the tendency to start theology mostly from African cultural presuppositions and not from biblical and Christian theological ones. We shall return to this issue later on.

For many African theologians African theology is also a quest—a quest for identity, as Kwame Bediako insists. Andrew Walls notes that the African theological quest for identity has become rather urgent now that the Western value-setting pre-eminence of Western Christianity has diminished or has been rejected by many Africans. The question is where this leaves the African Christian whose identity as a Christian had been closely tied to the Western sources of his or her Christian faith: Who is he? What is his past? Walls maintains that since a past is vital for all of us, "the prime theological quest for African Christian theology today is about his [the African Christian's] past and about the relationship between Africa's old religions and her new one."[13] For many African theologians, then, theology is personal, in that it is a search for a place in the Christian sun, so to speak. The same applies to African Christian churches themselves. For these churches, African theology is as well a search for self-identity and relevance as the world grows more and more into a single place, as the center of gravity of Christianity moves more and more south, and as many new challenges arise on the African continent, putting the traditional Christian answers to the test as old formulations are found not to provide adequate insights for grappling with many of these issues and situations. There is no greater evidence for this truth and for the anxiety of the churches about this situation than the various regional and international assemblies of the Christian churches over the years and the different structures erected by the churches to help them address these challenges on an ongoing basis. We will consider some recent efforts of the Roman Catholic Church on this matter in the last chapter of this book.

One suggestion for ensuring that Christianity survives and thrives on the African continent is to make sure that Christianity is "integrated with the indigenous culture and religion," for "without such integration its [Christianity's] future remains bleak."[14] In this view, the onus is on Christianity to prove itself worthy of its presence on African soil. However, while it is true that the faith in the African context needs to be deepened, one must be careful not to reduce African theology to just one of its aspects: catechetics. Theology is broader than that. As Saint Anselm puts it, theology, generally speaking, is an undertaking by "one who strives to lift his mind to the contemplation of God, and seeks to understand what he believes." It is "a meditation on the grounds (i.e., the basis) of faith." It is "faith seeking understanding."[15] The key word of theology is the word *God*—indeed, etymologically, theology is "God-talk" or discourse about God. This word (or some more or less equivalent word), as John Macquarie has noted, lies behind everything that the theologian says, and integrates all the separate areas of theology into which the theologian's investigations may lead him. "Whether the theologian talks of revelation or grace or justification or the last things, these are all understood as acts of manifestations of God, so that if one could give an account of the logic of the word 'God' one would have gone far towards giving an account of the logic of theology as a whole."[16] Even though theology is a different kind of science, it also claims to be an intellectual discipline and it aims at truth. The business of theology is to explain and interpret, to make intelligible and credible, and these are characteristics that it has in common with other intellectual disciplines. "This implies that theology has its own standards of methodological integrity, different no doubt, yet no less strict, than the standards accepted by the historian or the chemist in their fields."[17]

*So far I'd like to see Odozor's work engage Alexandrian Scholars of Coptic or Ethiopian Variety. Do they provide any insights here?

African theology is faith seeking understanding, in this case, within the African reality. Like all forms of theology, African theology is an exercise of reason informed by faith; it is a reasoned reflection "on the gospel, the Christian tradition, and the total African reality in an African manner and from the perspective of the African world-view," ongoing changes in African culture included.[18] Just as in every other part of the world, Christian faith in Africa is facing, has faced, and will face the problem of integration, deepening, and stimulation. The gospel has always been faced with challenges since its initial proclamation, therefore creating the need for deeper reflection on the faith and for better understanding of its content and meaning.

Although we often speak of African theology, it is also correct to talk of African Christian theologies. For if, as Bernard Lonergan says, the context determines or at least helps set the agenda of any theology, one must not forget that the African context is varied. Thinking historically, for example, it must be remembered that different African historical epochs have given rise to different issues—slavery, colonialism, apartheid, the various liberation struggles on the continent, and so forth. The theologies produced at this time and within the various regions of Africa reflect, have reflected, and are bound to reflect the historical circumstances and issues that give rise to them. Black theology in South Africa arose as a response to apartheid, and African liberation theologies have arisen, first in response to various liberation struggles on the continent, and today serve as reflections based on the struggles of minorities and marginalized people in Africa. Some other forms of African Christian theological reflections on the faith have arisen from concerns with socioeconomic and political issues.[19] The issue of poverty too has attracted much attention from theologians, as have questions concerning ethnicity, ethnic rivalries, the place of women in church and society, and governance, among others. In fact, reflection on the so-called social questions is one of the most thriving aspects of African theology, especially among Catholics. Given the proliferation of literature on this issue, it might even be considered more prominent than the larger question of inculturation in African theology and that of women in the church and society in Africa. However, despite the various interests and sub-specializations of African theology, it is still true that "the chief non-biblical reality with which the African theologian must struggle is the non-Christian religious tradition of his own people."[20] This, as Kwame Bediako points out, makes African theology "something of a dialogue between African Christians and primal religions and spiritualties of Africa."[21] Clearly, discussion on inculturation and on the relationship of African Traditional Religion has continued to be a staple of African theology, and for good reason.

The Contemporary Subjects of African Theology

Although theology is God-talk, it is God talk for and by a people. God does not need theology. People do. What kind of people are the subjects of African theology? In a nutshell, the contemporary African subject of African theology is one whose psyche has been affected by so many historical circumstances such as colonization, missionary evangelization, and slavery.[22] Ali Mazrui has referred to the colonial period in Africa as "the era of *territorial imperative*."[23] European contact with Africa, which began initially as a trading relationship, soon turned into a slaving relationship, which was later followed by full-fledged colonization.[24] The colonial arrangement was ratified in 1885 at a conference in Berlin when the European powers partitioned Africa into spheres of influence. Lord Lugard, one of the principal architects of British rule in Africa, points out that "the partition of Africa was . . . due primarily to the economic necessity of increasing the supplies of raw materials and food to meet the needs of the industrialized nations of Europe."[25] Colonialism in Africa, among other things, allowed the European nations to meddle in African political, social, and economic affairs, mostly with disastrous effects for Africa. Consider the following three brief examples. The first has to do with the fact that Europeans arbitrarily redrew the map of Africa, in some cases bringing together peoples of different backgrounds and histories into one state, while in others dividing peoples with the same ancestry into different states. An attendant effect of this arbitrariness is there for all to see in the intractable wars and conflicts in many parts of Africa since independence. The second example has to do with the absorption of Africa into a world culture that is still primarily Eurocentric, an absorption that has in some ways been beneficial to Africa but in the main has had devastating effects in the area of values and norms in Africa. It is right therefore to say that globalization is nothing new to Africa. What has always made globalization in whatever form difficult for the continent is that Africa's absorption into the global order has always (even presently) happened at a pace and on terms supplied by others. A third noteworthy effect of colonialism in Africa is that of the role of European languages in Africa. As Mazrui points out, "The significance of English, French, and Portuguese especially in Africa's political life can hardly be overestimated. . . . Rulers are chosen on the basis of competence in the relevant imperial language. Nationwide political communication in the majority of African countries is almost impossible without the use of the relevant imperial medium."[26]

African consciousness has also been shaped by the proselytizing activities of Islam and Christianity. The history of these two faiths in Africa is a long one. North Africa was home to Christianity from the very beginning of the Christian faith up until the emergence of Islam in that part of Africa in the eighth and ninth centuries. Although the spread of Christianity in this region was halted by the so-called barbarian invasions there and subsequently by the emergence of Islam, the spread of the Christian faith in much of sub-Saharan Africa in modern times has been phenomenal. This growth has occurred in two phases. The first phase ranged from the time of the European Middle Ages up until the 1960s, when many African countries got their independence. Christian evangelization was carried out by the so-called mainline churches, which were all European sponsored. The influence of these churches in the development of the African mind can be seen in three principal areas. The first is the obvious introduction of a new religion, which meant tampering with the foundational myths of most Africans who were converted from African Traditional Religions to Christianity. The second influence was that of the introduction of Western education with its means of communication and the opening up of worlds of insight hitherto unknown to the African. The third was the setting up of churches that were in communion with Christian churches in other parts of the world. The mainline Christian churches have sometimes been criticized for their attitude toward the various cultures of Africa, and accused of looking down on these cultures, sometimes waging all-out wars against those aspects that they considered devilish and uncivilized. The story is not that simple, as we shall see throughout this book. In any case, it is true that there has been a con-

tinuous "turf war" among the three major African religions: African
Traditional Religion, Christianity, and Islam.

The second phase of the growth of Christianity began with the
rise and spread of African-Initiated Churches (AICs). The late Nigerian historian/theologian Ogbu Kalu traces the origin of the AICs to
the emergence of African resistance to foreign domination and colonialism in the late eighteenth century and early nineteenth century,
and to the reaction of many Africans in postindependent Africa to the
failure of African indigenous leadership and the collapse of African
economies and infrastructure. This resistance, often referred to as Ethi-
opianism, "was a muscular movement that operated with a certain
theodicy claiming that God has not deserted Africans to their humili-
ations but has raised a people to restore Africa's glory. Countering
the white man's burden with an assertion of an ideology built around
the black man's burden, the Ethiopian movement believed that Africa
could be redeemed through Christianity."[27] But this was to be a home-
grown Christianity that was different in many ways from that brought
to Africa by Western missionaries. As a religious phenomenon it was
to be a Christian movement "with a radical mission of renewal and
reformation." In fact, as Allan H. Anderson points out, the AICs self-
identify themselves as "a reformation of over-Europeanized Christianity." Anderson argues that "the entire AIC movement in all its
many forms throughout the continent, but particularly in its most
prominent Pentecostal-type churches, represents such an indigenous
Reformation and transformation of Christianity on a continental scale
unprecedented in the history of the worldwide church."[28]

The response of African-Initiated Churches to the African
ecosystem—religious, social, civic, and political—varies tremendously from those of the mainline Christian Churches. For example,
the Pentecostal branch of the AIC movement, relying intensely on the
biblical faith that Christ is the redeemer of humanity, has argued at
times that African Traditional Religion is a creation of the evil one
which must be destroyed, and in this way undermining the rapprochement that the mainline churches have tried to forge over the years with
traditional African cultures and societies, and with Islam. Another negative aspect to the theology of many of these newer Christian churches
is a lack of commitment to the social aspect of the gospel. The worldview of many of these churches often lacks the usual Christian idea of

politics as a commitment to the wider human good. Political power is for many of them a means for proselytization. The challenge the AICs pose in this regard is how to acknowledge the lordship of Jesus Christ and also maintain a healthy respect for what the Second Vatican Council referred to as the autonomy of the earthly order and for the other religions of Africa as sources of God's grace in some ways.

Any discussion on the making of the modern African mind would be incomplete without considering slavery and its continuing effects on Africans and on African societies. So much has been written, and rightly so, about the external aspects of this phenomenon. The role of the various Western powers and the Arabs in African slave dealings has been well documented. In recent years the role some African rulers and potentates played in this despicable trade has also become more of an issue. Seldom acknowledged, however, is the continued devastation of this phenomenon on African societies. To this end, I wish to note just one area of the ongoing impact of the slave trade on Africa: the continuing stratification of many African societies. In many African societies, people are still divided into categories, freeborn persons and descendants of slaves, while some African societies still have caste systems. These are carryovers from the era of the slave trade. The many internecine conflicts in Africa today are in fact traceable to this issue. Consider for example the Hutu/Tutsi issue in Rwanda, as well as the Bassa/Gwari conflicts in parts of Plateau State in Nigeria. Even within homogeneous groups like the Igbo of southern Nigeria many communities are in a state of constant tension and many groups are marginalized because of the stratification of society. As a result, some African societies are among the most racist and ethnocentric societies anywhere, a fact that has yet to receive the level of attention it deserves in African theology.

Some of the current racial and ethnic tensions in Africa date back to precolonial times when various groups were engaged in intertribal battles for control of territory, trade routes, trade, or other particular local interests. However, much of the racial tension in Africa can be traced back especially to the policies of Africa's colonial masters. Consider the Rwandan case, for example. Although there had been tensions between the Hutus and the Tutsis for a long time, it was the policy of the Belgians in Rwanda that really awakened the ethnic demons of these peoples when in 1933–34 they decided on a radical policy to increase the power of their administration by solidifying Tutsi supremacy in the land. Applying the racial theories of the nineteenth century, they classified the Tutsis as belonging to the Hamitic race, the Hutus as Bantu, and the Twas as Pygmies. These identities approximated the racial prejudices that would later become meaningful to people in their lives. Here is how Bishop Mathew Kukah describes the situation:

> The colonialists created physical differentiations among the two peoples. Thus, the white people who assumed that their own superiority was taken as given were merely interested in making the best out of a very bad situation. If the white race was superior, the colonial mind reasoned, where do you find something in Africa that approximated the white man so as to make him a junior partner? This was why the white man believed that the Tutsis were superior. After establishing that, they went on to classify him as being tall, having long fingers and a nasal structure that looked like that of the white man. The Tutsis thus became the white black race of Rwanda. Tutsis then came to be associated with wealth and power. The instruments of power for them were ownership of cattle, the military career and administrative skills. The Hutus on the other hand came to be associated with farming, while the Twa came to be given the lowest rung in the ladder. They were the hewers of wood and drawers of water in the geopolitical power calculation. Indeed under colonialism, the process of power allocation was further delineated thus: if you had a herd of cattle, from ten upwards, then you were rich and Tutsi. If you had ten or less, then you were Hutu. This automatically raised the question of what would happen if a Hutu with two cows suddenly became blessed with ten or fifteen cows or if a Tutsi suffered loss of fortunes and his twenty cows came to eight. The answer lies in the fact these identity formations fluctuated, and so there was a sense in which nothing was ethnically permanent so to say: intermarriages also helped over time to blur the lines of identity.[29]

✗ The Tutsi were the ones with administrative skills who got the chance for education and for careers in the military. Since they were

⌐ potens e.g.)

the ones with guaranteed ownership of wealth, the economy was also in their hand—all this even though a national census ordered by the Belgians showed that they were less than 10 percent of the entire population. What the Belgians did in Rwanda, the British attempted also in Nigeria, though they did not succeed to the extent that the Belgians did. The British administration in Nigeria adopted a strategy of divide and rule in Nigeria through the indirect rule or native administration system. They favored one ethnic group, the Fulani, who like the Tutsi are fair complexioned and tall, with a nasal structure like that of the Caucasians, and with a penchant for administration and ruling. To the Fulani the British granted untold privileges with a view to making them the super race of Nigeria. The saving grace for Nigeria, if one may say so, is that unlike the Tutsi the Fulani were slow in accepting Western education because they believed it contaminated their Islamic faith.

These two examples show some of the ways the genie of ethnicity was let out in Africa. This genie has shown itself to be a demon, devouring African lives in the hundreds of thousands every year and preventing the kind of meaningful progress that can come only from peaceful coexistence. The Rwanda story is still too fresh. And let me say outright that nothing whatsoever justifies the genocide that was visited especially on the Tutsi people in 1994 and 1995. The Nigerian situation is still a story in progress, for the Fulani are emirs in lands that are non-Fulani, and they are prepared to do whatever is in their power to make sure that no one else rules Nigeria. They believe they have a God-given right to rule, and rule they must at all costs. Clearly, the ethnic tensions all over Africa represent a real challenge to African theology and to the gospel in general, first of all because of the sheer scale of the violence, death, and destruction that occurs in various African societies on this score; and secondly, because there is a refusal to accept the full humanity of the Other who is not from one's own tribe or ethnic group.

What kind of subject emerges in the context I have been trying to describe here? First, the African remains a deeply religious subject. Survey after survey has shown that nearly all Africans believe in a transcendent being. Secondly, the African is deeply historically conscious. What I say here must be qualified further. The historical consciousness I refer to sometimes seems to manifest itself more in negative memory than in positive. Hence, many Africans are acutely aware of the negative aspects of their collective past. These negative memories often translate into some of the conflicts bedeviling Africa today as the African political and economic consciousness still struggles to find its place in the universe today. All of these aspects of African life in various forms and to varying degrees inform or constitute the fiber of the African mind and tradition, and form the matrix of African theology.

Sources of African Theology

There are four sources for the development of African theology. The first is the Bible, which as the Second Vatican Council puts it, is "the soul" of all theology. During the 2008 synod of bishops on the word of God, Archbishop John Onaiyekan of Abuja, Nigeria, reported on the widespread attention to the Bible among African Christians generally.[30] Even though a large segment of African Christians assume "an uncritical approach to Scripture,"[31] the Bible is normative for Christian Africans as the word of God, canonical, and "fit for instruction" (2 Tim. 3:16). A corollary to the normativity of the Bible, Old and New Testaments, and a second source of African theology is the uniqueness of Jesus Christ as the revelation of God. He is confessed by the generality of African Christians as "true God and true man." The life of Jesus and his teachings are considered normative by the generality of African Christians. However, what this normativity implies is not always universally agreed upon, as we shall see later in this book. Suffice it to say for now that the generality of African Christians and theologians draw inspiration in some way from the life, teaching, and other events around the life of Jesus—although often not adequately so, as I argue later in this book, due in part to inadequate attention to Christology, which has been identified by some as a weakness in African theology.

A third source for African theology is African tradition. African theology tries to take the lived experience of Africans into account. As has been noted above, "the chief non-biblical reality with which the African theologian must struggle is the non-Christian tradition of his or her own people."[32] Understanding African traditions and the way they have continued to affect the lives of African societies and of individual Christians, and investigating the extent to which the church in Africa has tried to integrate Christianity into African cultures and tradition—these are major preoccupations of African theologians. Christianity came into an Africa that has "a rich and varied complexity of culture, economic, political, linguistic, social and religious ideas, practices and rites."[33] All these form the fiber of African tradition.

A fourth source for African Christian theology is the received Christian tradition. For African Protestant theologians this tradition encompasses basically the Bible and the works of the so-called trinity of African theologians of the patristic church: Tertullian, Cyprian, and Augustine.[34] For African Catholic theologians, the "inherited Christian tradition" includes the Bible, all the fathers of the Latin and Western churches, the theology that is shaped by later Christian writers, including the saints and theologians of the church up until our time—with varying degrees of authority and importance. Included as part of the tradition of the church, and having a special place in it, is the magisterium of the church: the teaching authority of the pope and the bishops of the church, as well as the teachings of the church's various ecumenical councils.

Emmanuel Katongole has pointed out an important lacuna in much of African theology today: the failure "to take the church seriously as the social and historical embodiment of the Christian way of life."[35] In a study of several African theologians, Katongole shows how some of the leading African theologians have minimized the importance of the church in their theology. In a review of Kwame Bediako's work, for example, Katongole points out that although Bediako asserts now and again that "the future of the church is in Africa," he does not do much to show "the type of future and the type of Christianity that will be associated with Africa"; instead he is taken up with "an abstract concern for Christian identity,"[36] an assertion that fails to uncover the complex challenges with which African Christians are faced. As in the work of many other African theologians Bediako's search for African identity stems from a need to sort out historical and theological challenges that arise from the presence of African Traditional Religion and from the complaint and attempt by many foreigners and ethnographers that Africa had no past worth remembering or celebrating. As Aylward Shorter points out, "In the colonial era Africans were made to feel ashamed of their culture. They were made to accept alien values and alien ways of life. They were completely passive."[37] Bediako therefore tries to justify the past of the African people by arguing that there was a historical continuity between African's pre-Christian past and Christianity in Africa today. The former was a kind of preparation for the gospel and finds fulfillment in Christianity, a fact historically vindicated by the massive conversions to Christianity in Africa today. Bediako consequently asserts triumphantly that "the era of African theological literature as a reaction to Western misrepresentations is past. What lies ahead is a critical theological construction which will relate more fully the widespread African confidence in the Christian faith to the actual and ongoing Christian responses to the life experiences of Africans."[38] The question for African Christianity then is whether it can find "viable intellectual grounds upon which to validate and secure its African credentials."[39] Katongole charges that Bediako is not only too optimistic about the prospects of Christianity in Africa, but that his adoption of the notion of Christian identity as central focus of his theology allows him the luxury of avoiding the rough and messy situation that characterizes much of African Christianity today—a situation that could have easily been appreciated had Bediako "invoked the far more basic and substantive category of church." Had he done so, Katongole contends, Bediako would have been able to see that Christian life and the formation of Christian identity find their locus in the concrete communities called church.

The lack of attention to the ecclesial dimension in the work of some African theologians today sometimes stems from a misguided effort at doing "ecumenical theology" on the continent or, as in the case of Bediako, a commitment to an evangelical form of Christianity which seems to show very little regard for the reality of the church after Augustine. Among some African evangelical Christians the church is seen as a great evil to be avoided because it has "distorted" the message of the gospel all these centuries. It is in some cases seen as "the great beast" of the book of Daniel or the great Antichrist with the 666 mark of the book of Apocalypse (13:18). Some contemporary African scholars (theologians included) delight in bringing up repeatedly the perceived atrocities of the church and the exploitation of Africa in the church's evangelization of the continent. "Missionary Christianity" has become a code phrase that usually refers to the evangelizing work of European missionaries in Africa and especially to a negative assessment of the effect of this work on African societies, real or imagined. Since the missionaries are agents of the older Christian churches, the tendency is then to ascribe to them much of what has gone wrong in all sectors of African life, including religion, cultural dislocations of all sorts, moral and ethnic decay; or, on the other hand, to accuse them of too close a rapprochement with and appeasement of African Traditional Religion. As indicated already, the church in this case is the Antichrist, the great Satan, or the great whore of the book of Revelation. For some of these African theologians, the proper theology and the authentic history of African theology are traceable only to the time they became aware of the Bible. Theology is the study of this short period, sans history, sans tradition, doctrine, teaching authority, or church order. The safe thing then is to speak of the gospel or of Christianity in the abstract. As Katongole insists, however, "Christianity will remain alien and non-liberating unless African theologians have the courage to provide a narrative display of the agency of African Christians and their historical and social context." In other words, it is not just enough to speak of the gospel in its own right and category. To try to unhinge Christianity from its historical past is to drive a wedge between the gospel and history, and "to trivialize the social, historical and cultural embodiment of Christianity."[40]

In the search for an African Christian moral theology, the category "church" is essential. It is important to ask what the church has taught as it tries to teach, live, and propagate the gospel, or what the church has done and what it has failed to do; what the church should do so that people can authentically live the gospel within the African context; and what the church is currently doing not only to bring Christ to Africa but also to make the continent a more humane place to live. This particular quest is what informs the last chapter of this book, which is devoted to the work of the two synods of Africa, especially the second. Bediako's point about the current phase of African theology as one of critical construction is important. However, African theology must now find ways to build on insights from all these sources mentioned above as it tries to find answers to the questions that various African contexts raise for Christianity in Africa, for African Christians, and for the peoples of the continent as a whole. Finally, African theology pays close attention to the work of other theologians both within and outside Africa. The theology that emerges from any particular theologian depends of course on the weight and value given to any one source or on how these sources are combined. All of these depend in turn on the interest, training, competence, and inclination of the theologian in question as well as on the subject matter of his or her work and on the audience to which the theologian's work is addressed.

THE SECOND VATICAN COUNCIL AND AFRICAN THEOLOGY

A very important source of African theology, one unique to Catholic theology, is the Second Vatican Council. Before we can discuss Vatican II as a source of African theology, however, we need to correct a number of wrong impressions standing in the way, to my mind, of understanding the history and nature of African theology. The first is that African theology properly so called began only when theologians of African descent started to put thought to paper and in that formal way to reflect on the data of the faith as it pertains to or as it is lived in Africa. If this assumption is true, then we have a problem of immense proportions that is limiting theology to only its academic variant. I would contend, to the contrary, that dating the start of African Catholic theology to that famous encounter between Tshibangu and Canon Vaneste in 1960 or to the publication of *Des prêtres noirs s'interrogent* in 1956[41] is correct only to a point. Modern African theology has a longer pedigree that must be acknowledged so as to assess properly the history of theological thought in Africa and to give proper credit to the true pioneers of African theology. These pioneers include the missionaries to Africa, their local catechists, and the many teachers of the faith who worked very collaboratively with foreign missionaries to Africa to interpret and teach the faith in various African contexts. The point here is that theology as done in the academy is only one type of theology. The work of these other teachers is also a legitimate type of theology that African theology can no longer ignore; or that it continues to ignore at great disadvantage to itself since the theological insights that many of us African theologians gained from our local catechists and teachers continue to be an important aspect of the worldview informing our works today. Take the Igbo church, for example; long before I knew of Tshibangu, I had already begun to feel the impact of the work of Catechist Modebelu of Onitsha, Catechist Maduforkwa,

Catechist Nwabugwu of Ihiala, and Nna anyi Mathew Onwuzuruike of Amucha, among many others.[42] These people, and many others like them, studied the catechism, appropriated it and became the interpreters of the faith to millions and to many generations. In this regard, we should also consider the impact of the compilers and composers of the *Igbo Hymn Book* on generations of Igbo Catholics, an impact that is palpable in all Igbo Catholic communities today all around the world. In fact, it is safe to say that to understand why Igbo Catholics are the way they are, for good or for ill, one has to take time to study *Mary Nne Jesu, Igbo Catechism, Igbo Hymn Book*, and so on.[43] These sources are fundamental to understanding and to the renewal of Catholicism among the Igbo because they constitute the wellspring from which the previous generation of Igbo Catholics drew and from which they fed their children. These children have now become priests, sisters, mothers, fathers, grandparents, and bishops. And even though they all have the trappings of modernity, and in some instances carry long lists of theological degrees after their names, they are still children of their church, the church founded by missionaries and brought to life by the teaching and theological work of the pioneers whom I have spoken about.

On another but related note, theological discourse in Africa today sometimes seems to pretend that missionaries to Africa did not do theology, or much of it, anyway. The fact is that they did. They had a theology of mission. They had theologies of church and of non-Christian religions. They operated out of a type of Christology. Some of these were written down, others were not. If African theology would claim Augustine and Cyprian and others as ancestors, it must also include these more recent pioneers in the canon, whether we feel comfortable with what they said and did or not. Many bishops and non-African theologians also left records and practices in Africa borne of their theological reflections and understanding of the African reality. Consider the Igbo church again as example. Long before the Second Vatican Council talked about pastoral or parish councils the missionaries in Africa had already established station and parish councils or committees. Long before the decree on the laity of Vatican II lay involvement in the teaching of the faith and the running of the church and Catholic schools was the norm. Long before people in the West started to reflect on the role of women in the church, the church in that part of

Africa had managed to involve women visibly in the running of the church in a way that is still not possible in the churches of the West today. Women were catechists and lay leaders at various levels in the various station churches. The Catholic Women Organization in several parts of Africa mirrored the secular organization of women's societies in the area, and as a body constituted a force for leadership in the church as a partner to other entities within the Christian community in evangelization, catechetics, and social service. Whether these initiatives arose out of necessity is out of the question. For after all, many of the advances in the church are made in that way and are subsequently given the necessary theological grounding that they need when it is necessary to do so. It is hard to understand why the missionaries to Africa were unable to influence their local churches at home in the West on these matters. I am not saying that all was well in the African missions. I am simply saying that the African churches were already operating full scale on very interesting and sometimes clear theological assumptions that must be part of the canon in the study of African theology. If one wants to understand Elochukwu Uzukwu or Cardinal Francis Arinze as theologians, or any other African theologian of whatever theological leaning, for example, one would have to return to these sources discussed here or include them in the study of the history of African theology. The main point here is to show that even though it is legitimate to study African theology on a general African basis, it is important to note that there are important confessional variations. Many of these variations can be accounted for historically by taking the reality of Vatican II seriously. This is to say that the Second Vatican Council has had a tremendous impact on African Catholic theology in such a way and to such an extent as to give it a distinct character and slant.

In addressing the impact of the council on African theology and African theologians we must first consider, even if briefly, the effect it has had on Catholic theology in general. In doing this we will not attempt to be comprehensive or exhaustive since to do so would not only take us beyond our interest here but would in fact be an impossible task given the enormity of such an undertaking. There are two aspects to the conciliar contribution to the development of theology in the Catholic tradition in recent times. "One contribution is in the tone that was set by the Council to theological discourse and to pastoral

practice. The other contribution has to do with specifics, that is, with
the actual teaching and directives from the Council."[44] A lot has been
written about the council's general affirmation of the world as a created reality and its invitation to Christians to take the world seriously.
"The Council took seriously the hopes and anxieties of all peoples, including very basic interests that have no obvious religious content. The
*Pastoral Constitution of the Church in the Modern World (Gaudium et
Spes)*, for example, emphasizes that the Church can learn from the
world and must help in critically evaluating what the world has to
offer. The important thing is that this critique must be made from a
positive understanding of the values under discussion."[45] The council
as well showed much regard for particular cultures and situations and
for the historicity of human institutions and laws.

Catholic theology since that time has in imitation of the council
shown a much greater appreciation of and openness to the human situation, to the fact of the historicity of human institutions; and an appreciation of the importance of the cultural matrix as a locus of God's
ongoing revelation of himself in human history. In addition to and
arising from this conciliar openness, Catholic theology in response to
specific injunctions, directives, and impetus from the council itself has
probed, investigated, examined, and dug into very specific aspects of
human life in the effort to be taught, to teach, to challenge, to be challenged by all these in light of the gospel of Jesus Christ. It is safe to say
that when future generations of Christians and others look back on
our theological times they cannot ever accuse us of being lazy or quiet
or unproductive, whatever else they say about our efforts. The theological efforts of our times have often been marked by a sense of optimism about the world as a created order, in spite of the evil and sinfulness obvious everywhere we turn. This sense of optimism contrasts
with an earlier one that carried over from the church's struggle with
modernism, as can be seen even in the opening statement of Pope
John XXIII at the council:

> In the daily exercise of Our pastoral office, it sometimes happens
> that We hear certain opinions which disturb Us—opinions ex-
> pressed by people who, though fired with a commendable zeal for
> religion, are lacking in sufficient prudence and judgment in their
> evaluation of events. They can see nothing but calamity and disas-

ter in the present state of the world. They say over and over that this modern age of ours, in comparison with past ages, is definitely deteriorating. One would think from their attitude that history, that great teacher of life, had taught them nothing. They seem to imagine that in the days of the earlier councils everything was as it should be so far as doctrine and morality and the Church's rightful liberty were concerned. We feel that we must disagree with these prophets of doom, who are always forecasting worse disasters, as though the end of the world were at hand.

The pope went on to assert, "Present indications are that the human family is on the threshold of a new era. We must recognize here the hand of God, who, as the years roll by, is ever directing men's efforts, whether they realize it or not, towards the fulfillment of the inscrutable designs of His providence, wisely arranging everything, even adverse human fortune, for the Church's good."[46] The two points that John XXIII passed on to the council, which in turn has become an accepted characteristic of the council, are the acceptance of the goodness of the earthly order and a renewed faith in history as the field of God's action. This faith is a realistic one and not a utopian faith. Rather, it is a faith that comes from the understanding that the God who brought us this far is not about to abandon us to our fate despite our sinfulness and our ineptitude as a human community. God is the Lord of history who has always sought after his people even when they sin and abandon him. The church had of course always trusted God and as a community of faith always believed in the Lordship of Jesus Christ and in the efficacy of his gospel. However, the theology of the manuals prior to the council had not always reflected this hope and a sense of optimism borne of the faith in the Lordship of Jesus Christ.

The council also left very specific imprints on many aspects of Catholic theology: the importance of scripture to theology; an insistence on returning to the ancient sources of theology; an expanded and more inclusive notion of church; respect for the autonomy of the earthly order; respect for non-Christian religions as sources of truth about the divine reality; interreligious dialogue; the importance of the laity in the life of the church; greater appreciation of the various charisms that make up the church; attention to human experience and to the signs of the times as possible sources of theology and

cf. O'mulley 'What happened at VII'?
This all all very Latin centered

of theological truth; attention to the human person integrally and adequately considered as the center of Christian morality; women; the ecumenical nature of Christian theology; an appreciation of theology as an integrated discipline; the importance of the liturgy as the summit and center of the Christian life; a new and deeper theology of the religious life; a fresh understanding of the nature of ministries in the Christian community; and so on. Someone else would undoubtedly come up with a different kind of list; nevertheless, the one truth is that Christian theology in every aspect of the Christian life has been very profoundly influenced by the Second Vatican Council in a lasting way.

AFRICAN THEOLOGY SINCE VATICAN II

In the spirit of Vatican II, African theology since the council has tried to be open to the world around it. Thus one of its main characteristics as theology has been its dialogical nature. African Catholic theology since the council has been in dialogue with African Traditional Religion, with the theologies of other Christian churches, with Islam, and with other theologies of the West. Virtually every African theologian writing today has had to, or will in the course of his or her theological career have to, engage African Traditional Religion. We have already noted Adrian Hastings's dictum that the African theologian finds that the chief nonbiblical reality with which he must struggle is the non-Christian religious tradition of his own people, and that "African theology in its present stage is shaping as something of a dialogue between the African Christians, and the other religions and spiritualities of Africa. These religions were immensely rich and significantly varied—just as the kinship and marriage systems of Africa were highly varied."[47] African theologians in general have undertaken to reinterpret African primal religion on its own terms, but also with a view to appropriating its riches for their lives and the community as Christians. As Kwame Bediako points out, by investigating African Traditional Religions theologically, "African theology may have been charting a new course in theological method. It is not that this discourse has no parallel in the totality of Christian scholarship . . . Rather, this new theological approach has no counterpart in the more recent Western theological thought forged within the context of Christendom."[48] The value of this engagement with African primal religions varies greatly among African theologians.

Inculturation

A second aspect of the impact of Vatican II on African Catholic theology which follows from the greater attention to African Traditional Religion is especially evident in the discussion on inculturation. *Ecclesia in Africa*, John Paul II's exhortation on the church in Africa, in fact considers inculturation to be "one of the greatest challenges for the church on the Continent on the eve of the Third Millennium."[49] The insistence on inculturation is to a considerable extent motivated by what Africans perceive to be a situation of imbalance in the contact between Africa and the Christianity introduced into Africa by missionaries from the West. In the words of one prominent African theologian, "Contact between Christianity and African religion has historically been predominantly a monologue, bedeviled by assumptions prejudicial to the latter, with Christianity culturally more vocal and ideologically more aggressive."[50] The insistent call for inculturation is therefore also a call for dialogue among the African worldview, the gospel, and other forms of Christianity from the Northern Hemisphere, Catholic and non-Catholic, which make up the world church as equals. At a most basic level, however, the call for inculturation has been a call for the creation of a Christianity that is authentic and African, yet also authentically Christian.

The search for an authentic African Christianity has gone through several phases even before Vatican II and among several theologians, Protestant and Catholic. In 1956, for example, a group of French-speaking Catholic priests openly published their positions on what it means to be African and Christian.[51] About two years later African Protestants met in Ibadan, Nigeria, in a bid to find a program for the emergence of a truly African Christianity. The ferment in Christian theology in Africa coincided with the emergence of African states as independent nations. As James Okoye points out, the year 1965 was eventful for African theology: "It saw the fourth consultation of African theologians and probably the first proposal of what would be African theology by Vincent Mulago. The consultation in Ibadan was appropriately on the Bible in Africa. The scholars compared and contrasted African beliefs and biblical concepts. The second ecumenical Vatican Council 1962 to 1965 and the all Africa Conference of churches . . . came at the right time to gather forces and carry the movement of African theology forward."[52]

The year 1965 was significant also in another way. This was the year when Bolaji Idowu published his now famous book *Towards an Indigenous Church*,[53] in which he strongly argued for the indigenization of the church in Africa, with Nigeria as his main focus. For Idowu the imperative of indigenization arises out of a number of considerations, including the types of questions many Nigerians were putting to Christianity, and the need for the church to secure its future in an independent Nigeria. Idowu contended that the church in Nigeria was being called upon to justify its purpose in the country and to prove that it was not an instrument of colonialism and the enslavement of Nigerians to foreign ideas and powers. "The various questions are all of a piece: they arise from the basic question as to whether Christianity is not, after all, a European institution which has no beneficial relevance for Nigerians, but which has nevertheless been imposed upon them as an instrument of colonial policy by their European overlords. And if that is so, what is the need for Nigerians to continue to accommodate the imposition at this time of day when they are wide-awake to their independent status as a nation."[54] Furthermore, Idowu believed that failure to indigenize the church was tantamount to a denial of the Lordship of Jesus, who belongs in every race and nation.[55] If the church is to survive in Nigeria, "she must respect, preserve, and dedicate to the glory of God anything that is of value in the culture and institutions of the country." For, after all, the purpose of Christianity is to fulfill and not to destroy, to make free and not to enslave.[56]

Bolaji Idowu understood indigenization then to mean that the church "should bear the unmistakable stamp of the fact that she is the church of God in Nigeria." The church in Nigeria must be a church that provides the people with the means to worship God as Nigerians and in a way compatible with their own spiritual temperament, by their own style of singing and praying to God.[57] Idowu compared the Christian church to a powerful stream that is alive, flowing into and through various nations and in the process giving of itself to enrich the peoples it touches, transforming their land, bringing to and from each place something of the chemical wealth of the soils it encounters on its way, "at the same time adapting itself to the shape and features of each locality, taking its coloring from the native soil, while in spite of all these structural adaptations and diversifications, its *esse* and its *differentia* are not imperiled but maintained in consequence of the living ever-replenishing, ever-revitalizing spring which is its source."[58] For Idowu the one big question for African theology and indeed for African Christianity in general is "whether in the pre-Christian history of Nigerians (and Africans in general) God has revealed himself to them and they have apprehended his revelation in however imperfect a way; whether what happens in the coming of Christianity and as a result of evangelism is that Nigerians have been introduced to a completely new God who is absolutely unrelated to their past history."[59] Idowu's answer is that there is only one God: "The God of redemption is the same as the God of creation. . . . He is the same God."[60] In other words, Christianity is neither introducing the idea of God to Africans nor bringing a new God to Africa. God has revealed himself to Nigerians. The question then for theology is to show in what ways this revelation has occurred, to establish the link between this revelation and biblical revelation, and to establish the relevance and meaning of Jesus Christ to the Nigerian context.[61] For Idowu what Christianity brings to the table is the absolute Lordship of Jesus Christ, who is the living Lord "in consequence of whom the church is a living and dynamic organism, sufficient for the present needs of each nation in every age and generation."[62] Jesus Christ is the only authority who should have preeminence over and should govern the life of the church in Nigeria. It is thus time for the church to allow Christian Nigerians the opportunity to hear Christ's voice, interpret his will for themselves, and worship him in a style and idiom that is in keeping with their temperament.[63] The Lordship of Jesus Christ is for Idowu the one nonnegotiable element in the indigenization of the church. Even though Idowu does not in this book engage with the issue of the implications of recognizing the Lordship of Christ for living in Africa, he does insist and indeed tries to show that some of the aspects of the life and teaching of the church need attention on this basis, including biblical translations, preaching, theology, and liturgy. Idowu insists that the Nigerian church, to remain relevant, must present a fresh and unconventional approach to worship; it must be led by Nigerians who speak in a language that is at the same time theologically sound and under-standable to the masses; it must supply the felt need of Nigerians for a church that is relevant to their lives. In other words, when Nigerians embrace Christianity they must not feel that something crucial is miss-ing from their lives. Rather, they must see that this religion touches and sustains them at every moment and in all areas of their life. Christianity as practiced in Nigeria must have the power to convince Christians of the sufficiency of God. They must hear the voice of God clearly telling them in their own languages, "My grace is sufficient for you."[64]

Inculturation is an ongoing concern for the whole church. Born into a Jewish world, the church soon found itself in non-Jewish envi-ronments; it has therefore always had to deal with the question of its relationship to the cultures in which it was taking root. As Luke Mbefo points out, the preaching of Paul at various places and the work of the apologists and early church fathers are proof of the church's interest in finding and maintaining a home in every culture. "The catechetical schools of Alexandria founded by Clement and ex-panded by Origen is a paradigm of theological inculturation. In the words of St. Augustine, in this catechetical school, 'the spoils of the Egyptians,' those truths and values learned from pagans and secular culture, were deployed in the service of the gospel much as later in Scholasticism, Thomas Aquinas baptized the pagan Aristotle and the Muslim Averroes."[65] Mbefo opines that since the abiding truth of the gospel never comes to human beings except in provisional, histori-cally conditioned forms, it is the responsibility of theology in every age to transpose the good news "as it enters new cultural regions."[66] Inculturation in its most basic sense implies therefore the attempt to preach the gospel of Jesus Christ in any human situation. I am refer-ring here to the situation in which the gospel is addressed for the first time to "peoples, groups, and sociocultural contexts in which Christ and his gospel are not known."[67] In this sense, inculturation is synony-mous with first evangelization. Whenever the gospel is preached for the first time in any context, a summons is issued to the context in question to accept the salvation God offers in and through Jesus Christ, an acceptance that must bring about change in the people's perception of reality and in their value system. This summons becomes the basis for the dialogue that often ensues between the gospel and the new host context.

The second sense of inculturation follows closely from the first: a process in which the faith embodied in one culture encounters another culture so as to become embodied in it.[68] Put another way, inculturation in this sense implies an effort by Christians in a particular place and time "to understand and celebrate their Christian faith in a way peculiar to their situation and context" while still sharing in the one, holy, and apostolic church.[69] The gospel of Jesus Christ is one thing; the matrix or the manner of handing it on from culture to culture is another. Thus one of the tasks involved in inculturation is the differentiation of the gospel from the cultural context of its transmission, such that the new host culture can receive it without losing its soul, while giving its own local expression to the gospel. Inculturation is therefore an expression of the awareness of cultural diversity both within a region or nation and even across national and international boundaries.

A third sense of inculturation is, as Pedro Arrupe, former Jesuit superior general, puts it, "the incarnation of Christian life and of the Christian message in a particular cultural context, in such a way that this experience not only finds expression through elements proper to the culture in question (this alone would be no more than a superficial adaptation) but becomes a principle that animates, directs and unifies the culture, transforming it and remaking it so as to bring about a 'new creation.' "[70] Arrupe's definition not only implies that inculturation is a continuous process of dialogue between faith and culture, but also creates the goal of all attempts at inculturation as a symbiotic fusion, as it were, of culture and faith into a new creation that is Christian because it is totally permeated by the spirit and teaching of Jesus Christ. This is not to say that inculturation takes over all facets of the human endeavor "for Christ." The Second Vatican Council specifically acknowledged that many people are afraid that "a closer connection between human activity and religion will prejudice the autonomy of humanity, of societies and of the sciences." The council sought to allay this fear by first distinguishing true from false autonomy. "True autonomy of earthly realities implies that created things, and societies also, have their own laws and values which are to be gradually discovered, utilized and ordered" by human beings. Thus, every created thing, by virtue of its being created by God, "possesses its own stability, truth and goodness, and its own laws and order."

These should be respected, as should "the methods which are appropriate to the various sciences and arts."[71]

Three important points arising from the preceding definitions are worth emphasizing. The first is that, as Aylward Shorter points out, "we are not only talking about the first insertion of the Christian message into a hitherto non-Christian culture or cultures," although this first encounter between Christianity and a new culture or cultures is extremely important because on it depends everything that follows.[72] The second point is that faith cannot exist "except in a cultural form." It is this reality and not just geography that makes it possible to speak of "American Catholicism," "African Christianity," "Asian Christianity," and so forth. It therefore means that to speak of inculturation is to speak of dialogue between a culture and faith in cultural form.[73] For this reason, African theology has been calling attention to the fact that Christianity came into Africa in a Western cultural form that is not necessarily part of the gospel of Jesus Christ and that must be unmasked to allow the faith to become African in a way that would be more recognizable and acceptable to Africans. As Mbefo points out with specific reference to Africa, "Inculturation is a gigantic intellectual effort in faith to find a coherent and cogent interpretation of Christianity for any culture different from its Eurocentric matrix."[74] A third point is that inculturation is a two-way process. While it is true that through inculturation "the Church makes the Gospel incarnate in different cultures," it is also true that through the inculturation of the gospel in various local churches "the universal Church herself is enriched with forms of expression and values in the various sectors of Christian life, such as evangelization, worship, theology and charitable works."[75]

That Christianity is always linked to a culture and transmitted in cultural forms that make it recognizable and palatable to a people in their world is both a mark of the pliability and adaptability of the gospel and a challenge to evangelizers to prevent its being co-opted by any particular culture in a way that is opposed to the spirit of the gospel itself. In his two encyclicals dealing with moral issues Pope John Paul II insisted that it is a task of theology to help the church keep a critical eye on cultures. In his encyclical on mission, he speaks of another aspect of inculturation, namely, the dialogue between the faith and the world of the so-called high culture, which he refers to as the modern Areopagus. The pope insists that "we will do well to pay attention to these modern areas of activity and be involved in them."[76] Thus, inculturation, according to the pope, also means "the intimate transformation of authentic human values through their integration in Christianity in the various human cultures."[77] Inculturation is therefore neither a matter for the faith in only one culture or set of cultures, nor is it something of interest only to liturgists and systematic theologians. Rather, inculturation is an ongoing issue for both the older and younger churches,[78] and inculturation as dialogue between faith and culture is a task for both liturgists and systematic theologians, as well as for moral theologians.

Perhaps the greatest achievement of African theology with regard to the discussion on inculturation since Vatican II has been to remind the church of a somewhat forgotten truth, namely that all theologies are contextual and the product of the circumstances within which they arise; or, as Bénézet Bujo would say, we all speak from our various cultural caves as we open our mouths to theologize. God speaks to people in their various contexts.[79] While these divine manifestations cannot be equated to the definitive revelation of God in Jesus Christ, they are not nothing. On the contrary, without this prior appreciation of what God is doing in the world through the particular cultures and histories of various peoples it would be difficult, if not impossible, for the believer to appreciate what God is doing or has done in Jesus Christ. Inculturation discourse in African theology comes from a very deep place in the African psyche: a memory of gratitude for God's abiding presence and abundant gifts. Like ancient Israel, which because of its living and deep memory of the abiding love of God had gratuitousness enshrined in its laws and commandments, African theologians in their inculturation work are making a simple but profound statement: God is good, God has been with us all this while; God has left God's imprints in our cultures and traditions through our creative geniuses and those of our peoples. Our job as theologians is to honor this presence and to get our people to do the same in gratitude to God for his great gifts. One reason inculturation is no longer much of an issue in European theologies seems to be that European cultures that once had this sense of God's presence in the world are now struggling under the weight of a secularist culture that has robbed it of the memory of or the capacity for appreciating the guiding hand of God at work in human history and cultures.

The Effect of Vatican II's Constitution on the Liturgy

When in *Sacrosanctum Concilium*, the Second Vatican Council opened up the liturgy to the vernacular and to adaptation to the riches of local cultures, it opened up the soul of the African church and of African theology. It is hard to imagine what the African church would be like today or to imagine any meaningful discussion on the distinctness of African Catholic theology without the effect of this document on African Christian religious life even beyond the Catholic Church. For this is the one conciliar document whose impact was immediate and whose spirit unknowingly and unwittingly permeated all the Christian churches of Africa. It is true that many of the African-Initiated Churches had long before the Second Vatican Council started to use the vernacular and to employ African instruments in church music, for instance. The truth was that most African Christians from the mainline churches tended to look down on people from these faith communities as less than Christian for the way they wiggled their hips in ecstasy like David dancing before the Ark of the Covenant (2 Sam. 6:14). *Sacrosanctum Concilium* made all that physical movement acceptable among not only Catholics but also by extension Anglicans, Presbyterians, Methodists, and others; and more to our purposes here, it made it respectable to theologize about the way to do these things. In at least four ways the constitution saved African worship and theology. First, it made it possible for African Catholics to do something that is in the genes of every African: to celebrate ritualistically. Faith becomes a celebration, one that engages the totality of the human person. Elochukwu Uzukwu's magisterial work *Worship as Body Language* succinctly captures this fact.[80] Second, it freed the African Christian aesthetic imagination. African art made its way into the sanctuaries of African Catholic churches and chapels, and African musical creativity was let loose. Third, African liturgical musicians were able to move to the forefront of a catechetical renewal in Africa. Through the music melodiously rendered in the various African languages and in ways that touch the African soul, they have also been able to transmit profound theological truths about God, Christ, the Holy Spirit, the Blessed Mother of God, the church, the various sacraments (especially the Eucharist), and have been able to teach moral truths about how to live well as human beings and especially as Christians in this world. Fourth, for many years African theology was almost completely synonymous with liturgical inculturation. Through the discussion on adaptation, indigenization, and ultimately inculturation, discussions that basically began in the liturgical area, and through the decree on the liturgy, the Second Vatican Council created and enlarged the African theological space for further explorations in all aspects of theology. Inculturation discourse in African Catholic theology is not comprehensible without this conciliar constitution. Perhaps the one word best describing the effect of *Sacrosanctum Concilium* on African theology is *revolutionary*. Why has this document had so much impact on African theology? Aside from its specific directives, this text touches on something central to most religions: worship. As Joseph Cardinal Cordeiro points out, worship is something which through its very nature "touches life, springs from life, and flows into the rumble and tumble of life." Life and worship are so inseparable and intimately connected that "freshness and newness in the mode of worship was bound to send ripple effects into the lives of the faithful."[81]

The council did not devote any special text to theology as such. While everything it says has theological implications, its directives concerning the renewal of theological studies in the church are contained in *Optatam Totius*. Numbers 13–18 of this document deal with the review of ecclesiastical studies in general. Here it insists, among other things, that students in preparation for the priesthood must be trained in Latin and philosophy, and be exposed to sound scholarly methods and to a coherent knowledge of the world, nature, and God, guided by the philosophical tradition of lasting value (presumably Scholasticism in general and Thomism in particular, as previously decreed by Pope Leo XIII in *Aeterni Patris*). The decree goes on to say, "Students are to be trained most diligently in the study of scripture which ought to be the very soul of theology." In addition, the council insisted that attention be paid to the study of the fathers, the medievals, especially Thomas Aquinas, and moral theology, which itself ought to be renewed through lively and intimate contact with scripture and other aspects of theology. Students should also be introduced to "fuller knowledge of the churches and ecclesiastical communions separated from the Holy See, and to knowledge of whatever other religions are most commonly found in the particular religion of interest to them or wherein they are located or most conversant with." The aim is to help them recognize "what by God's grace is good and true" in these religions, and to learn and reject what is false (in them) in order "to share the full light of truth with those who lack it."[82]

The Bible in African Theology

One very important effect of *Optatam Totius* on African theology is that it has drawn African Catholic theology to a deeper engagement with the scriptures. The late Justin Ukpong has divided the history of African biblical interpretation/studies into three parts: the 1930s to the 1970s; the 1970s to the 1990s; the 1990s to the present.[83] In the first phase African scriptural studies were reactive and apologetic, founded on a desire to legitimize African religions and cultures through the comparative method of the study of religions. In the second phase, scholars paid attention to the African context as a resource for biblical interpretation; this period was dominated by interests in inculturation and liberation. Ukpong states that the period from 1990 was proactive, recognizing the African reader as a subject of biblical interpretation. As he puts it, in this period "the African context is used as a resource in the hermeneutic encounter with the Bible." The two main approaches, which he identifies as inculturation and liberation, crystallize. "The inculturation approach is expressed in two models . . . all Africa-in-the-Bible studies and the evaluative studies. . . . The liberation approach is expressed in liberation hermeneutics, black theology and feminist hermeneutics."[84] In the third phase, African biblical interpretation was more confident, more proactive, seeking to make an original contribution to the discipline of biblical studies at large by reading the Bible in terms of specific African contexts, such as racial oppression in South Africa and throughout the continent. During this period African biblical interpretation sought to integrate the perspective of the ordinary reader in the interpretation it offers the meaning of the biblical text.

Two things must be noted in discussing the question of the Bible in African theology. First, several factors other than the directives of the Second Vatican Council influenced the growth of biblical studies. As Ukpong rightly shows, interest in the Bible in Africa predates the Second Vatican Council. This interest was originally located in the Protestant churches, for historical reasons predating the arrival of Christianity in Africa in the modern era. Second, even within the Catholic Church the rise in biblical studies owes its origin in modern times to the great renewal of biblical studies that started in the 1930s and was given a decisive push and direction by Pope Pius XII in his famous encyclical *Divino Aflante Spiritu*. The directives of the Second Vatican Council in *Optatam Totius* and in *Dei Verbum* for the renewal of biblical studies in some ways merely ratified what was already afoot within the church. Even so, we cannot underestimate the effect of the conciliar directive on the development of scripture studies and subsequently the effect it has had on African theology. With the council's blessing, biblical studies in Africa has been one of the areas of African theology that has shown the greatest ecumenical bent.

The impact of the Second Vatican Council on biblical studies in African Catholic theology extends well beyond biblical interpretation and into all aspects of the understanding of the Bible as word of God. In the first place, the general revision of the lectionary and the arrangement providing more biblical texts in the liturgy over certain cycles have increased biblical awareness on the continent. In many parts of the continent people have turned biblical passages into hymns and recited or sung the Psalms in their own local languages.[85] Partly in response to the council and to the challenge from the Pentecostal movement, Catholic biblical studies groups have sprung up and are flourishing in many parishes throughout the continent. This general openness to the Bible as word of God has in turn led many more Catholic priests, sisters, and laypeople into earning specialized degrees in the Bible from universities in Europe, North America, and sometimes within Africa.

Another important area feeling the influence of Vatican II's directives on biblical studies in Africa is that of the pastoral formation of the clergy. As a seminarian at Bigard Memorial Seminary in Enugu, Nigeria, in the 1980s, I witnessed firsthand the reality I am writing about here. We were required to study at least two years of intensive Hebrew and Greek in addition to classes in general and particular aspects of the Bible, Old and New Testament exegesis, and so forth. The second year of theological studies included oral examinations on Old Testament exegesis in which students were required to translate and parse passages from the book of Isaiah. For final examinations in biblical exegesis students were given whole passages from the book of Jonah. I mention this to show how even at that level of ministerial training African seminaries took seriously the injunction from the Second Vatican Council on the importance of scripture for theological education; this is hardly the case with their peers at that level of education in some other parts of the world. A quick look at the program of studies of a number of African seminaries and theological institutes reveals similar emphases on biblical studies all across the continent. I mention three of these institutes in no particular order of importance: Spiritan International School of Theology (SIST), Enugu, Nigeria; Tangaza College, Nairobi, Kenya; Facultés Catholiques de Kinshasa, Democratic Republic of Congo; and St. Augustine's College, Johannesburg, South Africa. Let us consider the programs of SIST and Kinshasa in some detail.

SIST offers a joint B. A. in religious studies with the University of Nigeria, Nsukka, and an M. A. in theology with Duquesne University in Pittsburgh, in the United States. The B. A. in religious studies taken in the third year of theological studies is a step toward obtaining the M. A. in theology in the fourth year of theological studies. The beauty of this program is that it incorporates the best in theological studies with the best in religious studies all at once; the offerings in the area of scriptural studies are strong. In the first year of study at SIST the student is required to take about twenty-three credit hours of classes in the first of the two semesters that make up the year, and another twenty-one credit hours in the second semester of the same year. This is the general distribution of work for the entire four years of study in this institute. In the first semester of the first year students take two credit hours of biblical Greek, three credit hours of biblical Hebrew, two credit hours in a course called "the peoples of the Old Testament: The history," and two credit hours on the Pentateuch. Thus, in this first semester nine hours of credits are devoted to biblical studies or studies related to it. This represents over one third of the course offerings in this one segment of the year. In the second semester of the same year five more hours are devoted to courses on the background to the New Testament and biblical Greek, leaving the rest of the space to other theological and ancillary courses. In the first semester of the second year of study, students return to the study of the first two synoptic gospels, Mark and Matthew. In the second semester they take up the gospel of Luke and Acts of the Apostles. Courses on Hebrew poetry, the theology of the Old Testament, prophets in the religion of the Old Testament, the close of the New Testament era, wisdom literature, and Paul take up a considerable amount of space in the second and third years of study. In the final year there are courses on themes in biblical theology and on the community of the beloved disciple. All of these courses are remarkably situated within a very busy program that incorporates the usual and expected aspects of theological studies at this level, in areas such as systematic theology, moral theology, pastoral theology, liturgy and practical theology, administration and music, and so forth.[86]

In Kinshasa we also see heavy emphasis on biblical studies in the curriculum of studies. In its program of studies for 2007–9[87] we observe that like the one at SIST this program is very much multifaceted. In the first year of theological studies at Kinshasa there are courses on the Old Testament, initiation into biblical exegetical methods, the socioeconomic context of the New Testament, and an introduction to New Testament Greek and to the Hebrew Bible. In the rest of this program there are studies in various biblical languages, the gospel of John, the works of Saint Paul, and various biblical themes, as well as courses on the synoptics and other New and Old Testament works. The same emphasis on biblical studies is observable in the published handbook of Tangaza College in Nairobi, Kenya.[88] Here, there are courses on biblical methodology, the Song of Songs, the parables, the shorter works of the Old Testament, biblical foundations for world mission, the epistles to the Colossians and to the Ephesians, biblical foundations of the charismatic movement, apocalyptic literature in the Bible, the historical books of the Old Testament, medical traditions in the New Testament, Hebrews, biblical hermeneutics, and so on. Of course there are also many courses on various biblical languages.

The discussion in this section is not meant to be exhaustive. Rather, the intention is to show that the Second Vatican Council's injunction on the renewal of theological studies in a scripture-centered way has had tremendous impact on theological education and training in many of Africa's theological schools. Two other areas of theological studies in Africa merit brief discussion: moral theology and mission studies. Moral theology was one of the last areas in the curriculum of African theological institutes to be affected by developments from the Second Vatican Council. For example, even as we were being taught the latest in biblical exegesis at Bigard seminary, we were still stuck in other areas of theology in the manualist tradition, which had been the hallmark of theological education in the Catholic Church before the Second Vatican Council. In moral theology, for instance, we were still debating in one of my classes how many drops of water would invalidate the sacramental matter. And even when it did catch up, in some ways moral theology in African seminaries has mostly been interested in applied aspects of the discipline. Thus, for example, much has been written about issues of poverty and development, marriage, the ethics of governance, and of course HIV/AIDS. Lacking for the most part has been a sustained discussion on foundational and methodological aspects of the discipline. In this regard one has to reckon with the pioneering work of Bénézet Bujo, Laurenti Magesa, and Lucius Ugorji, to name a few. Mission studies, on the other hand, have had a tremendous revival on the continent since the Second Vatican Council. The reason is not hard to imagine. First of all, international missionary groups on the continent had to reassess the very basis for their existence in light of the mission orientation coming out of the Second Vatican Council. Second, African theologians themselves in the years following the council devoted considerable energy to assessing the effect of the missionary enterprise on the continent's life and future. Third, African religious communities and even dioceses found themselves sending missionaries to other parts of the continent and of the Christian world in the years after the Second Vatican Council. Therefore, they had to think through some of the things they were doing, the reasons for doing them, whether they would continue to do them, and how best to do them in light of the teachings and orientations of the council on mission. In summary, therefore, some of the issues preoccupying African theologians and African theology for some time now may be described thus: "the need to develop an African theology that is African and Christian at the same time; a theology that respects and takes the African reality seriously; a theology which is both anchored in solid scriptural and ecclesial moorings but which is also independent and culturally distinct as an African contribution to the Church and to religious thought in general."[89]

African Theology beyond the Council

Just as it is correct to say that African theology had in many ways started to come alive before Vatican II, it is equally correct to assert that in spite of the impetus provided by the council, African theology has in many ways gone beyond Vatican II. While trying to stay open to or even to understand the spirit of Vatican II, this theology has also become ever more open to many other impulses. Much has happened since Vatican II: many more nations have become independent in Africa; many wars have been fought on the continent; various experiments at governance have happened there; two African synods have taken place; HIV/AIDS has become an issue; many African countries have become severely indebted; Islam has become more a challenge than ever before; the Internet has been invented; globalization has accelerated; the sexual revolution has taken new turns and twists; clergy sex abuse has become an issue of international concern; John Paul II has become pope, and so has Benedict XVI; Benedict XVI has resigned the papacy in a move that is unprecedented for the last six hundred years or so; Francis has become pope and is quickly putting his own stamp on the papacy; the seminaries and religious houses of many countries in the West have shrunk considerably; the churches of the Southern Hemisphere have become missionary churches in a serious way; women have found a voice in the church and in the world as never before—the list goes on and on. It is therefore a bit unrealistic to imagine that the council could have foreseen all these events or even been able to supply the guidelines for our theologizing about them. It needs to be said as well that in addition to inspiration from the council we must not forget that African theology owes a lot of its current vibrancy to another magisterial act: the Kampala declaration of Pope Paul VI, in which he insisted that the African church must develop its own brand of Christianity and even went on to suggest how this could happen.[90]

In the current African scene, many active younger theologians have arisen who in their training and historically have known no other church but that of the times after Vatican II. Even when we appreciate the fact that African theology is still grappling with the impact of Vatican II (as is the case with other theologies in the church), we must as well remember that these younger theologians have many interests and labor under a lot more influences than those coming directly from the council. For example, these younger theologians have shown interest in the question of the HIV/AIDS pandemic from various points of view.[91] Some of these theologians, like Bede Ukwuije at SIST, are involved in rethinking the very notion of God in African theology.[92] Bonaventure Ugwu,[93] his colleague at SIST, has shown considerable interest in pneumatology. Sylvia Nwachukwu[94] has devoted attention to the issue of Creation; Ernest Ezeogu has spent considerable time researching and arguing for the African origins of Jesus.[95] Anthony Akinwale has been working on ways to retrieve Aquinas for African theology;[96] Francis Oborji has continued the study of African religion from his location in Rome;[97] while Patrick Chibuko continues the work of liturgical inculturation with a focus on the various sacraments.[98] Léonard Santedi Kinkupu, from the Democratic Republic of Congo, studies inculturation from a dogmatic point of view;[99] while Anne Nasimiyu-Wasike continues the work of theologizing from a feminist standpoint of the critique of African and ecclesial structures,[100] as do several other women, including her compatriot Teresia Hinga,[101] who teaches currently at Santa Clara University. The list is indeed very long.

African theology is changing especially because the objects of its interest are becoming more varied. For example, due to the many changes taking place on the continent, the claim that ATR is the principal interlocutor of African Christian theology can no longer be asserted without qualification. The primal religions of Africa now share this honor with many other realities on the continent and with Islam. African Christian theology must pay increasing attention to these other voices. So far, as well, African theology has operated out of a limited theology of God. Beyond the very warranted assertion about African societies being suffused with the reality and knowledge of the divine, this has yet generally to lead believers on the continent into a full discourse on the reality of the one whom Jesus called Father, and on what this fuller understanding of the reality of God could mean for religious, social, and political life on the continent. It is my belief that African understanding of God needs to be completed and complemented, or even corrected, by the teaching of Jesus on God, as is the case all over the world and in all ages. This is a discourse several African theologians are, thankfully, beginning to pay attention to.[102] A third area needing attention in African theology is anthropology.[103] Traditional African anthropology, rich as it is, needs completion from the Christian point of view. This is another area where attention to the teaching of the Second Vatican Council could be of tremendous help. I will return to many of these questions later in this book.

African theology after Vatican II owes its vitality to quite a few other factors in addition to that council. The council alone cannot bear the weight of the differences in theological interests and tastes which are evident in work of the various generations of African theologians active since the conciliar era. There is sometimes a tendency in certain Catholic quarters to look at the council as the last word on everything. Thus, whatever came before the council was wrong or at best ugly and archaic in contradistinction to what came from and after the council. There is also a type of conciliar fundamentalism at work in the church today to which various sides on any given issue in the church sometimes fall prey, much as with scriptural fundamentalism. The council is often invoked in defense of or as refutation of all sorts of causes and ideas or as having provided guidance on everything about the faith. It is good to remember that the council has not abrogated all other aspects of the tradition and teaching of the church. Thus, as Joseph Ratzinger reminds us, "Despite all the good to be found in the text it produced, the last word about the historical value of Vatican Council II has yet to be spoken. If in the end it will be numbered among the highlights of Church history depends on those who will transform its words into the life of the Church."[104] Implied here is that fifty years is still too short a time to gauge the impact of such a monumental undertaking as the Second Vatican Council. This is not surprising, for after all we are still trying to grapple with Nicaea, Chalcedon, and Trent. This is a point to bear in mind even as we celebrate the great contributions of this monumental council.

AFRICAN CHRISTIAN THEOLOGICAL ETHICS

My interest in this book goes beyond the general discussion on African theology; it is rather to show how we can do moral theology today taking into account both the received Christian theological tradition and the African tradition(s) of morality, and by so doing contribute to the necessary engagement between African tradition and African Christianity from the point of view of theological ethical discourse. In other words, this work is not really about African theology in general. It is about African Christian ethics/moral theology, which of course is an aspect of African theology. As I have already indicated, many of the writings by African scholars on the encounter between Christianity and African cultures are generally concerned with several issues: correcting long-held erroneous impressions created and perpetrated by some Western scholars who believed that Africa had no significant cultures, traditions, or any significant religious insights before the advent of Christianity; showing that Africa was a deeply religious continent whose cultures and traditions needed very little enrichment from anyone else, Christian or otherwise; attempting to indicate ways African traditions and cultures can enrich and be enriched by the Christian message (inculturation). This book seeks to add to and to develop this last dimension of the discourse on the encounter between Christianity and African traditions, particularly from the point of view of ethics.

The search for an African theological ethics, Christian and African at once, is an important aspect of the larger discourse on inculturation in contemporary African Christian theology. This search is undertaken on three presuppositions. First, it assumes the uniqueness of the African as subject, and as agent, of morality. Africans (like any other peoples) have an exceptional sense of themselves, given the particular historical, economic, religious, and other social circumstances of their lives. Second, and more specifically, it assumes that African Christians, who are products of their African roots, also have had something "happen" to them as a result of their faith in Jesus Christ and as a result of their membership in the church of Christ. This faith and ecclesial belonging have shaped, should have shaped, ought to shape their attitudes, perceptions of reality, perspectives, and ability to make moral decisions and choices in such a way that these Africans have become, should have become, or should become "something different" from their compatriots who are not Christians. Third, it assumes, as many philosophers and theologians have pointed out in recent years, that traditions and cultures provide the most basic platform on which we all stand to name and make sense of reality by providing us with language and other tools for describing and evaluating reality—initially at least. Since this is no less the same for Africans, the search for an African moral theology would also be a search for the impact of the African traditions on the African Christian, and vice versa, in the search for what is right or wrong and in the ways these determinations are made. Thus, African moral theology is ethics; it is ethics done from an African perspective; it is ethics done from a Christian theological standpoint.

Exploring how these three aspects blend, or can blend, in order to provide a coherent basis for moral guidance, for moral decision-making, and for moral action—that is the task of African Christian moral theology as envisaged in this book. There are thus two very broad aims here: The first is to bring greater theological clarity to the issue of the relationship between Christianity and African tradition in the area of ethical foundations. The second aim is to provide a constructive example of what fundamental moral theology done from an African and Christian (especially Catholic) moral theological point of view could look like.

What I have said so far assumes that it is possible to speak of an ethic that is both theologically Christian and African. We are faced in this regard with a question that has been part of a larger issue within Christian ethical discourse in recent times, that is, the issue of the distinctiveness of Christian ethics, and even more particularly, whether an ethics that speaks from distinct subsets of human traditions is possible. It is difficult enough to conceptualize an ethic that is both ethic and Christian, and as the debate, which has gone on for a long time, has shown, it is even more difficult when we tag "African" to that complicated phrase. And considering that many people have trouble seeing how anything good can come out of Africa, the notion of African Christian theological ethics is even more daunting. Others might, out of sheer political correctness, voice agreement with such an idea, even though deeply convinced that such a notion as an African Christian ethics is nothing but an oxymoron.

It is perhaps pertinent at this stage to point to some further difficulties relating to classification in ethics in general and to African morality in particular. We have so far in this work used the terms *ethics* and *morality* interchangeably. Some moral philosophers use the term *ethics* to refer to "the articulated systematic thinking" that underlies society's moral codes and associated moral behavior.[105] *Morality*, on the other hand, is said to refer to "a set of social rules, principles, norms that guide or are intended to guide the conduct of people in a society, and as beliefs about right and wrong conduct as well as good and bad behavior."[106] This classification can be helpful to a point. In the first place it takes seriously the study of people's moral behavior as a legitimate field of inquiry. What are the core elements of a society's moral beliefs? What principles undergird the moral choices people make, either in their individual lives or as a group? What constitutes right and wrong choices, good or bad conduct, and on what grounds? Is it possible to study these? And if this is what is meant by ethics as a field of enquiry, then that is right. However, some moral philosophers, believing that "morality" as the practical aspect of the ethical enterprise implies an uncritical acceptance or assimilation of societal values, have chosen to characterize what they do as simply ethics. To speak of themselves as moralists or to characterize what they do as moral would be to descend from their imagined Olympian heights to the world of the uninitiated rabble that does not have the proper training or the disposition to differentiate critically or evaluate right and wrong.

For some time now, a debate has raged among African moral philosophers concerning how to characterize the study of morality in the African context: is it ethics or is it moral philosophy? At the root of this debate is the assumption shared by many scholars, present company included, that African ethics is at root a very religiously grounded type of moral reasoning, in which it is assumed that "most African peoples accept or acknowledge God as the final guardian of law and order and of the moral and ethical codes."[107] Some scholars object to this characterization of the African ethical discourse. According to the Ghanaian philosophers Kwesi Wiredu and Kwame Gyekye, "African conceptions of morality would seem to be of a humanistic orientation."[108] One reason is that Africans have never claimed "to have received a revelation from the supreme being intended either for the people of the community or all humanity." Consequently, one cannot speak of a revealed morality in the African situation. According to Kwame Gyekye, "If a religion is a non-revealed religion, then it is independent of religious prescriptions and commands. The characterization of traditional African religion would thus lead me to assert, to generalize on logical grounds that the moral system of each African society in the traditional setting does not derive from religion: thus, it is an autonomous moral system. Similarly, the claim about the social (non-individualistic) morality of the African society is closely related to the community and shared life of the African people. And so on."[109] As a humanistic ethic, therefore, African ethics is not unique "among the ethical systems evolved by the various non-African cultures of the world."[110] As Barry Hallen points out, one of the underlying concerns of scholars like Wiredu and Gyekye is also the fear that the characterization of African ethics as religiously based "would falsely portray African societies as communities where individuals mindlessly submit to moral values (characterized as 'traditions') that are inherited from the distant past, that continue to be enforced . . . unchanged in the present, and that will be passed on to future generations in an uncritical manner because that ultimate justification is itself an appeal to tradition."[111] Gyekye insists, to the contrary, that in Africa as elsewhere, all values are directly "derived from human interest" and that the family is the location where such values are transmitted through rigorous education in character. The aim is ultimately to teach the individual to act in ways or to make choices that promote the common good and the well-being of the community. African scholars who espouse an African humanistic ethics insist therefore that African ethics is a product of African reflections on the realities and circumstances of life—just like African religion itself.

This whole discussion raises a number of problems already hinted at. The first obvious issue in the positions of the African philosophers noted above is the misconstrual of religion as rigid revealed dogma. Religion encompasses much more than that, and as we have seen already and will consistently argue, African Traditional Religion is revelatory of God, even though it has no body of written scriptures or of writing prophets who speak in the name of God; and even though, from the Christian point of view, that revelation needs completion by biblical revelation, especially as occurred in the life and teaching of Jesus Christ. A second problem the position of these African philosophers raises is whether one can truly speak of an African ethics. The third, by extension, is whether one can speak of an African Christian ethics.

What is more important in all these issues is whether Africans have been able or are capable of any systematic and coherent thinking on matters of right and wrong, or whether, as Hallen points out above, they are only given to blind obedience to the dictates of some authority, whether human or divine. My answer is that even though Africans admit of the authority of divine powers in matters of right and wrong, they do also manage in very interesting ways to uphold the reality of human free agency. We will attend to this matter in chapter 8 when we consider moral reasoning in traditional African societies. The second question is also important: namely, whether it is possible to speak of an African Christian ethics. Although thoroughly answering this question would take the rest of this book, I will in this section begin to offer some ideas on the theoretical underpinnings that inform some of the claims made here concerning the possibility of this kind of ethics.

As John P. Reeder points out, religious ethics is generally concerned with "moral beliefs and their relation to a wider religious framework."[112] The difficulty here, as Reeder shows, is "to isolate moral norms from the other guides to conduct and character which occur in sets of religious beliefs"[113] or outside those beliefs. This signals two problems for us here. The first is to show what set of specific moral beliefs arise as part of the various frameworks that constitute either of the two religions of Africa, Christianity and African Traditional Religion, which are at the core of our investigation in this book. The other issue is to isolate or note those other moral beliefs that arise as a fact of the humanity of the African whether he or she is religious or not. There is a third issue: that is, whether there is or can be a hybrid of moral beliefs that come into existence in the life of the African Christian from the expanded, wider religious framework out of which the African Christian functions as heir to two religious traditions. As some African scholars have pointed out, contrary to the views of scholars like Wiredu and Gyekye, it is clear that African Traditional Religions are laden with moral norms that are part of the prescriptions of their set of religious ideas.[114] The same goes for Christianity, the debate about the specificity of these norms in recent theology notwithstanding. Even if this is clear in the various religious traditions from which the African Christian mind works, we need to establish how this is so in the Christian tradition of African ethics. In other words, what ethical commitments, if any, pertain to the specie of tradition called African Christianity? In this discussion we will sometimes have to employ ethnographic or historical evidence to show the content of this particular form of ethical tradition, how it differs from others—in other words, what it brings to bear on Christianity and to African Traditional Religion or brings from both—and how it has changed over time.

This book is a religious ethical inquiry. This inquiry is carried out not simply as a phenomenological exercise. The kind of religious ethics intended here is theological, and it springs out of the author's commitment as a Christian. It is even more specifically Catholic in that it also seeks to dialogue with the lived realities and traditions of Africa from a set of Catholic theological and ethical presuppositions about right and wrong, virtue and vice, good and bad. Ultimately, it is ethics, no more, no less, since it presupposes that even though our discussions here arise out of particular memory—as in all human discussions, since no one speaks from nowhere—its insights are applicable to other human situations in that they are persuasive and given that every ethical discourse "involves claims, arguments, narratives, examples, and other conceptually contentful objects in terms of which ethical topics can be specified."[115]

*This makes a lot of sense. But how does it fit within a more global context or framework. Does that make sense

Cite this

African Tradition and Traditional Religion as Foundational Issues in African Christian Theology and Ethics

Chapter Two

TRADITION, RATIONALITY, AND MORALITY

Any discussion on African theology must include the concepts of tradition and of African Traditional Religion, and thus the next three chapters will be devoted to these issues. Any theology worth its name has to be engaged with tradition, no matter how this is understood. This is as true in Africa as elsewhere because traditions generally provide the world of meaning on which people, including Africans, stand to make sense of all reality; they are a basic source of morality as well. This realization has led to a great outpouring of discussion on the subject of tradition and its relation to rationality and morality in contemporary philosophical and theological literature. In this chapter we will first revisit a bit of this discourse and then relate our discussion to Africa. The questions here are what we understand as tradition, and what role tradition or traditions play with regard to the way we construe reality, especially to how we determine right and wrong. Our discussion here has the added intention of vindicating or setting the stage for some of the assertions made in this book concerning the traditional bases of African Christian morality in Africa.

DEFINING TRADITION

Tradition can be understood in a variety of ways: as the transmission of particular beliefs; as that which is transmitted, an object or content; as the source of particular transmission; as memory of the past.[1] The term *tradition* could thus imply conservatism, community, and/or continuity. As conservatism it means a body of rules, a certain stockpile of directives (usually considered complete and unchanging) which govern life within a given human community. In this understanding of tradition all that those who live in a particular human community have to do is to reproduce as faithfully as possible the rules of the past, and apply, equally faithfully, old answers to contemporary problems that are in any way analogous to the old ones. The problem with this view of tradition is that it tends to pay little or no attention either to the possibly fresh nuance of the issue in question or to the complexity and hence the difference in its setting. The Preacher's view that there is nothing new under the sun seems to be the motto here (Eccles. 1:9–14). Every religious group, indeed every community, has its share of people who hold such a view of tradition. The Roman Catholic Church has its Marcel Lefebvres and its Lefebvrites. The Protestants have their various evangelical groups and characters. Islam has its Ayatollah Khomeinis and its various "morality police" squads whose raison d'être is simply to keep the "tradition" pure. In Islam, the *hadith*, made up of the Koran, the *sunnah* of the prophet, and the *ijima* of the *ulama*, is also an example of this rigid conservatism. However, here, as in many other instances, this conception of tradition is very hard to sustain and to defend. For example, since the close of the Islamic canon, Muslim scholars, faced with contemporary problems that Mohammad could not have known or foreseen, and in order to answer to these needs, have continued to chip away at the tradition through the *qiyas* (analogies), which to all practical purposes serve to give new meanings to old rules and even to further the ambience of the sharia.[2]

Tradition also connotes continuity. As in the case above, tradition here is synonymous with ethos, an ethos that bestows identity, provides a means of communication, and establishes continuity among a set of human beings. Tradition as continuity is dynamic, as opposed to being a rigid reproduction of the past, and arises out of dialogue between the past and the present in dynamic tension. As Edward Shils notes, tradition often involves changes that are unrecognized by its recipients, because between generations "changes by variations so small as not to be perceived as significant changes" occur.[3] Thus, although tradition is here also founded on memory, the memory referred to in this case is living and active, eager to learn and build on the past but never imprisoned by it. Therefore, if tradition is a continuity that goes beyond conservatism, it must, as Yves Congar insists, also be a movement and a progress going beyond mere continuity on the condition that, "going beyond conservation for its own sake, it includes and preserves the positive values gained, to allow a progress that is not simply a repetition of the past."[4] Tradition in this sense involves something like the "back-and-forth movement" that happens in a genuine conversation. It involves "an ability to listen, to reflect, to correct, to speak to the point," all in the effort to understand, to know, and to seek truth.[5] In a final sense of the word, tradition refers to a community of shared values and goals, and a common history. It is the embodiment of an ethos in a living community of human beings, a community of shared values which is nonetheless always on the quest for meaning and for deeper understanding of its nature, goal, and purpose.

Tradition as a World of Meaning

Ludwig Wittgenstein's theory of language games and forms of life is important to our discussion on tradition as both a world of and a continuing quest for meaning because of the influence it has had on subsequent discussion on the importance of the relationship among tradition, rationality, and morality. Language, he says, acquires its meaning from the various procedures and through the particular uses we put it to in the course of our life. Any discerning person should be struck by the great diversity of language in use. Wittgenstein argues that this diversity shows there is no overall unity in our language; what we have are language games. Although there are family resemblances among several language games, nothing is necessarily common to all of them. Each language is complete in itself. Religious language, for example, "does not need to be supplemented or taken over by theoretical or explanatory kind of language." That is, it is irreducible to anything other than itself. Its meaning can be disclosed only through religious language and behavior.[6] H. O. Mounce contends that for Wittgenstein the concept of language games was meant to refute the view that logic constitutes the a priori order of the world, and is thus prior to all experience. Mounce understands Wittgenstein's position to be that logic is found within the various language games themselves, not outside of them. The conclusion then is that we cannot question the sense of any language game. If logic is found within the language games, so of course are the canons of rationality, the criteria for distinguishing sense from nonsense.[7] These views raise a number of questions. Consider religion, for example. Does this mean, as some critics allege, that religious beliefs are cut off from all other aspects of human life? Does it turn religious language into "a protected discourse" or deprive religious statements of "ontological" and "metaphysical" significance, as John Hick charges?[8] D. Z. Phillips, one of Wittgenstein's foremost interpreters, has denied these charges on the grounds that if religion were to be seen as some esoteric and meaningless language, "it would not have the importance it has for so many people."[9] Language games are unquestionable not because we would fail if we tried to question them, but simply because to do so would be to assert that logic lies outside of them. Even so, says Phillips, language games, including religious language games, are not beyond criticism. To say otherwise is "to indulge in conservatism and protectionism," to misrepresent Wittgenstein's position.[10]

Closely related to the issue of language games is the question of the forms of life. A form of life is a wider context of human life within which we see how a language game is taken. For example, ritualistic songs and dances have little or no meaning in themselves apart from the context of a religious celebration. The institutional narrative is nothing but a set of words when taken out of the context of the Eucharistic liturgy. In other words, the power and meaning of utterances do not reside in the words themselves; the context is also very important for understanding the meaning of utterances. For Wittgenstein, therefore, the distinctive language games found in religion and ritual, for example, do not need justification, foundation, or verification from without. Just as the ritualistic response as a language game cannot be appreciated in isolation from the form of life of which it is a part, so also other types of action. Hilary Putnam has argued on this basis that we do not have notions of things or of the truth of things that are "independent of the versions we construct and of the procedures and practices that give sense to the talk of 'existence' and 'truth' within these versions."[11] For Putnam, as for Wittgenstein, truth is a context-dependent notion in the sense that it is these traditions that provide the rational basis for such determinations and the warrants that make such a notion possible in the first place. Kai Nielsen disagrees with this claim. He considers Wittgenstein's position as fideistic and refers to Wittgenstein himself as a conceptual relativist for believing that "what is to count as knowledge, evidence, a fact, an observation, making sense and the like, is uniquely determined by the linguistic framework used." Nielsen argues that if our very conceptions of intelligibility, knowledge, and so forth, are a function of the linguistic system we use, "it is impossible for us to attain a neutral Archimedean point in virtue of which we could evaluate the comparative adequacy of our own and other linguistic frameworks."[12] Nielsen's concern is well founded, although he seems to forget that even the very notion of an Archimedean point is not value-free or neutral. Thus, should such a point ever exist it could not exist independent of all conceptual schemes of reference. In other words, although the opinions of individuals cannot necessarily be taken as criteria for truth and correctness, and although majority opinion is not necessarily also the criterion for truth or falsehood, still, truth and falsehood are notions whose meanings sometimes depend on an on-going form of life. The point is that traditions, cultures, and history deserve to be emphasized as they are, not by those who seek Archimedean points in epistemology and ethics. These constitute our public language and the basis for assessing what is meaningful and what is not. But, as we shall argue later, Nielsen is not totally wrong in seeking a framework for evaluating the adequacy of our utterances and actions beyond what our particular form of life (read tradition) says about life, about rationality, and about the right ordering of life in this world. Such frameworks constitute some of the best safeguards we have against relativism.

Alasdair MacIntyre

Perhaps the best known and most influential contemporary exponent of the indispensability of tradition, culture, and history as the basis for judging rationality is Alasdair MacIntyre, for whom "the narrative of any one life is part of an interlocking set of narratives."[13] Even though MacIntyre's position on this issue is well known it bears recapitulating here in order to put the issues involved in this discussion in proper perspective. Contrary to the position of positivism and liberalism, which tends to see the individual as detached from the entanglements of history, society, and his or her own past, MacIntyre argues that the human subject is both a story-telling animal and a being with a story and a past. The individual can arrive at self-conscious selfhood only because he both has a story and is capable of telling stories. Consequently, human actions should not be seen as isolated bits of behavior independent of the agent's setting, beliefs, and intention.[14] Thus, the self finds its identity—moral or otherwise—through membership in a family, city, neighborhood, and so forth. These bestow moral particularity on the agent. Although the self does not have to accept all the limitations this particularity entails, it cannot be itself without it.

As part of a community with a past, the individual, MacIntyre says, is a bearer of tradition. Traditions themselves are shaped by, transmitted, and borne through practices that themselves have histories. These practices, on the other hand, are also shaped, borne, and transmitted through particular traditions. Traditions as worlds of meaning define or at least try to set the parameters for defining what are relevant human goods. However, these goods are not defined once and for all. Thus for MacIntyre, a living tradition, as opposed to one that is dead, is one in which this search for the goods is not settled and sealed. Rather, "a living tradition . . . is an historically extended, socially embodied argument, an argument precisely about the goods which constitute that tradition." It is within traditions that the individual generally conducts his or her search for the goods.[15] If MacIntyre is right to say that the individual's search for meaning is carried out within specific traditions, then a few conclusions must be drawn. MacIntyre himself draws those conclusions: "The conclusion to which the argument so far has led . . . is that there is no other way to engage in the formulation, elaboration, rational justification, and criticisms of accounts of practical rationality and justice except from within some particular tradition in conversation, cooperation, and conflict with those who inherit the same tradition. There is no standing ground, no place for enquiry, no way to engage in the practices of advancing, evaluating, accepting, and rejecting reasoned argument apart from that which is provided by some particular tradition or other."[16]

If we grant then that traditions are worlds of meaning from which we make sense of all reality, we must also inquire whether and to what extent there can be contact between traditions or whether, as Kai Nielsen would argue, we are doomed to hopeless relativism for espousing such a view. One issue here is that of communication between various traditions. Is there room for cross-cultural understanding? Is it possible for persons brought up within or trained in these various worlds of meaning to understand each other or to acknowledge some common basis for rationality and moral action, or would speaking from our various traditions lead to a human scientific equivalent of fideism and return us to the situation where all moral discourse consists only of incommensurable fragments, languages, and speeches whose histories are lost, lights that no longer shine? In other words, is the attainment of truth possible? And what is truth? These questions are assuming greater urgency today, not only because of the disagreements evident in various traditions found within the same geographical space, but also in light of the phenomenon we commonly refer to as globalization. We will discuss this issue in some detail later.

The first step in the quest for cross-cultural dialogue between traditions is for traditions to understand one other. This they can do via a set of historical transformations that enrich the traditions in question. MacIntyre notes that when such an understanding occurs, the result might be the rejection of one by the other, the conclusion that the issues separating and dividing the traditions are minimal and forgettable, or in some cases the judgment that "by the standard of one's own tradition the standpoint of the other tradition offers superior resources for understanding the problems and issues which confront one's tradition."[17] This moment when the agent becomes aware of the superiority (at least in some aspects) of a rival tradition has been described by MacIntyre as a moment of epistemological crisis. An epistemological crisis can occur when an individual realizes that a schema upon which he or she had hitherto based interpretations of social life has led him or her into error or deception. It could also occur when a rival tradition presents what the agent recognizes as a schema superior to the one he or she knew from the previous tradition. People sometimes react to an epistemological crisis by capitulation to the new tradition, but more often by skillfully co-opting the aspects of the rival tradition that are seen to give it the edge it has over the old one. "The first is akin to conversion, 'a change of course and direction.' "[18] The second reflects "a platonic confidence in the process of dialectic, that is, in the movement from a lesser to a greater knowledge of truth."[19] In either case what is involved in the resolution of epistemological crises is the construction of new narrative. A function of this new narrative is to enable the agent to understand how he or she could have intelligibly held on to his or her original beliefs and how he or she could have been misled so drastically by them.

Epistemological crises therefore can bring about two things in their wake. One is the dissolution of any propositionalist notion of truth that the agent might harbor. The second is the acute awareness of the limit not only of the agent's scheme of reference but also of the agent's ability to grasp or comprehend reality. This has consequences not only on the metaphysical assertions the agent makes, but on his or her ethical positions as well. Something similar to what I describe here has occurred in Africa. For, however we look at it, the arrival of Christianity on the African continent and the acceptance of Christianity as an alternative scheme of reference to the one provided by African Traditional Religion amounts to an acceptance in some ways of the inadequacy of the latter as an explanatory schema. A new narrative has emerged, therefore, which arises in some way from the fusion of Christianity with elements of African tradition. What emerges from this fusion still has to be recognizable to both the Christian community to be acceptable as "Christian," and to the African community to be acceptable as "African." This is the issue at the heart of the discourse on inculturation in African theology today. And it is not an easy task. From official Christian perspectives, however, certain anxieties come with this effort. As Robert Schreiter puts it, these include questions about unity and uniformity and what amount of diversity Christianity can accommodate in the name of inculturation without losing unity; what the point of demarcation is between a genuine expression of the faith and syncretism; to what extent one can in a Marcionite fashion ignore or write off aspects of the Christian tradition that had been accepted by other Christian traditions before; and when is it really necessary in the name of inculturation to challenge older expressions of the faith and when is it not necessary to do so.[20] In chapter 5 I will try to provide answers to some of these questions when putting forward some guidelines for inculturation in theology today.

Thanks in part to globalization there are epistemological crises of one sort or the other in various traditions around the world. An attendant result of globalization is the entrenchment of pluralism. It is my view that "not only does globalization imply a pluralistic consciousness; it also highlights the inadequacy of any single answer concerning human values and human life."[21] In this regard the best indication of the inadequacy of such single answers can be seen in the way traditions have reacted to globalization. Across the board these traditions are not handling the crises well. The ongoing ferment in the Catholic Church over contraception, homosexuality, ordination of women, and dissent from authoritative teachings is indicative of this crisis in the Catholic Church. The Islamic world is increasingly jittery over the erosion of cherished values and ways of life; the rise of fundamentalism and terrorism within it clearly indicates the inability of this tradition to deal with this crisis. The Western liberal tradition is increasingly incapable of justifying its answers on some key issues concerning the life and destiny of the human person, and has in recent years resorted to using the powers of coercion available to it—that is, the law and the police, powers it came to control in its heyday—to clamp down on dissent. African traditions, which have been under siege by so many external forces for so long, are struggling to survive, adjust, or renew themselves in the face of so much change, so much disequilibrium, and so much flux. One of our tasks in this book is to discuss not only how these traditions have handled their encounter with Christianity, but especially how both traditions, Christian and African, can on matters of right and wrong (ethics) continue to engage in dialogue to the ongoing enrichment of both.

TRADITION AND MORALITY

To start exploring the role tradition plays in moral discourse we will first turn to Henry David Aiken's discussion on the various forms or levels of moral discourse.[22] In his famous work on this topic, Aiken identifies four levels on which moral discourse takes place: the expressive-evocative level; the moral level; the ethical level; and the postethical or human level. Partitioning the levels of moral discourse in this way is useful only to a point, however, especially because these demarcations are not always strict since the contexts of moral discourse tend to shift. Thus, any moral discourse is likely to proceed on more than one level. Since moral discussion tends to be practical, the connections between the levels are more pragmatic than logical, more functional than deductive.[23] The expressive-evocative level is one of spontaneous expression of pleasure or displeasure, an expression that serves mainly to vent our emotions. As expressions of personal feeling they do not invite a reply; they cannot be challenged; questions of "truth" or "validity" cannot be raised in regard to them. Aiken concedes, however, that even here cognitive meanings begin to show themselves. In other words, even the spontaneous expression may in some sense be a raw expression of deep moral dispositions.

The next level, the moral, is the one where serious questions begin to be asked: What ought I to do? Is this object I admire so much, really good? And so on. Here, in short, there now appears a problem of conduct and a problem for appraisal and ultimate decision. Two sets of utterances are involved in attempting to justify one's answer to such a problem: "(a) factual appraisals of relevant means and consequences and (b) rules or procedures in relation to which alone the moral relevance of such appraisals can be established." Either of these is often ignored: "When the facts are sufficiently plain, attention may be directed exclusively to the interpretation and ordering of the relevant rules. At other times there may be no question concerning the meanings, order, or application of the rules, but only a problem as to the facts themselves."[24] Since we cannot do without moral rules or neglect the role of factual premises in our moral deliberations, the neglect of either, as Aiken points out, results in some form of irrationalism. Human beings always rely on some rule, often implicitly, to resolve their moral problems. And ultimately it is these rules that determine what factual reasons are to be accepted as relevant to the case, or what consequences have a bearing on the moral problem. The role the moral rules play is to present us with some standard of propriety, some reason it acknowledges one action "good" or "bad." The moral level is the one where communal codes operate. Thus even the moral rules considered relevant to the problem at issue are communally determined. The level of flexibility of these rules varies from one society to another as do the criteria for reasonableness, normality, competence, good sense, and so forth.[25]

Let us reflect briefly on the point Aiken is raising here with examples from the areas of sexual conduct and homicide. The permitted range of sexual conduct in the Christian, Muslim, and Jewish traditions, for example, exhibits some striking differences. Whereas in the Christian tradition sexual chastity rules out polygamy and any other forms of sexual contact outside of a valid monogamous union between a man and a woman (and even sometimes recommends celibacy), this is not the case in Islam or even African Traditional Religions. Islam not only allows polygamy, but also under certain conditions sanctions concubinage, and encourages men (who presumably had only one or two wives) to marry up to four. Differences also show up with regard to killing. In Islam and Judaism anyone whose conduct threatened the community (for example, adulterers or apostates) should be killed. Also, in Islam, killing for God in the name of a holy war is enjoined. Although Christians have killed others, even for the faith, such action has no warrant whatsoever in the New Testament. The Christian scriptures, on the contrary, enjoin love for the sinner, although also abhorring sin, and encourage people to turn the other cheek in the face of aggression. It is no use to deny these differences or to minimize them, arguing, as Ronald M. Green does, that they "are manifested against a background of basic similarities in moral teaching."[26] Although it is true that these traditions share some "basic similarities in moral teaching," they also harbor some fundamental dissimilarities as well, as the above examples show.

The next level in Aiken's construction is the level of ethical principles. At this level reflections on moral rules and principles take place. Here, one is obliged to ask occasionally "whether an action which is prescribed by existing moral rules *really* is right and whether, therefore, one ought to continue to obey them." The effect of such a question is to cast doubt on the validity of the rules themselves. The source of the question may lie in the perception that the rules are in conflict with some other moral rules, or in the realization that the rules can no longer be justified based on current human experience and need.[27] The questions raised on this level place moral discourse on an impersonal level, and set apart the questions and answers in which they occur from ordinary practical deliberations. "Perhaps the most distinctive feature of ethical discourse is its so-called 'autonomy.' It makes no promises of future benefit to the individual; nor are its principles justified by an ulterior consideration of expediency."[28] Here, too, ethical language begins to lay claims to universality and ideality.

On the postethical or human level the problem can best be understood in terms of the question "Why should I be moral?" Like the second and third levels of moral discourse, this is a limited sphere of discourse "with its own distinctive criteria of relevance and validity." Thus every question one raises in regard to the validity of a moral rule can be answered only by another moral rule, which in turn can be answered only by another rule, and so on. Kant's answer to this question was that every rational being recognizes that he is bound by moral laws. Thus to be moral is to be rational. But such answers cannot really be considered answers; they beg the question. Nor is the consequentialist alternative the solution. To answer that I should be moral because of some effects or some consequences from my action still leaves open the question about the justification of all moral discourse. In the end, the most compelling answer to the question of why one should be moral seems to be supplied by one tradition or another. Religious traditions, for example, give various answers to this question. For some the reason for being moral is that it is the will of God that this should be the case. And when God is perceived to be a Shylock who on Judgment Day will demand and get the just pound of flesh, the element of retribution becomes an important factor as well. Even here there are also interesting nuances since various religious traditions regard this qualification of the retributive scheme differently.[29]

We are back full circle—that is, to the acknowledgment of the particular nature of morality as derived from tradition. We are back also on Aiken's second level, the moral level, where, again, the questions are: What am I to do in this situation? Is this object that I admire so much really good? Is it really worth having? We are here dealing with questions about the nature of the good, the nature and criteria of value, and the criteria for moral choice. And answers to these questions are supplied, at least initially or even rudimentarily, by particular traditions. In other words, I contend that these are the three elements of moral discourse that are conditioned by our particular traditions. The answers we give to these questions, on the other hand, initially come from the first level, the expressive-evocative level. As Richard McCormick has pointed out, our moral convictions do not originate from rational analyses or arguments. For example, "we do not hold that slavery is humanly demeaning and immoral chiefly because we have argued to this rationally. Rather, first our sensitivities are sharpened to the meaning and value of human persons. We then *experience* the out-of-jointness, inequality, and injustice of slavery. We then *judge* it to be wrong. At this point we develop 'arguments' to criticize, modify, and above all communicate this judgment."[30]

When we speak of the place of tradition in morality we must therefore not forget the traditioning or socialization process. Through this process one comes to possess an identity, and acquire a language, as Wittgenstein and MacIntyre would say. The lessons learned from this process show up even unconsciously, at the evocative level, as Aiken has pointed out. In this area, therefore, tradition has the greatest impact on morality. Through the traditioning or socialization process we come to acquire both a picture of the world and a moral vision. An important element in the traditioning or socialization process is the symbol. Consider the way God can function as symbol for someone brought up in the Christian tradition. God as creator, savior, and one who cares for us so much that he sent his son, Jesus, to redeem the world is a very powerful symbol for a Christian. The implications and the lessons many Christians draw from this in their daily lives are beyond calculation. The thought of Christ on the cross and of the resurrection can be a powerful symbol of hope for someone who is at the point of despair. Also, someone brought up in the Christian tradition may see the value in a celibate life, or the reason for living simply and not acquiring many possessions. In other words, by ordering our values, tradition delineates our perspective, shapes our loyalties, and indicates ways through which the central symbols of the community can be brought to bear on our particular moral problems as members of the particular community in question.[31] One of my contentions in this book is that the crisis in moral discourse in contemporary Africa is partly traceable to a lack of clarity about some of the symbols (e.g., the idea of God) that have significant impact on the way people order their lives. As I see it, there is confusion among many African Christians due to an unresolved tension in the traditional African understanding of deity in several African Traditional Religions. This lack of clarity forms the background for receiving the Christian faith in most African societies, and the idea of God that comes through in the New Testament and in the teachings of the Christian church. I have argued elsewhere that the result of this lack of clarity is a kind of moral "schizophrenia" among many African Christians, and will revisit this discussion in chapter 6.

There is of course always the possibility that the views of Wittgenstein, the neo-Wittgensteinians, and Alasdair MacIntyre will lead to radical relativism, to a form of life one can confess or describe from inside but never in principle explain or criticize. This does not take away from or diminish the importance of the views herein discussed. The positions discussed here so far are not a political attempt to overthrow the entire epistemic context characteristic of pluralistic societies, nor "an irresponsible willingness to abandon public discourse and critical thought altogether—a kind of fideism whose natural social expression is sectarianism."[32] On the contrary, acknowledging the important role played by particular traditions in the way people conceive of the good and of moral value, and in the way they make moral judgments is crucial to any public discourse properly so-called today because it amounts to a recognition that we are all capable of arriving at truth; that no tradition or group of people has a monopoly on truth; and that even when the truth is found, it needs continued dialogue to refine it further for greater clarity. If there is any criticism to offer against MacIntyre's account of tradition as a series of developments in an ongoing debate around a certain set of common conceptions and values, it is that this account does not adequately, for theological purposes, address the idea of tradition as an "embodied" reality in the church. As John Cavadini points out in a very different context, it is not enough, for theological purposes to speak of "the Catholic intellectual tradition" only in the abstract. "Appeal to the 'Catholic intellectual tradition' apart from some explicit relationship to the Church risks reducing the tradition itself to an abstraction. And again I do not mean an imaginary Church we sometimes might wish existed, but the concrete, visible communion of hierarchic and charismatic gifts," the people of God, the communion of the faithful united by one faith, one baptism, one faith in the Lord Jesus, a community "at once holy and always in need of purification in which each bishop represents his own church and all of [the bishops] together with the Pope represent the whole church . . . (*Lumen Gentium* 1.4, 8; 3.23)."[33] In other words, my understanding of tradition in this book includes the church as an "embodied" and living entity that has both a doctrinal core and a moral vision that is consequent upon that core. This tradition in its embodiedness is capable of engaging in intellectual activities and has engaged with Africa as with other traditions and entities, and it is capable of opening up to the experience of others and to enter in conversation with them, in a global faith community, including Africa.

A number of questions arise from our discussion so far and need to be addressed, albeit briefly, in this part of the book. The first is whether the moral positions or the conclusions that people from a particular tradition adopt on a given issue are open to them only on account of their particular stories and to no one else. Let us take abortion or euthanasia or suicide, for example. Is the Christian story the only way to know that committing abortion or suicide is a wrong thing to do? Can human reason working independently of revelation and in other traditions come to such a conclusion? We must conclude that it can. Catholic tradition also reaches this conclusion, as is clear from the church's espousal of the theory of natural law. Natural law in this tradition is understood to imply that moral values and obligations are grounded in a moral order known by human reasoning reflecting on experience. Consequently, knowledge of the moral law is neither based solely on any faith nor limited to any one tradition since it is disclosed through the order of creation which reflects the reason of God. The point then is that although the various traditions to which we belong shape our perceptions of the world and of the moral order, they neither have exclusive hold on our reasoning nor offer exclusive insights into normal moral dilemmas and problems. The corollary is of course that "the notion of a moral order must always be tempered by the understanding that 'objectivity' in this sense does not mean 'something out there' to which we must all conform irrespective of our particularities. It is an objectivity that is structured by our subjectivities but not held captive by them. The moral law does not exist independent of who we are and yet it is prior to us, to our traditions, and to our caprices and whims."[34]

The second issue is that recognizing the role of traditions in shaping who we are also paradoxically exposes the fragility of our situation as a human race. The more the world becomes a single place,

the more it becomes clear to all of us how hard it is for the various traditions to come to agreement on many of the burning issues of our
day, some of which are literally issues of life and death. Apart from the
clash of civilizations that Huntington has so brilliantly chronicled in
his famous book by that name, one can also speak of several other
clashes going on in the sphere of morality: the clash within the West—
that is, the clash between some versions of liberalism and some versions of the Christian tradition; the clash within Catholic moral theology in various forms—liberal versus conservative; the clash within
African traditions between Christian religions and African Traditional
Religion. There are so many influences and cultural memories at work
today in the construction of subjectivity in the world that we are sometimes tempted to raise our hands in despair and bemoan our situation.
Consider the following story, for example.

In an episode of *Law and Order*, the NBC television series, an
American man married to an Egyptian woman decides to kill his uncle
because of the latter's involvement in a plan to perform a clitoridectomy on his niece. The attempt by the American father to stop what
he referred to as the "mutilation" of his daughter led to serious arguments with his uncle, an argument that turned violent and deadly.
The girl's Egyptian mother, her Egyptian grandmother, and some other
members of the family from the Egyptian side of the family, with the
active connivance and involvement of the defendant's uncle, had ar-
ranged to bring an Egyptian ob-gyn into the United States to perform
the procedure, which is customary in Egypt and in many other parts of
the Muslim world but is not allowed in the United States. The family's
justification was that in this way the tradition could ensure the young
woman's honor; cutting off her clitoris would spare her the temptation of sexual dalliance and the attendant evils of promiscuity and un-
wanted pregnancy which could result. The young girl's father vehemently opposed this idea, considering it barbaric to perform such
surgery on his eleven-year-old daughter, or on any woman at all, a view
shared by the New York deputy district attorney, herself a woman,
who, on discovering the killer and his reasons for killing the uncle, became almost unprofessionally sympathetic to the defendant. In the
end, through a series of plea bargains the defendant was convicted on
a manslaughter charge and given a very light sentence.

Several issues are evident in this drama. The first is of course the reality of the clash of traditions, Western and Middle Eastern/Islamic. In this case the clash is occurring not on metaphysical or theological grounds, but on ethical grounds. One culture describes clitoridectomy as "barbaric," another considers it a lesser evil and even a desirable price to pay to safeguard what it considers to be a greater good, the sexual uprightness of the young woman in question. A second point to note here is that each culture is laying claim to superiority over the other. The Egyptian relatives of the young girl were obviously scornful of what they regarded as the immoral Western way of life. They believed the Western tradition to be oversexed and dangerous to the morals of women; clitoridectomy was therefore in the best interest of the woman and her family since it prevented her from experiencing lust and the desire to enjoy sex. The American characters in the drama, on the other hand, considered the procedure inhumane and an unjustified mutilation; it was too high a price to pay for what they considered a secondary good. Sexual uprightness was an important good worthy of realization, but it was not to be realized at the cost of a higher good, such as the bodily integrity of the young woman in this case. In fact, the defendant himself told the police investigators that his Egyptian wife (the mother of the girl) had spent her life in physical and mental pain over the consequences of her own clitoridectomy, and that he was not prepared to see any other woman in his life go through the same torment. There was apparently no way to adjudicate between the competing claims of these two rival traditions. In the end, the defendant was sent to jail for manslaughter, which was the least penalty the law could impose to ensure that people do not take the law into their own hands. In other words, the sentence was handed down to preserve the justice system, no matter how minimally. The Egyptian relatives of the young girl lost because they were in the "wrong" country; if the incident had taken place in Cairo rather than New York, it was obvious that the defendant would have received the maximum sentence and his daughter would certainly have been circumcised.

For some African feminists, however, there is much more to this issue than is immediately apparent. Obioma Nnaemeka argues that the discussion over female circumcision, or female genital surgery as some would prefer to call it, speaks to "the complexity of the imperialist project by exposing it as a question of location ('where one is coming from,' literally and metaphorically) that transcends race and history."[35] According to her, much of the characterization of female circumcision is driven by "arrogant notions of superiority" that propel the word *barbaric* from its "original meaning of 'foreign' (*barbarikos, barbaros*) to an over-determined configuration of baroque proportions—monstrosity, abnormality."[36] Thus characterized, the practice becomes easier to condemn. Sondra Hale maintains in this regard that the debate on circumcision has given many Western women like the district attorney in this story "the license to let their ethnocentrism free associate!"[37] She asks, "What is the 'debate' about? Where does it take place? Who is participating? What is at stake in the sense of whose interests are being served or not served? What are some of the problematics of this debate?" These for Hale go a long way toward showing what is at stake here. In response to these questions Hale argues that there "is a great amount of racism and ethnocentrism being expounded in the name of participation in either a feminist struggle or a human rights struggle . . . one part of the world is defining human rights for the rest of the world." Another issue for Hale is that Western feminists who are so preoccupied with this matter are, in her words "starting from the wrong place"; they should rather go clean their own house first. "For example, feminists in the United States might want to begin to look at the abuse of women and children here in the United States: the rape capital, the child abuse capital, arguably the domestic violence, and one of body mutilations capitals of the world! We might want to look at our society, where more women are hurt and killed by the men in their lives than in any other way."[38] In Hale's view, therefore, the "evil" of female circumcision must be neither exaggerated nor trivialized, and must not be seen in isolation from a host of challenges evident all over the world with regard to the treatment of women.

As both Nnaemeka and Hale acknowledge, however, there is a deeper issue here of how to read and interpret or evaluate various cultures and traditions. On one hand is the view of culture relativists, who maintain that "all cultures are ok on their own terms,"[39] and that all cultural practices are acceptable because they are necessary for maintaining the culture, even if they might be found to be unpleasant or even sometimes unhealthy. On the other side of this debate are culture "universalists" who proffer global solutions to local questions.

Hale wonders "how and why so many Westerners, especially (but not only) white feminists, are becoming active in either scholarship or politics around the issue without knowing anything about the practices or without having a single conversation with a circumcised woman!"[40]

Both positions assert points of view that do not fit into our view in this book on the relations between the gospel and tradition. One important point is that although traditions and cultures are to be respected as the basis on which we stand to make sense of reality, they are not beyond criticism, even when we do not always know why they sanction some of the things they do. This implies a delicate dance between the universal and the particular, between the global and the local, between ancient histories and modern realities, and ultimately between the gospel as a more recent phenomenon in Africa and African Traditional Religion as a much older reality of the life of African societies and individuals. There is another subtle issue that lies hidden in Hale's position. Her position, that of a Western feminist who is sympathetic to Africa, unwittingly reinforces what Gavin Kitchling has described as the Siamese twins of endemic European (read Western) guilt about Africa and the endemic psychological dependence on the African side, attitudes that characterize a lot of the discourse about Africa in the contemporary academic world. These attitudes make truth telling (about Africa) hard and the adult taking of responsibility harder.[41] The truth is that female genital mutilation, for whatever cultural reason is used to justify it, is at best medically suspect. People can critique it wherever it occurs, including Africa, without being termed imperialists or neocolonialists. Africa stands to gain from outside criticism on some of these issues if it is not to succumb to "intellectual and cultural penury, a condition in which the mind virtually refuses to engage reality in a creative way that could open up more possibilities than there have been."[42]

TRADITION AND MORALITY IN AFRICA

Clashes like the one just described in the television drama have become a part of everyday life for most people in the world and are often exacerbated by the phenomenon known as globalization. The clash of traditions is something Africans have known too well and lived for very long. In dealing with tradition and morality in Africa, we must briefly note two issues that have continuing relevance for our discussion throughout this book. The first is whether to speak of African traditions or of African tradition in the singular. The second concerns the connection between African tradition /traditions and African religion/religions. There are different possible ways of considering the first question. One is to say that given the multiplicity of peoples on the African continent and their various histories, there would necessarily arise many and different communities of shared ethos arising from shared history and values, and that therefore it is impossible simply to speak as some people do of "African tradition." The other possibility is to assert a contrary claim, that when one looks at the African continent today one must notice a single community with a single history of common and shared ethos and values arising from that history. Thus, in spite of all differences, there is a commonality among Africans both as regards their histories and their attitudes and approaches to life and reality in general; this makes their differences so unimportant that we can make general statements about African "tradition" just as one can speak of European tradition, even though we know that the English are different from the Scottish and the French, who are only a boat ride away. As a defender of this view has put it, due to some important historical reasons, Africa has "emerged as an operative concept, which can be applied to an entire area of existence and historical experience. . . . This notion, starting as an ideological construction, has developed beyond this contingent factor to assume the significance of objective fact: there is today the sense of an African belonging that commands the vision of an entire people regarding their place in the world."[43] Both of these views have their defenders and rationale for claiming validity. I have no intention of attempting to settle this matter at this point in our inquiry. This means that even though I will, more often than not, speak of African tradition, I will also sometimes speak of African traditions when doing so would help bring out variations in local cultures, histories, or practices.

Another preliminary point to make is that the African tradition belongs to that group of traditions that Alasdair MacIntyre has differentiated from those of Western modernity in that it is a tradition largely bound up with particular religious beliefs. To understand this tradition is to understand African religion/religions and vice versa.

Despite all the aggressive proselytizing by Islam and Christianity, African Traditional Religion has proved very resilient and has continued to present itself, especially at the most critical junctures of many people's lives, as a viable alternative to the two world religions. The ongoing interaction between Christianity and African Traditional Religion can constitute a gain for African Christian theology in that, as Kwame Bediako points out, it offers the Christian theological world the opportunity to regain what Europe has lost, which is "the opportunity for . . . a creative and serious theological encounter between Christian and primal traditions."[44] African Traditional Religion is integral to the memory of the African—both memory and tradition are inextricably tied to a religious worldview in the African context. Anyone even remotely aware of the African scene knows that African life and reality are suffused with theistic concerns. Indeed, what A. G. Leonard wrote of the Igbo of southern Nigeria in 1906 is also true of other groups on the continent: "They eat religiously, drink religiously, bathe religiously, dress religiously and sin religiously."[45]

African Traditional Religion is a dialogue partner with Christianity, and so it is necessary to indicate some of the issues and areas involved in this exchange. One such area concerns the understanding of God that informs African Traditional Religion and Christianity. Some African moral theologians have written extensively on the idea of God in the African consciousness—that is, on the idea of God found in African Traditional Religion. They often wish to show what African traditions understand about God and to indicate what common ground there is between the African understanding of God and the Christian understanding. A theologian who has done extensive work in this area is the Tanzanian Catholic theologian Fr. Laurenti Magesa, who in his widely read book on African religion points out that all across Africa, "God is seen as the Great Ancestor, the First Founder and the Progenitor, the Giver of life, the Power behind everything that is. God is the first Initiator of a people's way of life, its tradition."[46] Like John Mbiti before him Magesa maintains that ethical commitment in Africa, as elsewhere, is anchored in the people's concept of the God they worship. Some would argue against this monotheistic view of God, in view of the many instances in Africa where polytheism can becloud the sense of the existence of a supreme God. Yet in the multiplicity of deities in such societies there appears ultimately to be a supreme being that represents primacy. A case in point is the Yoruba pantheon in which there is a multiplicity of gods, at the head of whom is Olódùmarè, the Supreme Being.[47] In Africa, God as primal ancestor and ultimate source of the people's traditions "possesses certain moral qualities that human creatures must emulate."[48] God is kind, relational (toward creatures), all-knowing, and protective of his creatures; he punishes sinners but is also merciful.[49] How the thought of God affects African tradition will be discussed in a later chapter.

Tradition and Social Location

It is important to note immediately, however, that as with everything else how one evaluates African tradition depends on one's social location. In other words, the moral rules upon which these traditions operate, the social organization that characterizes them, and the ethos that they enshrine and espouse affect various people and segments of society in very different ways. Laurenti Magesa characterizes African tradition as one of abundant life, that it is basically life affirming and life enhancing. This characterization is accurate in many respects, but it would be taken differently by different people at various points in their lives. I would like to offer some examples here to buttress my point. The first concerns a widow's view of the way widows are treated in an African tradition.

Regina Igwemezie, a widow from Nigeria, has written a book whose title, *Widowhood: A Harrowing Experience*, speaks directly to the concern some Africans have about some aspects of African tradition.[50] In this book, Igwemezie chronicles her ordeals at the hands of relatives and extended family acting in the name of "tradition," or *Omenana*, following the tragic loss of her husband in a car crash in 2005. She describes the way widowhood practices almost reduced her to a nonperson. During her husband's lifetime, she enjoyed many prestigious associations, earning awards for her work within and outside her local society, and had been received in very high places and admired by so many. At her husband's death she came to the quick realization that "all these honours and freedoms" were accorded her because of her husband. In her own words, "I did not know that these honours and freedoms were a result of the fact that my husband was alive. I was enjoying them under his protection." Even though Mrs.

Igwemezie had standing in her own right as a teacher, she soon came to realize after her husband's death that all of that meant nothing because traditionally she "stood under her husband." After her husband's death, she experienced tremendous indignities not necessarily because of anything personal to her, but as part of the traditional widowhood rites and the treatment given to widows in this part of Nigeria. Her movements were restricted, her feeding was regulated and supervised, and she was forced to shave her head as part of the mourning rites. Igwemezie still considers the forced shaving of her head one of the most terrible things she had to endure.[51] Here is how she puts the matter: "Another terrible experience I had was that of being made to shave my hair. Though every widow goes through this process, this exercise made me feel sad, highly disappointed and very badly humiliated. From the moment my hair was shaved, I lost my confidence and could hardly walk confidently or talk well. I still feel drained by the entire ordeal, two years after the event. To this day, I no longer have the same personality I had before. My boldness is gone. I feel highly insecure."[52] Among other things that bothered Igwemezie was the fact that the tradition rendered her invisible during the entire year during which she had to mourn for her husband. As she puts it, "The tradition requires you in a rural setting not to appear at public functions and public places such as the market square and at traditional celebrations for the whole period. Even those widows who live in cities are also required to curtail their movements. They cannot attend meetings, seminars, conferences, or visit friends," as they may like, during the six-month or one-year period of mourning.

Some African societies go even further than what Regina Igwemezie describes in her book. As Ifi Amadiume reports, in some African societies widows are sometimes accused of being responsible for the death of their husbands, and "victimized, tortured and generally regarded as unacceptable in society." In some of these societies widows are "made to sit on ashes, dress in sacks, go without food or bath, and forced to eat from broken plates," all as part of the tradition of mourning for their husbands.[53] The plight of widows in much of traditional Africa was such a troubling issue to the participants in the Second Synod of Bishops for Africa in 2009 that it was listed among the fifty-two propositions of the synod that were submitted to the pope for inclusion in the postsynodal exhortation to be issued later.

In Propositio 50, the synod states that "the synod Fathers condemn all acts of violence against women, e.g., the battering of wives, the disinheritance of daughters, the oppression of widows in the name of tradition, forced marriages, female genital mutilation and several abuses of women, such as 'arme de guerre' or sex slavery. All other inhumane and unjust acts against women are equally condemned." A tradition in which such ills occur cannot unequivocally be termed a "tradition of abundant life" no matter what other redeeming features it may have.

Mercy Amba Oduyoye, who once served as deputy general secretary of the World Council of Churches and whom many regard as the dean of African feminist theologians, and a world-class theologian by any standards, has also argued that African traditions cannot be unambiguously classified as "traditions of abundant life." Writing from a feminist perspective, she argues that these traditions have been used to oppress women and have been woven around myths, histories, folktales, and cultural patterns that were generally meant to reinforce their domination by men and to perpetuate it. For this reason, she says, "Each time I hear 'in our culture' or 'the elders say' I cannot help asking, for whose benefit? Some people or group may be reaping ease and plenty from whatever follows. So, if that harvest seems to be at my expense, then, I shall require the proceeding to stop until I am convinced that there is good reason for me to die that others might live."[54] In her book *Daughters of Anowa*, Oduyoye returns a damning judgment on African traditions concerning the treatment of women in African societies. For her, African cultures are systematically sexist, and lead to "cultural compliance, submission, and depersonalization of women."[55] Oduyoye begins by stating that several African mythical accounts acknowledge that "all human beings, male and female, are of divine origin and live because the breath of God has been breathed in them," and "enshrine the idea of the equality of men and women as part of the divine ordering of life."[56] She argues, however, that this egalitarian image has been largely subverted by other African foundational stories that stress not only gender-based roles, but inequality and the oppression of women as well. Oduyoye uses two myths—the myth of creation among the Yoruba of southwestern Nigeria, and the Ozidi and Ogboinba myths from the Ijaw of the delta regions of Nigeria—to illustrate what she sees as the disparity in the ways African traditions treat women and men.

According to Oduyoye, in the Ogboinba myth, a woman is punished for challenging her destiny; and in the other myth, the Ozidi saga, the murderous Ozidi, who had spent much of his life on a murderous spree, initially in revenge for the assassination of his own father but later for his own advancement, "enjoys the admiration of all," is given a bride, and later placed in a shrine.[57] In the Ozidi saga, there is emphasis on the "crude" use of power and its incompatibility with being a woman in African society. Oreame, a female character, is not praised when she uses her "powers" to protect and enable a man to fulfill his ambition. By contrast, admiration is heaped on Ozidi during his career of blood-letting; he is considered a hero when on his quest to avenge his father's death he massacres those standing in his way. "On the other hand, when Ogboinba set out to change her destiny, she conquers others; in doing so, she incurred the anger of the creator and had to take refuge in pregnancy, the only state that protects a woman from execution."[58] Oduyoye concludes from these examples that in this part of the world, "a woman does not wield power, at least not in life denying ways."

The Ogboinba myth is sometimes read as an attempt to explore the contradiction between power and femininity; this alleged contradiction between power and femininity has been used to manipulate women. Oduyoye tells and retells other African myths and folktales, especially from Nigeria and Ghana, to buttress her point about the oppression of women in these societies and to emphasize that these oppressive measures are embedded in the foundational ethos of African societies as evidenced in these stories. On the basis of these stories she asserts that in Africa, "men kill, beat, and rape women."[59] Women, on the other hand, "are not allowed to use physical means to challenge male oppression."[60] Sometimes the only avenue left for women as protection for themselves is that of "mythical powers," which often are labeled "witchcraft" by society. She concludes that "when a woman resists being sacrificed or taken advantage of, she is classified as being other than normal, perhaps even a witch."[61] The secret societies of some West African communities constitute means for excluding women and for making them feel like inferior beings. Oduyoye cites as examples the Ogboni and Oro societies in Yorubaland and the Poro societies of Sierra Leone. "The annual demonstration of male power over women in these religious festivals helps perpetuate women's inferiority in the minds of boys and girls and to ensure all that patriarchy reigns where once there was parity or, perhaps, even female leadership."[62] What is now needed is for women to break the silence about oppressive structures in African tradition. They should rise up and prophetically denounce these injustices or else "lose their vital role as the communicators of life in its pristine wholeness."[63] The rest of Oduyoye's book is devoted to doing just that: indicating aspects of African tradition that need to be corrected, changed, or done away with completely.

It bears repeating that the central issue to which Oduyoye draws our attention is that African traditions do in fact include elements that can be unhealthy for some segments of society, in this case women. However, some quick questions arise. The first is whether she is not misreading these folktales, mythical accounts, and proverbs, for these myths could perhaps be interpreted in other ways as well. The Ogboinba story could, it seems to me, be interpreted also as a story of someone who refuses to accept the destiny assigned to him or her by the gods. Such characters abound in African creation stories of people who simply go ahead and challenge their lot, sometimes with great success but usually at great cost to themselves and to humanity in general in other ways. One is immediately reminded of Ojadili in Igbo folklore who refused to stay content with the role assigned to him as a human being by the gods, and who eventually in a bid for supremacy over the gods challenged his *chi* (destiny) to a wrestling match. Although he lost woefully, he sent an important signal to the divinity, reminding the gods that human beings have a need and a capacity to assert their autonomy. In a creation story from the Malozi of Zambia, we hear of the way human obstinacy and pride, forced the gods (Nyambe and Nasilele, his wife) to withdraw from the world into the sky, leaving human beings the worse for it. Especially horrifying to Nyambe and Nasilele, the gods of creation, were the human aspiration to be like the gods and the tendency to violence. Nyambe made all the animals and fish as well as Kamunu (the human being) and his wife. "Kamunu distinguished himself quickly from the other animals. When Nyambe carved a piece of wood, Kamunu also carved his own. When Nyambe carved a wooden cup, the man also carved his own. When Nyambe forged iron, the man also forged iron. Nyambe was amazed, and he began to fear man. Then man forged himself a lance, and one day he killed the male child of the big red antelope.

He killed other animals as well, and ate them." Nyambe was really horrified at the human penchant for violence and queried Kamunu, the man, "Why do you kill? These are your brothers. Do not eat them: you are all my children together." Since man would not repent of his ways, Nyambe "chased him away, and sent him afar off."[64] Although Kamunu continued in his evil ways and in many ways tried to oust God and usurp his authority, he had to abandon his quest when he realized how futile and impossible it was. Today, he is constrained to worship God. "Now Kamunu abandoned his efforts to find Nyambe. But every morning when the sun appears, he says: 'Here is our king. He has come.' He bends his forehead to the ground, clasps his hands, and says: '*Mangue, mangue, mangue Muyete*' (Glory, glory, glory to the one over us!)."[65]

To return to the Ogboinba story, Oduyoye cannot read it as simply a story in which a woman who dares to change her destiny is punished. It is more a tale of the struggle for supremacy between man and the gods or the spirits in African cosmology. Such stories are everywhere one looks in Africa. This in turn is part of the human quest for autonomy and for emancipation from the grip of the divine, a celebrated part of many ancient mythologies and accounting for much of the secularist and atheistic sentiment even in our day. Nor is it right for Oduyoye to read from this story the idea of pregnancy as punishment for woman's rebellion against "patriarchy." Stories also abound all over Africa celebrating pregnancy and honoring the roles of women as mothers. As for the Ozidi saga, as J. P. Clark-Bekederemo has shown, both in the transcription of the oral performance and in the dramatic adaptation of the tale,[66] the focus is the narrative of nationhood in which Ozidi, the hero, fights fourteen battles against evil forces that stand in the way of social progress. That is not to say that Oduyoye cannot take liberties with her own interpretation of the saga, or narrow its concerns to an expression of the horror in Ozidi's ascendancy. It is instructive to note, however, that it was Oreame, Ozidi's maternal grandmother, who fortified the yet unborn child with admirably mystical powers that would enable him to triumph throughout his exploits. So, clearly these are complex stories that can be interpreted in a variety of ways.

Even Oduyoye's point that African societies are often stratified along gender lines and feature definite gender roles, true as it may be, does not unambiguously indicate oppression of women or work to their detriment. For example, writing with particular reference to women in Igbo society, the late Nigerian anthropologist, herself a woman, Josef Thérèse Agbasiere, notes that "Igbo women, by virtue of their membership of bounded groups, are vested with some measure of political power." Women have traditionally wielded power in this particular society in various ways: through "the association of women who have attained the age seventy or over, and who are usually titled women"; more significantly through "the meeting of *umuada* or *umu-okpu*, daughters of the lineage"; and through the association of *ndiyom* or *inyondi*, "wives of the lineage."[67] Agbasiere notes that "under modern conditions, Igbo women continue to exert their pervasive political influence through their various open or bounded groups," through age grade associations, or through religiously based associations. Agbasiere thus concludes that some colonial and contemporary writers "have failed to give an adequate picture of the Igbo woman and her political status within society." She opines that the reason might be "due to an inadequate understanding of the traditional organs of power sharing" and a "failure to recognize the basic differences, especially between the *umuada* and the *ndiyom*," a failure that Agbasiere blames on the "masculine ideology of the colonial service."[68]

Again, just as it is true that African traditions, like other traditions elsewhere, contain elements that are life-enhancing, they can also, again like other traditions, contain life-negating and oppressive elements as well, both for men and for women. There is a story in Chinua Achebe's novel *No Longer at Ease* that warns us also against straightforward glorification of African traditions as "traditions of abundant life." In that novel, the main character, Obi Okonkwo, falls in love with Clara, another Igbo, while both are students in England. Obi and Clara look forward to their return to Nigeria and the opportunity to marry each other. But on returning to his village, Obi is forced by relatives to sever the relationship when it is discovered that Clara is an *osu*. G. T. Basden describes the *osu* as a cult slave, as distinct from the indentured slave. Other Igbo scholars have added to this definition, stating that the *osu* is "a living sacrifice, something or someone totally dedicated to a divinity. Only natural death can terminate its existence on this side of reality."[69] The *osu* in this sense is the property of the god to whom he or she is dedicated and has no prospect of redeeming his or her freedom; the *osu* is also restricted to the precincts of the shrine to which he or she is attached. Today, even though the *osu* is no longer physically circumscribed, his or her plight is not that much better, because in much of Igboland, once an *osu*, always an *osu*. This means, as in the case of Clara, for example, that as a descendant of an *osu* one remains an *osu*, and is not free to marry or be married into free society or, in most cases, to aspire to positions of leadership within the community. In short, in many parts of Igboland "an *osu* is a non-person, sacrificed to a local deity."[70]

Although we will discuss this issue a bit more in a future chapter, I introduce it here to show that the assumption that African tradition is straightforwardly one of abundant life is certainly not shared by a character like Clara in Chinua Achebe's *No Longer at Ease* or by many other groups or persons in African societies who are classified as nonpersons in the view of African Traditional Religious beliefs. African traditional life has its strengths and its weaknesses, like all other traditions, and we must not exaggerate either. In other words, whereas such a characterization as provided by Magesa is correct in some ways, it is very sweeping in other ways and can detract from the necessary work that must be done to unearth the deep structures of sin embedded in African tradition, as in any others—structures that need to be exposed to the saving effects of the gospel. There is no one way of reading African tradition. And whatever way one reads it, one is bound to see that, like every other tradition, African tradition, as the basis on which people understand and negotiate reality and within which they determine moral rightness or wrongness, is fraught with challenges that must be faced as we search for foundations for an African Christian ethic.

So far in this chapter we have discussed the role of tradition in determining what is rationally warranted and morally acceptable. African moral discourse is traditional not because it blindly accepts the dictates of any authority, divine or human, but because like all moral systems it makes its judgments about right and wrong based on its understanding of life, and on what in both religious and humanistic terms it understands to be right. In chapter 1 we noted the views of two African scholars, Kwesi Wiredu and Kwame Gyekye, who argue that African ethics is not a religious ethic, partly because African religion is not a revealed religion and has no prophets. I believe this view misses the point of what it means to say that African ethics is a religiously based ethic. As I have stated repeatedly here, in Africa religion is the culture and the culture is religious. Although this does not mean that everything is explicitly stated as religious, it does show that religion permeates every aspect of life. It is faith informed by reason, much like what obtains in Catholic ethics or in any other ethical systems related to religion. Its conclusions have room for both reason and faith. And although it is true that African Traditional Religion has no prophets who in certain historical circumstances issued a set of dogmas or revelations, this does not mean that African religion is not revelatory in some way, or that it does not manifest or mediate the presence of God. If this is the case, then, as is clear to every believer, faith has implications for life. Africans in their wisdom have also come to know this and to try to codify through various means what these demands are that arise from belief in the divine presence.

In discussing African tradition, no matter how the term is understood, we face the issue of how to determine the significance of Africa's past and its relevance to the African present.[71] There is no doubt, as Abiola Irele points out, that through the mediation of Christianity, there has emerged a new African consciousness. One must then ask what the content of this new consciousness is or should be, how it is being formed, and what meaning it is being fused with. In his novels Chinua Achebe chronicles in very deep ways the emergence of this new consciousness: the struggles, the distortions, and anxieties it creates. Some of these features are evident in Achebe's *Things Fall Apart*, which offers "a clear recognition of the decisive break in the African experience of history occasioned by the colonial fact," but the book also includes, especially for our purposes here, a recognition that with the introduction of Christianity into Africa something did indeed change with regard to the way Africans view the world and the way they organize life. What has changed? What has remained the same? And what should change? These are some of the issues we will be dealing with.

Chapter Three

AFRICAN THEOLOGICAL EVALUATIONS OF AFRICAN RELIGION

African traditions and African Traditional Religion are inextricably tied to each other; to understand African tradition one has to understand African Traditional Religion. This is to say that anyone engaged in the study of Christian theology in Africa must study African Traditional Religion as an aspect of African tradition and evaluate it both in itself as a particular religion that sometimes makes rival claims to Christianity; and as a non-Christian religion that is part of the constellation of religions with which Christianity has had to reckon as it makes claims about the world and about reality in general, and as it engages in missionary and proselytizing activity through space and time. In the first chapter we dealt briefly with the contention of some African scholars who argue, contrary to the generally held opinion, against the assumption that African ethics is a religious ethics because, they say, African Traditional Religion is not "a revealed" religion with "official" prophets, and no codified system of ethics that follows or is derived from any written and canonically approved scripture. As was noted in the last chapter, the reasons adduced by these scholars for their claim miss the point about the nature of religious ethics. An ethics can be religious because it is understood as being divinely dictated and codified, as is the case with certain understandings of the sharia in Islam, or with various understandings of the Ten Commandments and other teachings of Jesus in Judaism and Christianity. It does not matter whether these sets of rules have resonance anywhere else. What matters is that they have been remodeled as it were to fit the ethos or the general message of the community of faith in question. Or, an ethics can also be religious if it derives its raison d'être from the general ethos of the community of faith. I believe that this is what Segun Gbadegesin is alluding to when he states, "Traditional Africans believe that God gives the moral sense to each person, and they use the moral sense to fashion the moral order and its structure. The moral sense includes the sense of right and wrong, the sense of decency, the sense of fittingness, appropriateness, beauty and ugliness, the sense of straightness and crookedness, etc. . . . Human beings create the moral order through their use of the moral sense given them by God. This is the case with traditional Africans."[1] Further on in his essay, Gbadegesin concludes that in Africa as well "various contents of our moral norms are also influenced and shaped by religion."[2] Even though Gbadegesin stops short of stating that these moral norms come out of the religious views and sense of the people, he points to something obvious to any observer of the African religious moral scene, namely, that many Africans are generally influenced by their religious sense to act in several ways, to make or shun certain things, or to seek to acquire several virtues and avoid certain vices. We will return to this issue later in chapter 8 when we discuss moral decision making in African communities and the consequences of faith commitments to that process. What is important here is that there are many reasons for taking African Traditional Religion seriously. One such reason, as has already been indicated, is that it supplies the most important substratum for the African as a religious being in his or her encounter with Christianity.

This connection has to be taken seriously, more so now that African Christianity has become a missionary Christianity. Not only is Christianity growing in Africa at an incredible rate, African Christians are among the most active Christian missionary agents in the world today. Nearly all religious missionary societies of the Catholic Church with African foundations have received a new lease on life as missionary agents of the church through the involvement of their African foundations in their various missions old and new. The same goes for locally founded African religious/missionary societies of men and women. These too are to be found in large numbers all over the world, including the West. African Catholic priests are also serving in very large numbers as *fidei donum* priests—that is, as priests who, although ordained for particular dioceses, have been sent abroad to other dioceses in good faith arrangements between two local bishops (the sending and the receiving bishops) to help out in a diocese other than their own for a period of time or even indefinitely. The picture of African missionary involvement in all parts of the world gets much bigger when one factors in the many new Christian religious movements and churches that have originated in Africa and now have branch churches all over the world, including Europe, Asia, and America, and within Africa itself. The Africans involved in these Christian missionary engagements from Africa also carry with them worldviews that are partly shaped by African Traditional Religion through some form of osmosis, or they have been affected by a tacit personal or explicit theological encounter with African Traditional Religion. For this reason, even though we are more particularly interested in the ethical aspects of African religiosity—Christian or traditional African—it is necessary to discuss African Traditional Religion, both as a theological category and in its relationship to Christianity, before we delve into the particular concern of this book, which is the discussion of how these two religions interact, can interact, or should interact on the ethical plane in Africa.

Christian missionary and evangelizing work in Africa and elsewhere is a statement both about other religious traditions and about Christianity itself. The question is what Christianity is saying through its involvement in Africa about African Traditional Religion and about other religions in general. These are the questions we seek to answer in this chapter and in the next. It is crucial to address this issue not only with a view to ascertaining what Christianity brings to the table theologically, but in order as well to determine what it contributes to a theologically based ethical tradition such as we claim the African Christian ethic is. For the African theologian, then, the evaluation of African Traditional Religion is not a clinical one, as one might perform, say, of Babylonian religions, which are "dead" in that they no longer constitute or inform the worldview of any group of people in a decisive way. It is an existential and personal quest since the African theologian is in this case "handling dynamite, his own past, his people's present."[3] In other words, through his or her work on these issues the African theologian is on a quest for personal discovery and identity (as was pointed out in chapter 1) in a way that may not be the case with his or her theological colleagues and counterparts from Europe and North America. That is to say, the African theologian is studying a phenomenon that determines the way large numbers of people construe reality and organize their lives. While this chapter is devoted to evaluating African Traditional Religion as such, the next takes up the same question in the much wider context of Christian theological discussion of non-Christian religions.

CHRISTIANITY AND AFRICAN TRADITIONAL RELIGION

Despite its many successes Christian presence in Africa has been a hard pill to swallow for some African intellectuals in pre- and postindependent Africa. For some of them the arrival of Christianity on the continent was a net negative event with regard to Africa's cultures, customs, traditions, and religion, and African life in general. Mazi Mbonu Ojike, one of Nigeria's foremost nationalists, who fought for Nigerian independence from Great Britain, recounts a conversation he had with a European missionary working in Nigeria; they met at a house party in Brooklyn, New York, during his student days in the United States sometime in the 1950s.[4]

> Ojike: "What is the future of Christianity in Africa?"
> Missionary: "Just as Europe is now Christianized, Africa will eventually be Christianized," he said.
> Ojike: "You mean that Muslims and Omenanans[5] will have to be converted to your Christian ways?" asked another African.
> Missionary: "Not by force! Christ said, 'I am the way, the truth and the life. No one cometh unto the Father but by me.' So you have it in the Master's own words," he said.
> Ojike: "Why do you go to Africa to preach to people whose religion produces better results than yours?" I asked.

Missionary: "We were sent," he said.

Ojike: "By whom?" said I.

Missionary: "By God."

Ojike: "Is that God different from ours?" I asked.

Missionary: "No."

Ojike: "Suppose we had come to Europe in the 12th century and claimed we were sent, what would you have thought of us?"

Missionary: "But you were not sent."

This encounter captures the essence of the African intellectual challenge to the Christian presence in Africa then and now, especially as regards its relationship to and dealings with African Traditional Religion. For some African intellectuals Christianity has been a foreign and destructive presence on African soil. For them, conversion to Christianity appears unwarranted because not only is Christianity not superior to African Traditional Religion, it has no morally superior insights and ideas to offer as well. As Ojike suggests in his encounter with the missionary, Christianity was considered by this segment of the African intellectual elite to be morally inferior to African Traditional Religion. In the dialogue above, Ojike reads European historical moral failures down the centuries as evidence of Christian moral inferiority. Consider his question to the missionary: "Why do you go to Africa to preach to people whose religion *produces better results than yours?*" (emphasis added). Later on in the essay Ojike concedes that missionaries to Africa have done some good for the continent through building schools and hospitals, but he quickly adds that "no learning or hospitalization can help a people who have been denied religious, social, political and economic freedom, which is the basis of national growth."[6] Here is another issue characterizing the discourse on the relationship between Christianity and African Traditional Religion: the issue of Christian presence in Africa among certain African intellectual elite, who equate the Christian presence with European colonial exploitation of Africa. Much has been written on this subject, and some of it is true. However, there is need for careful distinctions on this matter. The situation of Christianity in Africa during the missionary era was not always one of superior arms or of great political clout, for in many cases in Anglophone Africa, at least in the Catholic Church, the missionaries were Irish; they had no significance politically, and in relation to the British, who were one of the principal colonial powers in Africa, were in fact themselves a colonized people. Ojike is right, however, that in some circumstances the Bible and the sword did go together in Africa. This issue in African history has been much discussed and so will not occupy us here to any extent. Finally, for these African intellectuals, Christianity is "a superimposed religion" that does not and cannot touch "the depth of the African mind because its theories do not square with the fundamentals of African society. Yet it renders the African impotent because it imprisons his deeper culture."[7]

Ojike's encounter with this unnamed missionary is in some ways reminiscent of an encounter between Ambrose of Milan and the pagan philosopher Symmachus which Arnold Toynbee reports in his book *Christianity among the Religions of the World*.[8] After Christianity had become victorious in the Roman Empire, the new imperial government went about forcibly closing pagan temples and places of worship in the western part of the empire; it also decided to remove from the Senate house of Rome the statue and altar of victory, which had been placed there by Julius Caesar. "The spokesman of the Senate at the time, Quintus Aurelius Symmachus, had a controversy with St Ambrose on the subject, and the documents have survived. Symmachus was beaten, not by argument, but by overwhelming force. The government simply closed the temples and removed the statue. But, in one of his last pleas, Symmachus has put into the record these words: 'It is impossible that so great a mystery should be approached by one road only.'" According to Toynbee, "the mystery of which he is speaking is the mystery of the universe, the mystery of man's encounter with God, the mystery of God's relation to good and evil."[9] From the encounter between Ojike and the missionary the challenge to African Christianity is clear—say something about your faith: What do you bring to the table in Africa? Why should we be converted to Christianity? What is wrong with our traditional way of worship? What moral insights does Christianity bring or add to the African way of life which are not already part of African tradition and which cannot be inferred or learned from African Traditional Religion? As is evident from the encounter between Ambrose of Milan and Symmachus these questions have been put to Christianity before in other contexts. The flip side of these questions is the one that forces Christianity to say something about the non-Christian religions, and about why it invites people away from them and eagerly welcomes them into its fold. This issue will be examined in the next chapter.

Mbonu Ojike's questions to the missionary continue to reverberate in Africa today even as Christianity continues to grow. Two of these questions, concerning the moral superiority of the Christian faith and the efficacy of the Christian God, continue to provide the greatest challenge to the Christian faith in Africa. I will illustrate this point with two short stories. The first case concerning Christian moral superiority came in the form of a remark addressed to me by the priest of Ogwugwuapku Okija, a deity in Okija, a town close to Ihiala, Anambra state, Nigeria, where I worked as associate pastor following my ordination to the priesthood in 1984. I had just been in this parish for a few months when an incident connected to the struggle for succession to the royal throne of the Oluoha of Ihiala blew up and nearly threatened the very fabric of the town. At some point in the squabbles, one of the families involved in the case decided to invite the high priest of the Okija shrine to come to provide the rites of protection and cleansing over them. The families involved in this case not only were Catholics, but also had prominent roles in the church as lay leaders. In fact, the most prominent person in this case was the head of the Catholic Women Association (CWO), which in Nigeria is the umbrella organization for Catholic women in the local station, parish, diocese, and nation. The president of the CWO is a very powerful person in every one of these settings. Any pastor who wants to succeed had better work with this person or be prepared to face the consequences. Thus, it was a most disturbing development when the president of the CWO in this very large and prominent parish turned out to be involved in what is considered idol worship. It was telling too that this family chose the mediation and the prayers of the high priest of Ogwugwuapku over and in spite of that of us, the Catholic priests in the parish.

We got wind of the impending visit of the priest of the deity from Okija through some very concerned Christians, and since the ceremonies were to be held in the open, I was asked by the pastor to go to find out what was actually happening. When I arrived in my cassock I made a point of standing away from the center of events but at a point where I could clearly observe the proceedings. The lady of the house (the CWO president who was the organizer of the event) came over to greet me, as did many other members of the parish who had come to observe what was going on. At some point in the ceremonies the high priest began to sprinkle a greenish-reddish concoction that he had prepared and prayed over. He then made a point of coming directly at me and sprinkling me with the material (needless to say, that was the end of my white cassock). The more interesting thing, which has stayed with me for nearly thirty years after this event, was that while splashing me with his concoction he kept shouting at me in Igbo, *"Obu ala ndi uka mebishiri ka anyi biara ka anyi dozie!"* (We are here to restore the cosmic/moral order which the Christians have destabilized!). In other words, for this man, my Christians were the problem of the community. And it was they who had invited him to come clean up the mess they had made and the moral disorder they had created. In a context where all the participants in this power tussle were Christians, what the Okija priest said has stayed with me. In other words, Mbonu Ojike's question is still an issue today in African Christianity and for Christianity everywhere. What is the proof of Christian moral superiority? Can we point to history in any form for this proof? Not unambiguously. For even though Christians have done great things in history, we have also done terrible things. If history does not provide unambiguous moral proof of Christian moral superiority, where can such a proof be found? On the other hand, the question must also be asked whether Christian claims about the validity of the faith actually hinge on a claim to being morally superior. As we shall see in the next chapter, the primary Christian claim is that in Jesus Christ, God has entered into human history, to give life and salvation to all. Of course the Christian faith has consequences for how we live or should lead our lives. Christianity is not a code of morality; it is a movement and a community of people who, having found the offer of grace from God through Christ attractive, have embraced this offer in faith. Although it is beholden on them as "a new creation" to live out in every way the implications of their lives in every word and deed, they are still sinners, who in spite of their privileged status as the "New Israel of God" (Gal. 6:16; see also *Lumen Gentium* 9) have to work out their salvation one step at a time, "in fear and trembling" (Phil. 2:12).

A second brief story is about the efficacy of the Christian God as one who redeems and punishes. During the election that brought Olusegun Obasanjo to his second term of office as president of Nigeria in 2003, there was massive rigging and stealing of votes. Some politicians simply took the ballot boxes to their homes and had them filled up there, eventually returning them to be "certified" by electoral officers who had been heavily bribed to produce favorable results for the ruling People's Democratic Party (PDP). Some Christian churches, including the Catholic Church, did everything in their power to ensure accountability at the polling centers. In this regard, many young people, including vowed religious, were trained and posted to serve as monitors at various polling centers. In spite of all these efforts, the elections were "won" mostly by those who had the means to buy their way to power. I happened to travel in Nigeria around this period in 2003, and I heard many very disturbing stories of irregularities during these elections. One that stuck in my mind concerned two young female religious sisters (in their early to mid-twenties) who, while working at one of the polling centers as local observers for the Justice and Peace Ministry of the Catholic Church in Nigeria, observed a PDP candidate carting ballot boxes away and under armed police protection, getting them all filled up in his favor at his home. These two young nuns decided to confront him when they realized that everyone else seemed unable to do so. After trying to appeal to the politician's better moral sense of judgment to no avail, they reminded him that God was observing him and would in due course punish him for his wrongdoing. The sisters told me that at this point the politician looked up at them and roared with laughter, saying, "God? Your God cannot punish anyone. He is powerless!" The politician "won" his seat in the federal parliament and was duly sworn in, to the utter dismay of these young sisters, who were left wondering where God is in all this! One point of this story is that there is a certain aspect of African religiosity that wants "proofs"—that is, indications that God is "powerful" and able to wreak instant vengeance and retribution, and to fight one's cause against one's enemies. Any "God" who is seen to possess power for instant retribution wins; the one who cannot produce instant rewards loses out.

The question then boils down to the reason for conversion to Christianity among African religionists. In his book on the meaning of Christian conversion in Africa, Cyril C. Okorocha points to the fact that at least in the case of the Igbo of southeast Nigeria, "the nature of the traditional religion is the key . . . to conversion." Socioeconomic factors are only a catalyst. "The people converted to Christianity in search of salvation, in search of power. . . . This is what determines their response to the new message."[10] Okorocha's position seems to be borne out by incidents like one reported in Chinua Achebe's *Arrow of God* in which one village, Umuaro, was contemplating war against another, Okperi, which had killed an emissary sent to them to make peace. In the course of the deliberations about finding a proper response to the killing of their kinsman by the people of Okperi, some people at Umuaro were eager to go to war against their neighbor. The spiritual leader of Umuaro, Ezeulu, vehemently opposed the war; in response the chief proponent of war on the Umuaro side, Nwaka, in a secret meeting with his men, later replied: "We have no problem with Ulu. He is still our protector. . . . We shall fight for our farmland and for the contempt Okperi has poured on us. Let us not listen to anyone trying to frighten us with the name of Ulu.[11] If a man says yes his Chi also says yes. And we have all heard how the people of Aninta dealt with their deity when he failed them. Did they not carry him to the boundary between them and their neighbors and set fire on him?"[12] In other words, when a deity can no longer live up to expectations, people reserve the right to change it or abandon it for a "more potent" one, for the deity is there to attend to human needs, or, as Nwaka puts, to be "our protector."

As a serious discussion partner with Christian theology and with the gospel, African Traditional Religion provides a unique opportunity for, and many challenges to, African theology in that it forces Christianity as well to give an account of its claims and assertions about God, the human person, human destiny, the world, and the nature of the good. One issue in African Christian theology is the extent to which both religions—Christianity and African Traditional Religion—are in sync in what they say about reality, God, the human person, and so on. Especially for the African Christian, the issue in question is what is "usable" in the African past for his "new" life as a Christian.

There is therefore a deep sense in which African Christian theology has never been just Christian theology. For, "from its earliest times, written African theology has always sought not merely to dialogue with African traditional religions and African culture, but also to make sense of the complex world of African traditional religions."[13]

This concern with the non-Christian religions of Africa is a sign of realism and maturity. African theology has always been inter-religious, seeking to be more than a proselytizing theology without denigrating Christianity. In other words, it is with good reason that African Christian theologians have had to ask themselves, and be asked by others, "Why do we continue to seek converts to Christianity from the devotees of African Traditional Religion?"[14] The question here is precisely what value to accord African Traditional Religious beliefs from a Christian theological standpoint. Another related but often neglected point is the issue of history and evolution in African Traditional Religion. As Edward Fasholé-Luke has pointed out, much of the material for the study of African Traditional Religion is in oral form, particularly the myths and legends. There has, however, been a tendency "to neglect the historical dimensions and developments of traditional religions, and to describe their beliefs and practices in a continuous present tense." For this reason, Fasholé-Luke concludes, African theologians need "the insights that can be gained from the methodology of historians of Africa who have patiently sifted and carefully pieced together the vast mass of oral tradition and converted them into coherent historical patterns."[15] In other words, apart from the usual challenge posed by geography with regard to the notion of African Traditional Religion—that is, whether we should be speaking of African Traditional Religion or of African Traditional Religions—another problem is posed by history since African Traditional Religion is itself a living entity, bound by that fact to react to and sometimes to adapt to changes from its various contexts and as it passes through various epochs. One could therefore ask, which African Traditional Religion are we speaking about? In what age? Questions like these also invite us to consider what constitutes the perennial core of this religion as in any other religion or tradition. In the next section we will briefly do two things. First, we will restate the basic outlines of African Traditional Religion that are pertinent to our discussion, as some scholars of African religion see them. The second brief task is to offer a brief theological evaluation of African Traditional Religion, again from the point of view of some of these scholars. This evaluation will lead then into the much wider discussion on primal religions, which will be undertaken in the next chapter.

EVALUATING AFRICAN TRADITIONAL RELIGION:
THE DESCRIPTIVE TASK

One scholar who has written extensively on African Traditional Religion is John Mbiti, a Kenyan whom many consider the dean of living African theologians. An important preoccupation of Mbiti's work has been to show that knowledge of God and the worship of God have been staples of African life from the earliest times on the continent. In other words, he shows that the sense of the divine was not something introduced to Africa by missionaries or by anyone else; that the knowledge of God in African religion was not much different from the idea of God that Christian missionaries preached in Africa; and, more specifically to our purpose here, that belief in God engendered a moral response that for centuries before Christian arrival in Africa directed moral life and interaction on the continent and among its peoples. According to Mbiti, Africans came to believe in God by reflecting on their experience and through observation of the created universe. Specifically, by reflecting on the wonder and magnitude of the universe, they came to the conclusion that God must exist: they posited the existence of God to explain the existence and sustenance of the universe. Rooted in the belief in God as the Creator, Africans believe in various dimensions of the created universe, such as visible and invisible (the spiritual realm), heavenly (skyward) and earthly (and in some ethnic groups there is a belief in the underworld). Commonly, God is believed to dwell in the skies. In most cases, the earth is conceived as a living thing, a goddess, "Mother Earth." According to Mbiti, the earth is symbolically viewed as the mother of the universe, while the heavens/sky are seen as its male counterpart.[16] While the universe has a beginning, many Africans believe that it does not have an end—either spatially or temporally. The ordering of the universe and its continuance depends on God. Mbiti emphasizes that Africans view the universe religiously. Since God is seen as the Creator, various aspects of the universe are permeated by the sense of the sacred—the religious mentality affects the way people see the universe. Therefore, the universe has dimensions of order and power as follows: first of all, there is order in the laws of nature. This order, established by God, guides the functioning of the universe, preventing it from falling into chaos; and it ensures the continuance of life and the universe itself. Thus, everything is not completely unpredictable and chaotic because of this order. This is the function of God's providence and sustenance of the universe. These laws are controlled by God directly or indirectly through God's intermediaries. Secondly, there is moral and religious order. According to Mbiti, Africans believe that God has ordained a moral order for humans, through which they came to understand what is good and what is evil, so that they might live in harmony with one another and safeguard the life of the people. This order, according to Mbiti, is knowable to humans, by nature. Thus, it is because of the existence of this order that different communities have worked out a code of conduct. This happened in the past, and these codes were stipulated, considered sacred and binding, by the community leaders. "Moral order helps men to work out and know among themselves what is good and what is evil, right and wrong, truthful and false, and beautiful and ugly, and what people's rights and duties are. Each society is able to formulate its values because there is moral order in the universe. These values deal with relationships among people, and between people and God and other spiritual beings; and man's relationship with the world of nature."[17] Mbiti further adds, "The morals and the institutions of the society are thought to have been given by God, or to be sanctioned ultimately by him. Therefore, any breach of such morals is an offense against the departed members of the family, and against God or the spirits, even if it is the people themselves who may suffer from such a breach and who may take action to punish the offender."[18]

The moral and religious order in the universe is articulated and expressed in a variety of taboos and customs that prohibit specific actions contravening such order. Taboos and customs cover all aspects of human life: words, foods, dress, relations among people, marriage, burial, work, and so forth. "Breaking a taboo entails a punishment in the form of social ostracism, misfortune and even death. If people do not punish the offender, then the invisible world will punish him. This view arises from the belief in the religious order of the universe, in which God and other invisible beings are thought to be actively engaged in the world of men."[19] A part of this belief in the moral and religious order is belief in the invisible universe, which consists of divinities, spirits, and the ancestors (the living dead). These act as God's associates, assistants, and mediators, and they are directly involved in human affairs. Human beings maintain active and real relationships with the spiritual world, especially with the living dead, through offerings, sacrifices, and prayers. These act as a link between God and the human community.

There is also a mystical order of the universe. Africans believe in the existence of a mystical, invisible, hidden, spiritual power in the universe. This power originates from God but is possessed hierarchically by divinities, spirits, and the living dead, and it is available to some people, in various degrees. This is a universal belief among Africans. Those to whom this power is accessible can use it for good, such as healing, rainmaking, or divination, while others can use it for harm, through magic, witchcraft, and sorcery. This power is not accessible to everyone, and in most cases it is inborn, but the person has to learn how to use it. Mbiti says that "access to this power is hierarchical in the sense that God has most and absolute control over it; the spirits and the living dead have portions of it; and some human beings know how to tap, manipulate and use some of it. Each community experiences this force or power as useful and therefore acceptable, neutral or harmful and therefore evil."[20] According to Mbiti, human beings have a privileged position in the universe. Everything is said to center on them. Human beings are the link between the heavens and the earth, between the visible and the invisible universe. This view influences the way humans relate to the universe: on the one hand, they strive to maintain harmony between themselves and the invisible universe by observing the moral and religious order; at the same time, humans see the universe in a utilitarian way, from the point of view of what is beneficial or harmful to them.

Some of the ideas from Mbiti's works are pertinent to our discussion here: Africans believe in a hierarchy of beings, from the ultimate being, God, to lesser ones, divinities, spirits, the living dead, human beings, animals, plants, and inanimate beings. Mystical power is found in all of them, in diminishing degrees. This hierarchy is also evident in human society, where there are chiefs, clan heads, family heads, older siblings, and so on. Second, Africans believe in a moral order given by God, stipulated by the ancestors in the past. Observing this moral order ensures harmony and peace within the community. "Many laws, customs, set forms of behavior, regulations, rules, observances and taboos, constituting the moral code and ethics of a given community, are held sacred, and are believed to have been instituted by God."[21]

Furthermore, a person acts in ways that are good when he or she conforms to the customs and regulations of the community, or bad when he or she does not.[22]

Mbiti makes a very controversial point when he claims that in African societies there are no acts that would be considered wrong in themselves. Acts are wrong if they hurt or damage relationships or if they are discovered to constitute "a breach of custom or regulation." To buttress his point Mbiti states that in certain African societies "to sleep with someone else's wife is not considered 'evil' if these two are not found out by the society which forbids it, and in other societies is in fact an expression of friendship and hospitality to let a guest spend the night with one's wife or daughter or sister."[23] Mbiti's assertions must be read as a limited reference to some African societies and in some limited settings. As I have discussed elsewhere, for example, some African societies are so conscious of the implications of crossing the line on some ethical matters, like adultery, incest, and murder, that anyone who engages in these acts is considered automatically to be putting the very survival of the community in danger. Thus, to assert as Mbiti does that there are "no secret sins" or that "something or someone is 'bad' or 'good'" only according to "outward conduct" is too careless a statement to make.[24] With regard to the issue of offering one's wife in generosity, this practice, as Laurenti Magesa has shown, applied to a very limited number of African ethnic groups, such as the Masai, and in very tightly controlled situations among friends within the same age group fraternity and on very limited occasions.[25] This practice, no matter how limited it is, again shows how untenable the blanket assertion is that African moral traditions are those of abundant life. No matter how one looks at it, to "offer" the female members of one's family as a mark of "hospitality" to a stranger is morally wrong, not just from the point of view of Christian morality but from a purely natural law point of view as well. Inculturation, as we will argue later in this book, sheds the light of the gospel on cultural practices like this one to reveal what is sinful in them and to show that human beings, especially women, in this case, deserve better treatment than this.

Ronald M. Green of Dartmouth College in Hanover, New Hampshire, a non-African scholar of African religion, has also written about African Traditional Religion and about religion and morality in Africa.

He has useful insights to add to our discussion and in many ways corroborates the statements other scholars like Mbiti have made about African religion.[26] Green points out that there is a rational basis to African Traditional Religion that shows, in Kantian terms, that there is a "deep structure of universal moral and religious reason to it."[27] The three requirements of reason at the heart of this structure are: "first, a basic rule or procedure of moral choice; second, a metaphysic grounding the possibility of strict moral retribution; and third, . . . 'a transmoral' suspension of retribution in the face of self-confessed and inescapable human wrongdoing."[28] Green notes a similarity between this "deep structure" and that which has developed in Christian theology over centuries of effort at "grounding human moral striving in the face of the experiential difficulties that assault moral idealism." In this Christian theological system, the idea of God as creator and sovereign expresses the moral requirements of impartial regard for all. As judge, God is understood to uphold this standard by ultimately punishing its violations and by rewarding the righteous (usually in some eschatological domain). In the face of persistent human iniquity, God is believed to furnish means of atonement and forgiveness, "thereby tempering justice with mercy."[29] However, although Christianity and African Traditional Religion share some striking similarities, closer examination of African traditional beliefs reveals that the contrasts are far more striking than the similarities. An important area Green points to has to do with the role of God in these two systems of thought. He contends that although African Traditional Religion generally refers to God as creator and sustainer of the universe, morally good, omniscient, and caring toward humans, "yet even where this is held to be true, the high god in Africa is very often regarded as distanced from human affairs." And even when he is considered benign, "the high God is morally otiose, having little direct retributive relationship with humankind."[30] In some situations, the high God is cast in unfavorable terms as one who creates and who kills. However, in African religious thought God is distanced from the task of moral affairs because the task of moral retribution and maintenance of effective moral norms is usually performed by spiritual agents of much lower standing—that is, "by spirits of various sorts, by ghosts and even by human practitioners of spiritual arts."[31] Other characteristics that show the contrast between (Western) Christian thought and African Traditional Religion, according to Green, are the nonexistence of concepts of heaven and hell in African Traditional Religion, the lack of messianic expectations and hope, and the absence of eschatological thought with God "stepping in to right all wrongs or to punish wickedness."[32] And although African Traditional Religion affirms the continuation of life after death, where the person is believed to join the spirit world of the ancestors to continue life in some ways similar to the life before death, this belief does not constitute a hope for improved existence or for ultimate reward and punishment since a person's moral depravity or moral rectitude "[does] not count in the beyond and whatever penalties or rewards those may bring have no bearing on life after death."[33] Mbiti makes this point too when he stresses that "the majority of African peoples believe that God punishes in this life." Although God is concerned with humanity's moral life and upholds the moral law, "there is no belief that a person is punished in the hereafter" for his or her wrongdoing in this life. "When punishment comes, it comes in the present life."[34] Whatever the difference in the deep structures that undergird the moral life in the Christian conception or in Africa Traditional Religion, Green, like Mbiti, concludes that Africans believe in a morally saturated universe. "Theirs is a world in which all really significant interpersonal relationships, including important relationships between humans and spiritual beings, have moral content and are governed by moral considerations. If it is approached at the *right level*, African traditional religion can be seen to be powerfully shaped by moral concerns."[35]

The role of intermediary agents and spirits in maintaining moral order in African Traditional Religion is quite remarkable, as we have already seen from the work of Mbiti. These intermediary agents include the ancestors, members of the community who at death become idealized. "Devoid of essential personal characteristics they represent the essence of what might be called structural personality. Their significance lies in the genealogical positions and the rights and duties which derive from them."[36] Ancestors uphold right conduct by punishing moral violations, demanding respect and attention, and getting angry when not given due respect. Belief in the ancestors presents the idea of reciprocity in the African traditional moral world. Dependence here functions like a two-way street, with the dead needing continued respect from and support by the living, and the living needing at least benign neutrality on the part of the dead. Green opines that although superficially regarded, this may seem to be a minimal moral relationship—more like a kind of egoism on one side and fearful propitiation on the other—it also shows, however, the profound role that respect for age and for the fulfillment of lineage and familial duties play in this traditional setting.[37] Other spirits with a significant role in maintaining the African traditional moral world include ancestors and lineage spirits "who operate in specific social contexts where their will is expressed through misfortunes," and some other spirits "who do not act directly but who rely on human agents to effect their will." These spirits underlie the power of spirit mediums who, as mediators between space and the human world and by virtue of the moral authority this confers, are able to arbitrate between living human beings. The spirit medium is required to possess moral probity and integrity. "The Spirit medium is in many ways a subordinate agency within the layer of retributive order." The voice and action of the spirit medium "connect the community with these moral and spiritual entities who help shape human destiny. The spiritual medium is the physical embodiment of the religious retributive order in which Africans know themselves to stand."[38]

The final aspect of this deep structure of moral reason in African Traditional Religion Green refers to as "morally intentional" transmoral "safety valves" such as are found in the doctrine of grace or atonement in Weston religions (Christianity) or of liberation from the world of moral causation in Eastern religions. In short, the question is whether the notion of "mercy" exists in the moral order of African Traditional Religion and whether the sacrifices of African religion amount to an expiatory understanding in African religious thought. Furthermore, the issue is whether a strict order of retribution cannot be tolerated if human ambition gets in the way of realizing enduring moral virtue and well-being.[39] At stake here is nothing less than the question of human culpability and ultimate redemption, which has to do with the traditional Christian topic of sin and grace. We will return to these issues later, but for now it is enough to ask whether the similarities in the deep structure between the two religions are indeed as similar as Green suggests. By Green's own admission, and as we shall see later, there are as many divergences on the architectonic hinge of these deep structures—God, the human person, and the material world—as there are similarities. These differences, I will argue, have significant impact not just on the way people conceive of the moral world or with regard to moral intentions, but also on moral practices.

A third scholar of interest to us here is Laurenti Magesa, the central thesis of whose book on African religion is captured quite succinctly in the subtitle: African religion constitutes a tradition of abundant life. Like Ronald Green, Magesa argues that African Traditional Religion is in the background of all African religiosity, both in Christianity and Islam, and supplies the basic attitude or worldview of most African Christians. So, basically, to speak of African tradition is to talk about African Traditional Religion. To understand African tradition, one needs to understand the position of African Traditional Religion on God, the human person, and creation.[40] Magesa discusses the African tradition in its various manifestations: its understanding of the human person and of life in general; aesthetics, politics, ethics, and of course religion, which he shows to be the architectonic basis of these other expressions or manifestations of African tradition. Like Mbiti and Green, Magesa notes that the world of African Traditional Religion is a hierarchically ordered place where "God is seen as the Great ancestor, the first Founder and the Progenitor, the Giver of Life behind everything that exists. God is the first Initiator of a people's way of Life, its tradition. However, the ancestors, the revered dead human progenitors of the clan or tribe, both remote and recent, are the custodians of this tradition. They are its immediate reason for existence and they are its ultimate purpose."[41] On the lowest rung of the ladder are spirits, who are active beings distinct from humans and reside in nature and phenomena such as trees, rivers, rocks, or lakes. God, the ancestors, and the spirits are all moral powers whose actions affect human life in various ways and to various degrees. They are thus "moral agents." It is the ancestors, however, the custodians of tradition, who determine the way these agents act, and it is tradition that "supplies the moral code and indicates what the people must do to live ethically."[42] African traditions carry out their role as ethical guides in many ways, including myths and rituals. Some of these myths explain the origin of the universe, the nature of the relationship between creation (including humanity) and God, and the source and cause of the human predicament and of evil in general; they also provide "a synopsis of the forces comprising the African moral conception of the universe."[43] Religious rituals provide a means by which the community seeks redress and repairs wrongs that have been committed and that call down calamities and afflictions from spiritual beings—all this to restore the status quo ante or even "to maintain the existing good status quo that society or an individual may be enjoying."[44]

In the hierarchically ordered world of African Traditional Religion, God is the ancestor, par excellence.[45] All life, power, and existence flow from God, and by "right of their primogeniture and proximity to God by death God has granted the ancestors a qualitatively more powerful life force over their descendants." Who constitutes the world of the ancestors? These are "the pristine" men and women, the originators of the lineage or clan or ethnic group. They can also be "the dead of the tribe, following the order of primogeniture. They form a chain through the links of which the forces of the elders [now with the community] exercise their vitalizing influence on the living generation."[46] For Magesa, the ancestors are primarily authority figures whose being implies "moral activity" in that they are the maintainers and enforcers of "norms of social action." Although they are entrusted with these roles in their relationship with humans, "any capriciousness of the ancestors is not taken kindly by the living, just as it would not be acceptable from any elder in society."[47] The ancestors are beyond reproach. "People may complain to God and the ancestors, but they will never accuse them of any moral wrongdoing. Moral culpability is always on the shoulders of humanity."[48] The same hierarchy evident in the relationship between God, the ancestors, and humanity is also present in the relationship between the animate and the inanimate world, the former being superior to the latter. It is also present in relationships between persons, based on age and function. Thus, for example, older persons not only possess a more powerful vital force but a greater responsibility in society and more intense mystical powers.[49] African religion's behavior is centered mainly on the human person and his or her life in this world, "with the consequence that religion is clearly functional, or a means to serve people to acquire earthly goods (life, health, fecundity, wealth, power and the like) and to maintain social cohesion and order."[50]

This should make it clear why some African intellectuals would question the relevance of Christianity on the continent. African Traditional Religion appears to be a self-sufficient system, both from a theological point of view, in that it provides answers to questions of ultimate reality and meaning, at least to its adherents; and from the point of view of morality, in that it provides the moral rules, norms, and instruction in virtues by which human beings can live upright moral lives. The vibrancy of African Traditional Religion in these two aspects—theological and moral—creates a unique opportunity for Christianity in Africa, one that, as Bediako points out has been lost to Christian theology in the West, "for a serious and creative theological encounter between the Christian and primal traditions." [51] It is therefore very important for African theology to ascertain the meaning of African Traditional Religion, both because of the service this tradition renders to Christian theology as "a dialogue partner," and because the very self-awareness of the African theologian and of African theology itself to a large extent hinges on a proper articulation and appreciation of Africa's pre-Christian past.[52]

EVALUATING AFRICAN TRADITIONAL RELIGION: THE THEOLOGICAL TASK

African theologians have tried to take stock of African Traditional Religion in a number of ways. One approach concerns the continuity between African Traditional Religion and Christianity. Simply put, the thesis of the continuity school runs like this: There is only one God, who has revealed himself in Jesus Christ. Christianity in Africa is a historical manifestation, albeit a unique one, of the truths that God has revealed to humankind in various ways, including African Traditional Religion. African cultures and traditions are the purveyors of the revelation of God to Africans. Therefore, "conversion to Christianity in Africa must be coupled with cultural continuity."[53] Basically, theologians of this school speak in language resembling that of Clement of Alexandria about the Christian faith as "a living stream which flows into and through the nations, giving of itself to enrich the people and transforming the land, borrowing from and depositing in each place something of the chemical wealth of the soils which it encounters on its way, and at the same time adapting itself to the shape and features of each locality, taking its coloring from the native soil, while in spite of all these structural adaptations and diverse variations its *esse* and its *differentia* are not imperiled but maintained in consequence of the living ever-replenishing, ever-revitalizing spring which is its source."[54]

The continuity school of thought considers the core of the Christian faith to be the same as the belief in African Traditional Religion on many issues. Thus, for example, as regards the central issue in both Christianity and African Traditional Religion—God—E. Bolaji Idowu, a leading proponent of the continuity school, has this to say: "There is only one God, the creator of heaven and earth and all that is in them; the God who has never left himself without witness in any nation, age, or generation; whose creative purpose has ever been at work in this world, who by one stupendous act of climactic self-revelation in Jesus Christ came to redeem a fallen world . . . He is the same God."[55] According to this school, the problem with the Christianity brought into Africa is that it is heavily clad in European cultural garb and in this way seems like a foreigner. The task of indigenization accordingly therefore is to find ways to divest African Christianity of its European garb since "conversion to Christianity must be coupled with cultural continuity."[56] The church in Africa (Nigeria) "should bear the unmistakable stamp of the fact that she is the Church of God in Nigeria." She "should offer the Nigerians the means of worshiping God as Nigerians; that is, in a way which is compatible with their own spiritual temperament, of singing to the glory of God and praying to God and hearing his holy word in an idiom which is clearly intelligible to them."[57] Indigenization is not to be seen as an attempt to remove any mark of foreignness from the African church. To do that would make the church in Africa "cease to be a living cell within the whole Body."[58] It is instead a call for the Christian church and message to adapt to local situations. Whatever adaptations might be made, the church in Africa must acknowledge the Lordship of Jesus Christ and would continue to make him real to Africans.

The theme of continuity between African Traditional Religion and biblical religion is perhaps most evident in the theology and practice of the African-Initiated Churches. These churches, "founded in Africa, by Africans, and primarily for Africans,"[59] were often established as a rebellion against the mainline Christian denominations. One important characteristic of the AICs is their enthronement of the Old Testament (the Hebrew scriptures) as their foundational charter. It is not that the New Testament is not considered canonical; rather, they simply find the Hebrew scriptures closer to their religious sensibilities as Africans. Thus, even the names many of these churches take speak eloquently of their sense of connection with the Hebrew scriptures and with Judaism; for example: The Holy Sabbath of God Church, Cherubim and Seraphim Church, Mount Zion Church, New Bethel Church. In his book *Prophecy and Revolution*, a study of the role of prophets in African Independent Churches, Nathaniel Ndiokwere has indicated a number of ways in which the AICs have cultivated and maintained an Old Testament and Judaic flavor. These include a strong emphasis on prophecy, and the existence of a group of prophets in the AICs who identify themselves with the prophets of Israel and see themselves more or less as heirs to the prophetic ministry in Judaism. These churches, sometimes made up of the lowliest persons in society, often "compare themselves with the Jews, oppressed but virtuous."[60] One author argues that it is not that the members of these churches feel themselves oppressed like the Jews but that they feel that "they like the Jews are special recipients of divine favor, with positive spiritual benefits."[61] Another point of contact between the AICs and Judaism is found in what Ndiokwere refers to as "the Zion-Jerusalem ideology." This includes the belief that Zion is God's dwelling place where God has chosen to manifest himself to peoples in diverse ways. Thus Zion is the spiritual and cultural center, par excellence, the scene of the great festivals and the center of pilgrimages. There is deep hope in these churches as well that "the destroyed Zion will be restored in the messianic age. Thus, these churches also, like Judaism, harbor a messianic expectation. The figure of this messiah is identified in various ways such as 'Immanuel,' the servant of the Lord, 'The son of man,' Cyrus, Zerubabel, 'Simeon Bar Kohba,' etc."[62] In the AICs the figure of Moses is greatly revered. In fact some of the prophets in these churches see themselves as exercising their ministry just as Moses did, amid a new Israel whom they are called to lead out of slavery.

African Independent Churches have also appropriated, in their own ways, many of the essential laws of Judaism. For example, some of these churches observe the Sabbath. All the ones I know enjoin circumcision as a religious obligation. For many of them the divine name is better spoken in Hebrew, and thus they speak of Yahweh, Jehovah, Elohim, and El Shaddai. One can discern the impact of Judaism on this brand of African Christianity in two other ways: liturgy and theology. Briefly, Christian liturgy in these African churches has a very Jewish flavor, to say the least. The Psalms have been translated into virtually every African language and sung in all of them. The sentiments of prayer, supplication, thanksgiving, protest, pain and anguish, but hope in God before tribulations and trials—all these have become African sentiments as well. In fact the average African Christian knows these Psalms very well by heart, chapter and verse, and can sing many of them in as many languages as he or she can speak, to the shame of many a biblical scholar. The Hebrew scriptures are very well known and are used in the liturgies of African-Initiated Churches. Theological work on the Old Testament, especially on some aspects of the Old Testament religion and of later Judaism, abounds today. This heavy tilt toward Judaism notwithstanding, most African-Initiated Churches consider themselves part of a Christian reformation movement, which, in reaction to an over-Europeanized Christianity, "has discovered and implemented some of the major theological concerns being expressed elsewhere in the world concerning the reformation of the Christian Community."[63] Spurred on by the vernacular translations of the Bible, this reformation in its various manifestations in the different AIC churches encompasses distinctive liturgies, healing practices, church leadership, and appreciations of African Traditional Religion. In short, the AICs are the branch of African Christianity that emphasizes continuity with African Traditional Religion the most, although they also acknowledge in some ways their distinctness as a Christian or Bible-based religion.

Another approach to the question of the theological relevance of African Traditional Religion insists that African Traditional Religion does not need to be interpreted by anyone who is not a practitioner, Christians included. So long as the African religious past is studied either from the point of view of anthropology or sociology, that is not a problem. Efforts at theological interpretation of the African religious past, however, have tended to be viewed with suspicion and skepticism.[64] In any case, since religion is distinguished at least in part by the claims it makes concerning ultimate reality and meaning, it cannot but be evaluated theologically by other religions with which it comes in contact. This is even more the case in the relationship between African Traditional Religion and Christianity because Christianity and

Christian theologians have to show not only what is different between Christianity and African Traditional Religion, but also why Christianity has to seek converts from the latter and what it brings to the table that warrants or justifies the kind of dislocation of the African psyche that all conversions entail. As mentioned earlier, Kwame Bediako makes the issue of the relationship between Christianity and African Traditional Religion one of identity. He points out that the question of the foreignness of Christianity to African contexts has deep historical roots and deep precedent in Christian antiquity. For example, he notes that the attack of Celsus on Christianity in the time of the early church was fundamentally because of its "foreignness," the same note often sounded by critics of Christianity in Africa such as Mbonu Ojike, Okot p'Bitek, and other African intellectuals. Bediako responds that "if African theologians are to answer these critics effectively, a clear distinction of African Christian identity and how it integrates into an adequate sense of African selfhood will doubtless form part of the response."[65] In other words, as the project of this book implies, the African theologian has to show that it is possible for an African to be both African and comfortably Christian.

As to the larger question that this school of thought raises—that of the legitimacy of the theological interpretation of African Traditional Religion—there are two brief answers to give here for now. The first is that since African Traditional Religion makes theological claims about people's lives and ultimate end, these claims must be subjected to a theological critique, as in all other religions. The danger, however, is that this critique is often carried out from the critic's own background. Thus, for example, one often hears people talk about "salvation," "eschatology," and so forth—notions that are definitely foreign to African Traditional Religion and do not amount to the same thing, even where they exist in the African primal worldview. On other occasions, African theologians have often given or sought to give Christian content to commonly used terms such as *God* and in such situations embarked on an endless quest for similarities of meaning for that idea in Christianity and African Traditional Religion. The second answer is that, practically speaking, the reality today is that many Africans are living what can be considered schizophrenic lives because they must contend with two opposing frameworks for explaining reality. It must be the task of African theology to destroy the syncretism at the root of this religious schizophrenia; this will help clear the confusion regarding ultimate reality and meaning which is characteristic of religious discourse in Africa today.

The best response to the question of the theological meaning and relevance of African Traditional Religion does not lie in insisting that there be a complete break with Africa's religious past, as some African Evangelicals insist. This radical discontinuity school argues that African Traditional Religions should be kept at arm's length in African theology. Theological reflections by some of the leading Evangelical theologians in Africa such as "Kato, Tile Tienou, Tokumbo Adeyemo, Cornelius Olowole, Roy Musasiwe and many other African Evangelicals emphasize the need for the African convert 'to make a complete break with the past.'"[66] Birgit Meyer notes that while other groups in society, among them leading Catholic and Protestant mission churches, try to come to terms with local traditions and reconcile new and old ideas in order to develop a genuine African synthesis, "Pentecostalists oppose this revaluation of tradition and culture. They emphasize the 'global' character of their variant of Christianity . . . and the necessity to break away from local traditions."[67] Meyer argues that this call for rupture enables these Pentecostals in many parts of Africa to go on to draw a line of demarcation between "God" and the "devil," "us" and "them," "then" and "now," "modern" and "traditional." Meyer also points out that the Pentecostals cast themselves as heirs to secular modernity in terms of their embrace of progress and continuous renewal. It is hard to see, however, how Pentecostals can actually consider themselves secularists or heirs to modernity in that sense. Nevertheless, Meyer is quite on the mark when she states that the Pentecostals she studied in Ghana consider Christianity "modern" in opposition to African Traditional Religion. Christianity is "modern" in that it supersedes all "fetish" worship. Further, "traditional" means, for these groups, worship of the devil. Consequently, conversion to Christianity would entail repudiation of this traditional past with all its rituals, beliefs, and other cultural accretions, and to be born again in Christ, putting on "the new man." What this shows is that the Pentecostal approach to African Traditional Religion in fact takes the latter very seriously as a living faith. As a result, there is in the interaction of Christianity and African Traditional Religion, according to these Pentecostal groups, an ongoing "clash of covenants." For African Pentecostals, as

Ogbu Kalu points out, the African quest for identity and survival through religious power in Africa creates a power encounter. African Pentecostals employ the concept of covenant to indicate the binding relationship between Africans and their gods. Christians, through the Holy Spirit, are bound to Christ in an eternal covenant; African Traditional Religionists are also bound to their deity or deities. These two commitments run parallel to each other. When they meet, as they have done in Africa, a clash ensues. This clash of covenants "challenges the church's method for doing mission." In this encounter, "Pentecostals argue that mission churches had compromised and that the failure to adopt the right counteraction explains why the spirits that guard the gates of communities have remained unconquered, thereby creating a dilemma for Christianity and calling for a refining of inculturation theology."[68]

Curiously, the approach of African Pentecostals to African Traditional Religion is also very paradoxical, in that this branch of Christianity has borrowed most from African Traditional Religion in many ways. For example, African Pentecostals have taken wholeheartedly to the position of African Traditional Religion that the earth is a war zone of contending and inimical spirits. The human person is at the heart of this eternal power struggle between inimical powers, and faith in Jesus Christ is a weapon for survival in this world. Thus, material failure in any form indicates the triumph of the devil in one's life, or can be attributed to the machinations of evil persons and forces. In this way, African Pentecostals have taken over hook, line, and sinker the African traditional belief in witchcraft and sorcery. Most sicknesses are attributable to these sources, hence also the inordinate desire for leaders and persons with extraordinary healing powers. In this view, Christian religion should be a form of insurance for success in business, in relationships, and in finding and keeping life partners. In this regard, as in African Traditional Religion, "salvation is squarely and solidly reduced to the mere horizontal level, which is akin to the African system of thought."[69] In summary, African Pentecostals, as Kenneth Enang points out, have "constructed a new religious atmosphere . . . in which some aspects of African traditional beliefs and certain aspects of biblical systems of thought are combined to form a new identity. In this way, they are presenting a new culture intended to bury the old one of pain and suffering, but this has not been completely successful because many in the Pentecostal Churches still believe that the past remains in the present. The old enemies are those of the present age, and are enemies of both a spiritual and human nature."[70]

✕ Certainly, the greatest contribution of African Traditional Religion to life in Africa is the deep sense of the divine presence in human life and history, and as part of reality in general. Belief in God—that is, the pervasive sense of the presence of the divine—has serious implications for the way Africans construe the world morally. One area where this influence is felt acutely is in that of human relationships. It is important to remember that Africans recognize life as "life-in-community." For the African, "we can truly know ourselves if we remain true to our community, past and present. The concept of individual success or failure is secondary. The group, the village, the locality, are crucial in one's estimation of one's self."[71] This sense of solidarity is fostered and maintained by an active sense of relatedness to the deity, who frowns on selfishness. Growing up in Nigeria, I recall being told moonlight tales meant to reinforce the idea that the gods reward those who look out for others and punish those who are selfish. In one such tale, a woman is left to care for two young children, her own and that of another woman who had gone away to the farm. At about noon, in the midday heat, the children became thirsty and began to ask for water to drink. The woman who was minding the two children, having run out of drinking water, went over to the neighbor's house (i.e., that of the woman whose child she was taking care of) to take water from the water pot for the two children. On her return from the farm the other woman noticed that her child-minding neighbor had been to her pot of water and insisted that she replenish the supply. This would not have been a problem except that she also stipulated that the water come from the dreaded river from which the gods had forbidden humans to collect water. For reasons only known to her, the woman who owned the water and was now demanding it back, was hoping that her neighbor, the child-minding woman, would perish in the process. When she approached the river, the dreaded god, Amadioha, the Igbo god of thunder, reacted angrily to the human intrusion into his space. The woman, trembling with fear, told Amadioha her story: how she had done a good deed by giving water to the two thirsty children; how her neighbor had been angry with her about this; and how she would be satisfied with nothing less than water from the river of the god.

After listening to her story, Amadioha let her collect the water, and in a surprising twist of benevolence loaded her also with food for her family and jewelry for her use. When this woman got home alive, and with water and many rich gifts to boot, her wicked neighbor, filled with envy, decided to go to the dreaded river herself to fetch water in the hope that she too would receive gifts from Amadioha. The only gift she got from the god was death, for Amadioha killed her.

With stories like this one, African communities have tried to drive home lessons about the importance of human solidarity, the maintenance of family cohesion, the sacredness of human life, and the importance of living morally upright lives.

Chapter Four

ISSUES IN THE THEOLOGY OF NON-CHRISTIAN RELIGIONS

ſ In the encounter between Christianity and African Traditional Religion two basic issues must be attended to, mostly from the Christian perspective, one particular and the other more general and thus more foundational. We dealt with the first issue in chapter 3, namely the question of Christian evaluation of African Traditional Religion in its various aspects. Also, within that discussion we dealt with the questions some African intellectuals have put to Christianity itself. In this way, one might say there is some sort of dialogue going on between these two religions. The problem with this dialogue, however, is that since African Traditional Religion has no written texts and no official spokespersons or prophets, the task is often left to other voices, usually Christian ones, to speak up on behalf of African Traditional Religion and to articulate its tenets. These articulations are not always immune to bias from the detractors of the religion or to overstatement by its overzealous nonparticipant theorists.

ƙ The second question with which we have to deal here concerns the Christian understanding of non-Christian religions in general. This is important for completing the picture of African Traditional Religion because it goes to the heart of the motivation for Christian evangelization everywhere, including Africa, and thus answers the question people like Mazi Mbonu Ojike put to the missionary for justifying Christian proselytization in Africa and elsewhere. Moreover, a better understanding of Christian theological attitudes toward other religions would help to highlight some of the bases for Christian moral insights and demands. I will argue in the subsequent chapters that to understand Christian moral teaching one has first to understand Christian teaching on God. But that is not all. The Christian position on God is also evident in the way Christians have over the centuries reacted to other religions, and to their quality as revelatory channels of God's grace and as sources of moral guidance. In order to achieve my aims in this chapter I have chosen to survey several theologians who have had some significance in discussing Christian approaches to other religions. I use the word *approaches* quite deliberately because there is no one Christian approach to other religions. Some of the theologians I have chosen to discuss here—Schlette, Barth, and Tillich—in various forms and to various degrees either represent or have articulated some strands or aspects of Christian positions on non-Christian religions in general. The same is true of John Hick and Paul Knitter, although in their case they take the question further by addressing the very nature and centrality of Jesus as revealer of God. These theologians are therefore important here because the positions they represent or even help to articulate continue to be influential, one way or the other, in the dealings of various Christian churches and persons with non-Christian religions in general and with African Traditional Religion in particular.

THE EVOLUTION OF CATHOLIC MAGISTERIAL POSITIONS ON NON-CHRISTIAN RELIGIONS

Christian appreciation of non-Christian religions has gone through several phases based on certain exigencies at various historical epochs. Even so, there has always been an optimistic strain running through scripture in regard to humanity's status before God and in positive appreciation of humanity's "extra-biblical religious experience and institutions."[1] God knows no partiality (Rom. 2:6, 10–11), but desires the salvation of everyone (1 Tim. 2:4–6). Following Paul, Christians link the fate of the whole of creation to Adam's fall in Genesis. The consequence of that fall has been universal. Consequently the fruits of the redemption wrought by Christ are also universal. Christ appeared for the destruction of the sins of all (Heb. 9:26–28) and brought about a universal grace that knows no boundaries. According to Justin Martyr, "It is our belief that those . . . who strive to do the good which is enjoined on us have a share in God; . . . Christ is the divine word in whom the whole human race shares and those who live according to the light of that knowledge are Christians, even if they are considered as being godless."⟨Justin, Origen, and Clement of Alexandria are some of the early church writers who not only carried forward that optimistic strain, but amplified it. They saw the *logos* present in a hidden way even in the pagan religions predating Christianity, hence the talk of those religions as being imbued with *logoi spermatikoi* or *rationes seminales*. Clement and his school went even further, refusing to accept the popular opinion that paganism was an invention of the devil, insisting instead that it had actually been willed and planned by God—as the law of the Jews had been—in the guise of a *paidagoges*, the slave who leads the truth-seeker to Christ.[3] The non-Christian religions were therefore a *preparationes evangelicae*, the slave son who was only holding the fortress until the heir appeared.

There is as well what one may regard as a negative strain in Christianity in its evaluation of non-Christian religions. This became even more pronounced when Christianity was thought to have extended to and secured a firm lease in the whole of the inhabited world, when for a brief moment it seemed the whole *oikumene* (the inhabited world) had become Christian. Given this limited geographical perspective, it was easier to formulate an axiom like "no salvation outside the church." This axiom's roots and precise formulation, both negative and positive, date back to Ignatius of Antioch, Irenaeus, Clement of Alexandria, and Cyprian, and have undergone many interpretations. First, the statement was taken literally to mean that damnation awaited anyone, pagans and Jews alike, who was outside the physical confines of the church—that is, the nonbaptized. With increasing numbers of heresies and schisms in the church, it came to be understood, as in the formulations of Boniface VIII in the now famous papal bull *Unam Sanctam*, to mean that "it is altogether necessary for salvation that every human being to be subject to the Roman Pontiff."[4] In 1442, the Council of Florence, following Augustine's disciple Fulgentius of Ruspe, gave a more critical turn to the axiom: "The Holy Roman Church firmly believes, professes, and proclaims that none of those who are outside the Catholic church—not only pagans, but Jews also, heretics and schismatics—can have part in eternal life, but will go into eternal fire 'which was prepared for the devil and his angels,' unless they are gathered into that church before the end of life."[5] Experience soon forced many in the church to rethink such assertions. For, faced with an expanded world and with the attendant variations in peoples and cultures, as well as an ever-accelerating pace of change in culture, science, and technology, the church itself could no longer make such an assumption. The sheer impossibility of baptizing every soul on the face of the earth (the efforts of the Francis Xaviers and the Peter Clavers in the church notwithstanding) forced the church to concede membership in the church even to those who had not received baptism, either because of invincible ignorance or physical incapacity, but who could have accepted baptism had they known its value or had occasion to be baptized. Still, the church maintained, in the words of Pope Pius XII in *Mystici Corporis*, that "even if they [non-Catholics] are related to the mystical body of the Redeemer by desire, still they lack many divine gifts and helps which can only be enjoyed within the Catholic Church."[6]

Many of the official Catholic pronouncements on non-Christian peoples especially in the years immediately preceding the Second Vatican Council conveyed the sense of urgency and concern with which the church viewed the plight of those who had not yet received the Christian faith. Interestingly, this was the era when Africa was most intensely evangelized by several missionary groups. The influence of these official church statements on the work of the missions in Africa is unmistakable, as is the fact that given the pastoral and theological climate of this period, missionary work in Africa was an act of love, a love that took the lives of many and which bore many rich fruits for Africa.[7] For example, in *Maximum Illud* Benedict XV insists that "an anonymous number of souls must be saved from the proud tyranny of Satan and be brought to the freedom of the children of God. . . . In their misunderstanding many people are still very far from the true faith. . . . What type of people needs brotherly love more than the nonbelievers who do not know God at all? Bound by blind, unrestrained passions they languish in the worst possible slavery, that of the domination of the devil."[8] Although Pope Pius XI in *Rerum Ecclesiae* describes these non-Christian peoples as "heathens," "savages," and "semi-civilized," he also calls on the clergy and religious of the rest of the church to work hard for the conversion of these pagans, who "even in our day number almost a billion." Said the pontiff, "Since no one can be thought so poor and naked, no one so infirm or hungry, as he who is deprived of the knowledge and grace of God, so there is no one who cannot understand that both the mercy and grace of God shall be given to him who, on his part, shows mercy to the neediest of his fellow beings."[9] Pius XII also talked of about 85 million people in "darkest" Africa who still worshipped their "heathen gods."[10] All these statements were very different from those of a few years later, when the Second Vatican Council would proclaim that "God is not remote from those who in shadows and images seek the unknown God since he gives to all people life and breath and all things (Acts 17:25–28), since the Savior wills all people to be saved (cf. I Tim. 2:4). Those who through no fault of their own, do not know the gospel of Christ or his church, but who nevertheless seek God with a sincere heart, and, moved by grace, try in their actions to do his will as they know it through the dictates of their conscience—those too may achieve salvation."[11]

Much as this statement represents a recapitulation of the basic official Catholic position on the issue of non-Christian religions, it is also the first official statement suggesting that salvation can occur outside the church. This too has had its attendant difficulties. Does this statement really represent a significant shift from "outside the church there is no salvation"? Those who think it does talk of the great openings the statement has created and how the prospect for dialogue with other religions has been tremendously enhanced. Others who think that the statement is merely a reframing of the original axiom have on the other hand gone on to reinterpret the concept of the church and to show how the council was really not saying anything new. The problem, they argue, is one of faulty ecclesiology (not with the teaching church). Therefore, a whole new ecclesiological orientation has arisen to try to show what "church" should be understood to mean in this statement. In any case, the recognition can no longer be retracted that God acts in whatever way God wills, and that consequently it is inconceivable that God might not be acting and saving within African Traditional Religions or other non-Christian religions of the world, for example. Some Catholic theologians have in fact already taken the extra step and declared the non-Christian religions to be ways of salvation. However, as Hans Küng also points out, there is a difference between saying that the religions are ways of salvation and that they are true: "If Christian theology today asserts that all men—even in the world religions—can be saved, this certainly does not mean that all religions are equally true. They will be saved, not because of, but in spite of polytheism, magic, human sacrifice, forces of nature. They will be saved not because of but in spite of all untruth and superstition. To this extent the world religions can be called ways of salvation only in a relative sense."[12] Two things are responsible for the modern theological concession that religions can be ways of salvation: one reason is scriptural, the other is demographic. From scripture, theologians cite instances of God's universal salvific will and purpose. Demographically speaking, it is obvious that most of humanity has never been and might never be Christian. Then arises the perplexing question whether all of these people are a *massa damnata* or whether God does intend their salvation as well. The answer to this question has taken many twists and turns, and involves several issues at the heart of our discussion here and of the enterprise called African theology in general. As mentioned earlier, we will in this chapter do the following: first, we will undertake an extensive discussion of the theology of non-Christian religions from a number of Western scholars, Catholic and Protestant; and second, we will provide a brief synthesis of the issues herein discussed as they pertain to the main interest of this book: the search for foundations for an African Christian theological ethics.

We begin the discussion here by examining the work of the German Catholic theologian Heinz Robert Schlette, who approaches the question of non-Christian religions from the salvation history context. The problem as Schlette sees it is how to reconcile God's professed universal salvific will with the teaching that "outside the Church there is no salvation," and how to reconcile the indispensability of Jesus for universal human salvation with the stark reality that the vast majority of human beings are not Christians and have no intention of becoming Christians. A few presuppositions form the background to Schlette's thinking on the non-Christian religions: that following Vatican II, it is correct to say that a genuine possibility for salvation exists in the non-Christian religions; that in the dictum "outside the Church there is no salvation," the word *church* cannot be understood in the sense of "the juridically constituted" Catholic Church but as "an objective principle defining a category," and implying that "if and to the extent that anyone is saved, he is so by reasons of the church, through the Church, through its representative capacity conferred on it by God."[13] As has already been noted, following the acknowledgment by the Second Vatican Council that a genuine possibility of salvation exists in the non-Christian religions, some Catholic theologians have gone a step further to say that these religions can also be "ways of salvation." Schlette is one of these. How did he come to this conclusion?

Central to Schlette's salvation history approach to the theology of non-Christian religions is the historical character of human existence and the recognition of the history of humanity as one open field for God's salvific action toward the human race. "Man never exists except suspended . . . between past and future. . . . The past is never totally past, but always present and future as well, and the future is never totally future but always adumbrated in the past and so contributes to determine the present."[14] Thus, the historical character of human nature is the very basis of the possibility of history in general and constitutes the basic feature "which makes redemptive history possible." All history whether sacred or secular is materially, at least, co-extensive, and viewed as an arena where God acts to save mankind, all history is sacred history of redemption. Schlette defines sacred history as "the sum of all that has occurred and does occur in the history of mankind on God's part for the salvation of the human race; and which corresponds to the fundamental structural feature of the human situation [which] we term its genuinely historical, freely decided character."[15] But who decides which history is sacred or profane? Or how does sacred history come to realize itself as such? Schlette answers that this realization is the result of the history of revelation having actually occurred in history. Being aware of itself, sacred history takes on the task of assigning value to all history. But this history that is able to recognize the other as "other" must be different from the other and special. Schlette calls the other general sacred history and this latter special sacred history.[16] Following G. von Rad, Schlette argues that the Yahwist was able in Genesis 1–11 to build a "universalist conception of world and sacred history" and to limit the absolute origin believed in with the history of Israel. Schlette discerns, especially in chapters 6–9 of Genesis, that "a fundamental sanctioning of all non-Israelite religions is recognized as deriving from God himself"; and as "an expression of Israel's knowledge of its faith, Israel was seeking to understand itself from this comparison with the general covenant concluded by Yahweh."[17] This is important not only as regards method, but above all because here the distinction between general and special history is implied.[18] Furthermore, it could be inferred, according to Schlette, that sacred history in the most general sense as a saving relation between God and mankind "goes back to the beginning," since it has always been the will of God that all people should be saved.

After dividing sacred history into general sacred history and special sacred history, Schlette further divides the latter in two: Israel, and the new people of God in the New Testament—the church. General sacred history concerns salvation, which Schlette describes as the "whole life and existence of mankind as ordered according to God's intention." If God's covenant with Noah indicates that salvation can occur "within the state," the evil and depravity in that state notwithstanding, it means that God has always given humanity as a whole in principle and universally a genuine chance of salvation. Following Karl Rahner, Schlette argues that if human nature and existence are historical in character, and "if precisely this character, which belongs to the constitutive features of human life, expresses itself as sociability, followership, communicative association and personal relationships, then it must be admitted that a religious activity situated on the plane of general sacred history is never merely interior, subjective and individualist activity . . . that the experience of God and consequently the real chance of salvation in the state of general sacred history is manifested and accomplished in a definite social way, that is to say, in the form of religions."[19] The non-Christian religions are thus tangible expressions of God's will to save, a divine offer of salvation deserving confidence. One can be religious only within the religion known to the people of one's time and place. To imagine that God would only enter into a saving relationship with the individual in a religion alien and unknown to him or her is a contradiction of what is known about God; it would interiorize religion and make it a purely transcendent thing without any "tangible predicamental element and [would] consequently annul the principle . . . that every actual real religion is a social thing."[20] The question is this: If the religions (general sacred history) are proper and legitimate channels through which God offers salvation to human beings, what is the relevance of special sacred history? Why mission?

Schlette further argues that the meaning of special sacred history is very well brought out by the term *representation*—that is, chosen to stand for *all*. Thus Israel and the Old Testament become for other nations and religions a representative chosen in a historically concrete manner for God's saving action in Jesus Christ. With reference to the New Testament, Schlette states that the question of the meaning of special sacred history can no longer satisfactorily be answered by reference to "the perdition and estrangement from God from which God has delivered us by Christ's atoning death . . . the peril to salvation of individual immortality could not have been a sufficient ground for special sacred history and in particular for the logos." After all, the religions could have mediated salvation for the individual. Rather, the essential significance of special sacred history and of the incarnation of the logos lies in "the freely bestowed revelation and communication of his nature before the eyes of men, that is, in their history. It can also be said that in the revelation of the divine *doxa* to men or in the complete epiphany of God, there is to be seen the fundamental meaning of special sacred history and also of general sacred history as far as what applies to the former also applies to the latter."[21] The individual, even prior to the concrete historical appearance of special sacred history, is already called to a saving relationship with God. The individual's ruin or salvation lies in his or her attitude to this historically mediated divine call. So, the motive for special sacred history is the glorification of God (John 17:1, 22), which would reach its fullness when "the son surrenders" all things to the Father (1 Cor. 15:27–28) so that the restitution of all things occurs. It is a fundamental affirmation of the New Testament and of all Christian theology, Schlette says, that all sacred history has come to an end with and in Jesus Christ, and all distinction between Jew and Gentile has been abolished (Gal. 3:28) "*a limino*" and suspended "*and must now be accepted by faith in the risen Christ and so make way for God's reign . . .*"[22]

Confrontation with the absolute eschatological fulfillment and the faith to accept the offer therein being made are both God's gifts,

given to whomever he will. Meanwhile the religions continue to be ordinary ways of salvation for those who had neither the offer nor faith
in the offer extended to them. Such is the mystery of divine election.
The church is therefore an "eschatological community called together
from the four winds which by its existence in the world is to bear witness to the goal to which the ordinary ways of salvation (the religions)
lead, and which at the same time demands in the name of God that the
ordinary way should be followed in obedience and humility."[23] The
church is "extraordinary" because it is always the *truth* and the *life*. It
is superior not because it offers a more advantageous chance of salvation. Rather, its superiority consists "in God's freedom (by choosing
the Church) to reveal his glory before the world by the way of special
sacred history."[24] Thus, for Schlette, Mbonu Ojike's question as to the
moral superiority of Christianity, important as it is, would be a secondary one. More important is that the church as a community of those
who have been called together by God is, as Vatican II would say, the
sacrament of Christ in the world. It is chosen to bear witness to God's
enduring love for humanity. Although the moral ramification of this
election is important, it does not trump its importance as kerygma.
The choice is free and must not be seen as a discrimination against or
as a devaluation of other religions by God. The validity, or, to use Rahner's term, the legitimacy, of religions as ways of salvation lasts, however, until the religions actually refuse the divine offer after a genuine
confrontation with "the absolute claim of special sacred history, that
is, the *Kairos* situation."[25] But the religions as structurally constituted
social institutions can never be confronted with the claim of the eschatological message to absoluteness and finality. Only individuals who
belong to those religions can be so confronted. "It is really only individual human beings belonging to a certain religion who find themselves in a decision or crisis and who if they accept the claim are extri-
cated from the religion that surrounds them. In this way there occurs
in the individual what has happened for each of the baptized in faith:
a sharing in the death and resurrection of Christ (cf. Rom. 6:3–8)."[26]
As for the religions that themselves are not placed in a situation of crisis and therefore of choice, those remain legitimate—that is, ways of
salvation—as long as there are people who are sincerely convinced of
their legitimacy.

Clearly, therefore, the reason salvation history must take place in the religions, according to Schlette, is that this is demanded by humanity's social nature.[27] However, to conclude from humanity's social nature that the religions were *the* ways of salvation for pre-Christian humanity raises a host of questions. First, there is no reason whatsoever in humanity's social nature as such to credit it with salvific qualities. Even if there were, there does not seem to be sufficient ground to make a purely religious grouping the only possible channel for God to carry out his salvific intentions. It is even more difficult to prove conclusively that the religious mode of bonding is universally the primary (prior) mode of human bonding. What about bonding to hunt or to gather food? Are these religious activities in the sense Schlette understands religion?

TWO PROTESTANT REPRESENTATIVES: KARL BARTH AND PAUL TILLICH

Karl Barth

Only one revelation has occurred in all human history as far as Karl Barth is concerned. It occurred between 1 and 30 AD in the person of Jesus Christ and was the time of fulfillment. Earlier, there was the time *ante Christum natum*, the time of the witness to expectation of revelation; the Old Testament belongs to this time. The time of the witness to expectation also belongs to the time of fulfillment, although it was also quite different. The Old Testament is "the genuine expectation" of revelation, which raises it high above the other times *ante Christum natum*. In regard to the Old Testament one can talk of revelation only in the sense of an expected revelation or of an expectation of revelation, because revelation has "broken into the peculiar context of the Old Testament, from an exalted height." Otherwise, the Old Testament would just be seen as "one remarkable phenomenon . . . of piety in the ancient East."[28] The Old Testament by itself is not capable of recognizing itself as the expectation of revelation. Revelation alone, Jesus Christ, makes it aware of this by his death and resurrection. Jesus is manifested in the Old Testament as the expected one. This is clearly demonstrated in the many Old Testament covenants between God and man, each important though bearing no stamp of finality but only expecting the revelation of Jesus Christ as the covenant between God and man; it is also demonstrated in the many spokesman "mediator" agents of the Old Testament—Abraham, Moses, David, Solomon, the servant of Deutero-Isaiah, the kings and prophets of Israel—all representatives of God with regard to the law and in anticipation of the one man who himself would be prophet, priest, and king, and then God's representative par excellence.[29]

There is also a time of recollection of revelation: the period *post Christum natum*. It is the time of the New Testament and is closely bound with the time of revelation through a relation that has nothing to do "with the relation of historical cause and effect." In fact this connection "can as little rest upon the illuminating historical relation, say, between New Testament religion and its founder, as previously upon the relation between Old Testament religion and the original religious personality of Jesus as rooted in it."[30] The question arises, therefore, why the New Testament, this particular monument of a religious past among many others, will have to be regarded as documents of the revelation of God. The answer to this question lies in understanding the New Testament in terms of its peculiar assignment, its formation on the basis of revelation. Only in view of these can one sensibly speak of the New Testament as documents of the revelation of God. But this knowledge is open only to those within the perspective of revelation, who have been granted the power to participate in revelation itself. In other words, even in relation to the New Testament claim to revelation, we are pointed to Jesus Christ himself, to the act of lordship in which he gives the Holy Spirit of hearing and obedience to whom he will.[31] The truth of God's revelation is grounded in him and proved only by him. The New Testament is a record of recollection of this event and is concerned with showing that the sanctification of man, which was the goal of the Old Testament, has been carried out by God himself who has become man. The Old Testament and the New Testament are both expectations. But unlike the Old Testament the New Testament knows who it is that is expected: the Christ "who it already knows as very God and very man."[32]

Revelation is the action of the self-revealing God. In revelation, God encounters the human person and possibly determines his or her existence. Thus there is a human aspect to revelation as something that may be grasped historically and psychologically. Here, precisely, we come up against the issue of man's religions. If revelation also has a human aspect, can we judge it by or try to understand it in terms of other things human? That is, can we really regard revelation as unparalleled in human experience? Is not Christianity in the first instance only a particular instance of the universal called religion? Could not Christianity be regarded as "a species within a genus in which there may be other species"? According to Barth, human beings have always necessarily shown that they are aware of forces and influences beyond them, influencing their lives and world, and have consequently sought to relate every aspect of their lives to something ultimate and decisive, "which is at least a powerful rival to their will and power." This wholly "other" is reverenced by individuals and groups as the source of the dedication to and sanctification of human life. It is difficult, therefore, Barth argues, "to find any time or place when man was not aware of his duty to offer worship to God or gods in the form of concrete cults. . . . It is difficult to find any time or place when it was not thought that the voice of the deity has been heard and that it ought to be asserted and its meaning investigated."[33]

The "main" religions have holy books that, like the Christian Bible, grapple with questions basic to human existence: the origin and destiny of the world and of humanity, religious and moral law, sin, redemption, and so on. Why does Christianity claim any special importance? The fact is, Barth says, that in his revelation God has allowed his own reality and possibility to be expressed in ways analogous to human realities and possibilities. By revealing himself under these categories, "the divine particular is hidden in a human universal, the divine content in a human form, and therefore that which is divinely unique is something which is only singular."[34]

Even the Christian religion regarded as a particular concept "within general observation and experience, as a content of human form" and therefore as a member of the series designated as "religion," belongs to the category of man's realities and possibilities. Karl Barth believes that theology and the church made a mistake by allowing God's revelation to be subsumed under the category of religion. The issue is determining what it means to regard God's revelation as man's religion and therefore as religion among other religions. Which determines the character of the other, religion or revelation? A task for theology today, Barth insists, is to return religion to the status of a problem in theology and to stop seeing it as *the* problem of theology; to abolish the understanding of the church as a religious brotherhood and begin to regard it as "a state in which religion is 'sublimated' in the most comprehensive sense of the word"; to begin to regard faith as "a form of judgment and grace of God, which is naturally and most concretely connected with man's piety in all its forms and not as a form of human piety." Barth believes that the reversal in the conception of the relationship between religion and revelation among Europeans stemmed from vacillation in regard to what has taken place once and for all in Jesus Christ. He claims that the "discovery" of religion belongs to that era when Europeans, in continuation of an earlier movement in Greco-Roman antiquity, went back to discover man, his nature, his possibilities, his capabilities, and his humanity. Theology did not remain unaffected by the Renaissance spirit. But rather than "participate in the trend and lovingly to investigate it," theology fell prey to the absolutism with which man of that period made himself the center and measure and goal of all things.[35] By cooperating thus with the zeitgeist, theology became "religionistic." Theology's sin, however, was more that of omission than of commission, a sin of unbelief, too, that failed to proclaim Jesus the Christ as the *One* and *All* but sought instead to "liberate" humanity from Christ's lordship and ownership. By so doing, theology lost its object: "revelation in all its uniqueness. And losing that, it lost the seed of faith with which it could have moved mountains, even the mountain of humanistic culture."[36] And this by exchanging its "birthright" for the concept of religion. To correlate revelation and religion in the form of comparison or delineation or for whatever reason is a category mistake. Religion can be considered only in the light of revelation, never as an independent issue to be first taken seriously and then related to God's revelation. Whatever will be said of religion has to be said in the light of God's sovereign action on man — and man only as he is revealed in the light of revelation. Theology has therefore to investigate the phenomenon of religion only from the standpoint of revelation and faith.

According to Barth, "Religion is unbelief, a concern, indeed . . . the one great concern of godless man."[37] All religions, including the Christian religion, must be so considered. Religion is a human thing and a type of unbelief that tries to anticipate what revelation would do as its proper work: to teach the truth to human beings that God is God and our Lord. In doing this, however, it replaces the divine reality offered and manifested to us in revelation with a concept of God that is nothing but the result of "human insight and constructiveness and energy."[38] Religion is therefore a contradiction of revelation. Truth can come only from truth (revelation). But in religion human beings try all by themselves to grasp at truth in an a priori manner: they try "to grasp at God." Revelation on the other hand is radical— assistance from God to us unrighteous, unholy, and lost creatures— and thus presupposes our helplessness. Humanity should not have been so unrighteous, unholy, lost, and helpless since it was created in God's image and meant for salvation and not for destruction. But humanity fell from its blessedness, a truth made present to it by the revelation: Christ Jesus. On his own, man cannot declare himself righteous, holy, and saved. In Jesus the Christ God reconciles the world to himself and replaces all human attempts at justification, salvation, sanctification, and conversion which the religions represent. To believe in Jesus Christ is to recognize and to accept that everything has been done once and for all in him. The efforts religions make to sanctify, justify, and save apart from revelation again constitute an alienation from and a shutting of the door against God. God himself had taken care of the sin of the world, and he wills that "all our care should be cast upon him because he careth for us."[39]

Religions are for Barth, therefore, an ultimate non-necessity (at least in their origin) and are fundamentally mere empty externalizations and expressions.

Christianity too is unbelief. Like every other religion it constitutes an opposition to the divine revelation and is an "active idolatry and self-righteousness." However, Christianity is the true religion; it has been so declared by revelation. Like a "justified" sinner it has been upheld, sanctified, and justified by revelation. All religion is sin. But because Christianity is the religion of revelation "it is sin committed with a high hand." We can thus speak of the truth of Christianity "only within the doctrine of the *justificatio impii*."[40] When the Christian realizes that his religion and he himself both contradict the grace of God, he comes to this realization through "the righteousness of God which makes an infinite sanctification" for his sins.[41] This amounts to a tenacious clinging to grace in spite of the contradiction of grace which he lives in. The symptom of the truth of the Christian religion is in this: that the Christian is able constantly in faith to confess his sinfulness and that of his religion. Barth argues that when we ground the truth of the Christian religion upon grace, "it is not a question of the immanent truth of religion of grace as such, but of the reality of grace itself by which one religion is adopted and distinguished as the true one before all others. It is not because it is a religion of grace that this happens, nor is it because it is so perhaps in a particularly insistent and logical way. But conversely, it is because this happens that it is a religion of grace in an insistent and logical way."[42] In the Christian religion we come face to face with an act of divine creation. The Christian religion has no autonomous "self-grounded existence." It has been brought into existence by the name of Jesus. Here we are also dealing with an act of divine election: the name of Jesus alone makes Christianity a divine creation and a true religion on the basis of a free election and God's good pleasure. The Christian religion is also an act of justification or forgiveness of sins freely given by God and thus making it worthy to be the true religion. Lastly, in the relationship between the name of Jesus Christ and the Christian religion we are also dealing with an act of sanctification. Christianity is differentiated from other religions by this association with the name of Christ. It historically manifests and reveals this name. Christianity is an eloquent proclamation of an event from God's side. There is also a corresponding event issuing from man's side, which is determined in the Old Testament, and God is seen both by Christians and Jews as acting and saving. Even if the later revelation in Jesus would be final and absolute—that is, the source of the efficacy and authentication of the Old Testament revelation (in what sense this can be said would have to be clearly worked out)—it cannot be denied that in the Old Testament too, God has spoken and has manifested himself as God and Lord. The Old Testament makes this claim prior to Christianity, as Christianity even acknowledges. The New Testament authors often express their indebtedness to the Old Testament event and strenuously seek to show that the groundwork of what they have inherited had been worked out there.

Barth's position is of course based on the general Protestant stand on grace and salvation as mediated only through Jesus Christ. His

theology of religions is a high-water mark of Christian uniqueness—
a fact that has spawned many misunderstandings and misreadings,
particularly on the African religious scene. There are today in Africa
many Evangelical pastors and groups who parrot Barth's dictum about
the sinfulness of religion, relating their views to African Traditional
Religion and its various manifestations. Of course none of this is to
be blamed on Barth. But some of these groups, lacking the sophistication of Barth and in total disregard of the other aspects of his views on
the matter, vehemently oppose African religion as merely a human creation with little or no merit whatsoever. These groups, contrary to
Barth, divide the world into a *massa damnata* and a group saved by a
free election in Jesus Christ, and consider any attempt to understand
African religions, let alone learn from them or dialogue with them, as
sin. There is also within this Evangelical group a palpable disdain for
the institutional church and for historical Christianity. The history of
Christianity, when they grant that such a history exists at all, begins
with Christ in the gospels and sometimes continues through some of
the early fathers of the church. Anything after Augustine is sin. That
history resumes with the rise of Evangelical Christianity in modern
Africa. In this group, there is no thought of a church order or church
teaching that is continuous and truly representative of God's will expressed in Christ, and rather than speak of church, we should only
speak of Christianity in nondenominational terms. In discussing the
relationship between African religions and Christianity, this group,
whose members are increasing in number, presents a challenge to the
mainline churches and the theologians therefrom with regard to the
extent they can acknowledge African religion as in some ways revelatory or, even more specifically for our purposes here, sources of moral
insights and truths.

Finally, although I believe Karl Barth is right in his doctrine of
Christian uniqueness, I would take a position that serves as something
of a foil to his, one that is strong on the Christian side but is less dialec-
tical and dichotomous. In other words, I believe that one can hold that
the religions, especially in this case African religions, have value as
channels of God's grace and are therefore avenues of salvation for
those who have not had the offer of salvation made to them in Christ
through his church; and that one can argue this case without giving in
to the confusion that characterizes much of theological discourse today

about what is revealed and what is not, and about any non-Christian religions as "true" religions, however that term is construed. Christians cannot be too assimilationist on this issue. They must continue to accept, as Justin Martyr and some of the early church fathers did, that the truth of God's self-disclosure is available to humanity in its absolute fullness and uniqueness in Jesus Christ and is witnessed to through his church, while granting as well that God continues to show his face to those who sincerely seek him in other contexts and who, out of no fault of their own, cannot come to explicit faith in him through his Son in the church.

Paul Tillich

Like Karl Barth, Paul Tillich has a strong belief in revelation as the starting point for any discussion on religion and the religions. But that is as far as the similarities between the two men go. The place and especially the content each of them gives the notion of revelation sometimes appear irreconcilable. Paul Tillich defines revelation as "a special and extraordinary manifestation which removes the veil from something which is hidden in a special and extraordinary way."[43] Revelation takes the veil from what concerns us ultimately, the ground of our being. It is always revelation "to someone in a concrete situation of concern." There is always a giving as well as receiving side in revelation. There cannot be any revelation if there is no one to receive it as his ultimate concern. And every reality, thing, or event can be a medium of revelation; nothing is in principle excluded from this role. Since everything participates in being itself, no medium of revelation is such due to any special qualities it possesses. There is, however, a difference with regard to the truth and significance of revelation which a given medium mediates. Consider a stone and a person, for instance. The one "represents a rather limited number of qualities which are able to point to the ground of being and meaning" while the other represents the central qualities, and by implication all qualities which can point "to the mystery of being."[44] Mediums of revelation do not in themselves possess a revelatory character; they reveal only that which uses them as a medium and bearer of revelation. Under special conditions, history, groups, and individuals can enter into "the revelatory constellation" and thus become revelatory. "If history points beyond itself in a correlation of ecstasy and sign-event, revelation occurs. If groups of persons become transparent for the ground of meaning, revelation occurs."[45]

All revelation occurs in history, the medium notwithstanding. But only when an event is experienced ecstatically as miracle[46] and through history can the revelation that occurs be described as historical. Persons or groups of persons can become mediums of revelation as either "representatives" or "interpreters" or as both. This does not make them exclusive mediums in any sense. "The prophet, although a medium of historical revelation, does not exclude other personal mediums of revelation. The priest who administers the sphere of the holy, the saint who embodies holiness himself, the ordinary believer who is grasped by the divine spirit, can be mediums of revelation for others and for a whole group."[47] It is neither the priest's function as such nor the moral or religious perfection of the saint which makes these mediums of revelation. They are so only because they are transparent for the ground of being. Tillich states that there has occurred a universal revelation and a final or actual revelation. Though Tillich has said that revelation occurs through history, he is quick to point out that the history of revelation is not the history of religion. That is, "there is revelation outside the religious sphere," and there is much in religion that is not revelation. But there has occurred a final revelation, and also a universal revelation that was preparatory for the final revelation and has created the symbols and the religious experience that help to make the final revelation understandable and receivable.[48] Universal preparation gets ready for the final revelation under different guises: by the conservation of the sacramental object (through the priest), "which keeps alive the power of original revelation by making new individuals, new groups, new generations enter the revelatory situation";[49] by criticism in the form of mysticism, which devaluates every medium of revelation and tries to unite the soul directly with the ground of being and make it enter the mystery of existence without the help of a finite medium; by rational criticisms "directed against distorted revelations"; by criticism in the form of a "prophetic attack against distorted sacramentalism," an attack that "subject[s] the concrete mediums of revelation and the concrete sacramental symbols and priestly systems to the judgment of the divine law, to that which ought to be because it is the law of God";[50] and lastly, by anticipation—that is, the Old Testament religion, which

Tillich regards as the immediate preparation for the final revelation. "The universal revelation as such could not have prepared the final revelation. Since the latter is concrete, only *one* concrete development could have been its immediate preparation. . . . The other religions, albeit in a minor scale, also represent 'the maturing process' working in all history and moving towards the *Kairos*—the time of fulfillment as the Christ."

In spite of his insistence on the religions as representing only one medium of revelation among many, Tillich for all practical purposes traces the beginning of revelation to the appearance of religion in man's horizon, and vice versa, thus making the history of revelation synonymous with the history of religion. Tillich defines religion as "the state of being grasped by an ultimate concern, a concern which qualifies all other concerns as preliminary and which itself contains the answer to the question and meaning of our life."[51] The history of revelation, on the other hand, is "the moment man becomes aware of the ultimate question of his estranged predicament and of his destiny to overcome this predicament."[52] The point should be stressed that this moment when one becomes aware of the ultimate questions in one's life (that is, the beginning of the history of revelation) is the same as the moment when one is grasped by ultimate concern (religion) and therefore the start of the history of revelation and of the history of religion.

There has occurred in Jesus a final revelation. This is the very basis of Christianity. *Final* is here to be understood in the sense of "the decisive, fulfilling, unsurpassable revelation, that which is the criterion of all the others."[53] Every revelation is conditioned by its medium. Final revelation is one that has been able to sacrifice its own finite condition and become perfectly transparent to the mystery it reveals. This medium thus becomes one with its ground of being without "separation and disruption." Jesus achieved the status of final revelation by "conquering the demoniac forces which tried to make him demoniac by tempting him to claim ultimacy for his finite nature,"[54] through trying to induce him to sacrifice himself as medium of revelation by avoiding the cross and thus become an object of idolatry. But Jesus would not succumb to this temptation. In his cross, therefore, Jesus negated "that medium of revelation which impressed itself on his followers as messianic in power and significance."[55] He sacrificed his flesh and consequently became "Spirit" and "New Creature" and

thus Christ and final revelation. Following Paul's letter to the Philippians Tillich argued that the Christ is Christ "only because he did not
insist on his equality with God but renounced it as a personal possession (Philippians, ch. 2)." Therefore, a Jesus-centered religion or theology would be wrongheaded because "Jesus is the religion and theological object as the Christ and only as the Christ. And he is the Christ
as the one who sacrifices what is merely 'Jesus' in him. The decisive
trait in this picture is the continuous self-surrender of Jesus to Jesus
who is the Christ."[56] Jesus as Christ is therefore final revelation on
two grounds: he was closely united with God; he was victorious over
all attempts to make him exploit this unity with God to his personal
advantage. Christianity is universal not because it is superior to other
religions, but because it witnesses to final and universal revelation.

According to Tillich, "where there is revelation there is salvation."[57] To speak of universal and final revelation is to speak of universal and final salvation. The concept of salvation includes that of revelation and emphasizes "the saving manifestation of the ground of
being."[58] We do not mean by revelation here "information about divine matters . . . to be accepted partly through intellectual operations,
partly through a subjection of the will to authorities."[59] Nor should
salvation just be seen as the ultimate fulfillment of the individual beyond time and history. Salvation, Tillich says, is to make whole and
healthy—whether of sickness, demoniac possession, or "servitude to
sin and to the ultimate power of death." Seen in this sense, therefore,
salvation like revelation takes place in time and history. Both are un-
shakably and objectively founded "in the event of Jesus as the Christ,"
an event which "unites the final power of salvation with the final
truth of revelation."[60] Revelation as received by man in his existential
condition is fragmentary; so is salvation. It is not total. Nor must salvation be total (that is, identical with being taken into the state of
blessedness, as against total condemnation to everlasting pain or eternal death), argues Tillich. Salvation to eternal life should not be made
dependent on an encounter with Jesus as the Christ and with "acceptance of his saving power." Were such to be the case, Tillich adds,
only a few will reach salvation.[61] Only in Christ, however, is the healing quality (salvation) complete and unlimited. The salvation (healing)
with which human beings are in contact in history is not enough. All
human persons need to participate in the power of the new being in

history. Even the Christian religion "remains in the state of relativity with respect to salvation."[62] Like the rest of the religions, and indeed like all human beings, Christianity too is in need of "a religion of paradox" or of the "concrete spirit" that is realizable by means of "a symbol of a divine mediator"—found only in Jesus the Christ, bearer of the new being and mediator of the reconciliation between God and man. When is this religion of the "concrete spirit" to make its appearance? In the evening of his life Tillich admitted that "the religion of the concrete spirit . . . can happen here and there within the religions."[63]

What we have seen so far in the work of Tillich is part of his larger systematic theological work. Paul Tillich presents an impressive and penetrating study of revelation and consequently of the religions. This study, we must remark, is only a part of his very comprehensive systematic theology. To understand his thinking in the area of revelation and the religions, one needs to study his systematic theology fully and therefore be able to set these ideas in their right places. As with Rahner, therefore, one must be slow to offer commentary on Tillich. However, that does not mean we have in Tillich's system a perfect system. He falls prey to two diseases that plague much of Protestant thinking on the religions: the near obsession with the historical-physical necessity of Christ for salvation, and the "epistemological-psychological necessity of Christ for salvation."[64] The religions are revelatory and therefore salvific, but in a fragmentary way; complete and unlimited salvation is possible only through historical-physical contact with Jesus. And this is possible only in the so-called religion of paradox or of the concrete spirit. What exactly does Tillich mean by incomplete and fragmentary salvation? Tillich talks of universal revelation as that which witnesses and prepares for the final revelation. Christianity is universal revelation, just as the Old Testament is final revelation, on the grounds just mentioned. However, it is understandable to talk of Christianity as witnessing to Christ (final revelation). Can we also rightly talk of it as preparing for the final revelation? Or is Christianity a stage to be surpassed on the way to the religion of the concrete spirit? It would appear also that Tillich has stretched the doctrine of the kenosis (Phil. 2:6 ff.) too far and unwittingly used it to create thought patterns he himself cannot accept. To talk of the Christ as being final revelation because he has been able completely to negate the medium that he is and has succeeded in letting the ground of being shine forth unrestrainedly, is to create room for many revelations. Christ has thus become one final revealer among many (cf. the Buddha, Muhammad, et al.). The Christian claim that the Christ is absolute and unequaled stands threatened by this idea.

ONE GOD, MANY ABSOLUTE CENTERS

Next, we will quickly consider two authors who have carried Paul Tillich's relativizing tendencies to their logical ends, each in his own way. The issues involved are very much the same as those forming the basis of Roman Catholic theological thinking on the non-Christian religions: Christianity's self-understanding as the authentic religion versus the plurality of religions; the belief in Christ as God incarnate, absolute and sole mediator of salvation versus the notion of a universal salvific will in God. But if the questions raised by this theocentric theology represented by Paul Knitter (Roman Catholic) and John Hick (Presbyterian), among others, are the same, the answers put forward by both parties are a world apart.

Paul Knitter opines that whereas today's Catholics could understand and accept their religion as *true*—that is, as *a* source of salvation to all human beings—most of them would be "turned off" by the claim to absoluteness that their religion makes, on several grounds, such as the fear that such a claim leads to: an idolatry of authority and dogma; a ritual and ethical practice that becomes superstition; a morality that degenerates into legalism, even hypocrisy; and a sense of reality that becomes "false consciousness and hubris towards outsiders."[65] Because the world is experiencing religious pluralism "in a qualitative new way," Knitter argues, the time has come for Christianity to revise its self-understanding as absolute religion—the one ultimate self-disclosure of God, definitive and valid for all times and for all people. He claims that the first stages of this revolution started at the Second Vatican Council. On the whole, the evolution consists in a shift from ecclesiocentrism to Christocentrism to theocentrism. The first phase— the shift from ecclesiocentrism to Christocentrism—involves the recognition and proclamation "that the church is not to be identified with the kingdom or with Christ"; and that "none of the religious forms of Christianity—creeds, codes and cult—can be absolutized into one and only, unchanging statement of truth." The church is meant instead to serve and promote the task of the kingdom "by being sign and servant, wherever that kingdom may be forming. Therefore the church is not necessary for salvation."[66] Knitter maintains that the church's move away from ecclesiocentrism amounts to a recognition on its part that the saving grace and presence of the Universal Christ is active beyond the Catholic Church. This shift was especially fostered by ecumenical dialogue with other Christians and by the realization that the Roman Catholic Church was an obstacle to such dialogue.

According to Knitter, it is recognized today in relation to the wider ecumenism that it is not just the concept of church that constitutes an obstacle, but that the understanding of Christ among Christians impedes this dialogue in a very special way. At this point precisely the shift from Christocentrism to theocentrism begins to occur. To allow that other religions are also ways of salvation but only by the grace of God in Christ is to see the other religions from the point of view of Christian absoluteness and ipso facto to disqualify them as independent and efficacious entities. The question to ask today, according to Knitter, is whether absoluteness, either exclusively or inclusively, is a necessary ingredient to the doctrine of the incarnation and to other traditional Christological claims. Knitter's position is that it is not. For him, whereas the totality of Jesus is the Christ, the "Cosmo-theandric principle, the universal revealing and saving presence of God . . . the totality of the Christ is not Jesus and cannot be contained in and limited to him."[67] Christ belongs to God (1 Cor. 3:23). As Jesus, the Christ is nowhere in the New Testament "simply identified with God." Jesus is unique. Through him Christians meet God and so can quite rightly say of him that he is absolute. Yet this absoluteness, though it demands total commitment, does not rule out the possibility of recognizing other absoluteness. Nor does it feel duty-bound to make Jesus normative in regard to "other great figures of history." Jesus is a particular revealer of God. The recognition of this fact is, Knitter concludes, essential for authentic religion and authentic religious dialogue. A revision is called for in the Western consciousness, which up to the present equates the true with the absolute. In the new understanding of the truth (especially religious truth), "a true religion will no longer be founded on the absolutely certain, final and unchangeable possession of Divine truth but on an authentic experience of the Divine which gives one a secure place to stand and from which to carry on the frightening and fascinating journey, with other religions, into the inexhaustible fullness of the Divine truth."[68]

John Hick, for his part, insists that Jesus is neither divine nor the Son of God incarnate. The implications of such belief are too serious to fathom. For if Jesus was literally God incarnate, and if it is by his death alone that humanity can be saved, and by their response to him alone that people can appropriate that salvation, then the only doorway to eternal life is Christian faith. It would follow then that the large majority of the human race so far has not been saved.[69] But Jesus is not God. Nor is he in any way divine. In Hick's view, Jesus was merely a victim of the tendency in religions to exalt human figures and turn them into divine ones of universal power, as in Mahayana Buddhism where the human Gautama was turned by his followers into the preexistent logos or divine son. Hick rejects the resurrection as proof of Christ's divinity. We do not know for certain what the resurrection event consisted in. Nor can we say of it that it was a guarantee among Jesus' own contemporaries of his divinity. In any case, Hick says, the raising of the dead to life, understood in the most literal sense, did not at that time, in those circles, constitute an earth-shaking and nearly incredible phenomenon as it does to the modern mind. This, Hick says, is evident from the numerous raisings of the dead referred to in the New Testament and in the patristic writings. Therefore the resurrection claim merely "indicated that he [Jesus] had a special place within God's providence, but this was not equivalent to seeing him as literally divine."[70] Above all, the Nicene understanding of Jesus as "God from God," "light from light," "true God from true God," "begotten of the father before all ages began," and the Johanine logion that the word (God) became flesh are both as far from anything the historical Jesus can "reasonably be supposed to have thought or taught as is the doctrine of the Three Bodies from anything that the historical Gautama can reasonably be supposed to have thought or taught."[71] Hick also endorses the call for a Copernican revolution in theology—that is, for a move away from a church-centered, Christ-centered theology and faith to "the realization that it is God who is at the center, and that all religions of mankind, including our own, serve and revolve on him."[72]

John Hick notes that human beings have had a long history as religious animals. There is a great variety of religions and religious experiences, the first recorded instances of which, he says, occurred in the period between the third and the second millennia before Christ. The period 800–300 BC is regarded as "the golden age of religious creativity." The reason, Hick says, is that there occurred in this period "a remarkable series of revelatory experiences all over the world; experiences which deepened and purified man's conception of the ultimate, and which religious faith can attribute to the pressure of the divine Spirit upon the human spirit."[73] In Israel this was the age of the classical prophets who spoke "in the name of the Lord" and had faith in him. It was also the age of Zoroaster in Persia, of Lao-tzu and Confucius in China, of the Upanishads and Gautama the Buddha in India, as well as that of Mahavira, the founder of the Jain religion. This was perhaps also the time when the Bhagavad Gita was written. At the close of this age came the Greeks: Pythagoras, Socrates, and Plato. "Then after the gap of some three hundred years came Jesus of Nazareth and the emergence of Christianity; and after another gap the prophet Mohammed and the rise of Islam."[74] These were all moments of divine self-revelation to humankind, an indication that the divine revelation has been a continuous process. Therefore, God did not reveal himself just in a "single mighty act," nor did he do so through one single human revelation to mankind.

The various revelations have in turn evoked different and valid responses due to geographical, ethnic, climatic, economic, sociological, and historical variations. These responses have in many instances been championed by some "spiritual outstanding individual or succession of individuals" and have over time developed into "the great religions"—cultural phenomena we call the world religions. Therefore the different encounters with the transcendent in various religions are all "encounters with one reality, though with partially different and overlapping aspects of that reality."[75] Hick sees in the current tendency among the religions to "mutual dialogue and observation" a possibility that these religions may be gradually moving toward a convergence in the future; to a time when such terms as Christianity, Buddhism, Islam, and Hinduism "will no longer describe the then current configurations of men's religious experience and belief." In this future time the different religions of today "will constitute the past history of different emphases and variations within a global religious life."[76] John Hick's view here again corresponds very closely to that of Paul

Knitter, for whom the present state of the religious climate calls for a joining together of the religions in a "unitive pluralism of religions." Knitter's hope is that through speaking to each other in their various efforts to come to "a fuller understanding and living of the Mystery," the religions will evolve from the level of mere "unitive pluralism" into a higher form of religious unity and to an acceptance of Jesus the Christ as the symbol par excellence for such unity.[77]

The questions raised by Knitter and Hick go to the very heart of Christian self-understanding: the denial of the divinity of Jesus Christ, the relativization of the absolute claim of Christ's followers for their master and their church, and the establishment of "absolute" centers in the so-called world religions—issues that demand more attention than we can give them here. For now, however, I must touch on two issues that are germane to African Traditional Religion and to African theology. The first issue is that John Hick exhibits a deplorable disregard for creations other than the European, and sometimes (as in the case of religions) the Asian, which characterize much of Western thought. Hick's concept of religion is imperialistic. Only European and Asian religions are considered world religions, just as only the world religions are considered revelatory religions. Every other religion constitutes a crude fantasy that will one way or another grow into (or empty itself into) the "sophisticated metaphysical speculations" that the world religions represent. Two facts stand out clearly: Hick in the end falls back into the same faults he set out to fight: the absolutizing of some religious experiences to the exclusion of others. The other issue is that the rather too optimistic hope shared by Hick and Knitter for a possible fusion of the religions in the future is both a veiled religious version of Hegel's hope for the emergence of the absolute spirit, and a return to, albeit outside Christianity, an absolute religion.

JESUS CHRIST, THE CHURCH, AND OTHER RELIGIONS: AN INITIAL REFLECTION

Every Christian theological inquiry into the problematic of non-Christian religions must sooner or later come to grips with the issue of Jesus Christ both in the Christian religions and therefore in relation to other religious confessions that do not center on him. Because such inquiry is a human project it has to speak from "somewhere"; because it is a Christian venture it proceeds from certain assumptions about Jesus, history, and the church. Here precisely the inquirer runs into no small difficulty. What should these assumptions be? What is the "final" and "accurate" point of view from which to proceed? In other words, what is the really Christian approach to non-Christian religions? It is clear from our inquiry so far that these are all very contentious questions both outside and within Christianity itself. In short, we have come to recognize how difficult it is to talk of a Christian approach to non-Christian religions. That is not to say that there are no commonly accepted beliefs in Christianity. Nor does it mean that there are no "nonnegotiable" articles on the Christian agenda for dialogue with non-Christians, including African Traditional Religion. However, even when Christians commonly accept the centrality of Jesus the Christ, or rather his uniqueness or even the uniqueness of the church, to mention a few, their interpretations of the import of these realities differ nearly to an irreconcilable point. All the same, basic to Christian self-understanding is the belief that God the creator of all things did in time become a human person in Jesus Christ. Jesus is truly God and truly man, God's absolute and unsurpassable self-disclosure of himself. It is Christian belief that "in this name and in no other is salvation given to human beings" of all ages and all places. This understanding of God's purposes in the world is the kernel of the good news and constitutes a summons to all Christians to go out on mission and invite peoples everywhere to faith in the name of the Father and of the Son and of the Holy Spirit. In the apostolic exhortation *Evangelii Nuntiandi* Pope Paul VI insists that "neither respect and esteem" for other religions, "nor the complexity of the question raised" about this teaching "is an invitation to the Church to withhold from these non-Christians the proclamation of Jesus Christ" (no. 53).

Christians affirm that in Jesus of Nazareth God has done something unique, extraordinary, and unrepeatable. In him God has eminently manifested his intention to save all humanity; in him we are in "direct" contact with God. That is, in Jesus we are in direct contact with a divine person whose significance stretches beyond his visibly finite existence to all ages, all peoples, and all times. *Dominus Jesus,* the document issued in 2000 by the Vatican Congregation for the Doctrine of the Faith "on the Unicity and Salvific Universality of Jesus and the Church," makes the same point when it asserts as central to Christian belief that "it must be firmly believed that, in the mystery of Jesus Christ, the Incarnate Son of God who is 'the way, the truth, and the life' (Jn 14:6), the full revelation of divine truth is given."[78] We have seen all these assertions in their more precise formulations in the course of this chapter. Also, we have noted not only the almost total lack of a uniform view of the reality and significance of Jesus, especially in relation to other religions, but also the fact that there has often been an outright rejection of such basic Christian claims as the incarnation, the divinity of Jesus, the resurrection, and consequently the importance of Jesus Christ for the non-Christian religions. Thus, at the heart of the theology of Christian religions is the person of Jesus of Nazareth: his identity, what he says about himself, how his disciples saw him, and what can be said of him on the basis of all these. The New Testament is the confessional documentation of various early Christian communities with regard to the reality they perceived in Jesus. Even though it is largely historical, it was not intended to be a purely historical account of the life of Jesus. Rather, it was to be an act of faith based on the historical experience of the proto-Christian community's *memoria Jesu*. Jesus left no written records, nor is there any string of *verba et facta ipsissima*. "What he did leave—only through what he was, did and had said, simply through his activities as the particular human being—was a movement, a living fellowship of believers who had become conscious of being the new people of God . . . an eschatological liberation movement for bringing together all people, bringing them together in unity, universal shalom."[79] This movement's basic confession about Jesus is summed up by Peter at the gate called Beautiful (Acts 3:10): "For all the names in the world given to men, this is the only one by which we can be saved" (Acts 4:12). The New Testament is therefore a record kept by those who have found definite salvation for all human beings in the carpenter from Nazareth. Moved by this experience, the early members of the Christian movement sought to dress the man whom they said was centrally important for their salvation in many honorific titles—Son of Man, Messiah, Christ, Our Lord, Son of God, and so forth. Basic to the New Testament affirmations about Jesus is that Jesus is "the way, the truth, and the life" (John 14:6). He is "light for revelation to the gentiles, and for the glory of Israel" (Luke 2:32); the one anointed by God's Spirit "to bring God's saving reality within the experience of those who were open to God."[80] In him all national religions, all social and sexual differences are abolished (cf. 1 Cor. 12:13, Gal. 3:28, Eph. 2:11–21). In other words, Christians have always ascribed a universal dimension to the Christ-event, even if due to cultural blinkers this fact was to take a long time to be appreciated and at such great cost to men like Paul. To say that something has universal significance means that the thing in question has a "determinative effect on every person in settling the ultimate purpose of his life." That is, his life "is settled by a fundamental and . . . freely accepted reference to this universally valuable thing. It is a reality that imparts universal meaning."[81] Or it means, as Karl Rahner puts it, in speaking of the Christ-event, "that a historical event which lies far in the past still touches my existence."[82] Rahner also talks of the Christian ascription of a universal significance to Jesus of Nazareth as meaning that in him "we are dealing with the definite salvation of the whole person and of the human race, and not with a particular situation of man."[83]

We have of course seen the many objections that some raise regarding the Christian claim about Jesus of Nazareth. While some object to this claim on the grounds that it is by "definition an extra-cultural utterance" that runs counter to the "fundamental pluralism of human culture,"[84] others, like Hick, find it unacceptable since the claim implies that "God can be adequately known and responded to *only* through Jesus." According to Hick that claim was tenable as long as "Christendom" lasted and was synonymous with Europe, and had not come in contact with other cultures. Today we need instead "a global religious vision which is aware of the unity of all mankind before God. . . . We must acknowledge that a single revelation to the whole earth has never in the past been possible . . . and that the self-disclosure of the divine, . . . working through human freedom within the actual conditions of world history, was bound to take varying forms."[85]

The grounds on which the rejection of the universality of Jesus is based are difficult to accept. Behind all this relativization lies a whole world of ideas from the Enlightenment which see Jesus as an embodiment of religious ideas and as an ideal like the great religious teachers, and no more. According to this view, no historical religion that has been handed down to us has an intrinsic significance, since they possess no "immediate experiential evidence." They might constitute only a particular religious experience, part of God's pedagogic design toward mankind. Thus Jesus would be an example of a unique religious experience valid for his own time perhaps, and mediating new religious values and an "original religious experience. But this historical mediation must not itself be universalized."[86] Opinions like these are too dogmatic and ascribe to themselves a false knowledge of all possibilities that can be. To limit every religious mediation to a place and to a time in an a priori and arbitrary manner is to beg the question, or as Schillebeeckx has put it, to give "a negative answer before an enquiry has even began." The issue is one of method and fails to take note of the great discovery in the study of religions today, the intransitivity of values: the fact that every religious truth can be validated or invalidated only within the religion in question. No one person or school of thought has the right to seek to limit what a religion is saying about itself and about its world. What Hick, the Enlightenment, and the neo-Enlightenment figures seem to be doing in the guise of comparative religious studies is unacceptable. Comparative religion, insofar as it remains valid and true to its goals, can employ only a phenomenological approach as its method. It is not within its province, I think, to make declarations about, or set limits to, the value of any particular religious experience; this is the work of the theology of the religion in question. Granted, eponymous tendencies in literature and religions abound, and human figures can sometimes be turned into divine powers; yet this very human tendency does not say anything for or against (that is, in regard to its veracity or otherwise) the Christian claim of a universal significance for the man from Nazareth. Whether Jesus was divine or not, whether he has universal significance or not, must be argued on grounds other than this.

Finally, to ask a religion to abandon its central claim on the ground of discovery of other religions and for fear of "offending" the sensibilities of these religions is again unacceptable. The truth cannot be arrived at by leveling down of all claims, no matter how offensive these might sound. To do so would be to cause untold harm to the religion. To ask Christianity to abandon its claim that Jesus has universal significance is to deny it of its central foundation, to kill it. Religions involve issues of ultimate concern, to paraphrase Tillich—that is, they constitute sources of life for their adherents. The Christian religion is built around the community's experience of Jesus Christ as Lord—that is, as the one upon whom all human destiny rests. The claim is stupendous and might really sound to an "outsider" like saying too much. But to abandon it would be to abandon the Christian faith in Jesus. The community would then be merely a social club. If any other community of faith feels like making a similar assertion about its spiritual originators, that community is free to do so, provided of course the claim is in agreement with the basic experience that brought the community into being. Dialogue between the religions cannot proceed on the lines of "doctrinal compromise."

One question arises: How can a historically particular individual have universal significance? In other words, where in Jesus can a unique universality be located, in his being as man or as God or both? The question of Jesus as referent for all human beings and for all ages is a religious one. To be a useful and worthy referent Jesus must be shown to have the complete backing of God and to be truly a member of the human race (see the letter to the Hebrews). Karl Rahner among others has tried to show how Jesus is universally significant through a transcendental Christology that sees in Jesus the example of what it means to be human; or in Rahner's words, as that which happens "when God wants to be what God is not," or as "the historical manifestation of the question which man is and the answer which God is." This makes him, Jesus Christ, the unique mediator between the divine and the human, able to bring about a binding rapport between the two. The figure here presented by Rahner does not, to my mind, conform to anything the human mind has experienced. He is neither God (or he is half so), nor is he man (at least not in our real sense). Christianity should not accept this Christology of a Jesus Christ who is "a universal human being." Rather, Jesus should be seen as the universal highest expression of God's love, the God with a human face, who intentionally goes in search of the lost sheep, the poor, the unloved, the outcast, and the sinner, primarily to bring them "home" to God—that is, to offer them salvation. The universality of the church can only be one of mission. But it is a mission "born from the command of Jesus Christ . . . and fulfilled in the course of the centuries in the proclamation of the mastery of God, Father, Son, and Holy Spirit, and the mystery of the Incarnation of the Son, as saving event for all humanity."[87] It is a mission grounded in the fact that the church is mysteriously united with Christ as an indispensable instrument of salvation for every human being. Jesus' message was for all humanity. The church is sent by the Spirit to proclaim the message of the good news of Christ. As such, the church is, as the Second Vatican Council puts it, the sacrament of Christ, in that through its work of evangelization it shares the good news of Christ with everyone; through its works of charity, it brings the love of God to all humanity, poor and rich alike; and through its liturgical celebrations it offers and mediates God's love and salvation in a concrete way. How this ecclesial role has played out in Africa and what it means in this concrete situation vis-à-vis African Traditional Religion has been the stuff of much discussion, as we have seen. What would be unacceptable as African Christian theology would be to water down the universal and absolute significance of Jesus as Lord and Savior or to put African Traditional Religion on a par with Christianity as means of salvation. To proclaim Jesus as the way, the truth, and the life (John 14:6) is to acknowledge that "in this name and in no other is salvation offered to human beings" (Acts 4:12). "Offensive" as this may sound, it is the kernel of the Christian faith. To hold otherwise is to remove oneself from the faith. Any African theology that is Christian must start with this faith, even though it must also listen to insights from African Traditional Religion about the divine presence in Africa and in our world, and, for our purposes here, consider what implications faith in the divine presence can contribute to the way Africans build their communities and to the way they treat or interact with one another.

PART THREE

Foundations of an African Christian Theological Ethics

Chapter Five

AFRICAN MORAL THEOLOGY AND THE CHALLENGE OF INCULTURATION

In parts 1 and 2 of this book we dealt with the nature of African theology in general as well as with the question of African Traditional Religion, which I consider an essential aspect of African tradition within which African Christian theology is carried out. As Kwame Bediako has repeatedly pointed out, African theology has an opportunity that has largely been lost to its Western counterpart: the opportunity of being in close and constant conversation with a living primal religion. Thus, whereas the Western theologian who engages in discussions about non-Christian religions does so from some "safe" distance as an avocation, the African theologian does so from a situation of immersion. Even if the African theologian has no first-hand knowledge of African Traditional Religion, situations, events, and people in the surroundings often so impinge on his or her space that the theologian is forced to take note and react to the presence of African Traditional Religion, both in its particularity and with regard to the questions and issues it raises concerning non-Christian religions in general. Now that we have attended to this aspect of our discourse, I will focus attention in the next section on the central concern of this book, the search for firm foundations on which we can construct an African moral theology. As I point out repeatedly here, African moral theology, as both theology and ethics, has its tentacles both in the world of theological discourse in general—hence our interest in the theological issues in African religion and in the issues that religions raise for Christian theology in general—and in the world of ethics—hence our concerns in the chapters ahead with issues of both normative ethics and metaethics. That is to say, we will be dealing with issues pertaining to the nature of African Christian ethics, the bases for making moral decisions in African ethics—in short, with the foundations for and methodology of African Christian ethics.

African moral theologians have generally shied away from issues pertaining to the foundational aspects of the discipline. A notable exception to this rule is Fr. Bénézet Bujo, who has made a lifelong career of trying to show that the foundational aspect of moral theology is as much an area for inculturation as any other in African theology. Bénézet Bujo has tried to articulate and develop the foundations of an African ethics that is also Christian. In the next two chapters, I will keep Bujo by my side, so to speak, as an interlocutor as I embark on the search for firm foundations for an African moral theology that is both Christian and African. I will begin by piecing together, as much as possible, the basic outlines of the moral theology of this great African pioneer in order to show what has already been achieved as well as to delineate the contours of my own modest contribution to the discussion.

THE MORAL THEOLOGY OF BÉNÉZET BUJO

Born in 1940 in Drodro in the Democratic Republic of the Congo (DRC), Bujo is a priest of the diocese of Bunia and was for many years professor of moral theology and social ethics at the University of Fribourg in Switzerland. He was educated at Murhesa Major Seminary, Bukavu; at Niangara Major Seminary, Njiro; and at the Louvanium in Kinshasa, all in the DRC. He earned his doctorate at the University of Würzburg in Germany with a dissertation on the autonomy of morals and the specificity of moral norms in relation to the insights of Thomas Aquinas on moral norms.[1] In 1983 Bujo produced another work on Aquinas for his *Habilitation*, also at Würzburg.[2] The list of

Bujo's publications is long.[3] His most mature insights on methodological and foundational questions in African ethics are found in *The Ethical Dimension of Community: The African Model and the Dialogue between North and South*; *Foundations of an African Ethic: Beyond the Universal Claims of Western Morality*; and "Differentiations in African Ethics" in *The Blackwell Companion to Religious Ethics.*[4]

In *Foundations of an African Ethic* Bujo frames the thesis that animates his work in African ethics. Like many other African theologians, he begins with the claim that Western culture, introduced into Africa and made more ubiquitous by globalization and modern popular media, is destroying Africa. Even when this "new culture" espouses lofty ideals such as "democracy," it despoils Africans' traditional world. The further result of the disparaging and destruction of African culture by that of the Western world is the emergence of a monoculture. This situation is good for neither Christianity nor Africa. For, "if the good news of Jesus is to make its home among every people, it cannot identify itself with one specific culture, not even a global monoculture."[5] The imperative for inculturation arises, therefore, from the fact that Western culture does not have either the last or necessarily the superior word on what it means to be human and/or on how to construct the *humanum*; nor does the expression of Christianity with which it is identified constitute the only or best possible expression of the Christian faith. Like many other African theologians, Bujo opines that Western culture and Western Christianity in their encounter with the African world did not believe that Africans had any culture or religion worth preserving. The result was that "genuine dialogue between Christianity and African religions was seen as irrelevant." Thus Bujo's inculturation theology elaborates on the foundations of an African Christian theology, and in particular on an African Christian ethic, to create a better understanding of the realities that from a genuinely black African context can help Africans connect with and live their Christian faith as well as engage in meaningful dialogue with the rest of the world.[6]

There are two trajectories in Bujo's search for methodological foundations for an African Christian ethic. The first involves the rejection or critique of certain notions or approaches in traditional Catholic moral theology or of the way norms are determined in some aspects of this tradition; the second is a constructive one, involving the search for elements for the foundation of an authentically African Christian ethic.[7] These trajectories cohere within certain tendencies and trends in recent Western Catholic moral theology which Bujo absorbed in his studies in Europe during the 1980s when debates raged on fundamental issues in the discipline. The mark left on Bujo by this experience will be evident in what follows.

First Trajectory: Critique and Repudiation

One researcher has discerned two phases in the development of Bujo's thought. The first, which includes the period between Bujo's seminary studies in the DRC and his *Habilitation* in 1983, is marked by a concern "to found morals on something other than the natural law in view of the dialogue between Christianity and non-European cultures."[8] An important presupposition that Bujo articulates in this period arises from his reading of Aquinas's ethics through the prism provided by the work of the "autonomous ethic" theologians, especially Alfons Auer, whom he admired.[9] A quotation from one of Bujo's later works captures this presupposition: "The Bible has not invented moral norms— not even Jesus has—but . . . everything goes back to man created in the image and likeness of God and questioned by his word in order to deepen and radicalize the existing, or better pre-existing ethos. The Christian must, starting from the word of God, criticize, stimulate and integrate the human ethos. Even the ecclesiastical magisterium up to now ought to think in such categories, if it does not want to reduce Christians to the level of puppets."[10] Two important insights influential in the second phase of Bujo's work on African ethics are evident here. One is the notion of ethical autonomy already mentioned. Human beings as creatures of God are capable of generating norms that guide their lives without receiving any other explicit norms through revelation. The second insight is that the involvement by the church's magisterium in the search for norms is not necessary and might sometimes be no more than an authoritarian imposition.

Bujo's positions here must be placed in the context of the post-conciliar debate on how to construct a moral theology that is truly scriptural, Christian, and human. Vincent McNamara notes three important historical stages in this effort to build a Christian/Catholic morality that is theological in character.[11] In the first stage the overriding principle was that Christian morality should be understood as a new life of grace in Christ. This theory was built around the axiom *agere sequitur esse*. Grace as an entitative elevation of the soul and its faculties gives the human being "a new esse, a new ontology which was the basis of and which demanded a new kind of moral life."[12] If action follows being, the reasoning went, this supernatural essence demanded a supernatural morality that would be radically different from the merely natural. A second notable effort at constructing a truly Christian moral theology was that of Gérard Gilleman[13] and René Carpentier, who argued that the distinctiveness of Christian ethics is to be inferred from the biblical stress on charity. The third effort was that of Bernard Häring, who attempted to construct a theology around the theme of the law of Christ. These attempts proved largely unsuccessful in their bid to argue for a distinctive Christian morality, because they could not answer the question whether the newness of Christian morality referred to content, motivation, or stimulus. Was there in fact a revealed morality different from what Catholic teaching had always held to be within the grasp of everyone, Christian and non-Christian alike? If there was not, how can one continue to talk of a distinctively Christian morality? If there was and is, what would be the content of such a morality? One school of thought in recent Catholic moral theology, the autonomous ethic school, denies the existence of any specific Christian ethics.[14] Alfons Auer, a prominent proponent of this view, denies any concrete ethical normativity to Christianity. "Neither the individual Christian nor the Church," he says, "has any revelation about what is or is not the concrete expression of the moral demand."[15] Although Bujo would insist that his ethic is not totally synonymous with Auer's, the connection is unmistakable. Bujo also rejects basing moral justification on natural law, since its appeal is limited to reason: "Does there not exist a legitimate pluralism in argumentation and the ways in which norms are established, a pluralism that can ultimately lead to divergent (though not contradictory) forms of praxis?"[16] And although he argues that to reject natural law reasoning is not to call into question "the possibility of universal validity" in ethics, he repeatedly criticizes the *Catechism of the Catholic Church*, *Humanae Vitae*, *Veritatis Splendor*, and a host of other church documents for speaking of intrinsically evil acts—that is, those the tradition categorizes as wrong or sinful irrespective of culture or any other extenuating circumstances.[17]

Second Trajectory: Constructing an African Ethic

Whereas the first phase of Bujo's work is characterized by rejection of some of the foundational supports on which traditional Catholic moral discourse stands, the second phase of his work is marked by an attempt to rebuild the moral tradition, especially in its more recent phase in African Christianity, on new supports that include specifically African materials, including African traditional ethics. According to Bujo, African traditional ethics is based on a relational network that is simultaneously anthropocentric, cosmic, and theocentric. This means that African moral norms arise through a reciprocal relationship among all three of these poles in the process of "palaver"—that is, open communal discourse. Therefore African ethics is essentially communitarian, unlike Western ethics, which tends to be rationalistic and discursive, or Christian/Catholic ethics, which is based largely on natural law. Recognition of relatedness is important for proper appreciation of how Africans make moral judgments. "African ethics . . . is concerned with the significance of the community for the discernment and laying down of norms and for ethical conduct as a whole." This sense of relatedness goes beyond the concrete visible community to embrace the dead as well. And "indeed even those not yet born constitute an important dimension."[18] This reality of the relatedness of everyone to everyone else and to the cosmic order further implies that black Africa, in principle and in fact, rejects the Cartesian *cogito ergo sum* in favor of *cognatus sum, ergo sumus* (I am known, therefore we are) as decisive for moral thinking.

For Bujo, the slogan *cognatus sum, ergo summus* enshrines the conviction that human beings become human only in fellowship with others, and that human beings act more effectively to the extent that they are in solidarity with other human beings. The slogan also implies a universal perspective in ethical thinking in black Africa. Thus in black Africa, for example, "hospitality, daily friendship, and dialogue with the members of other ethnic groups are vital laws from which no one is excepted. One who is not a member of my own group is ultimately also the 'property' of the other just as I myself am, and this means that I owe him respect and esteem. Thus one is ultimately related to all human beings."[19] It is this principle of solidarity rather than metaphysical considerations or natural law reasoning that is at the heart of the search for moral norms in African ethics. As noted above, Bujo's African ethic is an "autonomous ethic" where people, created in the image and likeness of God, in open dialogue with each other, search for the way to respond to the summons of conscience by "palaver" or the "word."[20] The "word" is part and parcel of the search for what is right or true or just or good in African communities. Africans consider the "word" powerful, for "a word can be medicine, just as it can be poison; it has a life-giving power just as it is capable of bringing forth death. In Africa, words are something drinkable or edible; one chews and digests them. Badly chewed and digested, they can destroy the individual and a whole community, whereas in the opposite case they bring to life."[21] The palaver is where one discovers "not only norms but personal and communitarian identity" as well.[22]

There are different kinds of palaver: therapeutic palaver, which represents "the dialogue between the traditional healer and the patient and his or her circle"; family palaver, which includes the living and the dead, the ancestors, and the yet-to-be-born; and extra-family or administrative palaver. Whereas the sage or the traditional healer is in charge of therapeutic palaver, family palaver, which is the locus for elaborating, grounding, reinforcing, or developing family ethics, is overseen by the elders of the particular family in question. Administrative palaver "is not just a kind of appeals court dealing only with cases beyond family authority"; it is also concerned with totally new cases that go beyond isolated frontiers and applies to several clan communities as well. Hence administrative palaver has a political dimension and character.[23]

At various points in his writings, Bujo tries to show that, although African ethics shares many elements with the discourse ethics of Jürgen Habermas and with certain forms of North American communitarianism, it differs from them on some key issues. For example, whereas discourse ethics is somewhat elitist in that the communication it espouses usually occurs among individuals with exceptional intellectual capabilities and who are alive and able to speak, African palaver ethics is interested in all persons living, dead, and yet to be born, as well as with the entire cosmos. More importantly, perhaps, is that whereas discourse ethics is secular, in that it brackets consideration of religion, African ethics has a religious dimension: God and the world of the ancestors are an integral part of palaver.[24] And even though this is the case, African ethics is neither secular nor religious. For although the emphasis is on interhuman relationship, God plays a role as an "unquestioned postulate" who, though rarely mentioned, is assumed to be the one without whom "nothing comes about and nothing survives."[25] Integrating God, the ancestors, and the world in its determination of right and wrong does not deprive palaver ethics of its ability to be critical. However, reason must not be turned into an instrument of oppression or power. Palaver ethics is a consensus ethic and, as such, is open to other experiences in its search for moral truth. It believes that in the search for this truth and in the proclamation of morality, "one must stop imposing from on high one particular ideal of virtues" on other peoples, because many of these ideals are contextually and culturally conditioned.[26] Thus, African palaver ethics holds that one "must always speak in a locally defined manner, out of the 'cultural cave.'" Even though this is the mode of operation in this ethic, it also acknowledges that the right of specific communities to formulate obligatory norms impels them to dialogue with other communities in the search for moral truth.[27]

An Appraisal

The first broad question raised by Bujo's work which we have so far considered is whether it is better to speak of African culture and tradition in the singular or in the plural. This question has received much attention in the literature on Africa and has been addressed in the second chapter of this book.[28] Here I will devote attention mainly to three issues: (1) structurally negative aspects of African traditions and cultures; (2) the question of periodization; and (3) the African as moral actor today and the realities he or she must deal with. Regarding the first issue, one of the many strengths of Bujo's work is that it forces us to remember that, as Alasdair MacIntyre and others have pointed out, and as we have also seen in the second chapter of this book, traditions supply the basis on which to make sense of reality and by which we determine what actions are rational and right or irrational and wrong. What Bujo has not sufficiently adverted to, however, is that African traditions as living traditions are extended arguments about the good and are, as such, an ongoing construction. This is not to say that there are no constants in African traditions and cultures. Indeed, there are numerous such benchmarks that give African traditions character and identity. Bujo himself has identified many: the life-giving and life-enhancing impulse and structure in the tradition; the role of ancestors as custodians of life and "participants" in the determination of norms; the anamnetic role of the community in which the memory of the people resides; the role of stories, music, dance, the arts, and sacred persons in articulating and inculcating virtues and in the preservation of community ethos and identity; and so on. These constants are embodied in and by African Traditional Religion as a living tradition and as such constitute veritable sources of moral insight and enrichment for the African Christian as for everyone else. These are important and significant African contributions to the dialogue on morality and to the search for that hybrid, an ethics that is truly African and truly Christian.

My concern with Bujo's presentation on the role of African communities and cultures in the search for moral truth is that it is a bit one-sided. This fact is evidenced by or results in idealizing Africa's past and giving insufficient attention to the structurally negative and damaging elements in those traditions. For example, Bujo argues that in black Africa, "hospitality, daily friendship, and dialogue with the members of other ethnic groups are vital laws from which no one is excepted. Even those who are not members of one's own group are also worthy of respect and esteem since they too are ultimately also the 'property' of another person or group like everyone else." Thus, "one is ultimately related to all human beings."[29] This assertion expresses much that is true and much that is questionable. African hospitality is legendary. So too is African solidarity with family, friends, and kinfolk. But whether such solidarity rises to a universal norm in traditional African societies is open to question. In fact, it could be argued to the contrary, as I do later, that many traditional African societies do not appear capable of extending or willing to extend to persons beyond their immediate purview the recognition of full personhood and hence the same hospitality and friendship they would show to members of their families and clan. The slave trade in many ways benefited from this fact, for example. The history of Africa is replete with stories of raids by one village or clan or one ethnic group on another in search of slaves. We are only now beginning to come to grips with the enormity of the role Africans themselves played in this horrendous trade, first between Africa and the Arab world and later between Africa and Europe and the Americas. The slave trade is a counterargument to claims like the one Bujo makes above. Another counterargument can be made of the ethnic strife that has become a hallmark of the modern African world. As the Nigerian pogrom of 1966, the Liberian/Sierra Leonean massacres, the Hutu/Tutsi genocides, and all other such cases show, one common factor in all of them is the question of ethnic superiority and the unwillingness to confer equality on some people who are not of one's own family or stock. If it is indeed correct, as Bujo asserts, that the African sense of solidarity is devoid of any moorings in metaphysics and natural law, then we have arrived at some important reasons for the slave trade and for continuing African ethnic strife. For if people do not see any binding reasons—whether religious or humanistic—for treating others fairly, then all attempts at "solidarity" can easily become no more than ideological attempts to impose on another or to push an agenda. But even though I criticize the African traditional conception of hospitality as sometimes lacking in universal import, I cannot accept Bujo's claim regarding the lack of metaphysical or natural law grounding for either African ethics in general or even for African solidarity. I criticize it only for not being able to carry what is a legitimate insight to its more universal conclusion. The point here is not to join in the devaluation of the contributions of African societies and cultures to the search for universalizable moral truth, but to advise caution and a more critical attitude toward the facts about African history and culture.

My second question about Bujo's work apropos of African cultures and traditions is that of periodization. Which period in African history or tradition must be the focus of retrieval and of our theologizing? One could argue that we should talk only of African tradition as it is now. The problem with this approach, however, is that tradition as where people are today may be a superficial appreciation of an ethos arising from a shared history. Where we are today may be a betrayal of who we are. However, what Bujo has done in his stress on African traditions and culture is to call attention to the enduring values that can constitute the basis for an African Christian ethic.

Regarding the third issue, the African as moral actor, Bujo's views on the role of palaver in African ethics bring home quite clearly how community conscious Africans are and how community oriented African ethics is. Bujo himself has addressed both the strengths and the weaknesses of the character of African ethics with its emphasis on community with regard to questions about individual freedom and personal responsibility, sin and conscience, and so forth.[30] However, the search for moral truth by the process of palaver is not without concerns in other areas as well. One concern I have is that Bujo has not given enough consideration to the elements of the demonic in the process of palaver. I want to illustrate my point with two stories, one from a real-life situation, and the other from Igbo folklore. The first story is about an incident I witnessed in a town in eastern Nigeria where I was sent to work as a young seminarian. The town had recently experienced a spate of robberies. The town union, which in many parts of eastern Nigeria functions as a de facto town assembly, decided to do something about the situation. One step was to invite all able-bodied townsmen in every part of the country back home for a covenant ritual (*Igba Ndu*). Part of the covenant involved having every able-bodied male (ten years and above) swear an oath based on these terms: (a) that he has never stolen, (b) that he would never steal, (c) that he would not invite others to steal, (d) that he would not join others to steal anything anywhere, and (e) that he would not maliciously or willfully take lives or injure anyone or force anyone to give up his or her property. Before the ceremonies started, various people from the town rose up to speak in the true spirit of palaver, as described by Bujo, generally in support of the covenanting process and in the hope that this action would eradicate the robberies. At some point in the process a man stood up and signaled only partial acceptance of the terms. He wanted the community to expunge from the list any of the conditions that would prevent anyone from the locality who wanted to "do business" elsewhere from doing so. It was plainly understood by everyone present that "doing business" here meant cheating and stealing from other people who were not members of the clan. The man who made this proposal was quite rich and eloquent, and had two sons who have since been apprehended by the police for armed robbery. His motion would have carried had not another man, known to be an upright and honest Christian, stood up to oppose him. It was only then that others had the audacity to speak up against this man.

My second story, from Igbo folklore, tells of a situation where things had been going badly in the animal kingdom—there was disease, famine, and death everywhere among the animals. They decided to meet and to see what could be done to change the situation. Every animal was present for the meeting except the hen. Other animals who had passed by the hen's house on the way to the meeting had reminded her that it was time for the community assembly. The hen replied that she was too busy to attend the meeting but would abide by whatever the community decided. At the meeting word came from the gods that they were angry and that all the diseases, famines, and deaths were manifestations of the gods' anger toward the animals for a certain transgression. Life would become normal again if the animals would decide to make a sacrifice of one of their own to placate the gods. The animals deliberated long and hard but could find no one who would volunteer to die for the rest. Someone then remembered that the hen had indicated that she would abide by whatever the animals decided. Someone placed in motion the idea immediately to offer the hen as a sacrifice to the gods. The motion carried, so the hen was sacrificed as "a willing holocaust."

Many lessons can be drawn from these stories. Perhaps the most obvious is that palaver is not a foolproof approach to determining moral norms, because it is open to being hijacked by demagogues and to distortion by community and individual biases. One could reasonably argue in reference to the first story that the inability of the rich and powerful man to have his way is itself proof that the process works. However, one would also have to wonder what might have happened had the other courageous man not been present to insist that taking another's property against that person's reasonable wish is wrong anywhere and at any time. In the second story we do not have the dissenting voice that is influenced by other considerations. Instead, the determining factor in the search for what is right is selfish interest disguised as community interest. It is the Caiaphan principle at work: better that one man should die than that a whole nation perishes (John 18:14); if it takes a whole community ganging up against one person to achieve this goal, so be it. The point is that palaver alone cannot insulate any human community from the point in ethics where "everything is negotiable, everything is open to bargaining,"[31] even the most fundamental human rights, such as life and conscience.

One of my proposals in this book is that African Christian ethics cannot afford to dispense with the natural law as a means for moral justification. Bujo rejects what he regards as the rationalistic approach of natural law and the process this "rationalism" takes to justify certain conclusions about certain moral questions such as polygamy and homosexuality. He questions whether truth "may be grasped by one kind of methodology, via a 'one-way' street."[32] The answer is of course that it may not. He also points to certain conclusions Aquinas reached on the equality of men and women, on polygamy, and on masturbation as indications of the limits of natural law as a means of moral justification.

There are certainly many examples of the bad and ideological use of natural law throughout the church's history. But as Martin Rhonheimer points out, it would not be correct to ascribe the philosophical shortcomings or the mistaken attempts at moral justification by some authors, including Aquinas, to the works of the natural law tradition as a whole: "Mistaken or provisional hypotheses can occur in every field of knowledge, and can create the condition for progress by encouraging a deeper investigation of certain difficulties."[33] What African Christian ethics needs to do is to engage in a proper and ongoing careful articulation of the essence of the natural law as guide and conversation partner in the arduous task of searching for moral truth. This search for the essence of natural law reasoning could begin with a reflection on the famous no. 16 of *Gaudium et Spes* of Vatican II. The council states that "deep within their consciences men and women discover a law which they have not laid upon themselves but which they must obey. Its voice, ever calling them to love and to do what is good and avoid evil, tells them inwardly at the right moment: do this, shun that. For, they have in their hearts a law inscribed by God. Their dignity rests in observing this law, and by it they will be judged."[34] Even though the council does not explicitly call this law natural law, there can be little doubt about its inference. As Joseph Boyle points out, "This conviction of Vatican II expresses the core of natural law as understood within Catholicism—namely, that within the foundations of the conscience of all human beings there are nonconventional, nonarbitrary moral standards which make possible genuine moral self-criticism, and so true moral knowledge even for those who have not received the moral instruction of divine revelation."[35] Three pertinent

points from this understanding of the natural law are important to
the search for Christian ethical foundations for ethics even in Africa:
(1) it is possible to know right and wrong; (2) it is possible to choose
freely right from wrong; and (3) there are moral standards "which
are not simply the results of personal preference or choice or of social
conventions."[36]

The idea of moral standards that are exempt from cultural determination can sometimes appear as a culturally insensitive imposition.
But it ought not to be. In an ethic that is also Christian, the search
for such standards is ongoing and must be carried out in partnership
with revelation and culture. For example, revelation supplies key truths
about the human person such as this: Creation in the image and likeness of God and the consequent truth that the person possesses a dignity not conveyed by society or status and not based on gender, race,
ethnicity, or any other such characterizations of human existence in
this world; fidelity in relationships is an essential human attribute; and
human action in this world has a telos beyond this world. Africa needs
these and similar standards. I do not imply here that Africa has no
moral standards. In fact, as I will show in chapter 8, Africa not only has
standards for moral reasoning but also has managed to arrive at some
of these standards based on natural law. Those standards, like standards anywhere, need the universal justification of natural law and
the searchlight of divine revelation. Ethics is more than an attempt to
find compromises. It also involves a summons, as Vatican II says, to
rise above one's cultural and personal inclinations to do more and be
more, to reach beyond oneself for something higher.

As Bujo says, African ethics is anamnetic—that is, "the ancestors' words and deeds, the norms they set, are made available to the
current generation so that it has life and continues to look after the
deceased, and so that prepares the future of the not-yet born."[37] Bujo
adds that through regular evaluation of the ancestors' words and deeds
the community, not individual conscience, acts as the "highest court of
appeal" for moral decisions. Thus, "communal conscience, above all,
measures and determines the individual conscience."[38] This issue will
be addressed later, but I must indicate again, as stated above, that the
danger of communal coercion and demagoguery is real in the inversion
that Bujo makes here of this relationship between the individual and
individual conscience.

African Christian/Catholic ethics must also be anamnetic—in a more inclusive way than that identified by Bujo as being the case in African traditional ethics. First of all, the subject of remembrance must begin with Jesus Christ and the saints of all ages and places, including, of course, the African ancestors whose lives and deeds are worth remembering. In this way, the African Christian has a host of witnesses to rely on in the journey of life. But African ethics must also be anamnetic in another way. It must recall in shame the deeds of those African ancestors whose ruinous neglect—the "particularist greed"— manifested in four exhausting centuries of bloody exportation of their kind and in four centuries of political disorientation and social disorganization in the face of European incursions into Africa, has left the continent in shambles. As Chinweizu has prayed, "May their souls sleep without rest in our memories to warn us away from any repetition of their ruinous neglect."[39] But African Christian ethics as an anamnetic ethic must not stop at merely exposing the misdeeds of the past. It must also be a constructive ethic of reconciliation. Too many people in Africa are going about with memories wounded by historical wrongs, real or imagined. It must therefore be the task of Christian ethics as theology to help find ways of healing memories in Africa through conflict resolution. In the end, African ethics as Christian ethics must be an ethics of discipleship. As William Spohn observed, this means that Christian ethics in Africa, as anywhere else, must be an ethic that takes seriously what Jesus took seriously. For Africa this would include (but not be limited to) emphasis on forgiveness as a central Christian moral imperative; love as the center of Christian ethical life; attention to the poor and the marginalized; recognition of the equal humanity of all persons, irrespective of ethnicity, gender, or religion; and continued vigilance over the culture to make sure it does not harbor, condone, or nurture any tendencies harmful to the welfare of the human person integrally and adequately considered.[40]

GUIDELINES FOR THEOLOGICAL INCULTURATION IN AFRICA

I have stated before that this book is a search for an ethic that is both Christian and African. In other words, it is a search for ways to engage in inculturation in African ethics. The first chapter closed with a discussion on the history and meaning of inculturation. I want to conclude this chapter with proposals on how I believe the task of inculturation in African moral theology should proceed. These points are useful for any project of inculturation anywhere. They are neither exhaustive nor limited to any branch of theology. And since our interest here is in ethics, these guidelines are offered much more specifically for the discussion in the rest of this book and in view of the search for foundations for an ethic truly African and Christian. The broad discussions here on inculturation are premised on my stated position in chapter 1, namely that all theology is contextual and in some ways an exercise in inculturation.

The first point I want to note here is that inculturation must be built on strong Christian theological convictions. As Paul Ricoeur has noted, "No one speaks from nowhere." The theologian who is engaged in the work of inculturation must first of all be conscious of himself or herself as a Catholic theologian and not as an apologist for African tradition or for any other non-Christian tradition and must speak confidently about the soundness of this tradition. The theologian of inculturation must be convinced of the role faith (revelation) plays in shaping reason—that is, by the way faith contributes to the formation of human attitudes and dispositions. The phrase "reason informed by faith," which is a staple of Catholic moral discourse, implies that reason is shaped, not replaced, by faith. Revelation and personal faith influence ethical decisions at a most profound level of our being. Thus, "one's choice of issues . . . and the dispositions she or he brings to these issues can be profoundly affected by one's personal appropriation of revealed truth, by one's prayer life, by one's immersion in the values of poverty, humility, compassion, characteristic of the Gospel"—in other words, by what Richard McCormick often refers to as the Christian story.[41]

The Christian story, as McCormick has summarized it, takes its bearing from what he calls "God's relentless gift of himself" in Jesus. Jesus Christ is God's absolute gift of God's self to the world. The believer's response to God's love, to God's stunning deed, is total and radical self-commitment. For, in the words of Joseph Sittler, to be a Christian "is to accept what God gives."[42] What God gives is himself. For McCormick, faith in Jesus as God's self-gift entails that: (a) the event of the life, teaching, and mission of Jesus is "an absolutely originating and grounding experience"; (b) Christ is both law and law-giver; (c) God's deed in Jesus reveals and presents to us "a new (Christocentric) basis or context for understanding the world"; (d) Jesus as new fact and center of thinking finds "its deepest meaning in the absoluteness and intimacy of the God-relationship"; and (e) "the empowered acceptance of God's engendering deed in Jesus (faith) totally transforms the human person."[43] "Stamped" at such a profound level, the Christian is able to construe the world theologically. Thus, for example, the Christian is able through reason informed by faith in the life, death, and resurrection of Jesus Christ to come to an appreciation of life as a basic but not absolute good; the essential equality of all human beings; and the need for a special care of the poor and the needy in our communities. The fact that Christ has overcome death and lives, that we are pilgrims now guided by him and will also live with him hereafter, yields a general value judgment on the meaning and value of life as we now live it. This value judgment has immediate relevance for the care of the ill and dying. "It issues in a basic attitude or policy: not all means must be used to preserve life. . . . There are higher values than life in the living of it. There are also higher values in the dying of it."[44]

Christian faith is not the only source of moral truth, nor are insights from faith without resonance in other contexts of moral evaluation. However, "even though Christian faith is not an arcane source of moral judgements, it has a good deal to contribute to the formation of human attitudes and disposition."[45] Thus, for example, the Christian story is not the only cognitive source for the radical sociability of persons or for the immorality of fornication, adultery, and abortion, and so forth, even though these insights may historically be strongly attached to the (Christian) story. "In this epistemological sense, these insights are not specific to Christians. They can be shared by others."[46] However, seen through Christological lenses these commonly shared insights assume totally new meanings and significance.

Some African theologians engaged in the work of inculturation start by regarding culture as the normative principle. As noted earlier, they often begin by pointing out how much damage the West has done to African culture through colonialism and a Christianization that was more or less Westernization in disguise.[47] To remedy this situation, they make every attempt to give priority to African culture in the dialogue between culture and faith. What can sometimes ensue from this effort is an uncritical presentation of culture, suggesting that because something is seen as coming from one's culture, it must be good or adequate and without need of further challenge, even by the gospel. On the contrary, the point of inculturation is that the believer who already is caught up in "God's engendering deed" in Jesus sets out to find ways to make the news and effects of that deed take flesh in his or her cultural milieu, so that the word would indeed take flesh among his people. There is a noteworthy insight here: The Christian faith, not cultural pattern, should provide the theologian with the primary lens through which to view life and reality in general. Only in this way can the theologian perceive the strengths and the distortions and evil in any culture. The theological work of inculturation must be unmistakably Catholic/Christian and theological, and not merely another exercise in cultural anthropology. And even though, as many African theologians and others have amply demonstrated, the Christian story is not an arcane or only source of moral insight, it must be for the Christian the primary criterion for measuring the soundness of any other source, and not the other way round.

Secondly, therefore, inculturation must be based on very clear assumptions about God, as revealed by Jesus Christ and attested to in the longstanding theological tradition of the church. Bénézet Bujo points out that "though the human person stands in the centre of African morals, the position of God is distinctly emphasised."[48] The question here is, which God? In Bujo's theology, two notions characterize God: creator, and defender of the moral order. Beyond the assumption of the fact of the incarnation, Bujo does not extensively discuss God's nature and purpose in the world. Instead, Bujo's work is composed mainly of discussions that assume total commensuration between the notion of God in African religions and Christianity. For example, referring to the Masai belief in God to show that Africans believe in God, Bujo asserts, "The Masai are monotheistic. For them God is a spiritual being, creator of all things, almighty, ubiquitous, omniscient, merciful and eternal. Because he rules everything, he is also the guardian of moral laws and of morality in general."[49] This understanding of God is Bujo's working model of God. I do not find sufficient emphasis in his work on the triune nature of God and what this might imply for African Christian moral theology. Missing is the radicalness of the God of Jesus, the

God who so loves the world that he dies on the cross for *all* humanity, the prodigal father of Luke 15:11–31, and the God whose radical gift of self in Jesus Christ makes us more and invites us to be more. Authentic African ethics cannot be built on minimalist assumptions about God found in African culture as in all cultures. Rather, African ethics can be an effective transforming ethos only when it takes into full consideration the implications of God's stunning deed in Jesus. The God of Jesus is new to every culture, including African culture. Attention to this newness has been and can still be transformative of human lives and human societies everywhere, including Africa.

A third important point for the work of theological inculturation is that the theologian of inculturation must have a deep knowledge of the culture in which he or she is working—that is, a deep appreciation for its strengths and honesty about its weaknesses. This is to say that cultural criticism has to be an important ingredient in inculturation. Otherwise, the theologian runs the risk of succumbing to culturalism, an uncritical appreciation that can go so far as to insist that the gospel be judged by the culture, rather than the other way around. As John Paul II observed, "Since culture is a human creation and is therefore marked by sin, it too needs to be healed, ennobled, and perfected" by the gospel.[50]

The connection between culture and morality runs deep. Although this truth is obvious, we often do not advert to it or to some of its most obvious implications. Consider this story. There was a certain society that considered it part of their culture to put twins to death. Thus, on some given days in the year, a cultural festival was held at which recent twins were brought out and ceremoniously executed. This practice was meant to appease the gods and thus to ensure the safety of the tribe. There were "twin hunters" whose job it was to attend every birth and to report every twin birth to the appropriate authorities. This was the cultural practice; human beings should not give birth to twins, only animals do. It happened that on one occasion one of the twin hunters from this village was visiting another village and there witnessed a cultural festival where people were making much merriment, with music and dancing. On closer inquiry the twin hunter discovered that the center of attraction here was twin babies. In this case, however, rather than being executed, the babies (and their mothers) were beautifully dressed and adorned and were being loaded with all sorts of presents.

First, the twin hunter was filled with apprehension as he waited for the gods to visit the community with destruction. When this did not happen, his fear turned to anger at the flagrant disobedience of these people. However, as he went back to his village, he could not erase the scenes he had witnessed from his mind: the radiant and proud glow on the faces of the mothers of the twins, the healthy-looking babies that were the object of everybody's admiration, the proud and happy husbands and fathers, and the very happy and contented community that had put on this show in gratitude to the parents and to their gods. As a result, he began to harbor solid doubts about the alternative practice in his own community, about its rightness, and about his own involvement in the whole affair. We have here the classical components of what Alasdair MacIntyre refers to as an epistemological crisis. In this situation, the scheme of reference that had held the twin hunter's worldview had begun to disintegrate. For him, things were beginning to fall apart, to paraphrase Chinua Achebe. Convinced of the wrongness of the cultural practice of twin hunting, our twin hunter embarked on a crusade to effect change in his community. After much toil and opposition he managed to draw a sizable proportion of his community to his side, and thus, the practice was stopped. The community not only reversed its previous practices but in fact set aside another day when, like their neighbors, they celebrated twins and atoned for the twins they had killed over the years.

Note in this story how a morally reprehensible act is initially and for a long time held and enforced in the name of culture as a morally right thing to do. What was needed to effect a change here was the conviction of one person who himself had to undergo a conversion experience. Note also the point I made above concerning the intrinsic connections among culture, morality, and law. In this story, a moral conviction is expressed in public celebrations and rituals and put into effect by sanctions imposed by the law. The relationship between culture and morality reminds one of the proverbial quandary about the relationship between the egg and the hen: the hen gives rise to the egg and the egg gives rise to the hen. In this case, however, the analogy limps quite badly since, as I contend, it is indeed what people believe and hold as right or wrong that becomes enshrined as culturally right and acceptable practice.

Most cultural practices are therefore inherently changeable because they are at best only partial approximations of value or the good. In fact some of them contain a very large dose of imperfection and could cause harm to certain segments of society, even if inadvertently. Thus we need to revisit them periodically to ensure that they protect the good for which they were enacted in the first place, and to determine whether the values they enshrine are in line with reason and revelation and whether they still promote the common good. Some aspects of culture are outright immoral and must be changed as soon as we become aware of their immorality; failure to do so could otherwise make us morally complicit in them. Morally conscious Christians, and indeed morally conscious citizens, have a duty to work to change such immoral practices. Christians do so from the point of view of who they are: people tutored and informed by faith. This is the essence of inculturation from a moral point of view. The attitude of the church to law and culture is shaped by a fundamental self-understanding that enjoins the church to respect everything of value in any culture, to recognize what *Gaudium et Spes* refers to as the autonomy of the earthly order, which implies the right of human societies everywhere to arrange for the proper running of people's lives and institutions without undue interference from institutions like the church; the church's attitude also derives from a belief that the light of the gospel helps the church and human societies to discern the truth about how to construct a just and morally upright polity. Cultural criticism must, however, proceed from a deep knowledge of the culture.

Anyone involved in the work of inculturation must also have more than a fleeting knowledge of the Christian (Catholic) tradition. In an interview at the University of Notre Dame in 1992, Richard McCormick described how well versed he was in the moral tradition of the Catholic Church in all its aspects, beginning with the manualist tradition: "I started moral theology at a time when we had to teach from the manuals. I got to know the manuals very thoroughly. I read six or seven manuals for every single presentation of every single subject. I got to know the tradition as it was presented in those manuals very thoroughly. I am grateful for that because it exposed me to a point of view which I think had an awful lot of good balance to it."[51] Walter Burghardt verifies this testimony:

Richard McCormick knows the Catholic moral tradition—and much more of our broader theological tradition—from scripture through medieval scholasticism to the twentieth century. From long experience and contemplation it is resident in his bones and blood. I trust he will be a living reproach to a generation of scholars who know Augustine only as a born-again Catholic who foisted on the western world a hellish doctrine of original sin and a pessimistic view of marriage; who cannot spell Chalcedon, even though a quarter century ago Harvey Cox argued that apart from Chalcedon technopolis is unintelligible; who can anathematize Aquinas and scuttle scholasticism without ever having read a word thereof; who sneer at the mere mention of "medieval," as if the middle ages were darker than our own; who could not care less about a papal pronouncement, much less peruse it.[52]

The theologian involved in inculturation must have a thorough and deep knowledge of the Christian tradition in all its ramifications. Thus, when he disagrees with it, he knows very well what he disagrees with. Although much of the Christian tradition has been forged in contexts foreign to Africans, one must at least know what the tradition teaches in order to dialogue with it or improve it or even modify it for African appropriation; otherwise one runs a number of risks, including chasing after red herrings, reinventing the wheel, or even engaging in outright heresy. Further, the theologian of inculturation must involve himself or herself actively in an ongoing conversation with the culture creators of the day, the new Areopagites. There are those who set the pace and those who merely follow, those who set the ethos and those who merely benefit from it. As John Paul II stated with regard to what he referred to as "the immense Areopagus of culture, scientific research and international relations which promote dialogue and open new possibilities," we "would do well to be attentive to these modern areas of activity and be involved in them."[53] Anyone involved in the work of inculturation needs to be attentive to the work of this very important segment of society—the creators of culture—to learn their language, cultivate their friendship, and meet them in their forums.

A fifth guide for inculturation: the theologian of inculturation should always be conscious that inculturation is not only about the past. It is especially about the present. As an attempt to dialogue with a given culture and tradition, inculturation must be carried out with that culture in its living and breathing form. Let me qualify this. Current cultural practices can harbor significant distortions of a people's way of life and may need reform and renewal. Yet it is *this* same culture as known and lived by *this* particular people today that harbors or generates the values today's people hold important and by which they construe reality. Therefore, it is with *this* culture as carrier and index of life here today that we must be in dialogue. The past might participate in this discussion so as to inform, illuminate, or guide the present. Thus, even though the theologian of inculturation must be in constant dialogue with the deeply held assumptions of the societies of his day, he or she must also be aware of some deep-seated assumptions, a carryover from the community's history, as it were, which continue to inform the societies of the present day for good or for ill. Some African theologians involved in the work of inculturation seem glued to the past and have little regard for the present; they cloak this "past" with an aura of sacredness as if nothing were wrong with it and everything was Christian. On the importance of African ancestral tradition Bujo writes, "One can no longer talk about sacraments without including the African ancestral tradition in this doctrine. In my opinion, a genuine African Christology, an ecclesiology and a doctrine of grace have to take this tradition as their starting point. Even the doctrines on God and the Trinity, together with eschatology—to say nothing about ethics—find their starting-points here."[54] Statements like this simply focus too much on Africa's past and present potentials and can be a hindrance to proper and thorough catechesis, for they assume the presence of what is not there and by so doing make it difficult to present what is in fact uniquely Christian doctrine. In saying this, I do not mean to imply that Africa was not a very religious place and very fertile ground for Christianity. Historical developments have in fact proved that African traditions and cultures contained unique elements that made the continent a good and fertile ground for the faith and that continue to help in the growth of that same faith. All I am saying is that one must be cautious in asserting the compatibility of African ancestral heritage with the gospel. For often things are not as easy or as compatible as they might appear.

A sixth guide for the work of inculturation is that it must be a limited enterprise. Every person created in the image and likeness of

God is infused with the spark of divine light; therefore every culture as the creation of human beings is also infused with God's grace. Thus, while the church seeks to bring Christ to a particular culture because it contains seeds of truth, inculturation also helps make clearer to the church certain aspects of the truth of what is human and humane. Thus, inculturation as dialogue with any given culture can never imply a total assault on a people's way of life with a view to replacing it. Although the church has much wisdom to offer the world on many issues, it must be understood that wisdom is not only a gift: "it is above all a responsibility to learn and to be in discussion with other relevant and interested parties" on any given issue.[55] Therefore, for the church to absent itself from discussions aimed at seeking solutions to common human problems "or to enter them ill-informed, to share in them from a position of authoritative arrogance as if the Church were in prior possession of concrete answers—all such approaches would dim the 'new light' and almost assuredly compromise 'solutions which are human.'"[56] Implied here are two considerations for African theology. The first, as noted above, is that cultures evolve. Thus, contemporary Africans are a different set of people from their forebears, because they have been informed by a different set of realities and experience. The second is, as the American adage puts it, "If it ain't broke, don't fix it." The "new Africans" have new ways of doing things and are part of a cosmopolitan culture that has, in spite of its shortcomings, much to offer in terms of faith and belief. Insofar as these ways do not go against faith, morals, and humane living, there is no need to worry about the fact that they are not originally "African." Moral theology is, like all ethics, a practical science. However, what the theologian says on practical moral issues must be based on sound theoretical constructions. This theory must aim to be true to the gospel; it must be worked out in conversation with the church's tradition; it must be based on sound human experience; and it must be critical of both culture and the Catholic tradition in the search for sound bases for its assertions and claims.

Finally, theological inculturation has to be subject-specific. What is required in liturgical inculturation is different from the requirements of inculturation with regard to the area of dogmatic formulations or of ethics. In some aspects of inculturation the goal might be to see how closely the gospel can take on the colorings of the host culture, while in others the goal might be to see how much the gospel can challenge the aspect of culture in question to take on "the mind of Christ." The latter is certainly what is required in the area of morality. The reality is that although cultures and traditions all around the world can harbor much that is noble with regard to the issues of right and wrong, they are always faced with the challenge of resisting the least pragmatic and easy answers in favor of the truly good. True inculturation happens in the area of Christian morality when faith meets reason and helps it lift itself up to the truth that is life—the Lord Jesus himself.

Chapter Six

GOD AND MORALITY IN
AFRICAN THEOLOGY

Christian ethics (moral theology) like all other forms of ethical discourse is done from certain perspectives and based on certain assumptions. In the last chapter we tried to show that African Christian ethics takes inculturation seriously. We tried to show how the dialogue between this form of ethics and African culture can proceed. In this chapter the first assumption of Christian ethics is that it is theocentric. The intention is to engage in discussion on what this means in general and what it can mean for African Christian ethics. As James Gustafson points out, "For theological ethics . . . the first task in order of importance is to establish convictions about God and God's relation to the world. To make a case for how some things really and ultimately are is the first task of theological ethics. What the theologian writes about ethics must reasonably follow from these convictions."[1] For a theological ethics that is also Christian the task is even deeper and broader—namely, to establish convictions both about the God Jesus spoke of and lived for, and about Jesus himself, about his teaching; and to show what implications these convictions might have for life and for organizing life in this world. There are various ways to understand the notion of theocentrism in ethics. This is so because there are different ways of appreciating God among Christian theologians.

Thus, to speak of theocentric ethics from a Gustafsonian perspective is different from how that concept could be understood in Thomistic ethics or in African traditional ethics. We will start by discussing theocentrism in Thomistic ethics, in the ethics of James Gustafson, and in African ethics.

THREE EXAMPLES OF THEOCENTRIC MORALITY: AQUINAS, GUSTAFSON, AND AFRICAN TRADITIONAL MORALITY

Thomistic Ethics as Theocentric Ethics

Saint Thomas Aquinas offers us a good example of a theocentric ethics that is also Christian. Commentators often mention that the most fundamental point about Aquinas's ethics is that it is theological ethics and not "a self-contained moral theory of the sort constructed by modern moral philosophers." Aquinas, they point out, "was a moral theologian who thought about moral questions in light of God, grace, and the sacraments. He was not a professional ethicist merely drawing upon theological claims to solve moral dilemmas."[2] Aquinas studied all things, including the morality of human action in its relation to God. In this way, as M. D. Chenu indicates, "everything, every being, every action, every destiny was to be placed, known and judged according to that supreme causality, wherein their ultimate cause will be wholly revealed in the light of God Himself."[3] This is the *exitus-reditus* scheme that constitutes the plan of the *Summa Theologiae* and about which so much has been written in the manuals and in other places down to our own time.

Aquinas's idea of God stays very close to the inherited Christian scriptural and traditional construal of God. Aquinas's God is Trinitarian, the God who reveals himself as Father, Son, and Holy Spirit. This triune God is at once "creator and the satiating supernatural goal, to be possessed by man's intellect and will in the beatific vision which was the culmination of man's life of grace."[4] Aquinas takes pains to discuss the question of the Trinity in the *Summa Theologica*. Beginning with the discussion on the essence of God from q. 2 to 22 of the *Prima Pars* he moves on to discussion on the distinction of persons in the Trinity in qq. 27–43. It is clear in all of this that even though Aquinas pays attention to and indeed borrows ideas from various non-Christian sources as he tries to put across his ideas about God, he is very much a Christian theologian who consciously stays within the revealed and the inherited tradition on this issue and who tries not only to explain the Trinitarian doctrine but also to draw out its implication for Christian belief and life. "Knowledge of the Trinity is knowledge through faith."[5] As Aquinas himself puts it:

> It is impossible to obtain the knowledge of the Trinity by natural reason. . . . Man cannot obtain the knowledge of God by natural reason except from creatures. Now creatures lead us to the knowledge of God, as effects do to their cause. Accordingly, by natural reason we can know of God that only which of necessity belongs to Him as the principle of all things . . . Now the creative power of God is common to the whole Trinity; and hence it belongs to unity of the essence, and not to the distinction of the persons. Therefore, by natural reason we can know what belongs to the unity of the essence, but not what belongs to the distinction of the persons.[6]

The important thing here is the acceptance of revelation and the authority of scripture since only thus can the truth of revelation be manifested.[7] The *exitus-reditus* schema is supported by a tripod: first, God, from whom all finite beings proceed, then the return of the human person to God through human actions that compose an individual life, and then Christ, through whom all things return to God. As Jean Porter points out, "Moral theology is located in the second part of this three-part schema; that is, morality, broadly construed to include all aspects of human activity, is placed under the rubric of the person's return to God."[8] Therefore, for Aquinas, Christian ethics is God-talk, although it is also an effort of human reason to find solutions to human problems or to construct a humane ethical order not in spite of God but with God as the principal cause and enabler of human life.

Aquinas's principle has been manhandled in various ways down the centuries by many in the ethics community. There are those especially in the philosophical community who have completely ignored the heavy theological or metaphysical underpinning of his ethical theory. The schema also made its way into the moral manuals in a truncated way: "Questions related to creation (the exitus theme) and the role of

Christ, the mediator, were relegated to dogmatic theology," while leaving the practical aspects of the human being's return to the creator, now without much theological mooring, to moral theology.[9] Aquinas is instructive here as a theologian who sets out with the intention to make clear the understanding of God that is at the basis of such ethics and to help the community draw out implications for such understanding of God for daily living. The Trinitarian emphasis of this theology brings into sharp focus what is distinctive about God in Christian consciousness. This view of God corrects or completes other ideas of God everywhere else and must constitute the foundation for any theological discourse that claims to be Christian, whether in Africa or elsewhere.

The Theocentric Ethics of James M. Gustafson

In his magisterial two-volume work on theocentric ethics, James Gustafson outlined both his view of God and his ideas of what this view implies for Christian ethics.[10] When Gustafson looks out the window, so to speak, he sees a cultural environment saturated with an excessive concern for the human person to the detriment of God and God's universe. He believes that much of this rabid anthropocentrism has been engendered by a Christian theology that makes excessive claims for man and sometimes tends to say too little about God. He notes philosophies and philosophers who have unwarrantedly turned the human subject into the measure of all things and a deontic morality that he believes has transformed religions, and indeed all ethics, into a code of absolutes. For Gustafson the picture is not satisfactory, to say the least. A change is called for in the cultural ethos of the day, and that change must start in theology, for therein is contained many of the symbols and concepts that guide people's lives and actions. Thus a reinterpretation is required of these religious symbols: God, man, faith, piety, Christ; yes, even Christ. The purpose is to "provide a perspective from which the species is perceived and interpreted in relation to the rest of the universe, to . . . turn . . . from anthropocentrism to God as the primary object of attention" and to learn to perceive and interpret man "in relation to the ultimate power and orderer of all creation."[11]

For Gustafson a focus on God is different from a focus on Christ. That explains why Christ takes the back seat in this theology. It also explains why Gustafson seems to have no second thoughts about discarding those aspects of Christian belief that he sees as standing in the way of clear access to God. Christ is relevant to the extent that he "incarnates theocentric piety"; otherwise he seems to stand in the way of Gustafson's theocentrism. And by largely ignoring him Gustafson makes this very clear. In a typical Gustafsonian passage we read that "God is the ultimate power that brings all things into being; sustaining, ordering, bearing down upon them; and creating the conditions for possibility of change and development in them. God is the determiner of the destiny of all things."[12] God cannot be manipulated, and thus personal and moral agency is foreign to him. Jesus merely incarnates theocentric piety and cannot be said to be God-incarnate. The ideas of salvation, eschatology, and the resurrection of Jesus belong to what Gustafson refers to as "traditional affirmations of God [which are] incongruous with well-established data and explanations of the sciences." To be accepted as a valid assertion about God an idea must as it were pass a congruency test. Says Gustafson, "Substantial ideas of God cannot be incongruous (rather they must be in harmony) with well-established data and explanatory principles established by relevant sciences, and must in some way be indicated by these."[13] Thus from the data and theories of many sciences (1) we could support the religious sense of dependence upon powers beyond ourselves—that is to say, we could infer that human life is part of and dependent on the processes of nature; and (2) we could infer order and ordering in natural processes and developments, and though we can infer that "governance" is occurring, we cannot from this infer a telos for man or the universe. On the other hand, Christian doctrine of a moral God "invested with perfect righteousness and love, and demanding the same of his devotees" cannot be sustained scientifically.[14] Nor is there scientific support for a God who is for man, given that man is only a very latecomer to the story of the universe, and even a chance development among other possible forms of life. There is also no scientific support for Christian eschatology. For "as the beginning was without us, so will the end also be without us."[15] For Gustafson "what is called revelation is reflection on human experiences in the face of ultimate power and powers"[16] and therefore does not represent any special self-disclosure of God to humans. This being the case, then, how else can we arrive at knowledge of God as a powerful other? How do we know or discern processes of divine governance in the world? Gustafson answers that we discover God "in our experience, that is, in the ways in which our human experience mobilizes our affectivity."[17] For Gustafson, piety is of primary importance in the human experiential basis for knowledge of God. He writes, "I am persuaded that the primary moment in a religious view of the world, and therefore an assumption in theology, is the affection of piety: a sense of dependence on, and respect and gratitude for what is given."[18] Piety is a "basic disposition and attitude . . . towards the world and ultimately toward God."[19] In contrast to faith, which suggests knowledge of God apart from "the experiential basis of all our knowledge, including our knowledge of God," piety is an orientation toward God as apprehended by humans.[20]

Gustafson's critics have charged him with "a univocal notion of human experience";[21] with building up a God which is no more than the human construct Nietzsche declared dead long ago and criticized by Feuerbach, and which J. A. T. Robinson in his *Honest to God* declared a metaphor;[22] and with failure to distinguish properly between God and nature.[23] Against this last charge Gustafson argues that his insistence on God as creator and as mystery rules out any identification of God within nature.[24] I agree with Richard McCormick's criticism, and I also think that Anthony Blasi is right to say that Gustafson's God is an all-too-human construct. Although he explicitly states that the religious affectivities, piety included, do not prove God's existence but only provide "warrants and symbols for moving from particular experience to the experience of responding to an ultimate power,"[25] it is beyond doubt that the image of God that emerges from this experience is an all-too-human creation. The truth, however, is that no God-talk can totally escape this charge. Even the experience of God we have through revelation conveys something of the human recipients of the revelation, and every human language is woefully inadequate for expressing the reality of God, thus adding to the notion plenty of cultural, time-bound, and thus anthropocentric accretions.

To obtain a more complete picture of what Gustafson says about God, one must also take a look at what he says about the human person. To understand the human person in turn one has to take note of the scientific evolution of the universe. Gustafson believes that the human person, as a recent arrival in a universe with billions of years of history behind it, is a chance development, the product of a happy association of natural events. As for other forms of life there will also be a temporal end to human life. Says Gustafson, "There shall be a *finis*, a temporal end to life as we know it."[26] This position is supported by modern scientific accounts of the origins of the universe and of the origins and evolution of life on our planet, Gustafson says, and therefore has a central position in his (Gustafson's) development of theocentric ethics.[27] Here briefly are some of the salient points about the human person in Gustafson's ethics: (1) the human person is neither the center and crown of the universe nor the measure of all things; (2) the human person is part of a whole. And although in this "whole" the conscious development of human beings has far outstripped that of other life forms, this does not mean that other life forms are meant for man's self-aggrandizement; (3) human beings are participants in the patterns and processes of the interdependence of life in the world and therefore are not the proprietors of creation, with rights of ownership that authorize them to do with all things what they choose in the light only of their interest.[28] The salvation of humanity is not the chief end of God.

Finally, then, it remains to ask ourselves what theocentric ethics is, to find out how it differs from other forms of ethics. In the second volume of the theocentric ethics project Gustafson addresses these questions.[29] To help make clear what ethics from a theocentric perspective is I shall summarize the points Gustafson gives as defining the critical difference between this and the more traditional forms of Christian ethics. First of all, ethics from a theocentric perspective is indeed theocentric. Here, the human being is not the absolute center of value. And because of this, theocentric ethics espouses the view that there are occasions when a course of action that is beneficial to human individuals or communities will not be the best course to follow. Second, the "patterns of interdependence and development within human activity and life" constitute the basis, ground, and foundation of ethics from a theocentric perspective. This is in contradistinction to the idea of "the will of God" and "nature" as basis and grounds of ethics. From these patterns of relationship indications are drawn as regards "the right ordering of human beings and actions to the wider natural world, of society, culture, and history, and even of aspects of our individual persons." These are all objective referents for the determination of "right action, proper ends and fitting aspirations for human activity." Thus they ground moral values, principles, ends, and duties "in an objective reality of which human life is a part."[30] Third, the moral does not stand over against the natural and the historical like an alien force. "Moral thinking gives direction to our natural impulses and desires as individuals within the context of the arenas of life in which we act." Thus, whether these be institutions or policy or even our natural drives for sustenance and sexuality, they all involve the directing and ordering of existing powers in accordance with "moral principles, values, ends, and ideals."[31]

Fourth, ethics from a theocentric perspective is a religious ethics. Here the experience of the "ultimate power and of powers bearing down upon, sustaining and creating possibilities for action induces or evokes piety." That is, through its experience of God, the community in part lives by senses of dependence, gratitude, obligation, remorse, repentance, direction, and hope. Piety, the disposition of awe and reverence before the power/powers, evokes and sustains morality in theocentric ethics. Fifth, in ethics from a theocentric perspective, moral decision making is interactionally rather than individually oriented. The focus is on the large whole rather than on the specific and discrete individual or event. In this regard, human beings are agents participating in a larger sphere of interaction and in the development of the world. Theocentric ethics does not decide beforehand for or against the individual or the whole, but takes each case as it comes—always striving not only to keep the balance between the two but also to take into account the multicausality and individual human agency in understanding social, historical, individual, and cultural developments.[32] However, in the event of a conflict between the whole and the parts, "theocentric ethics will be weighted more readily . . . on claims for the common good of the whole."[33]

Sixth, unlike some other ethical systems, theocentric ethics, Gustafson says, has no moral principle to use to judge all cases. Rather, it "accents the experience of moral ambiguity and even in some particular circumstances the deeply tragic character of particular choices,"[34] though it does not license an existentialist or libertarian ethic. In the seventh place, self-denial, even self-sacrifice, Gustafson says, are central to theocentric ethics. These it requires as necessary for life in human communities. They "are part of the requisite ordering of life required even for proper individual self-interest, as well as for communities living together in the conditions of finitude. And they come to our attention also in our human dependence upon the natural world of which we are part."[35] Therefore, the first practical moral question from a theocentric perspective, Gustafson says, is, "What is God enabling and requiring us to do?" The general answer is that we "are to relate ourselves and all things in a manner appropriate to [our and] their relations to God."[36] Moral life in the theocentric perspective is one of "benevolence to being in general" and calls for a reordering of one's desires, ends, and purposes to agree with those of the power and powers that sustain and bear upon life.[37] Moral life in this setting calls for discernment—that is, a discriminating spirit, the preparedness and ability to attend to all the facets and details of the issue that one can reasonably get to. This is of course, as we have already stated, contrary to a deontic ethics that marries itself to a set of principles that make it difficult to be discerning in its choices and judgments. Theocentric ethics proceeds from an evaluative description of the occasion or circumstance in question. The basic ingredients of an evaluative descriptive process are the disciplined gathering of pertinent information; the delineation of the most significant casual factors in the event or circumstance, through an analysis of as much available and collectible data as possible; and judgment based on these.[38] Disciplined research and painstaking analysis do not in themselves always guarantee that a "correct" and "right" answer will be reached. However, they do ensure that nothing of importance to the case is left out in the process of discernment.

For Gustafson, the ethicist in theocentric ethics neither prescribes nor proscribes the conduct of others. Moral procedures are meant to bring moral agents to awareness and not to act as infallible guides to moral agents in their action.[39] In fact, as I have already indicated, he stresses that theocentric ethics neither resolves the deep ambiguities in moral choices in certain conditions nor eliminates the possibility of genuine tragedy as a result of a moral choice. Says Gustafson, "It does not provide a bland assurance that something good will issue from every circumstance, that every 'crucifixion' will issue in a glorious 'resurrection,' that all things work together for good for those who love God."[40] Theocentric ethics is consequentialist. Every moral discernment in this ethics arrives at a decision, taking account of the consequences of the moral choice in question across time and across space.

It is concerned for the consequences of its action for individual persons and for the entire human community, as well as for the common good of designated wholes like the family or the economy. "It seeks to discern patterns of relationships which require compliance in order to preserve possibilities for the future development not only of human beings but of the natural world."[41]

After the publication of these two books in 1981 and 1984, respectively, a question commonly asked was "What happened to James Gustafson?" What worried some people was the critical stance toward, and in some cases outright repudiation of, essential Christian articles of faith in these volumes. In other cases there was the perception that Gustafson was not only beginning to sing a new song, he was singing a strange song, given all that he had previously written about Christ, God, the human person, and ethics. Some commentators thought he was singing in a strange new voice as well. Stanley Hauerwas, however, was of the view that these reactions, which center mainly on Gustafson's doctrine of God, miss the mark;[42] Gustafson was only being consistent with regard to his views on God. In any case, by concentrating on this aspect of the work, one might miss both the trend of thought it pursues and the continuity that it establishes with Gustafson's earlier works. Anthony Blasi agrees. For Blasi, one should not read these volumes simply from the point of view of systematic theology, but also as a cultural statement from a theologian who believes that theology produces an ethos, an orientation toward the world or, in the language of Gustafson himself, a way of construing the world and all reality.

A careful reading of Gustafson's theocentrism in these two volumes, whether it is consistent or not, reveals a number of facts worth noting. The first, as already indicated, is that Gustafson's position limiting what can be asserted of God to what is justifiable by science is a rejection of the reality of the importance of faith and reason as ways of "knowing." To put it bluntly, his view is a form of agnosticism masquerading as Christian theology or religion. The second point is that because of his attitude toward the reality of Jesus, his ethics as expressed in this particular book is anything but Christian for it draws little or no specific warrant from either Christian symbols or from the teaching of Jesus. As Joseph Ratzinger points out in his book *Introduction to Christianity*, for Christians, Jesus is the way. Although someone who finds the way can forget the Buddha, it does not work in the same manner with Jesus. What matters for Christian faith is the person of Christ himself. "When he says, 'I am he,' we hear the tones of the 'I AM' on Mount Horeb. The way consists precisely in following him, for 'I am the way, and the truth, and the life' (John 14:16). He himself is the way, and there is no way that is independent of him, on which he would no longer matter."[43] It is Christian belief and understanding that to know Jesus is to know God, and vice versa. No ethics that ignores this fact is truly theocentric in the Christian sense. Third, Gustafson's approach to the nature of norms and the manner of ascertaining them is utilitarian in many respects. To make the large whole the focus of the rightness of any moral choice might sound good in some situations, but in reality it could lead to a slippery slope, with the individual sacrificed to group interests (as was discussed in the previous chapter with regard to Bujo's work). As with Bujo the problem is that Gustafson is entering into ethical discernment armed with little more than the intention to discern from experience what God is enabling the agent to do or think. In other words, the lack of standards to which one may appeal as a point of demarcation between good and bad, right and wrong, from the point of view either of reason or of faith makes Gustafson's work in these two texts problematic, to say the least. African Christian ethics cannot be theocentric in this way.

Theocentricism in African Traditional Ethics: A Brief Appraisal

One concern I have with the work of Christian ethics in Africa is that it is not sufficiently Christian, in that it has paid too little attention to the biblical doctrine on God. African Christian theological ethics, as a result, seems to be constructed on minimalist assumptions about God. I believe that, as James Henry Owino Kombo puts it, "what African Christians need is not the African concept of God. What African Christians need is a clear picture of the Christian view of God."[44] And yet, this is often lacking in much of African theological discourse. *Dominus Jesus*, the 2000 document issued by the Vatican Congregation for the Doctrine of the Faith, makes a distinction between faith and belief that might be helpful in the discussion here. According to this document "theological faith, which is the acceptance in grace of the truth revealed by the One and Triune God, is not identical with belief in other religions, which is religious experience in the form of the human quest for the Absolute."[45] For Christians, "the full and complete revelation of the salvific mystery of God is given in Jesus Christ. Therefore, the words, deeds, and historical event of Jesus, though limited as human realities, have nevertheless the divine Person of the Incarnate Word, 'true God and true man' as their subject" (DI, 6). Faith is the empowered response to the person of Christ as incarnate son of God. "For this reason," says *Dominus Jesus*, "the distinction between theological faith and belief in the other religions must be firmly held" (DI 7). Failure to adhere to this kind of distinction in African theology has led to a lot of confusion.

It is seldom clear what difference faith in God, who has manifested himself in Jesus Christ and who continues to abide with his church, would make to Christian ethical discourse in Africa. It is not enough to enumerate the attributes of God; for theology to be Christian it has also to draw the lessons from scripture and from the Christian tradition on God. What, for example, is the ethical import of the doctrine of the Trinity for Africa? What lessons are there for Africa in the God about whom Jesus Christ taught in the parables? What lesson is there for an African theological ethics that draws on Jesus' saying in John 3:16 and in many other such passages? How would the praxis of Jesus as regards women and the marginalized of society in his day affect the construal of relationships in Christian Africa? What warrant would the teaching of Jesus on forgiveness, personal and communal, provide for the ethics of forgiveness among Africans? We will take up these questions shortly. However, it is my contention that, as James Henry Owino Kombo laments, "the doctrine of God in African theology has remained at the level of African concepts of God for too long."[46] This is not sufficient for the Christian ethics envisaged in this book. As indicated earlier, the concept of God significantly influences the way people live and the choices they make. The same is true in traditional African societies. In these societies, how people relate to the world around them is largely influenced by their view of the deity, the spirits, the ancestral world, and the world of inanimate created beings.[47] There is already a crisis in God-talk in Africa resulting from a serious confusion between the ideas about God in African religions and those in Christianity—with clearly evident deleterious consequences for life in Africa.

Over the years African theology has devoted plenty of resources to "proving" that Africans have a deep sense of the divine. Some African theologians, like Bolaji Idowu, have gone to considerable trouble to show that Christianity did not introduce any new God to Africa. As Idowu puts it, "There is only one God, the Creator of the heaven and earth and all that is in them." This God "has never left Himself without witness in any nation, age, or generation." It is the same God, "who by one stupendous act of climactic self-revelation in Jesus Christ came to redeem a fallen world." Thus, Christianity did not introduce Nigerians (or other Africans) to "a *completely* new God who is absolutely unrelated to their past history."[48] What Idowu is saying can be broken down into a number of propositions. The first is that knowledge of God is universal among African peoples. This is an incontrovertible truth. As we have already seen, even ethnographers have asserted this fact. The second point is more contested, namely that the God of African religion is the same God as the one revealed by biblical religion. Here the answer is not completely in the affirmative. Pre-Christian Africa did indeed receive God's revelation in nature and through the conscience of peoples and the mediation of institutions and communities; yet "traditional Africa does not know that God has revealed himself in the Son and the Holy Spirit."[49] This is true of pre-Christian African societies as it is of all other societies in the world prior to their encounter with the Christian faith. Thus, to make this assertion about Africa is in no way the same as to claim that pre-Christian Africa was devoid of the sense of God or of the divine. Idowu's assertion echoes the views of Saint Paul in many places but especially in his famous speech at the Areopagus. But Idowu misses one part of the teaching of Paul here which implies that God, who had in various ways and at various times manifested himself, has definitively shown his face in Jesus Christ. This is an important claim that must not be glossed over. Since the choice to be Christian is a choice for Christ, every theology that is Christian, including African theology, must therefore begin by "painting an icon of Christ." Although this icon must be printed with "local" (that is, African) materials and on an African canvas, it must be painted with an eye on the "real thing," the person of Christ which appears in scripture and has been reproduced in many places and ways in Christian history and tradition, and never in spite of or apart from them.

African tradition has its myths and stock of ancient wisdom expressed in various symbolic forms. It has its stock of sages and philosophical and historically enlightened figures. To deny this is to deny that Africa has had its great civilizations. However, in the face of this great constellation of persons and despite this venerable tradition, Christianity, as in all situations, makes a bold assertion about Jesus Christ. It asserts that Jesus is not just another wise figure or sage who belongs to a particular epoch or cultural milieu: he is God incarnate, the very revelation of God, the one who definitively and absolutely reveals God's intention and purposes for the world. Although similar in many respects to the teachings of many wise people in different ages and places, his teaching is not to be reduced to wise insights and opinions but must be listened to and adhered to as the revelation of God's will for humanity. The African theologian, insofar as he is Christian, must accept this as a starting point for doing theology. His task must begin with trying to understand Jesus, his nature, his teachings, and his mission. He must go to Jesus to learn and understand what Jesus teaches and reveals about God and about God's intentions and purposes in the world. He must not stop there, however. For as Saint Paul states in the letter to the Romans, "Ever since the creation of the world his [God's] eternal power and divine nature, invisible though they are, have been understood and seen through the things he has made" (Rom. 1:20). This is a truth that applies to pre-Christian Africa as it does everywhere else. In his homily at the opening Mass of the Second African Synod on October 4, 2009, Pope Benedict XVI noted that "the absolute Lordship of God is one of the salient and unifying features of the African culture. Naturally in Africa there are many different cultures, but they all seem to be in agreement on this point: God is the Creator and the source of life." In this regard the pope refers to Africa as "the repository of an inestimable treasure for the whole world." He notes that Africa's "deep sense of God" manifests itself in a number of ways, including through its understanding of marriage as "the union between the man and the woman and in the birth of children; divine law, written in nature, and thereby stronger and prominent with respect to any human law."[50] Pope Benedict XVI further opined that although "when we speak of the treasures of Africa, our thoughts immediately turn to the resources and its land and its riches that, unfortunately, have become and continue to be a reason for exploitation, conflict and corruption, the Word of God, instead, makes us look at another inheritance: the spiritual and cultural one of which humanity has even greater need than it does of raw materials. As Jesus said, 'What gain, then, is it for anyone to win the whole world and forfeit his life?' (Mk 8:36). From this point of view, Africa represents an enormous spiritual 'lung' for a humanity that appears to be in a crisis of faith and hope." He quickly warned, however, that "this 'lung' can take ill as well. And, at the moment, at least two dangerous pathologies are attacking it: first of all, an illness that is already widespread in the West, that is, practical materialism, combined with relativist and nihilist thinking."

Therefore, the dialogue between African theology and African Traditional Religion must begin with an appreciation of what both traditions share: a deep sense of the reality and presence of God. However, this dialogue must not stop there or be content with the discovery of the lowest common denominator between the two faiths. From the Christian angle, it must continue with a clear and unambiguous presentation of the person of Jesus who is the good news of God, and with showing, as Saint Paul would say, that this name has a demonstrable and unique force and power. Some African theologians have tended to reduce Christianity to a religion that is acceptable to Africans only when it validates African culture and the African traditional dispositions of reality. In this way, the gospel has sometimes been robbed of its power to critique or change lives and cultures and indeed of its newness, especially for the African context. The fact is that the gospel is new in every culture, and African theology must explore its meaning and show how it can renew African societies. People in Africa need to know who Jesus is. They know about their traditions. They know that these traditions contain good and noble ideals, thoughts, and issues. They do not turn to African theologians and church people merely for an education in African traditional religious thought; they come to such people to help them make sense of their encounter with Jesus, or to help them see the face of Jesus in all his beauty, and with all the challenges this encounter entails. They come to be educated by him and to receive the salvation which he is and which he brings. They come hoping to hear what he says to them about how to live good and upright lives in this world, lives that accord with the will of God for them and for all humanity. African theology must help the African Christian in this encounter.

THE GOD OF JESUS

In the first volume of his work *Jesus of Nazareth*, Pope Benedict XVI argues that the goal of Christianity is neither world progress nor universal prosperity. In other words, it is not part of Jesus' message to usher in an earthly kingdom of prosperity and harmonious coexistence. What then did Jesus actually bring, if not world peace, universal prosperity, and a better world? Pope Benedict asks,

> What has he brought? The answer is fairly simply, God. He has brought God. He has brought the God who formerly unveiled his countenance gradually, first to Abraham, then to Moses and the prophets, and then in the Wisdom Literature—the God who reveals his face barely in Israel even though he was also honored among the pagans in various shadowy guises. It is this God, the God of Abraham, Isaac and Jacob, the true God, whom he has brought to the nations of the earth. He has brought God, and now we know his face, now we can call upon him. Now we know the path that we human beings have to take in this world. Jesus has brought God and with God the truth about . . . origin and destiny: faith, hope and love . . .[51]

In an earlier book, *Introduction to Christianity*, Ratzinger argued that to understand the biblical belief in God one must follow its historical developments from its origin with the patriarchs of Israel right up to the last books of the New Testament.[52] Ratzinger examines the Exodus story (Exod. 3) in which Moses encountered God in the burning bush. He considers this text central for the understanding of God in the Old Testament. The aim of the text is clearly to establish the name Yahweh as the definitive name of God in Israel and to give it meaning.[53] The theological significance of the name Yahweh consists in the differentiation of Yahweh as the God of Israel's fathers, the God of Abraham, Isaac, and Jacob. God is revealed to be God of human beings, not just of a locale, as some of the more ancient names of God in Israel imply. "He is not the god of a place but the god of men: the God of Abraham, Isaac, and Jacob. He is therefore not bound to one spot but is present and powerful whenever man is. In this fashion one arrives at a completely different way of thinking about God. God is seen on the plane of I and you, not on the plane of the spatial . . . He is nowhere in particular; he is to be found at any place where man is and where man lets himself be found by him."[54] For Ratzinger the explanation of the name Yahweh by the title word *AM* serves as a kind of negative theology that cancels out the significance of the name as a name: "Its effect is that of withdrawal from the only too well known which the name seems to be, into the unknown, the hidden. It dissolves the name into mystery, so that the familiarity and unfamiliarity of God, concealment and revelation, are indicated simultaneously. The name, a sign of acquaintance, becomes the cipher for the picture and the unknown and unnamed quality of God. Contrary to the view that God can here be grasped, so to speak, the persistence of an infinite distance is in this way made quite clear."[55] Even so, an essential characteristic of the biblical God is that he is personal. God by his name is personal. This implies not only that we can experience God beyond all other experience, but also that he can express and communicate himself.[56] In Jesus Christ God has become quite concrete and even more mysterious. God is always infinitely greater than all our concepts and our images and names. "The fact that we now acknowledge him to be triune does not mean that we have meanwhile learned everything about him."[57] Even so, the fact is that this God now has shown us his face in Jesus Christ (John 14:9)—a face that Moses was not allowed to see (Exod. 33:20).[58]

According to Pope Benedict XVI, in bringing the gift of the God of Israel to the nations Jesus has brought the gift of universality so that through him all the nations "recognize Israel's Scripture as his word, the word of the living God." This was the one gift God had promised Abraham, Isaac, and Jacob. "This universality, this faith in the one God of Abraham, Isaac and Jacob—extended now in Jesus' new family and all nations over the bonds of descent according to the flesh—is the fruit of Jesus' work. It is what proves him to be the Messiah. It signals a new integration of messianic promise that is based on Moses and the prophets, but also opens them up in a completely new way."[59] The vehicle of Jesus' universalism is the new family "whose only admission requirement is communion with Jesus, communion in God's will" (cf. Mark 3:34 ff.). "This universalization of Israel's faith and hope and the concomitant liberation from the letter of the law for the new communion with Jesus is tied to Jesus' authority and his claim to Sonship. It loses its historical weight and its whole foundation if Jesus is interpreted merely as a liberal reform Rabbi."[60]

Sources of Jesus' Teaching about God: The Parables

There is perhaps no better place to begin to study the teaching of Jesus on God than the parables of Jesus. As Arland J. Hultgren points out, "The English word 'parable' is a loan word from the Greek word parabolē (Παραβολή in Greek lettering)." Its basic meaning is "a comparison."[61] It is a story used to illustrate a point about reality. It is not, however, just a story; in its broad sense, it is "an expanded analogy which by drawing contrasts is used to explain or to convince."[62] As used by Jesus, "a parable is a figure of speech in which a comparison is made between God's kingdom, actions, or expectations and something in this world, real or imagined."[63] According to Joachim Jeremias, the parables "reflect with peculiar clarity the character of Jesus' good news, the eschatological nature of his preaching, the intensity of his summons to repentance, and his conflict with Pharisaism."[64] In these stories Jesus takes everyday experiences and weaves them into narratives that are at the same time highly realistic in terms of his hearers' world and their experiences "which have deep resonances with Yahweh's activity on behalf of Israel as these had been described in the Psalms and the prophets."[65] Generally, parables are used to convey certain important insights and truths. They do this sometimes by means of the paradox—that is, by means of some startling effects. Consider, for example, the parable of the sower (Matt. 13:1–24) who scatters his seeds so recklessly that some of them fall on rocky ground, others in places where thorns grow, others grow on pathways, and some others grow in good soil. In another parable those who work for one hour are paid as much as a person who had begun work at the crack of dawn. In yet another parable, the "mean girls" who refuse to share their oil with their friends are praised as wise. As Edward Schillebeeckx points out, these parables often shock not only us but the initial hearers of Jesus. The fact, however, is that "every para-ble turns around a scandalizing center," often standing things on their heads and startling the hearers to deeper thinking about reality.[66] In this sense, then, parables are "teasers," which set the familiar against an unfamiliar background, challenging us in the process to deeper thinking and forcing us to see reality more deeply and more clearly, and by so doing leading us to deeper truth. In a parable, "a narrative is told in order that the unknown might be illumined by the known."[67]

The parables of Jesus are part of a larger matrix within which Jesus conveys the essential message of his ministry about the approach-ing reign of God—a reign that has already begun and has been mani-fested in the ministry of Jesus, but which is still to come and for which Jesus invites his hearers to prepare themselves. "In the care he shows for man, and his record of suffering, for publicans and sinners, for the poor, the crippled and the blind, for the oppressed and for people torn apart by 'evil spirits,' Jesus is a living parable of God: that is how God cares for man. *In the story of Jesus is told the story of God*" (empha-sis added).[68] As we will see in a moment, although all the parables of Jesus are basically about God, certain features of Jesus' teaching on God will help us build up a theocentric basis for an African moral the-ology that is truly African and Christian.

Joachim Jeremias has provided a classification of Jesus' parables, similes, and other sayings. For example, some speak of the imminence of the day of salvation—that is, of a realized eschatology in the per-son and ministry of Jesus (e.g., Luke 7:22, Matt. 11:5); others speak of God's mercy for sinners (e.g., Matt. 21:28–31, Luke 7:36–50); and other parables provide various assurances about the kingdom of God, among many other types of parables.[69] We are interested here in the group that Andrew Greeley refers to as "the Great Parables": those of the sower (Matt. 13:1–13); the vintner (Matt. 20:1–15); the prodi-gal son (Luke 15:11–32); and the Good Samaritan (Luke 10:25–37). We will also discuss the story of the woman caught in adultery in John 8:1–11 and the case of the Samaritan woman (John 4:4–42). As Greeley points out, reading these parables, one comes to know who the Father in heaven is. "They represent Jesus' experience of the Father. They tell us who the God is that sent his son Jesus into the world to reveal him to those with whom he shared his humanity. The God of the great parables is the God of Jesus, the God whose kingdom began with Jesus and continues even today. The God who was embracing the world in his kingdom had to be a very large God and a very generous one—how large and how generous these four parables tell us."[70]

In the parable of the sower, we hear of a planter who scatters seeds lavishly to the point of recklessness. The seeds fall on every kind of soil, which either chokes them, helps them germinate and live for a while, or enables them to germinate and to do well, according to their circumstances. Although this particular parable is primarily about the reception of God's word and the need for the disciple to hear the word of God and be focused on it, it is still a story about "who God is and what God is doing and will do in Jesus' action."[71] Through the proclamation of Jesus, God is restoring Israel and establishing God's kingdom. In the end it is still all about God, the generous giver of grace. In the parable of the vintner we hear of a rich landowner who goes out at different times of the day to hire laborers and decides in the end to pay the last set of them the same daily wage he had agreed to with the first set of workers, who had been hired at dawn and had worked all day. The story of the prodigal son is about a young man who, contrary to custom and convention, insists on and receives a piece of his father's property, after which he sets off and squanders his share of the inheritance in a life of debauchery. When no longer able to sustain himself, he decides to return home in the hope of being hired to work for his father. But as soon as the father catches sight of him on his way home, he runs to his son, clasps him, and hugs him, announcing a feast to which he invites neighbors and friends, "for this son of mine was lost but is now found; he was dead but is now alive." We also see in this story how the other son becomes indignant at the sight of the revelry taking place on account of his wayward brother. Finally, the familiar story of the Good Samaritan introduces us to a traveler who is beaten and robbed by thieves on his way from Jerusalem to Jericho, but no one stops to care for him. Even fellow Jews traveling on the same route ignore him, for reasons not clearly stated in the story. At last comes a Samaritan, a non-Jew, who sees in this helpless victim a neighbor who needs assistance. The Samaritan takes the injured man to a place where he is treated for his wounds and makes a further commitment to pay any additional bills when returning from his own trip.

These well-known parables have been studied and analyzed for centuries. The characters in the stories have also been studied and many moral lessons drawn from their behaviors or from the way Jesus characterized them. However, it is safe to say as Greeley does that these parables are about God, the Father in heaven, and about his kingdom. "The Vintner is God, the Indulgent Father is God, and the Good Samaritan is God. These parables are about God—the God of the Kingdom, the God Jesus discloses to us—and his relationship to his people. They are about a passionately, insanely forgiving God."[72] Let us consider closely the parable of the vintner, for example. As several scholars have noted, this is perhaps the parable of Jesus that many people find most difficult to take because they consider the action of the vintner unjust, unfair, and even crazy. But the charge of unjustness cannot be levied against the vintner if we remember that, as Jesus told us already, he had agreed to pay a day's wage to the first group he hired. And this group of workers did indeed get what was agreed to and what they deserved. That is justice. But the weight of this parable does not lie on the perceived justice or lack of it. Joachim Jeremias describes it as one of the double-edged parables of Jesus (cf. Luke 15:11–32; Luke 16:19–31; Matt. 22:1–14). It describes two episodes. The first part of the parable (Matt. 20:1–8) describes the hiring of the workers and the instructions about their payments, while the second deals with the reaction of the other workers and finally with the vintner's response to the indignant workers: "Are you envious of me because I am generous?" (Matt. 20:15).

Hultgren, on the other hand, notes that the context in which Matthew places this parable would suggest a double audience. One audience would be those early disciples of Jesus such as Peter, James, and John who had wanted to know what their reward would be in the kingdom (Matt. 19:27) or whose mother had reportedly come to Jesus to seek favors on their behalf in the future kingdom (Matt. 20:21). To the Matthean community, "the parable indicates that those who are called first will have no advantage over those who are among the 'last.' The latter will also receive 'a hundredfold,' 'eternal life,' the same wages as those who had been disciples from the beginning. That is the way of God's ruling in grace."[73] Jeremias notes that this parable is also addressed to those who, like the Pharisees in this story, murmur and criticize Jesus for associating with the despised and the outcast.

Against such groups Jesus found himself repeatedly trying to justify his conduct and to vindicate the good news. So here he is saying, "This is what God is like, so good, so full of compassion for the poor." He is saying to them, "Such is God's goodness, and since God is so good, so too am I."[74] Thus, the story is not about economic justice or rational economic behavior. It is about God, a God who is so expansive, abundant, and loving in his generosity that people behaving with similar generosity would be considered insane. "By human standards, God is quite mad."[75] This second way of reading the parable goes deeper into the gospel of God that Jesus brought. Its point is that "we are accepted and loved by God, and saved by God, not because of our efforts but purely by God's own grace. God saves us not because we are lovable, but because God is loving in a radical way. This is the gospel. It is not from human wisdom."[76]

The same situation applies in the story of the prodigal son, or as some scholars prefer to call it, the story of the prodigal father. The father in this case is "crazy" enough to give in to the demands of a son who has no right whatsoever to ask for a share of the father's estate. When this "loser" son returns with prepackaged apologies the father is overjoyed at the sight of him and does not even allow him to read his prepared speech. Instead, in his "crazy" and overindulgent way he orders a big feast and celebrations for an "otherwise lost but found son." The reaction of the second son captures our normal human way of thinking: What? Has the old man gone mad? What example is he showing by "celebrating" "this son of yours . . . who has devoured your property with prostitutes" (Luke 15:30), as the other son puts it? But then, that is God for you. The older son's reaction is somewhat reminiscent of that point in the story of Jonah where, after reluctantly agreeing to preach to the Ninevites and finding that the people accepted his word and were pardoned by God, Jonah becomes angry with God and says, "O Lord, is not this what I said while I was still in my own county? That is why I fled from Tarshish at the beginning; for I know that you are a gracious God and merciful, slow to anger, and abounding in love, and ready to relent from punishing" (Jonah 4:2). The older son in the story of the prodigal son is equally stunned at the Father's prodigality. The God that Jesus presents in this parable, as in all other ones, is the forgiving and merciful God who is reflected in the actions and other aspects of the ministry of Jesus.

In his commentary on the parable of the Good Samaritan Andrew Greeley invites us to consider another angle to this familiar story. Although it had been read for centuries as a morality play that teaches a lesson of love toward anyone in need—and coming from an utter stranger—and rightly so, the story is indeed much more about God. The Good Samaritan here is God. Jesus is deliberately trying to shock his audience by making the Samaritan character in this story a God figure. "Outrageous, scandalous, shameful, disgraceful—think of any word you might want to add and all might apply. This story of Jesus was all of these things. Yet it remained in this tradition because everyone knew Jesus had said it. St. Luke couldn't leave it out, but he tried to tame it. That a Samaritan could be a good guy was acceptable, if by way of exception, but that it might be a symbol for the Father-in-heaven, how could he be that?"[77] The point then, Greeley concludes, is that the Father-in-heaven is "unacceptably surprising, especially when we are totally weak, utterly defenceless, and completely at the Father-in-heaven's mercy as we will be at the moment of our death. We might even cry out for mercy, even if you are Muslim or a Communist or an Atheist or a Bible-toting Evangelical."[78]

The way God acts becomes even clearer in Jesus' teaching about the reign of God. Through many other parables and the other teachings of Jesus and through his own actions we come to some understanding of the kingdom of God. As Pope Benedict XVI puts it, when Jesus teaches about the kingdom of God, he is speaking of God "who is as much in this world as beyond—who infinitely transcends this world, but is also totally anterior to it."[79] He is referring to God's actual sovereignty over the world, which is becoming an event in history in a new way. "When Jesus speaks of the kingdom of God he is simply proclaiming God and proclaiming him to be a living God, who is able to act concretely in the world and in history and is even now doing so."[80] This new proximity of the kingdom of which Jesus speaks—the distinguishing feature of this message—is to be found in Jesus himself. "God has here and now entered into history in a wholly new way, through the presence and action of Jesus. In Jesus, it is God who draws near to humanity, that is why 'now is the fullness of time' (Mk 1:15), and in a unique sense, the time of conversion and penance, as well as the time of joy." God is now the one who acts and who rules as

Lord—rules in a divine way, without worldly power, rules through
the love that reaches "to the end" (John 13:1), to the cross.[81]

Sources of Jesus' Teaching about God: The Praxis of the Kingdom

Jesus had a lot to say about the kingdom of God. Often, however, his
deeds spoke even more clearly about it. Two important stories of
Jesus' interaction with people, two women, to be precise, reveal a lot
about the reality of the kingdom of God pertinent to our inquiry here.
The first is the story of Jesus' encounter with an unnamed Samaritan
woman at the well known as Jacob's well in the Samaritan village of
Sychar (John 4:4–42). The other is the story of the woman caught in
adultery (John 8:1–11). In the first story a woman comes to the well
to draw water and there encounters Jesus, who asks for a drink. This
simple request leads to one of the most incisive and profound theological discussions in the New Testament. The woman is startled that
Jesus, a Jew, is asking for a drink from a *Samaritan woman*. When
Jesus tells her that she should be jumping for joy at this request—
"If you knew the gift of God and who it is that is saying to you 'give
me a drink,' you would have asked him, and he would have given you
living water"—the woman counters by making two points: (1) Jesus
had no bucket; and (2) Jesus, to her, might be overreaching himself.
She asks him, "Are you greater than our ancestor Jacob, who gave us
this well, and with his sons drank from it themselves?" To which Jesus
replies, "Everyone who drinks of this well will be thirsty again, but
those who drink the water that I will give them will never be thirsty
again." On and on the discussion goes, touching on issues about the
woman's life and leading to a point where Jesus discloses to the woman
his true identity as the Messiah. The woman says to him, "I know that
Messiah is coming (who is called Christ). When he comes, he will proclaim all things to us." At this Jesus replies, "I am he, the one who is
speaking to you" (John 4:26).

In her commentary on this story Sandra Schneiders regards this
woman as "a representative figure." She is symbolic "not only of the
Samaritans who come to Jesus through the witness of the Johanine
community but . . . of the New Israel who is given to the bridegroom
'from above.'"[82] This unnamed Samaritan woman is symbolic also,

I would add, of all women, all marginalized persons, and all those who are considered in one way or another to be disreputable, warranted on not, within their communities. There are two reactions to Jesus' encounter with this woman. The first comes from the woman herself when she responds to Jesus' request for water by asking him, "How is it that you, a Jew, ask a drink of me, a *woman* of *Samaria*?" (John 4:9). The point here is that Jesus is obviously breaking with Jewish tradition by speaking to and sharing implements with a Samaritan, a member of a group the Jews regarded with utmost disdain and contempt as "lowlifes." The second reaction to Jesus in his encounter with this woman came from his disciples, who, on returning from the trip to find food in the town, react with horror to the fact that Jesus was talking to this woman (John 4:27). Although Schneiders in her commentary spiritualizes that aspect of the story where Jesus notes that the woman had gone from one husband to another and was now living with her sixth husband, Christian tradition has long considered this woman an adulterer. Far from diminishing the woman, this latter point enhances her value and raises her symbolic worth as representing all sinners who come to Jesus as they are, warts and all. The interesting thing here is that Jesus refuses to pass judgment on her in any way. Instead he treats her with the utmost respect in spite of whatever had been her history. Being a woman can be a challenging reality in many societies, including those of Africa, just like being a member of a marginalized group in whatever sense, social, economic, or otherwise. Here in this story Jesus presents an alternative option to the dominant praxis of his day regarding women, the sinner, and the marginalized. He presents us with the goal of the kingdom of God where, with God in charge, everyone is treated with inclusive respect and with equal regard, gender, social status, or lineage notwithstanding. The kingdom of God as proclaimed by Jesus is, therefore, "an offer of salvation to those who do not belong."[83] This last point comes out even more clearly in the story of the woman caught in adultery (John 8:1–11). However we look at it, this is a story of God's superabundant mercy. It shows again, as Greeley points out, that "God's justice is not our justice. God's mercy far exceeds our mercy."[84]

Although Jesus was not the first to speak about God's approaching reign, his teaching on the matter is markedly different from that of the Pharisees and other religious groups of his day. The core of

Jesus' teaching about the kingdom of God, and indeed of all his good news, is charity. While the kingdom of God is God's utter choice and gratuitous offer, it also makes stringent moral demands on peoples everywhere. God is love, and those who worship him must love not only God but also one another, if their worship is to be sincere and acceptable to him. Thus, the first demand of Christian morality is love: God has loved us in Christ, and we must love God in return and love our neighbor as well because we have been loved by God. It is Christian belief that in and through his praxis of the kingdom Jesus is also pointing to his role and nature as God. He is that sign of Jonah that is sent by God, the eschatological prophet through whose life and activity people experience the saving presence and salvation of God.

An Initial Summary

One might ask what this whole discussion of the teaching of Jesus on God and on the kingdom of God is all about and ultimately what it has to do with African Christian ethics. In order to answer these questions we first need to summarize some of the basic insights about the Christian view of God which have become evident in our discussion so far, especially those pertinent to our search for the bases of an ethic that is truly Christian and African. There is no doubt that Africans take God seriously and that, as Pope Benedict XVI wrote in *Africae Munus*, "to deprive the African continent of God would be to make it die a slow death, by taking away its very soul."[85] The same Pope Benedict XVI pointed out in his opening remarks at the Second Africa Synod that the sense of God is something Africans are exporting to other parts of the world, which is in dire need of it today. My contention in this book so far has been that, speaking as a Christian, I believe the African sense of God needs completion or correction at some points from Christian revelation. From the analysis of the teaching of Jesus up to this point, we can discern three areas in which this completion can happen: the understanding of the nature of God; God's relationship with human beings and with the created order; and the universalism of God's love.

One lesson we learn from Jesus about God is that although God is the absolute Other, God has a human face, so to speak. The one who created us is the one who also redeemed us. As the fourth Eucharistic prayer of the Roman Missal put it, the God Jesus reveals is the one who "did not abandon us" even when we disobeyed him and lost his friendship; the God who so loves the world that he sent his son that we may have life and have it to the full (John 3:16), the God who is also in search of humanity—for humanity's own sake. Jesus is God's pledge of eternal friendship with humanity. He is Emmanuel—God with us and God for us. What this goes to show is that God is reliable; God can be trusted. By contrast, this is not the case in African Traditional Religion. The relationship between God and human beings in African Traditional Religion is one of fear. This accounts for the notion of the *deus otiosus*, the distant and withdrawn God, which some scholars speak of in African Traditional Religion.[86] The fear factor in the human-deity relationship is often the basis for right order in African Traditional Religion. To understand this better, let us revisit the *osu* caste system among the Igbo.

The *osu* question endures among the Igbo today, but not because the Igbo are callous or unmindful of the systemic injustice that the system implies—quite to the contrary. Since the 1950s efforts have been made to "abolish" the *osu* caste system in eastern Nigeria; in fact, it was officially abolished in 1956. Even so, it is still part of the psyche of many Igbo communities and individuals. What is keeping the system alive is fear of retribution from the gods to whom these persons had been consecrated. Few Igbo would want to interfere with "the property" of the gods, for fear that the deities in question would visit them or their families or descendants with rage and fury. Thus, the marriage of an *osu* to a non-*osu* would not only create the intermingling of bloodlines which would bring down the wrath of the divine, it would amount to daring the gods to act and think otherwise.

To say that the fear factor in African religion is paramount is not to negate the other attributes of God in African religion. In fact, in all metaphysically grounded ethics the reasonableness of moral commitment is to some extent grounded in "the promise of perfect retribution"[87]—that is, in the understanding that immoral behavior incurs divine wrath and is punishable in some form. In Christianity, for example, "the idea of God as Creator and Sovereign . . . expresses the moral requirement of impartial regard for all. As Judge, God is conceived to uphold this standard by ultimately punishing violations of it and by rewarding the righteous (usually in some eschatological domain). Finally, in the face of persistent human iniquity, he is believed to furnish means of atonement and forgiveness, thereby tempering justice with mercy."[88] The difference between Christianity and African Traditional Religion in this regard is in the nearness of God, in the understanding that God is not interested in anyone's death or suffering; that God gives everyone, especially the sinner, a second chance; that the Lord Jesus came for the sinner (1 Tim. 1:5), that he died on the cross for all (Matt. 20:28); in short, that God's love is for all. This is the essence of the universalism of God's love, of which we have spoken already. Divine retribution in Christian terms becomes a choice that one makes deliberately and in the *eschaton*, and is not something that is visited on people here and now because God is angry.

When we contrast these ideas with what goes on in African Traditional Religion, where it is understood that when "the high God" enters into human affairs "it is often to cause evils," then the point I am making here becomes clearer. For the truth is that in much of Africa, epidemics, diseases, and many other forms of physical evils are attributed to God. As Green notes, for this reason, "the common wish of African peoples is that God, who is far away from their lives, shall stay that way."[89] God is to be feared. That is the reason people in African Traditional Religion prefer then to deal with the lesser deities who are considered custodians of the moral order. Even these intermediaries of God, such as Ala, in Igbo religion, or the ancestors, are often considered to be moral enforcers, wrathful avengers of transgressions of the moral code.

The ethics of fear that arises from the kind of metaphysical grounding of ethics in African Traditional Religion which we have discussed so far can have dire consequences: when this type of fear factor is removed, societal breakdown often occurs. There is a lot of societal breakdown in African communities today. In many places where people no longer feel obligated to the ancestral forms of worship, and where the fear of instant retribution has disappeared, and where nothing has been found to fill this void, there has been a lot of chaos. This is evident in politics where people live and rule amorally; it is evident in people's personal lives and in their relationships. In these places, things have indeed fallen apart, because the center no longer holds. The blame for this situation is to be shared by many. In his homily at the opening Mass of the Second African Synod, Pope Benedict XVI noted that the deep sense of God that is evident in African culture and which makes Africa "the repository of an inestimable treasure for the whole world" is indeed at the moment under attack by certain dangerous pathologies, some of which have origins in other parts of the world and are already widespread within those societies. One source of the attacks on Africa is the West, the so-called First World, which is now exporting "its spiritual toxic waste that contaminates the peoples of other continents, in particular those of Africa." From this source come such viruses as practical materialism, moral relativism, "nihilist thinking," "religious fundamentalism, mixed together with political and economic interests." A second source of the attacks on Africa is that of religious fundamentalists who mix religion "with political and economic interests," as well as external "groups who follow various religious creeds" and are now spreading throughout the continent of Africa "in God's name" but follow a logic that is opposed to divine logic—that is, teaching and practicing "not love and respect for freedom, but intolerance and violence." In this sense, said the pontiff, "colonialism which is over at the political level has never really entirely come to an end." It is my contention in this book that Christianity too shares some blame for the God problem in Africa and for its attendant effects due to the haphazard evangelization in the area of God-language. In a bid to plant the faith in Africa, Christian missionaries quickly dislodged African divinities from their groves or quickly baptized them with Christian names without a corresponding change in the meaning they mediated. It is my view, therefore, that the place to begin to do Christian theology in Africa today is in the area of God-language. It is here we must begin the dialogue with African Traditional Religion.

African Christian theology must begin by providing a careful and loving portrait of the God whom Jesus called Father. African theology and catechesis must emphasize again in Africa that Jesus is Emmanuel, that God is for us, that God is our Father, that God so loves the world that he sends his Son for our redemption. God is not the vengeful Other. God is love, and Christian morality is a response ethic. It is a morality of love, a morality that begins with the acknowledgment of love. It is a morality that responds to love. It is morality of those who, believing that "nothing can come between us and the love of God made manifest in Christ" (Rom. 8:39), respond in kind to God's initiative through love of neighbor.

There is a second crucial element for African theology and African Christian ethics which the teachings of Jesus on God introduced to the God-language: the universalism of God and of God's love. Let us consider again the parable of the Good Samaritan. Noteworthy in this parable is that by his action in this story the Samaritan brings out the radical equality between himself and the man who had been beaten by brigands. This equality cuts through every other classification that separates the two men—race, class, and other circumstances of life. As Pope Benedict XVI points out, the assault victim here is the image of "Everyman" and the Samaritan is the image of Jesus Christ. "God himself, who for us is foreign and distant, has set out to take care of his wounded creature. God, though so remote from us, has made himself our neighbor in Jesus Christ. He pours oil and wine into our wound, a gesture seen as an image of the healing gifts of the sacraments, and he brings us to the inn, the Church, in which he arranges our care and also pays a deposit for the cost of that care."[90] As we shall see in the next chapter, the story of the Good Samaritan has moral significance in this regard in the moral demands it makes on us concerning human solidarity, and especially in the extent and reach of that solidarity. The lesson of this parable is clear: The God of Jesus is universal as creator, sustainer, and redeemer, and his love is inclusive and blind to ethnic and racial or class considerations.

Chapter Seven

ANTHROPOLOGY IN AFRICAN
THEOLOGICAL ETHICS

*O Lord, what are human beings that you regard them,
or mortals that you think of them?*

—Psalm 144:3

One of the most quoted passages in the *Summa Theologica* is the brief prologue with which Thomas Aquinas introduces the *Prima Secundae* (the first part of the second part). Aquinas says that "man is said to be made in God's image in so far as the image implies *an intelligent being endowed with free-will and self-movement:* now that we have treated of the exemplar, i.e., God, and of those things which came forth from the power of God in accord with His will; it remains for us to treat of His image, i.e., man, inasmuch as he too is the principle of his actions, as having free will and control of his actions."[1] What this means is that just as a proper understanding of the idea of God in Christian faith and theology is important for Christian ethics, so is a proper doctrine or understanding of the human person. As Klaus Demmer puts it, "The moral life of the Christian flows directly from his or her being; the imperative dimension, what one *ought* to do, is grounded in the indicative—what one *is.*"[2] In other words, our interpretation or theory of the human person—his or her nature, purpose, and destiny—has implications for what we say about the human person—his or her acts—since ethics is about the human person as a being and as a moral actor. In the theology of Thomas Aquinas we find an acknowledgment both of this reality and of the need for a thorough and comprehensive sketch of the human moral actor in ethics.

THE HUMAN PERSON IN THE AFRICAN WORLDVIEW

Earlier we saw that the African universe of beings is a layered universe: God, spirits, and human beings, in that order. Myths abound all over Africa that offer insight into what Africans think about the world and its origin and about human beings, their origin in the world, and their place in the universe. It is clear from all these sources of wisdom that Africans see the world as a result of God's creative act, although there are differences in these mythical accounts and theories of how the universe came about and how the first human beings were made. In his treatment of the Yoruba creation myths E. Bolaji Idowu makes this point when he states that, as regards the creation of the original man and woman and when it took place, "we are lost in the wilderness. All that is clear is that they were made by Olódùmarè, who also fixed their destiny." According to Yoruba oral traditions, "some creature who forms the nucleus of the human occupation of the earth has been in existence even earlier than the earth."[3] There is indeed a tradition different from that of the Yoruba of Nigeria which provides details of the story of the creation of the human person. Coming from the Fang of Gabon, it states that after Nzame (God) had created all things, he decided as well to create the human person. In this story, there are three who are Nzame, God: Nzame, Mebere, and Nkwa. After everything had been created Nzame called Mebere and Nkwa to show them his work. They answered, "We see many animals, but we do not see their chief; we see many plants, we do not see their master."[4] Thus, Nzame, Mebere, and Nkwa created a being like themselves to whom they said, "Take the earth. You are henceforth the master of all that exists. Like us you have life, all things belong to you, you are the master."[5] The name of this first man was Fam, which means power. Fam became proud of his sway, his power, and his beauty and refused to worship God again. God became furious at Fam and in anger sent thunder and fire, which destroyed Fam and all creation even though God had at creation promised that man would never die. When God saw the extent of the destruction, which he himself had wrought on the earth, "he felt ashamed and wanted to do better." Consequently, Nzame, Mebere, and Nkwa took counsel again: "they needed a chief to command all the animals: 'we shall make a man like Fam,' said Nzame, 'the same legs and arms, but we shall turn his head and he shall see death.'"[6] Noteworthy in this myth is that it tries to explore the human condition—the reality of suffering and death.

Like many other African myths of creation, this Fang story exhibits much that is similar to the Hebrew creation story. As a result, questions of dependence or even missionary influence on these stories have been raised, even though "the collectors of these stories have been able to rule out such a possibility."[7] Whatever the case may be, this is one of the few stories that actually detail in a comprehensive manner the actual creation of human beings. Most other creation myths try to explain either the origins of the earth, or the origin of suffering and death. While some ideas in these myths of creation might sound familiar to anyone acquainted with the Judeo-Christian or Islamic traditions, as is the case with the Fang creation story, other creation accounts from Africa might seem quite startling and unfamiliar to people in other parts of the world:

> In the Kono creation myth, Death is the original force in the world, existing before God; among the Malozi, God appears powerless to control man; among the Ijaw, man decides his own fate before coming into the world; the Wapangwa have a fantastic vision of the earth being created from the excrement of ants; the Yoruba regard the creator as guilty and responsible for deformities in man, and they also explain the existence of many gods, defining them as all forming part of the one divine being. These ideas are exciting and stimulating because they throw new light on man's relationship to God and attempt to come to terms with the supernatural and the inevitable.[8]

Death as an inevitable reality of the human condition takes up considerable space in African myths of human origin. In the end, many African mythological accounts generally blame the phenomenon of death on human choices at the beginning—the primordial past.

It is clear from their creation mythology that African societies regard the human person not only as a creature of God but as the crown jewel of God's creation. Among the Igbo a person is first and foremost "a being possessed of vital-breath or life force (*ume*); . . . and a composite of the material and the non-material." This complexity of his or her nature places the person above other visible living beings. According to some Igbo scholars, the term *mmadu*, the Igbo word for human being (masculine or feminine), is a composite of "beauty" (*mma*) and "life" (*ndu*) and thus illuminating the high regard for the human being as crown jewel of God's creation and the goodness of life, and as "implying the acme of existence."[9] Writing on this subject, Raymond Arazu, the Nigerian Spiritan liturgist and moral theologian, put it this way: "An Igbo contemplative animist confided in me once that Chukwu (God) looked on the world he had made and pronounced the sentence: 'Let goodness exist'—*Mma-du!* The result of this order from Chukwu was man as we see him today. Man's essence is an order from the Supreme Being: 'Let goodness exist.' The name is the nature. But man committed original sin in the fact that he pronounces his name without a pause in the middle of the word. Man sinned when he pronounced his name without thought."[10]

There is a widespread belief in African societies that "each person incarnates in the land through the creative act of the protective (dynamic) spirit assigned to the person by God. This is known variously in the West African sub region as *Chi* (Igbo), *ori* (Yoruba), *ka* or *kre* (Ewe, Asante), *ka* (Ancient Egypt)."[11] As Chinua Achebe has indicated, understanding the notion of *chi* is important to understanding the Igbo worldview, especially the concept of the person in that system of thought. "Without an understanding of the nature of Chi one could not begin to make sense of the Igbo worldview."[12] It is not my intention to go into a full-blown discussion of this concept here; I will mention only two aspects that bear on the discussion here on African ethics. The first is that each person has an individual chi that has "unprecedented powers" over that person's destiny. Even though, as Achebe is quick to point out, a person is not without say in his or her destiny (as the saying goes, "if one says yes, his or her chi would say yes"), it is also known among the Igbo that a person receives his portion in life, even his character, as an endowment from his chi even before he enters into the world. The second issue, then, is that of freedom. As Achebe puts it, even though there seems to be an element of bargaining at this primordial point, and even though the person seems to have some element of choice, it is that person's chi "who presides over the bargaining. Hence the saying, '*obu otu ya na chi ya si kwu.*'"

(Translation: this is his or her agreement with his or her chi.) Thus, sometimes "even a person of impeccable character may find himself or herself at odds with his or her chi." Achebe thus concludes that "chi is therefore more concerned with success or failure than with righteousness and wickedness."

But I do not see how Achebe could logically reach this conclusion. Isn't there an element of moral determinism here? Even though it is Ala, the divinity who is charged with moral rightness and wrongness, the Igbo seem to have evaded the logical implication of the involvement of one's chi in such a deterministic way in all other areas of the individual's life. What is at stake here, it seems to me, is the notion of human freedom. For if one's destiny has already been set without the agent's involvement, how can the agent as moral actor be held responsible for all of the things he or she does which lead to the person's activation of what was already determined for him or her? The problem of freedom comes up even more acutely in another crucial marker in African theories of the human personhood — relatedness.

According to Leopold Senghor, African societies put more stress "on the group than on the individuals, more on solidarity than on the activity and needs of the individual, more on the communion of persons than on their autonomy. Ours is a community society."[13] Other African scholars echo Senghor's views. Elochukwu Uzukwu opines that it is impossible among the Igbo to define the characteristics of a person without linking him or her to parents and even to departed ancestors who have become reincarnated in the person. Relationship, he concludes, "is not simply a way in which the subject may realize itself. It is the essential element of 'personhood.' The quality of a person is dependent on the intensity of maintaining these relationships." [14] A famous Belgian missionary to the Congo had earlier written that "the Bantu cannot conceive of the human person as an independent being standing on his own. Every human being, every individual is as it were one link in a chain of vital forces: a living link both exercising and receiving influence, a link that establishes the bond with previous generations and with the forces that support his own existence. The individual is necessarily an individual adhering to the clan."[15] What we have been speaking of here has sometimes been referred to as African communitarianism. According to Kwame Gyekye, "Communitarianism considers the human person as an inherently (intrinsically) communal being, embedded in a context of social relationships and interdependence, never as an isolated, atomic individual. Consequently it sees the community not as a mere association of individual persons whose interests and ends are contingently congruent, but as a group of persons linked by interpersonal bonds, biological/or non-biological, who consider themselves primarily as members of the group and who have common interests, goals and values."[16] As Gyekye points out, African leaders such as Julius Nyerere of Tanzania and Kwame Nkrumah of Ghana who advocated socialism in Africa in the days before and after independence did so on the grounds that African societies were "collectivist" and constituted by "an aggregate of individuals."[17]

It is necessary at this point to raise some preliminary questions concerning the positions espoused by the scholars we have so far discussed and by many other scholars on the person and the community in the African worldview. The first question is like that of the proverbial chicken and egg. In this regard one has to ask whether the cultural community exists prior to the individual, since the community consists of persons with shared interests and values, or whether the individual is not ontologically prior to the community, since the latter begins when a congregation of individuals forms. If we grant that the community has ontological priority over the individual, what then does this mean for issues of choice in moral decision making and in the question of moral autonomy and individual free will? Kwame Gyekye elaborates on the issues here in the form of two questions. In the first place he asks whether the communal and therefore the cultural character of the self implies that the self is ineluctably and permanently held in thrall by that structure; and secondly, whether the communal ethos can allow for new perspectives or further insights on communal values and insights. We have already raised these questions in our discussion of David Aiken's position on tradition and morality, and we will return to the issue later on in this chapter.

Another question raised by the discussion of the communitarian nature of African societies is that of its viability in modern state structures. One reason often adduced by scholars to explain some of the interethnic clashes in Africa today is that the state structures of most modern African nations are the result of gerrymandering by European colonial powers, which brought together unlikely "bedfellows" and forced them into nations in order to serve the European powers' interests. In this regard some point to the conflicts in Rwanda/Burundi and others on the continent as sufficient contemporary examples of the difficulties of operating these "new" African models of social organization. In his book *A Listening Church*, Elochukwu Uzukwu tries to answer the questions that have been raised as to whether the kind of African interconnectedness that operated within the kindred or tribal setting is tenable or usable within modern states structures. Uzukwu considers it pessimistic to assert that it cannot succeed in modern state structures in Africa. He points to the fact that African societies have had long experience as federating nations, nations founded on truth and linked together by spiritual forces, much unlike modern African states. "The conflicts which began during the slave trade and matured at the colonial period give birth to the lie which we call African states with their artificial boundaries."[18] What Uzukwu seems to be saying here is that modern African states have not been able to come to terms with diversity and plurality because they were founded on false premises and without the consent of the federating parties. He appears to be pointing to a fact that is often glossed over when we discuss the phenomenon of dysfunctionality within modern African states, namely, that many of Africa's current problems have more or less ancient roots. If this is so, it means that all that talk of African solidarity would have to be re-examined. It would thus be an unacceptable exaggeration to say, as Bénézet Bujo does, that among Africans "one who is not a member of my own group is ultimately also 'the property of the other,' just as I myself am and this means that I owe him respect and esteem. Thus one is ultimately related to all human beings."[19]

The truth is that African communitarianism is often limited to the known other. In his book on African American spirituality, Peter Paris wonders why and how a group so hospitable and so committed to community solidarity as Africans could engage in the heinous Atlantic slave trade without many qualms.[20] The reason, as I have pointed out elsewhere, is that these otherwise hospitable African societies were able to sell off their non–kith and kin because "they were unable to accord the same level of humanity to those who were not of their stock or kind. In other words, African societies have not over time developed a comprehensive theory of rights based either on religious or philosophical assumptions."[21] The reality of intertribal conflicts and the inability of Africans to construct modern states where citizens' rights are assured and protected, irrespective of ethnic or regional affiliations, is in many ways a direct result of the limitations of the African communitarian ethos.[22] Ultimately it results from the lack of a proper definition of the nature of the human person. The idea of relatedness, which scholars like Uzukwu and others offer as central to the African definition of the person, needs a boost to take it beyond mere blood ties to a universal vision. As I will argue later in this chapter, speaking as a Christian theologian, this boost can be given through close attention to some key ideas of the human person which are found in Christian scriptures and tradition. Uzukwu maintains that terms of union within African states have to be renegotiated in order to ensure justice for all by respecting the interests of the various groupings and regions. This is correct. However, such renegotiations cannot be carried out based on a tabula rasa; they must be grounded on solid principles. Again, Uzukwu is correct to assert that ancient African societies were not only homogeneous but also bound together by spiritual forces, through shared ethos and values, derived from a common vision of ultimate reality and meaning. If this is so, the renegotiation that is needed in Africa can be successful only if it calls forth spiritual forces relevant for today's Africans. Today's sub-Saharan Africans are largely Christians and Muslims. In conversation with their non-Christian partners, African Christians must draw from their own experience of God and other aspects of reality in the renegotiation of African societies. Finally, if the African scholars' speculation on the lofty nature of human beings within God's creative intention and purpose is accurate, the inevitable question would be, what happened? Why is the human person in such a dire situation in Africa today? In his post-synodal exhortation, Pope Benedict XVI proclaims that "Africa is facing an anthropological crisis." In this situation, he says, "Africa will have to rediscover and promote a concept of the person and his or her relationship with reality which is the fruit of a profound spiritual renewal."[23] I contend that, for this renewal to occur, African theology must rediscover Christian anthropology as an important contribution to the understanding of the human person as subject and moral actor in Africa.

ELEMENTS OF A CHRISTIAN THEOLOGICAL ANTHROPOLOGY

To determine properly the nature of the human person we will examine aspects of *Gaudium et Spes* (*The Pastoral Constitution of the Church in the Modern World* of the Second Vatican Council), for this document states some of the most basic themes in Christian appreciation of the human person. I will summarize the anthropological constants as supplied by this conciliar text and offer some reflections, followed by a relevant sketch of the human person as actor and subject of ethics in African Christian theology. Although useful, the sets of anthropological constants that appear in *Gaudium et Spes* are by no means new in Catholic theology. What makes them remarkable is that they are assembled together in this way for the first time in a magisterial text, giving the various elements, together and singly, a force they did not seem to possess before. As a result, these constants can now provide direction to the Christian understanding of and discussion on the human person as object of theology and ethics, which had not been the case up to this point. Previously, much of the discussion about the human person seemed to rely heavily on the definition of the human person given by Boethius: "an individual substance of a rational nature." This definition of the human person was found in the manuals of the pre–Vatican II era and was to some extent a one-sided caricature of the Catholic teaching on the subject; still, it was the definition uppermost in the minds of theologians like Bénézet Bujo and Elochukwu Uzukwu as representing the Catholic teaching on the human person.

Uzukwu's position is that what he refers to as "the static or ontic definition" of the human person was found in the classical Greek philosophy and Roman juridical culture and was passed on to medieval Western Christianity through the Boethian definition of the human person. This Christian tradition, "which influenced definitively the Western philosophical notion of person, was preoccupied with Christology and the doctrine of the Trinity." He contends that the Boethian definition with its emphasis on autonomy and substance may lead to "tritheism" instead "of a Trinity where relationship is anchored on divine substance." Uzukwu opines that medieval attempts to modify Boethius had several results. In the theology of Richard of St. Victor, it led to an emphasis on "incommunicability and singularity of existence"; in the work of Saint Thomas Aquinas it led to the idea of "being-for-itself (or subsistent being) of intellectual nature"; and in the work of Duns Scotus to the notion of "self-consciousness with a relationship of openness to God"—all of which are reflections of or precursors to the individualism that in his opinion characterizes much of the Western understanding of the human person. In contrast to the African social definition of person which regards the human person as a "subsistent relationship—in other words the person as fundamentally 'being-with,' 'living-with,' 'belonging-to'—Western philosophy lays emphasis on the absolute originality and concreteness of the human person, a being for itself."[24] Uzukwu concludes that although improvements have occurred in Western philosophical thought since the medieval period, in that there has been a recognition of "the universal openness of the human person to enter into relationship with being," this notion of relationality has not been understood as fundamental to human existence; it applied only to the divinity—that is, to the relationship within the Trinity.[25]

Gaudium et Spes begins with the well-known basic Christian belief that human beings are created by God in his own image and likeness. In other words, Christian tradition understands the human person as a creature, but a unique creature; as *Gaudium et Spes* puts it, he is "the only creature God has willed for its own sake" (GS 24), and as the one creature who alone has been called "by knowledge and love in God's own life."[26] As *The Catechism of the Catholic Church* points out, "Being in the image and likeness of God the human individual possesses the dignity of a person, who is not just something, but someone" (no. 357).

In Christian Trinitarian theology, the Father is a person, the Son is a person, and the Holy Spirit is a person. All are in communion with each other and relate with each other as such, each with its own identity. Creation in the image and likeness of God therefore gives us each an identity and implies that God can and does relate to each of us as persons with distinct identities. It also carries with it the moral obligation to acknowledge the identity of each human creature as well as his or her moral agency. As Karl Rahner points out, Christian insight on this matter comes from revelation, from which the human person is led to an experiential knowledge of his own human nature. Through revelation we come to the knowledge of the human person as a being without equal in this world, a being who is so truly personal as to be God's partner. . . . His position as a free spirit having eternal personal significance and value for God; his capacity to become a partner with God in a genuine dialogue or "covenant-relationships" which leads to absolute intimacy "face to face" in light inaccessible, to "partaking in the divine nature" where we shall know even as we are known; his capacity to disclose his own existence as an expression of God himself (God becoming man)—these are the things which really make man a being who is not in the last analysis a part of a greater whole (world). Quite uniquely he himself is the whole—as subject, a person, an individual rather than a thing.[27]

Therefore, creatureliness as a basic characteristic of the human individual is the most important mark of what it means to be human, in that as the characteristic that confers personhood on the human individual it enables the human person, a finite being, a being who is not God, to receive and be in dialogue with God.

Other noteworthy characteristics of human creatureliness in God's image and likeness include the fact that God made humans a pair, male and female. In this regard, one finds the Igbo adage *Ife kwuru, ife akwudebe ya* (one thing stands, and some other thing stands by it) an apt description of the human reality that we are not made to be solitary beings. This partnership of man and woman is the first and most basic form of human communion as well as the foundation of the wider community of the family. It is also a very important foundation of the Christian defense of marriage as an institution between a man and a woman based on complementarity. It is, as well, the basis of the radical equality of man and woman in marriage. In their being-man and being-woman, human beings reflect the Creator's wisdom and goodness. However, although being created in the *imago Dei* implies that human beings, all human beings, are representatives of God on earth, the converse is not true. In other words, as *The Catechism of the Catholic Church* puts it, "In no way is God man's image. He is neither man nor woman. God is pure spirit in which there is no place for the difference between the sexes" (no. 370).

Although created in God's image and for friendship with God, human beings rebelled against God. This assertion contains much that is central to Christian understanding of the human person. Aside from understanding that the moral evil we experience as part of our reality is not a direct result of God's creative activity, it also contains ideas about human freedom; explanations of the human condition in which we notice, as *Gaudium et Spes* says, that we as human beings are torn interiorly and engaged "in a continuous struggle between good and evil, between light and darkness"; and the idea of redemption, by which "the Lord himself came to free and strengthen humanity, renewing it inwardly and casting out the prince of this world (Jn. 12:31) who held it in the bondage of sin" (GS 12). Christian theology of the human person therefore not only acknowledges that our first human parents sinned and disobeyed God, it also holds that the sin of this first pair has somehow been inherited by all their human descendants. Two aspects to the question of human sinfulness are worth noting here. The understanding of sin includes the ideas of both original sin and actual sin, the individual rebellion of every human being. It is, as Saint Paul would say, an acknowledgment that "all have sinned and have fallen short of the glory of God" (Rom. 3:23). Sin in any sense of it implies the human capacity for knowledge and for volitional decision making. As a result of original sin, the entire human race and the entire cosmos inherited the tendency to rebellion from the human creature, its overseer. Thus in Augustinian theology all evil is a result of human sin. While moral evil is caused directly by the misuse of free will, physical evil—death, disease, natural calamities, and so on—is "God's just punishment for this moral evil."[28]

A third aspect to the question of human sinfulness has become very important in recent Catholic theology, and is also important to our appreciation of the human person because it affects the human person and his or her actions in this world. Christian tradition has always held that we are not born into a neutral environment in which we are absolutely unimpeded in our search for the good. On the contrary, this tradition acknowledges the fact of original sin as "the primordial situation of guilt in which our freedom and its history, from the very beginning, are situated and embedded."[29] The Catholic tradition and some Protestant ones have been divided on the extent to which the human environment has been conditioned by sin and concupiscence, as well as the extent to which the consequences of sin are woven into the fabric of human institutions. These divisions notwithstanding, the Christian tradition as a whole is in complete agreement about the existence of sin in our lives and in the world, and about the fact that we are all tempted to separate ourselves from God in order to lead our own independent and selfish existence.

Until recently, much attention was paid in the manuals of moral theology, and indeed in the whole of Catholic theology, to sin as especially an individual phenomenon. True sin was thought to be committed when a gravely evil action was committed by an individual with sufficient knowledge and freedom; every other sin was sin only by analogy. Although this is true, this truth must not be stretched too far, for two reasons. First, what is often classed as venial sin on the basis of a mere external observation of the triviality of the matter may in fact be only a pointer toward something larger and more deeply rooted. Thus a little lie may not be so little after all, and may indeed be more like a tip of an iceberg, small on the surface but harboring a much larger, sinister bulk underneath. Second, and somewhat related to this first point, treatment of the notion of sin as merely an individual phenomenon could lead to a situation where, as has been pointed out, one could in good conscience confess to an action motivated by greed "but fail to recognize one's collaboration in economic practices and structures which offered material benefits to the penitent at grievous cost to other (unseen) persons"; or one in which a slave owner "of good conscience" "could quite considerably recognize his or her cruelty to an individual slave but remain completely inattentive to the evil in the institution of slavery itself."[30] The privatization of sin in the Catholic tradition up until recent times was a result of a long and complicated historical process that we cannot go into here.[31] However, from the practice of communal confession of guilt in the early church, through the introduction of auricular confession of guilt by Irish monks in the sixth century, "sin itself came to be understood as a private matter with only a tenuous connection with the wider community."[32] This approach notwithstanding, the Christian tradition has indeed always recognized the social aspect of sin. For example, the priest at the confessional is required to impose some penance on the penitent in order to "heal the remaining effects of sins."[33] In recent times, however, the church has shown a greater awareness of the social dimension of sin, and thus these days it is very common to speak of social sin and of the structures of sin. This awareness is in consonance with the best of biblical tradition. In the scriptures, the prophets speak often of the collective blindness of the people, group egotism, and the pursuit of a lifestyle among both the people and their leaders which violates the terms of the covenant.

Social sin is different from personal sin in that its subject is the collective society and not the individual. Unlike personal sin, social sin is not usually produced by deliberation and free choice but by group blindness and inactivity. Gregory Baum identifies four aspects or modes of manifestation of social sin. In the first place, "social sin is made up of the injustices and dehumanizing trends built into the various institutions—social, political, economic, religious and others—which embody people's collective life." As people in such institutions go about their daily tasks, the dehumanizing trends built into the institutions which guide their lives will damage a growing number and destroy their humanity eventually.[34] A second level of social sin has to do with the destructive effects of religious and cultural symbols that are sometimes used to reinforce the unjust institutions "and thus intensify the harm done to a growing number of people." Baum refers to such misuse of these symbols as ideology. He states that the privatization of the notion of sin, which insists that the source of evil is only in the human heart while neglecting the root causes of oppression and the social devastation even of people's personal sins, would be an example of a destructive religious symbol. On a third level, to speak of social sin is to talk of "the false consciousness created by these institutions and ideologies through which people involve themselves collectively in destructive actions as if they were doing the right thing." Baum points out that it is on this level that people begin to wrestle against social sin. "For here, people, open to the Spirit, are able to become aware of, and turn away from, the taken-for-granted injustices built into their society. This is the level where conversion takes place."[35]

Finally, one can also speak of social sin in terms of "the collective decisions generated by the distorted consciousness, which increase the injustices in society and intensify the power of the dehumanizing trends."[36] Here, nations, communities, religious orders, and others may make decisions that appear to be the result of free choice but under close scrutiny prove no more than the results of "distortions built into the institution and duplicated in consciousness."[37] Thus, for example, tradition, as how a people live today, may represent only a superficial appreciation of an ethos arising from a people's shared history. Where we are today may be a betrayal of who we are. Some current prevailing "Christian" practices may be a betrayal of true Christian ethos, for example. Although we should not stress this point too far, as if any one age had all the right answers to what is authentically Christian, it is still possible, on the basis of our foundational story and inherited values accruing over the centuries, to describe a particular Christian era as one of decline or certain "Christian" practices as aberrant due to what Bernard Lonergan would refer to as major inauthenticities. Think of the crusades, or the participation of the church in slave dealing, or the Inquisition, for example. Among the Igbo, for instance, the present craze for chieftaincy titles and the yearning for a turn to feudalism more associated with some of their neighbors might be considered a betrayal of a deeply held republican ethos in Igbo tradition. In whatever way one understands social sin, its growth is fostered by the inattentiveness of the large majority of the people. The contradictions implicit in institutions initially go undetected. And even when after a time they begin to appear, they may not immediately be recognized as the effects of the system. Social sin is thus usually a sin of omission. Although it is sin by analogy, it turns into personal sin "if objective injustice is being or has been perpetrated, or when existing situations of injustice are maintained or allowed to continue in spite of a real possibility of changing them."[38] In other words, it can happen that one can be complicit in a situation simply by doing nothing. This is what the Catholic tradition means by the sin of omission; it is the point also where social sin and individual sin intersect. This is also the reason the Council of Trent taught that no one can be absolutely certain that he or she is in a state of grace—that is, of one's standing before God.

An important aspect of the Catholic moral teaching on social sin is the notion of "structures of sin." In his encyclical *Sollicitudo Rei Socialis,* Pope John Paul II writes that "the sum total of the negative factors working against a true awareness of the universal *common good,* and the need to further it, gives the impression of creating, in persons and institutions, an obstacle which is difficult to overcome."[39] These obstacles may be referred to as structures of sin. As in Baum's analysis cited above, these structures arise, according to the pope, through the "concrete acts of individuals who introduce these structures, consolidate them and make them difficult to remove. And thus they grow stronger, spread, and become the source of other sins, and so influence people's behavior."[40] The pope notes two attitudes and actions that, among many others, can lead to these structures. One is the thirst for power, "with the intention of imposing one's will upon others." The other is "the all-consuming desire for profit" (no. 37). Both are "indissolubly united" even though one of them may in certain circumstances predominate. Both individuals and entire societies can fall prey to this double attitude of sin. In this regard, the pope points out that some of the economic and political decisions made by nations and blocs are, if considered closely, "real forms of idolatry: of money, ideology, class, technology."[41] The pope's aim in this encyclical is therefore to help people become aware that in dealing with structures of sin we are dealing with a moral evil, the fruit of many sins.

The path to eradicating this evil is long and complex due to human frailty. But it is not an impossible task. According to the pope, there must first be a profound change of attitudes, moving from a situation where we have absolutized the desires for domination and excessive profit-taking, to one where individuals and nations become more aware of interdependence as a moral value and of solidarity as an essential virtue for human flourishing and survival. Solidarity, then, for the pope is a valuable key for overcoming structures of sin. This virtue is not to be equated with "a feeling of vague compassion or shallow distress at the misfortunes of so many people" (SRS 38). It is rather "a firm and persevering determination to commit oneself to the *common good*, that is to say, to the good of all and of each individual, because we are *all* really responsible for *all*." Solidarity makes us recognize one another as persons. It makes the more influential, who have a greater share of goods and services, "to feel responsible for the weaker and be ready to share with them all they possess." It imposes on the weaker members of society also the obligation to do even the little they can for the good of all (SRS 39).

Just as it stresses the fact of sinfulness, individual and social, the Catholic tradition has a lot to say about reconciliation. Again, just as a person can move away from inauthenticity to an authentic existence, so too can a whole society. The collective society can realize that certain things, or modes of acting or thinking which it had either actively promoted or cast a blind eye toward, have been damaging the humanity of some people. This realization could lead, in Lonergan's words, to "a change of course and direction."[42] Group conversion can be a drawn-out affair aided in part by the prophets and the holy people of the community. Ultimately, however, the fruit of this kind of change of course and direction would be the reconciliation among the various segments of society that had lived under, or helped to create, the dehumanizing structures and conditions that had hitherto characterized life in that society. Of course, reconciliation is always a continuous process. What is important is that structures and mechanisms be instituted that redress past wrongs and keep society on guard against relapsing into carelessness and inattentiveness to a creeping return of inhumanity, injustice, and degradation of any person or persons. A key point of *Africae Munus*, the postsynodal exhortation of Pope Benedict XVI, is the way it links the personal and social aspects of sin in its analyses of African societies in the early twenty-first century. In speaking of poverty in Africa today, for example, the pope points to the connection between individual greed and poverty on the continent: "The plundering of the goods of the earth by a minority" is detrimental to entire peoples on the continent and is immoral and unacceptable.[43] In another passage, the pope insists that one of the tasks of the church in Africa consists "in forming upright consciences receptive to the demands of justice, so as to produce men and women willing and able to build this just social order by their responsible conduct."[44] As we shall see in chapter 9, the Second Synod of Bishops for Africa dealt extensively with the issue of the structures of sin and with the need for greater solidarity among individuals and among peoples.

Closely related to the question of human sinfulness is the idea of human freedom. Basic to this idea is the understanding that human beings have the ability to say yes or no to God's offer of friendship; hence, Christian theology often categorizes this freedom as a mystery. The mystery concerns the way a creature who owes his or her existence to God can also be endowed with the capacity by God to choose to relate with God the creator or not to do so, with God seemingly unable to do anything about it. It is as if God is in awe of human freedom. This is the case not in the sense that God cannot do something about it, but rather that God would not invade this core sanctum of the human person. Post–Vatican II moral theology has been filled with discussions on freedom, with different perceptions of this complicated concept in the literature. There is first of all the understanding of freedom as the absence of physical constraint, as when I want to move

from point A to point B without hindrance or any constraint whatsoever. In this regard, for example, a stone falls freely from the top of a
mountain to its foot; a river flows through its course unhindered. In
these examples, freedom is a quality that can be shared by every entity, animate or inanimate. However, an aspect of this freedom is distinctive to human beings in that it involves not just physical hindrance
or lack of it, but also psychological compulsion. For instance, A and B
marry because even though A does not really like B and does not have
the intention clearly to enter into marriage with B, A goes along anyway to marry B because of a subtle or explicit threat from the parents
of both parties, who are bankers, to give away all their fortune, which
would have been A's or B's or A's and B's together, if either or both of
them refuses to marry the other. A goes on to marry B knowing that
this was not really his or her choice for a marriage partner. In this case,
A (and/or B) is not acting in freedom.

Some Catholic authors distinguish between freedom of choice and
basic or transcendental freedom. According to Josef Fuchs, we speak
of freedom of choice "in so far as we are able, in particular acts, to
apply ourselves freely to the many possibilities and requirements of
life as it unfolds before us in space and time."[45] These choices or acts
are "merely" personal acts since they "do not spring from a true commitment of the person." As such, "they are indeed moral acts, but only
by analogy and not in the full sense." That qualification belongs to acts
that emanate out of or are expressive of one's basic freedom. In Karl
Rahner's words, basic freedom (also known as transcendental freedom)
is that capacity which the subject has to decide about himself or herself, biologically, exteriorly, and historically, in his or her own single
totality. This is not a faculty "which is situated behind a merely physical, biological, exterior and historical temporality of the subject."[46]
Freedom is not the capacity to do this or that. Nor is it "the capacity
to do something which is always able to be reversed." Rather, it is
"the capacity to do something final and definitive. It is the capacity of
the subject who by this freedom is to achieve his final and irrevocable
self." Human freedom is that ability which the human subject has and
which is "actualized in a free and absolute 'yes' or 'no' to that term
and source of transcendence which we call God." Even though human
beings cannot grasp the essence of God they encounter him as the ultimate horizon and source of their being—in thematic, categorical

reflection in history. Human beings have the capacity then to affirm or deny, to accept or reject God. "We encounter God in a radical way everywhere as a question to our freedom, we encounter him unexpressed, unthematic, unobjectified and unspoken in all of the things of the world, and therefore expressly in our neighbor."[47] As a subject, a person is conscious of himself or herself as a subject "without reflecting on himself as an object."[48] Josef Fuchs notes further that "this self-consciousness lies much deeper than the subconscious or the unconscious as understood by psychologists, because the subconscious and unconscious are categorically and objectively defined."[49] The human subject by his very nature is oriented toward other persons in love. As a result we place ourselves unreservedly as persons "at the disposal of him who has the greatest claim on us because he—who is God—created us as persons."[50] Basic freedom is basic in the sense that it pertains to the determination of the self with regard to the totality of existence, the fundamental choice between love of self and love for or serving the Lord. Because the person's eternal salvation and basic standing before the God of salvation is at stake, such choices must involve a person's total disposition of himself or herself, out of the radical center of his or her being. Since this is the case, these choices will involve a depth of the person's being beyond formulating (or reflex) consciousness, and hence will escape adequate formulation.

In *Veritatis Splendor* Pope John Paul II points out what he considers to be erroneous notions about freedom in current culture and in recent Catholic theology. These ideas include: the exaltation of freedom "to such an extent that it becomes an absolute, which would then be the source of values" (no. 32); questioning the very existence of freedom (no. 32); the dissociation of freedom from truth; positing an alleged conflict between freedom and law; the belief that individuals or social groups have "the right to determine what is good or evil" (no. 35); and positing "a complete sovereignty of reason to the detriment of moral norms" (no. 36). There exists therefore a crisis in the understanding of freedom. At the root of this crisis, according to the pope, is an atheistic ethos that not only denies transcendence but goes so far as to make the individual conscience the "supreme tribunal of moral judgment which hands down categorical and infallible decisions about good and evil" (no. 32).

As Avery Dulles indicates, John Paul II always saw a connection between freedom and truth. While a bishop in Poland, he wrote in 1964 that "freedom on the one hand is for the sake of truth and on the other hand it cannot be perfected except by means of truth. Hence the words of our Lord, which speak so clearly to everyone: 'the truth will make you free.' "[51] In other words, when the pope wrote in *Veritatis Splendor* about ethical systems that are destroying "the dependence of freedom upon truth," he was pointing to a deep component of Christian anthropological understanding: that the human person does not live on bread alone but especially on obedience to truth, which is God himself. Thus, freedom goes hand in hand with, or rather entails obedience to, God's law. Obedience to God's law cannot be construed as alienation "as though God were a hostile power imposing terms on humanity as if on a defeated enemy."[52] The moral law is instead intended to safeguard human dignity. Human freedom and divine law both conspire to serve this end. Those who love God not only serve him freely but are also willing to do so even unto death, if necessary. The freedom to serve God can lead to martyrdom. This martyrdom is, however, "accepted as an affirmation of the inviolability of the moral order," and as a "splendid witness both to the holiness of God's law and to the inviolability of the personal dignity of man, created in God's image and likeness."[53] For John Paul II the martyrs therefore offer a supreme example of freedom in that when faced with the choice to deny the truth (God) or lose their own lives, they chose the latter, like Jesus, who in total obedience to truth gave up his life so that God's will would be done. The martyrs represent an achievement of freedom "beyond the capacities of the great majority of men and women. They inspire us by their example to rise above the more limited measure of freedom that we can claim for ourselves."[54]

The Catholic moral tradition has always taken the question of freedom seriously. The manuals of moral theology always included a vigorous treatment of this question in regard to conscience. I have treated this issue elsewhere[55] and will not discuss it in depth here. But one important issue to raise here is that of the relationship between individual freedom/conscience and the community. In the Catholic moral theological tradition conscience was considered "the authoritative guide of human conduct and the dictate of practical reason deciding that a particular action is right or wrong. As guide and judge, its role was the classification of the moral implications of the virtues as well as the discernment of the lawfulness of particular human actions."[56] In this sense, conscience functions as subjective norm of morality. As objective norm of morality, conscience "provides general information about the moral character of human actions."[57] While conscience as a subjective norm can err in that it can arrive at wrong conclusions as a result of bias, sinfulness, habit, sloth, or lack of knowledge, conscience as an objective norm cannot err because it is concerned with those first principles of moral action that every person can easily affirm—for example, be kind, be just, do good. The Catholic tradition therefore insists that every moral agent has the duty to form his or her conscience and to educate it in the wisdom resident in the human community, and in the church, for Christians. Although it appreciates the possibility of erroneous judgment by individual subjective conscience, Catholic moral tradition has always insisted on the supremacy of individual conscience. "Conscience is neither a dictator nor a slave. It is a discerning guide. As such, it must use all available means of enlightenment to dispel ignorance. However, it cannot be dictated to even when it is in doubt or clearly erroneous. Instead, it must be allowed to assume its rightful place in moral decision-making."[58] As Richard McCormick puts it, "The articulated wisdom of the community—the teaching of the magisterium—*enlightens* conscience; it does not *replace* it."[59]

The relationship between the individual conscience and the community can be a delicate one in every human community. In Africa this situation is made even more complex by the communitarian ethos in African tradition, something we have already discussed extensively. Let me briefly illustrate this point with two very familiar areas of African life: one has to do with the process of marriage, the other with the process of communal moral discernment. I will not go into great detail on these issues here, having done so elsewhere. I would like to emphasize the point, however, that this is another area of anthropological sharing between African tradition and the Catholic moral tradition.

African traditional marriage is an alliance between two families and sometimes between two peoples. As noted by the working paper of the Sixth General Assembly of the Symposium of Episcopal Conferences of Africa and Madagascar (SECAM) on marriage, held in Yaoundé, Cameroon, in 1981, all over Africa, marriage is considered a vital ministry of the life and future of the lineage. It is a covenant not only between two persons but also between the couple and their respective lineages. "One family gives to the other something of itself by giving one of its daughters . . . the other family acknowledges this gift by payment of a symbolic compensation. This is not a business deal, but a mutual commitment of each lineage calling upon fundamental human attitudes of confidence in the other."[60] It is wrong then to suggest, as Ifi Amadiume does, that marriage in Nnobi in eastern Nigeria is tantamount to the acquisition of sexual services and the reproductive and labor powers of the woman.[61] It is more correct to say that the new family of which she has become a member usually regards her much more highly. G. T Basden noted this fact long ago in these words: "What is generally forgotten is that it is not merely a man taking to himself a wife. It is more than that; it is the bringing in of another person into the family. She is something more than a wife; henceforth she is a member of the clan, and has her rightful place and share in all things pertaining to it."[62] The alliance between whole families that is apparent in African marriages raises the question about the individual's freedom of choice and interpersonal intimacy. For example, while praising African traditional marriage for its recognition of the familial and social nature of the marital bond and its relation to parenthood, as well as the progressive nature of human commitments, Lisa Cahill faults it for what she considers to be its "devaluation of interpersonal intimacy between spouses in favour of marriage's communitarian and procreative contributions."[63] Earlier she had praised the "Western marriage ideal" for recognizing equality, "especially as the freedom to choose a sexual, marital, or parental relation."[64] The inference then is that community involvement in African marriages works against the individual's (especially the woman's) right to choose a marital partner, and the "woman's role is seen almost entirely in economic and procreative terms, and is subordinated to the interests and needs of husbands and fathers."[65]

I believe the situation is much more complex than Cahill makes it out to be. The couple has the advantage that Western couples usually do not of structural (familial, societal) help in the course of their discernment. Of course, familial and societal biases may sometimes have undue influence in the discernment process. However, the role of the community in the life of the young couple, especially the woman, is not just to safeguard "the interests and the needs of husbands and fathers," but especially to ensure her happiness and well-being in her new home. On the other hand, Cahill's concern is legitimate and becomes much clearer when the situation is considered in reverse order. That is to say, the weight of the community in this area of personal choice becomes clearer on those occasions when the community, for whatever reason, refuses the choice the prospective bride or bridegroom makes of a marriage partner and therefore refuses to involve itself in the normal marriage process and ceremonies. In such a situation the individual who decides to go it alone does so with no community support and can in some communities be ostracized or punished in some ways. Although it is unusual for the community to force the bridegroom to take a bride he does not want, subtle pressure can be brought to wean a man or a woman away from the person of his or her choice and to direct his or her gaze toward someone else approved by the community or the family. This situation is of course not peculiar to the African tradition; it happens everywhere, more or less. However, it can be quite pronounced in the African situation because of the influence of the community in such matters of personal choice. The challenge for an African Christian moral theology is to be on guard against communitarian imposition that makes light of human individuality as the basis for free moral agency, while on the other hand avoiding the situation of excessive individualism in which the moral agent does not feel responsible to the community in any way for his or her moral choices.

Another aspect to Christian anthropology is the understanding that although they are made of spirit and body, human beings are not a duality but a unity; though sharing matter with the material world, they are not merely material beings; though having a soul and sharing their spiritual nature with God and the angels, they are not pure spirit. Human beings are embodied spirits. The issue here, as André Guindon points out, is how to acknowledge this reality of human beinghood. As Guindon puts it, "The moral task on this level of being consists essentially in sensualizing tenderness, *as befits an em(in)bodied spirit*."[66] Body and spirit have their own demands that must be held in dynamic tension. While on the one hand we must nourish our spirits, through prayer, various forms of spiritual exercises, and so forth, we must on the other hand take care of our body as well as discipline it through various forms of ascetic practices. What is called for is moderation. As

Vatican II puts it, people are not mistaken "when they regard themselves as superior to merely bodily creatures and as more than mere particles or nameless units in human society." People therefore are right to regard their bodies as good and to hold them in honor since "God created them and will raise them on the last day" (*Gaudium et Spes* 14). Christian anthropology insists that adequate attention be paid to the spiritual aspect of the human person. Thus, a hedonist philosophy that treats the human person as merely material and simply a product of the material environment would be antithetical to the Christian view of the human person.

Christianity's loftiest ideas concerning the human person are contained in the incarnation and the redemption of the human person in Jesus Christ. The incarnation is God's profound statement about the goodness of being human. It is an acknowledgment, as one author puts it, that "the author of reality is on our side. The ground of being is not far away, hostile or indifferent to us: the deepest dimension of the total reality facing us is for us. There is no reason to be afraid of the world . . . for the ultimate root of all being protects and favors human life. Despite the suffering and the evil in the world . . . we are summoned to believe that the ultimate principle of reality is love itself."[67] God is with us; God is for us. In the incarnation Jesus took all human flesh in his own flesh. He took the destiny of every person who has been or will be born into this world unto himself. There is something of Jesus in everyone. Consequently, everyone is equally a daughter and equally a son of God; everyone is equally loved and lovable before God. Through his redemptive work on the cross Jesus takes humanity several notches higher. Pope John Paul II's first encyclical was the first such document ever devoted to Christian anthropology;[68] the pope himself described it as "a great hymn of joy for the fact that man has been redeemed through Christ—redeemed in spirit and body."[69] In it we hear a strong affirmation of the loftiness of human life and destiny in Christ. The opening words of this encyclical are instructive for understanding what it is all about: "The Redeemer of man, Jesus Christ is the center of the universe and of history." Jesus, the word of God, became flesh and dwelt among us. The central truth of our existence is that God so loved the world that he gave his only Son that whoever believes in him should not perish but have eternal life (John 3:16). Pope John Paul II writes that in the mystery of redemption "man becomes newly 'expressed' and, in a way, is newly created. He is a new creation." Henceforth, in the famous words of Saint Paul, "there is neither Jew nor Greek, there is neither slave nor free; there is neither male nor female; for you are all one in Christ Jesus" (Gal. 3:28). Thus, the pope continues, anyone who wants to understand the human person and what he or she is must "appropriate the whole of the reality of the incarnation and redemption." Human worth can be gauged by the fact that God, the creator of the universe, gave his only Son so that human beings should not perish but have eternal life. Christ's redemption, which he accomplished on the cross, has definitively "restored dignity and given back meaning" to human life in the world, a meaning that had been lost to a considerable extent by sin. The good news is the essence of the deep wonder and amazement and human dignity and worth that Christ has wrought by his redemptive work. The mission of the church then is to proclaim this conviction and to help bring about an authentic humanism. This must be a humanism that has Christ as its center because Christ through his work has citizenship "in the history of man and mankind."[70] The human person, integrally and adequately considered—that is, "man in all his truth, in his conscience, in his continual inclination to sin, and at the same time in his continual aspiration to truth, the good, the beautiful, justice and love"—is therefore the "primary route" the church must travel to fulfill its mission. In fact it is the mission of the church, its very essence. For, if, as Saint Irenaeus says, "the glory of God is man fully alive, and the life of man is the vision of God" (*Adversus Haereses* IV, 20, 7), then it is clear that the human person in all his or her aspects and in whatever condition is a being of inestimable value and worth who is deserving of every effort we can muster to preserve his or her well-being. God has in Jesus already paid a price for the human person. God has also placed a non-negotiable value on him. This is a truth that African ethics or any other ethics that claims to be Christian cannot ignore or gloss over.

No discussion of Christian anthropology is complete without some discussion on grace. The second part of the first part of the *Summa* of Saint Thomas begins with the question about the end of human action and proceeds to the discussion on the intrinsic principles of human acts—human happiness, human will, goodness, malice, power, the emotions, habits, virtues, and vices (qq. 1–89); and then on to the extrinsic principles of human action, including law and grace (qq. 90–114). Aquinas speaks of grace as divine help that the human agent needs in order "to be moved to act well" (I-IIae, q. 109, a. 2). The human person as agent has need of grace. Aquinas makes some crucial distinctions as he treats the human need for grace.[71] First is the distinction between the natural and the supernatural order. The second distinction is between habitual grace, which is "infused in the soul and rooted in its essence," and *auxilium*, the help that God gives by "moving people to actions in accord with habitual grace."[72] The third distinction is between the human condition in the prelapsarian state and that in the postlapsarian; the need for grace is different in both circumstances. "In the state of perfect nature man needs a gratuitous strength superadded to natural strength for one reason, viz., in order to do and wish supernatural good; but for two reasons, in the state of corrupt nature; viz., in order to be healed, and further in order to carry out works of supernatural virtue, which are meritorious. Beyond this, in both states man needs the Divine help, that he may be moved to act well" (I-IIae, q. 109, a. 2). And even though the human person does not need grace to perform those acts that are natural to him as such, without grace "he cannot merit eternal life" (I-IIae, q. 109, a. 5). As is well known, Aquinas "gave his *Summa Theologiae* the form and plan of a journey."[73] Our life on earth is a journey with a definite beginning and end. It is a journey with its thrills, challenges, accidents, and pitfalls, but it is a journey whose end cannot be reached without the aid of the one through whose causality the journey was begun in the first place—God. The moral life is situated between two poles, creation and the eschaton, and Christian ethics as theology is meant to offer a reasoned roadmap for this journey. As M. D. Chenu points out, the *exitus-reditus* are not two separate movements to be studied separately in separate theological arrangements.

> Theology as a science is eminently one; dogma and morality are not two parts loosely put together, one speculative, the other practical, which some exterior pressure will tie together here and there. They are two sides of one reality, where the categories of speculative and practical, far from forming a real division, only play a part because of a constant surpassing of their technical differences. Human acts . . . are like the steps by which the end of human

nature, both beatitude and perfection, is realized upon the road of returning; practical knowledge of those acts and of their rules will be inserted into the most secret knowledge of human nature itself, according to the Divine plan and its predestinations. Thus the theologian mirrors the very wisdom of God, perfectly one because God "eadem scientia se cognoscit et ea quae facit" (God by one and the same science knows that which he has made).[74]

It is Catholic teaching that through the grace of God human beings can acquire certain stable dispositions that enable them to do good deeds worthy of the kingdom of God. In the parable of the foolish virgins (Matt. 25:1–13), for example, Jesus praises the prudence—that is, the preparedness—of the wise virgins who stuck it out to the end and were prepared to receive the bridegroom when he arrived at last with the rest of the wedding party. As Romanus Cessario puts it, in this parable "the burning lamps which they carry into the wedding feast symbolically portray Christian wisdom, the crown of the other gifts of the Holy Spirit and of the infused moral virtues."[75]

Morality is not simply about acting in conformity to rules. For Christians morality also seeks to transform the human person. The ultimate goal of human striving is personal union with God, for, as Augustine puts it in those famous words, our hearts are restless until they rest in God. The Lord Jesus himself taught that even deeds as little as giving food or drink or providing shelter to "one of the least of those who are members of my family" are actions done to him (Matt. 25:40). Human activity and striving are therefore necessary to living a good life on earth. However, although they can lead us so far, they cannot lead us to God by themselves. There is need for more. That more is the grace of God. In his teaching on the virtues, Saint Thomas Aquinas makes a distinction between infused and acquired virtues. Although he defines virtue as "a good quality of the mind by which we live righteously, of which no one can make bad use; *which God works in us, without us*," he reserves the last part of this definition to those virtues that he calls infused virtues. These virtues are given to direct us to our supernatural end—God—whereas the other virtues are those enduring traits of character that everyone has insofar as that person is a member of the human community.

Like Christians everywhere, the African Christian is one who is born again of water, and the Holy Spirit has had something done or happen to him or her. He or she has a new identity. It must be part of the task of African moral theology to help the African Christian claim this new identity or to nourish it constantly. What I have in mind here is something like what Paul said when he reminds his listeners often to have in them the mind of Jesus Christ (Phil. 2:5). It is not the role of moral theology to seek the lowest common denominator between the Christian and everyone else. Rather it is the task of a truly Christian moral theology to encourage the Christian to aspire to be more and to do more on account of who she or he has become—a son or daughter of God, made so by a new birth in Christ. The success of the Pentecostal and Evangelical churches in Africa stems partly from the fact that they often seek to inspire the African Christian to think of himself or herself as born again, that is, as "a new man" in Christ and as one who is therefore able through the grace of Christ to turn his or her life around and lead a more upright life, one in accord with his or her new Christian identity, no matter how this identity is construed or understood.

AN AFRICAN CHRISTIAN ANTHROPOLOGY

Our discussion in this chapter so far captures the essentials of the understanding of the human person which must guide African ethics. The notion of relatedness, as part of African traditional anthropology, provides two essential elements that work as important foundations for an African Christian anthropology. In the first place, this idea of relatedness provides resistance to any attempt to reduce an individual person to an atom or a monad—"an individual substance of a rational nature." The web of relationships that characterizes the personhood of the individual in Africa is sometimes beyond imagination. It is "like a vast network stretching literally (horizontally) in every direction, to embrace everybody in any given local group." In essence, every individual "is a brother or sister, father or mother, grandmother or grandfather, or cousin, or brother-in-law, uncle or aunt, or somebody else, to another person else. This means that everybody is related to everybody else."[76] This anthropological reality of the African world means that the family is necessary for defining the human person. Here, the African sense of family and family solidarity is one point where African anthropology and Christian theology meet. In a world where the individual is under threat and the family is under attack from all sorts of materialisms, a recovery even in Africa itself of this traditional sense of family and the place of the individual member in it is essential. Both the Christian and the African understanding present a stark contrast to the modern reality of the family in the West where the "family" is often construed as consisting of the parents and their children only. As Carolyn Osiek points out, this model of family is neither Christian nor ideal. In Roman antiquity household and family units included parents, "children, slaves, unmarried relatives, and often freedmen and freedwomen or other renters of shop or residential property."[77] This understanding of the family also became the norm in early Christianity. In other words, although the nuclear family existed and was recognized, it did not function as a social unit in isolation.[78] The group of Jesus' disciples (the church) now functions as family. "Family is not abolished but extended. The boundaries of kinship are not removed but reset. Those who will fulfill the role of true family members are those bound together not so much by blood or social structures as by Baptism and the Eucharist."[79] While holding on to the African traditional family affiliations and structures, African Christianity must also continue to push the boundaries and to help reset the structure of African family affiliations to a point where African Christians can appreciate the statement made by the fathers of the First African Synod: because "the same blood, the blood of Christ runs through our veins," African Christians must live in solidarity and peace with one another. In other words, the resetting of familial boundaries is a Christian project in Africa (as indeed everywhere). This renewed appreciation must arise out of an understanding of the bond that unites Christians, but also out of consideration for every human being as one whom God willed for himself, a creature whose dignity and worth has been enhanced by the incarnation and the redemptive mission of Christ.

A second area in which African traditional anthropology and Christian anthropology agree is in the understanding that there is a surplus and refractoriness to the being of the human person. In other words, not only is the human being not completely understood merely by his or her human affiliation, he or she is open to transcendence and is accounted for and accountable to a nonhuman other, no matter how this other is construed. At the heart of the relationship with an ancestral lineage which defines every African theory of the human person is a sense of transcendence. This sense of transcendence indicates "ownership." By *ownership* here I mean to imply that the gods and the ancestors have staked a claim to this person and are understood to wreak vengeance on anyone who takes the life of a relative, for example. Thus, when Bujo states that in Africa people are respected because they are understood to belong to another, he is not totally wrong. My only concern with this assertion is that Bujo fails to take into consideration the limitations of this respect and protection, a limitation that can be remedied, in my view, from the Christian point of view at least, when African theology takes into full account the resources within the Christian tradition itself, in principle at least.

Christian anthropology and African anthropology both agree that life is sacred because it is a gift from God. Although the two religions may not always agree on all the details of what this statement means, the basic assumption of the sacredness of life as a gift from God is a powerful basis for African theological ethics with regard to the life questions—abortion, euthanasia, and so on. Africa needs both the expanded vision of the human person which Christianity provides, and the agreement that the Christian tradition and the African Traditional Religion share with regard to the human person as Africa tries to find answers to the anthropological crises Pope Benedict XVI speaks about on the continent.

There is a lot of pessimism and cynicism about Africa today. Africans have been so battered by forces all around them that they have all but lost faith in the ability of any human beings or institutions to improve their lot. We have already spoken of the deep anthropological crisis resulting from this situation. Although I will return to this issue later, I would like to state, as I did earlier, that there are enormous resources waiting to be tapped by the increasingly influential Christian church to help effect an African renewal. African theology must be at the forefront of this renewal by honestly seeking those elements in Christian theology which can supply new impetus to the way life is construed in Africa today. The aim of the renewal would be to help Africans become more hopeful about their continent and its future and place in the world by helping them imagine an alternative world. The construal of this alternative world is possible only if we remember, as Vatican II teaches, that it is "only in the mystery of the Word made flesh that the mystery of humanity truly becomes clear . . . Christ the new Adam, in the very revelation of the mystery of the father and of his love, fully reveals humanity to itself and brings to light its very high calling." Christ throws light on our human condition, including the mystery of suffering and death, "which apart from his Gospel, overwhelms us."[80] African theology must refocus its attention on Christ as the basis for the anthropological renewal we seek on the continent.

Chapter Eight

MORAL REASONING IN
AFRICAN THEOLOGICAL ETHICS

In the preceding chapters, we discussed an inculturated theocentric ethics and the issue of an inculturated anthropology in African theology. Here we will take up the question of an inculturated mode of moral argumentation. The idea is both to show how this is done and to offer my own version. In chapter 5 we considered the views of the Congolese theologian Bénézet Bujo on moral decision making. Bujo engages Aquinas extensively on a number of foundational moral issues, especially on the theory of natural law.[1] He believes that the Catholic tradition has, through the work of Saint Thomas, "absolutized" the natural law theory as the basis for moral reasoning to the point that the tradition is no longer open "to an intercultural dialogue" on matters of morality.[2] Although he finds Aquinas's discussion on reason, its limitations, and thence the necessity of revelation helpful, Bujo also argues that Aquinas has limited relevance for African Christian ethics because of his position on a number of practical issues whose morality he believes could be better determined communally, and because of his mode of reasoning, which he believes to be flawed in a number of areas, such as masturbation, the equality of the sexes, human rights, and polygamy.[3] Bujo contends that Aquinas was prevented by the dominant anthropology, science, and philosophy of his day from discerning what is today taken for granted, namely, that our thoughts on these issues are culturally conditioned.

For Bujo, therefore, natural law morality is not good for Africa. Instead, what is preferable is a "context-sensitive" approach to ethics. The community can arrive at an ethical model not by reflection on metaphysics or through natural law.[4] And it must be left to the cultural context to determine what is intrinsically evil and what is not. Thus, for example, even though there might be shared agreement between African ethics and "Western" ethics on the immorality of incest, there is a difference in the way Western (natural law) morality arrives at this conclusion. The question is "not in the condemnation of what is to count as incest as such but . . . who determines what is to count as incest."[5] Throughout, Bujo maintains a contrast between natural law, which he considers rigid, and an African ethic, which he considers more flexible because it is "communitarian." African ethics, according to Bujo, justifies ethical conduct on communitarian terms—that is, on whether it builds or destroys community. This kind of justification applies to virtually every issue, including questions of personal, social, or sexual morality. Adherence to a communitarian form of ethics makes it possible for African ethics to distinguish between what is contingent and what is not in ethics. "We live in a contingent world, where contingent goods so compete with one another that we are able to recognize the absolute *bonum* only in the contingent *bona*. This differentiation might perhaps be better suited to carry on the dialogue between African ethics and Thomistic natural law ethics."[6] The dialogue between ecclesiastical moral theology, based on the natural law, and African ethics, which is communitarian, would be more fruitful if Catholic moral theology would in fact pay greater attention to the distinction contained in Thomistic natural law theory itself between *ius naturale* and *ius gentium*. The ultimate aim would be to "bring down to earth," through particular practices, the universal claims of the natural law and to expose natural law and all other moral theories that make universal claims to questioning in order to demonstrate their worth. Conversely, such a dialogue allows African ethics to be questioned by a principle that has been justified in formal terms. Through this process of interrogation and dialogue natural law ethics would come to learn from African ethics to involve the community actively in determining moral norms and in positing and applying these norms through the process of palaver.

In my earlier response to Bujo in chapter 5, I insisted that African Christian theological ethics cannot dispense with the doctrine of natural law. The idea of the natural law affirms the very thing Bujo is trying to affirm which is that human beings everywhere are capable of coming to know the truth. The natural law theory is indicative of "an optimistic strain running through scripture with regard to humanity's status before God and in positive appreciation of humanity's extra-biblical religious experience and institutions."[7] It fully appreciates the work of God in all cultures. But it also holds everyone and every culture accountable for what they do in this world. As Joseph Boyle reminds us, natural law theory provides an objective moral standard for distinguishing between sense and nonsense. Such a standard makes it possible to reject all forms of ethical skepticism according to which moral standards are simply the result of personal preferences or choice or of social convention. "All such preferences and convention are subject to evaluation by this standard."[8] As I mentioned earlier, palaver, the communitarian approach to moral discernment, needs the objectivity supplied by the idea of natural law, otherwise it becomes open to distortion by bias, ineptitude, or sheer demagoguery.[9]

Another problem with Bujo's use of palaver as moral method is that it elevates what can be a means for moral discernment in some situations into a principle. Palaver can be a process or a tool for arriving at moral truth in situations of moral conflict and unclarity. It is not, however, an end in itself. African ethics must and indeed does use other approaches to norms and ethical decision making that are available to anyone else. Finally, to base the judgment of right and wrong on the principle of community building can be a two-edged sword, lofty as the idea sounds. For one thing, it is difficult to indicate what community building really means and in what way or when such a goal can be or has been reached. When or where do we draw the line between demagoguery, the imposition of the will of some powerful people over others, and a legitimate goal that really serves the common good? Bujo is right about the process of palaver as a means for attaining moral truth in African ethics. What I worry about is that in rejecting the natural law outright as a Western imposition he risks leading the community onto the slippery slope of utilitarian relativism. In reality, however, African communities are generally not utilitarian, based on my own experience and knowledge. African ethical method tends to be a mixture of many things: deontologist on some issues, teleological on others, and pragmatist when it matters. The question is to determine in which situations any of these approaches to moral reasoning are considered appropriate and why. More importantly perhaps is that by rejecting the natural law morality Bujo runs the risk of depriving African ethics of the one important avenue it has of cross-cultural interaction and the search for moral truth with peoples everywhere. For, through the use of natural law we can discover "a set of precepts and values that, at least in their general formulation, can be considered as universal, since they apply to all humanity." Some of these precepts and values "can also have the character of immutability to the extent that they derive from a human nature whose essential components remain the same throughout history. It can still happen that they are obscured or even erased from the human heart because of sin and of cultural and historical conditions, which can negatively affect the personal moral life: ideology and insidious propaganda, generalized relativism, structures of sin, etc."[10] Although, as the International Theological Commission advises, we must be modest and prudent when invoking the "evidentness" of the precepts of natural law, "we must equally recognize in these precepts the common foundation on which we can base a dialogue with a view to a universal ethics."[11] This common foundation supplies, at least partially, the basis for our evaluation of the moral situations to which we will now turn.

MORAL REASONING IN AN AFRICAN CONTEXT

In this section, I will use two stories in Chinua Achebe's *Things Fall Apart* to illustrate the nature and the complexity of moral decision making—at least among some African groups. First is the famous story about the death of Ikemefuna; the second concerns the accidental death of a boy at the funeral of his own father. Both stories involve the main character of *Things Fall Apart*, Okonkwo. As every reader of this novel knows, Ikemefuna had come to Umuofia as compensation from Mbaino, a neighboring village, for the murder by the people of Mbaino of Ezeugo, the wife of Ogbuefi Udo, from Umuofia. In other words, Ikemefuna was a ransom paid to Umuofia as atonement for the death of the lady from Umuofia. The young boy was given over to Okonkwo for safekeeping within his family. He grew up here and in time became a beloved member of Okonkwo's family. Even Okonkwo himself became quite fond of the lad. After some years, however, the people of Umuofia decided it was time to get rid of Ikemefuna. When the decision was made by the village to kill Ikemefuna as expiation for the blood of the long-dead Ezeugo, Ogbuefi Ezeudu, a close friend of Okonkwo, came to warn him against any involvement in the young man's death. Here is how Achebe reports the encounter between the two friends: Ogbuefi Ezeudu to Okonkwo: " 'That boy calls you father. Do not have a hand in his death.' Okonkwo was surprised, and was about to say something when the old man continued: 'Yes, Umuofia has decided to kill him. The Oracle of the Hills and the Caves has pronounced it. They will take him outside Umuofia as is the custom, and kill him there. But I want you to have nothing to do with it. He calls you his father.' "[12] As it happened eventually, it would be Okonkwo himself who struck the blow that cut the young man down.

A lot has been written about this incident in *Things Fall Apart*.[13] For our purposes here, I want to draw attention to several features in the story that demonstrate my point about moral complexity in African moral discourse. First, this story illustrates everything that is wrong with the process of palaver. Although Achebe does not invite us to the meeting at Umuofia where the decision was made to kill Ikemefuna, clearly there had been long deliberations on this subject, in the true custom of palaver among the Igbo, and majority opinion had eventually carried the day. It is also conceivable that some people at this gathering had objected to the act as morally wrong. It is not unimaginable, for example, that someone like Ogbuefi Ezeudu had expressed dissatisfaction with the outcome of the deliberation. When he found himself on the losing side, he must have thought to himself that he could at least try to persuade his friend Okonkwo not to be part of this dastardly deed. The other point to note is that repulsive as this communal decision was, it was supported by a principle that could be put this way: the price for blood is blood, or maybe "a tooth for a tooth," even though that "tooth" happens to be an innocent young man who had no hand in the conflict that led to the death of the woman from Umuofia. This principle, or something similar to it, justified the killing of Ikemefuna in the minds of the Umuofians who made the decision or acquiesced to it. In another interesting aspect of this episode, although it was widely known that Okonkwo himself slew Ikemefuna, he was not in any way sanctioned by the community, even though his closest friends still thought he had committed an abomination. Okonkwo's defense, on the other hand, was that he was merely doing the will of the gods. Consider this exchange between Okonkwo and another of his close friends, Obierika, when Okonkwo goes to visit Obierika after the murder of Ikemefuna:

> "I cannot understand why you refused to come with us to kill that boy," he asked Obierika.
> "Because I did not want to," Obierika replied sharply. "I had something better to do."
> "You sound as if you question the authority and the decision of the Oracle, who said he should die."
> "I do not, why should I? But the Oracle did not ask me to carry out its decision."
> "But someone had to do it. If we are all afraid of blood, it would not be done. And what do you think the Oracle would do then?"
> "You know very well, Okonkwo, that I am not afraid of blood; and if anyone tells you that I am, he is telling a lie. And let me tell you one thing, my friend. If I were you I would have stayed at home. What you have done will not please the Earth.[14] It is the kind of action for which the goddess wipes out whole families."
> "The Earth cannot punish me for obeying her messenger," Okonkwo said. "A child's fingers are not scalded by a piece of hot yam which its mother puts into its palm."
> "This is true," Obierika agreed. "But if the Oracle said that my son should be killed I would neither dispute it nor be the one to do it."[15]

In this intense drama, Achebe captures the complexity of moral reasoning in an African setting. In this short exchange there is a bit of the divine command theory and the complications associated with that, a bit of deontologism, and even consequentialism all rolled into one. We are here reminded of the dilemma Socrates expressed in his exchange with Euthyphro when he wondered whether "the pious or the holy is beloved by the gods because it is holy or holy because it is beloved by the gods."[16] Another issue is that even though both men in this story agree that the gods have the right to command what ought to be done, they differ as to whether such commands, which are repulsive or morally evil, should be carried out. Obierika was persistent in his challenge to Okonkwo that he should not have done what he did. It is one thing for the gods to command evil, it is quite another for that command to be obeyed. In other words, human beings must exercise right judgment and act out of freedom, and must never allow themselves to become instruments for evil, even if it is to please the divinity. Okonkwo should not have led the way to Ikemefuna's slaughter. The Oracle should have found other agents to carry out its evil deed, for a father should not have been compelled or made to feel obliged to kill his son, even in obedience to the gods. And even though there might have been consequences for Okonkwo's disobedience, it was still not good to do evil to please the gods. If there is doubt that human beings feel bound to their consciences in traditional African ethics, this story is proof that they do indeed. For despite possible pressure from the community or from some interest groups within the community, Obierika's position makes it clear that, important as the community input is, the individual conscience is considered the ultimate guide and final arbiter in the choice an individual makes or in the position he or she takes on any given issue.

In another story in this novel, Okonkwo is inadvertently involved in the death of another young man during the funeral of his other friend, Ezeudu (who incidentally had initially advised him not to kill Ikemefuna). As the story goes, Okonkwo is attending the funeral and in honor of his old friend decides to fire some shots from his gun. These shots accidently kill the sixteen-year-old son of the dead man, Ezeudu. Following this incident Okonkwo is forced to flee from his village and into exile in his mother's village. As Achebe puts it, "It was a crime against the earth goddess *to kill a clansman* [emphasis added], and a man who committed it must flee from the land. The crime was of two kinds, male and female. Okonkwo had committed the female, because it had been inadvertent. He could return to the clan after seven years."

The contrast in judgment regarding the two deaths in which Okonkwo was involved is remarkable. Whereas in the case of Ikemefuna he was implicated intentionally, Okonkwo did not draw any sanctions from the community, presumably because, as he himself points out, he was simply obeying the divine command and by so doing had acted to save his community from divine wrath, and because the murdered Ikemefuna was not considered *a clansman*. In the second story he is severely sanctioned even though he had not intended the killing. He had shed a kinsman's blood and that was enough. It is also obvious that the two lives involved are not considered equal within this community. The principle seems to be that the kinsman deserves greater respect and protection at all costs—a right that could not be extended to the nonkinsman "outsider." In this example we see a critical weakness in African traditional moral reasoning—a weakness that partly explains the slave trade from the African end, and which may still be a contributing factor in the incessant ethnic strife and interracial violence plaguing Africa today. In other words, this principle may be a contributing factor to why some segments of African society still seem incapable of recognizing the human rights of others who are not part of their kinship group.

Some Pertinent Moral Categories

Before we can continue with further discussion on moral reasoning in African societies, it is important to take a brief excursus to explain the meaning of some moral terms and categories that are in use here. In chapter 2 we discussed David Aiken's stages of moral reasoning. At the fourth level, which Aiken labels the ethical level, people raise the question, why be moral? The answer depends largely on what people consider to be the goal of morality. Louis P. Pojman has noted several reasons why people think that morality matters: "to keep society from falling apart"; "to ameliorate human suffering"; "to promote human flourishing"; "to resolve conflicts of interest in just and orderly ways; to assign praise and blame, reward and punishment and guilt."[17] Pojman notes that although these principles might appear to be related, they are not identical. I would also add that they are not exhaustive from a Catholic moral theological point of view. For example, Catholic tradition has always held that beyond establishing humane living here on earth, what we do here or how we relate to others also has implications for our eternal well-being (*Gaudium et Spes* 38, 39). In any case, what is important here is that in order to achieve the desired moral aims people have different approaches to moral reasoning.

William Frankena classifies these approaches generally as teleological theories and deontological theories. According to Frankena, "a teleological theory says that the basic or ultimate criterion or standard of what is morally right, wrong, obligatory, etc., is the nonmoral value brought into being. The final appeal, directly or indirectly, must be the comparative amount of good produced, or rather the comparative balance of good over evil produced. Thus, an act is right if and only if it or the rule under which it falls produces, will probably produce, or is intended to produce at least as great a balance of good over evil as any available alternative; an act is wrong if and only if it does not do so." Only those acts and the rules under which they fall which will probably produce or are intended to produce a greater balance of good over evil more than any other available alternatives should be done.[18] In determining moral rightness or wrongness some teleological theories emphasize consequences alone as the basis for moral judgment. Although teleologism is often associated with utilitarianism, "which enjoins us to do what is likeliest to have the best consequences"—that is, produce "the greatest happiness for the greatest number"[19]—it must be borne in mind that not all teleological ethics is either utilitarian or consequentialist in the way the term is often understood in popular parlance. For example, one can rightly say that both Aristotelian and Thomistic ethics are in some sense teleological in that they argue that all persons act for an end which is perceived to be the good. In Aristotle that end is happiness. The same is the case with Aquinas, except that he adds that the happiness referred to in this case is life with God in the beatific vision. Bujo's ethics is also teleological to the extent that he believes that moral norms can be considered right or wrong based on their capacity for community building.

Deontological theories act differently from teleological theories since they assert that there are other considerations beside the goodness or badness of consequences which factor into determining the moral quality of an act. "A deontologist contends that it is possible for an action or rule of action to be morally right or obligated . . . even if it does not promote the greatest possible balance of good over evil for self, society, or universe." Such an action may be right or obligatory simply because of some other fact about it or because of its own nature.[20] Many approaches to ethics come under this classification. We have already spoken of the divine command theory in our brief analysis of the moral reasoning employed by Okonkwo to justify his killing Ikemefuna. In a divine command theory, "the central moral elements are related directly to the commands of the deity." Some people regard the Ten Commandments in the Old Testament and other injunctions based on them as evidence of this kind of theory. As mentioned earlier, in the *Euthyphro* Socrates captures one of the dilemmas of this theory—that is, whether God commands an act because it is right, or whether an act is right because it is commanded by God. If God commands an act because it is right, "then it appears that the fundamental standard of morality is logically independent of God's will or his commands although God's authority might still form the basis of our knowing our duty, or of our accepting it, or of our being motivated to do it." If the second part of this question is the correct one, then there appears to be no independent reason to agree to do what God commands. (This is alleged to make morality "arbitrary" or "capricious.")[21] Catholic moral theory is not a divine command ethics; although it teaches that God does indeed command certain things, it also holds that human beings are free agents who by use of reason process the divine intention and can in exercise of their freedom accept or reject it. Furthermore, there is, as we will elaborate below, a basic assumption here that makes Christian ethical reasoning very different: belief in the goodness of God and consequently in God's good intention in creation and toward all creation, including human beings. There is therefore no element of caprice in God, as with the gods of the Greek pantheon or of Igbo (African) cosmology.

There are therefore different forms of deontological ethics. We will not go into all of them here, but it is important to note at least two that have had considerable influence on moral reasoning. One of these is represented by Kantian ethics; the other by the Catholic moral tradition. As presented in the *Critique of Pure Reason* and in the *Prolegomena*, Kant's main intention in his theory of knowledge is to determine how much reason can know. In other words, Kant's central preoccupation was to determine the extent and the areas of knowledge open to humans as rational beings. Kant opens his discussion of morality in the *Critique of Practical Reason* by distinguishing between the theoretical and the practical use of reason. Whereas in the former case we are concerned with the critical examination of the cognitive powers of reason, in the latter, we are concerned with the "grounds for determining the will, which is a faculty either for producing objects corresponding to concepts, or for determining itself to the effecting of such objects, whether the physical power is sufficient or not."[22] Kant conceives of his task as that of isolating the a priori unchanging elements of morality. The question is whether pure reason by itself can determine the will or whether it can do so only through dependence on empirical conditions. To answer this question, Kant argues, it is necessary first to determine whether the human will is free or not. This task, in turn, demands a critical examination of practical reason generally. "Practical principles are propositions which contain a general determination of the will when several practical rules are under determination. They are subjective or maxims when the condition [determination] is regarded by the subject as valid only for his own will. They are objective or practical laws when the condition is recognized as objective, that is, as valid for the will of every rational being."[23] As a product of reason which prescribes action as means to an intended effect, the practical rule as a rule "is characterized by 'shall' expressing the objective obligation of the action and signifying that if reason completely determined the will, the action would inevitably take place according to this rule." Kant calls these practical laws imperatives. There are two sets of imperatives. One set determines the condition of the causality of the rational being as an efficient cause—"that is, merely in reference to the effect and the means of attaining it." Another determines "only the will as to whether it is adequate to the effect or not." The former contains mere precepts of skill, the latter are practical laws. Kant calls the former hypothetical imperatives, the latter categorical imperatives. The former are hypothetical because they do not determine the will simply as will but only in respect to a desired effect. The latter are laws and categorical because they are necessary, objectively valid, prior to any specific need for particular determination of the will, and independent of psychological conditions "that are only connected with the will by contingency." To be objectively and universally valid, rules must be without any "contingent subjective conditions" by means of which different rational beings are differentiated one from another. Kant's categorical imperative can be stated thus: "Act only on that maxim whereby you can at the same time will that it would become a general rule." Examples are "never break your promise" and "never commit suicide."[24] To put it in simple language, Kant's ethical theory not only asks the moral agent not to engage in a particular act, it enjoins him as a rational creature to consider what the world would look like if everyone were to act the same way on this matter. What would the world be if everyone told everyone else lies in their mutual dealings?

Roman Catholic ethics is also sometimes referred to as deontological ethics because it holds that certain things are never to be done because they are objectively or "intrinsically" morally wrong. Following Vatican II Pope John Paul II in *Veritatis Splendor* provided a list of some of these objectively or intrinsically evil acts:

> Whatever is hostile to life itself, such as any kind of homicide, genocide, abortion, euthanasia, and voluntary suicide; whatever violates the integrity of the human person, such as mutilation, physical and mental torture, and attempts to coerce the spirit; whatever is offensive to human dignity, such as inhuman living conditions, arbitrary imprisonment, deportation, slavery, prostitution, and trafficking in women and children; conditions of work which debase laborers as mere instruments of profit and not as responsible persons: all these and the like are a disgrace and so long as they infect human civilization they contaminate those who inflict them more than those who suffer injustice and they are a negation of the honor to the creator.[25]

The list also includes "contraceptive practices whereby the conjugal act is intentionally rendered infertile."

Although Roman Catholic ethics clearly holds that certain actions are wrong all the time and cannot be excused by any circumstances, or that certain actions are intrinsically evil and may never be done, it is not deontological in the Kantian sense. Certain absolute norms are derived from revelation and from the way the actions they forbid or regulate relate to human goods and the final good of union with God. Although in some areas, such as those listed above, the Roman Catholic tradition teaches that there are certain things one cannot do, no matter the circumstances and despite any other considerations, in other areas it is a bit more tentative and circumspect in both its approaches and its conclusions. Bruno Schüller has argued that the principal areas involved in the church's deontological approach "are the prohibition against false statements, suicide, and the killing of innocent human beings; the indissolubility of marriage; and the impermissibility of any sexual behavior which is regarded as going against nature, as is the case with the use of artificial contraceptives."[26] All other matters in Catholic morality, he argues, are decided on teleological grounds, such as the issues pertaining to the morality of war or of economic justice. The list of intrinsically evil acts in *Veritatis Splendor* shows, however, that this division is not as neat as Schüller's position might suggest. Some of the issues on that list certainly belong to social ethics in the classical Catholic categorization and not just to sexual morality or personal ethics like lying/truth telling. But the point remains valid that the tradition is certain on some issues and more inclined to be tentative on others, given that matters in these areas are more contingent and open to various calculations and interpretations.

Moral Reasoning in an African Context: Further Analysis

What people consider to be the goal of the moral life determines what approach they employ to arrive at moral truth. Put another way, since moral norms are brief statements about what values a society seeks to uphold, or what kind of person an individual wants to become, moral methods are important tools for achieving such goals. African theologians generally speak of the preservation of community as a central ideal of the moral life in African ethical discourse. Laurenti Magesa, on the other hand, argues that the achievement of abundant life is the central goal in African moral reasoning. Whatever may be the case, community building and the quest for abundant life are not mutually exclusive aims. To return to Achebe's *Things Fall Apart*, community cohesion leads Okonkwo to espouse a divine command theory: the community survives only when it stays together and obeys the command of the gods even when such a command might go against familial paternal feelings. If killing Ikemefuna would keep the gods happy and keep the community together and safe, so be it. Interestingly, as already noted, Okonkwo's friend Obierika did not see the matter the same way. Although he believed the gods had the right to command certain sets of action, he also believed in free human agency. If the gods command evil, they should be the ones to execute such a command or find someone themselves who would do their immoral act for them. No human being should feel compelled or be obliged to go along with others in committing moral evil. Obierika's character refutes Bujo's assertion about natural law and moral reasoning in Africa. In fact, African societies possess the resources to expose and correct the deficiencies of communitarianism and divine command ethics. African societies do not just discover what is right and wrong through the process of palaver. They do not make the rules as they go. Palaver, at its best, is used to determine the way to apply the rules in situations of moral conflict. In other words, it is a tool for casuistry in Africa—that is, for determining the right course of action when moral rules conflict. African societies generally hold that certain things are wrong always and everywhere. For example, they generally consider infidelity to one's spouse as adultery and morally wrong. African societies know that unjust killing of an innocent human being is wrong. The case of Ikemefuna is instructive in many ways, in that despite a certain set of opinions which justified his killing, there was another opinion, represented by Okonkwo's friend, which cringed at the prospect of Ikemefuna's death, even if on the narrow ground that by his long sojourn in Okonkwo's household he had also come to acquire the rights of a *clansman*. The point of all this is to show that African societies and persons do not all share one monolithic way of making moral decisions. Their world is as complex as anyone else's, and like people elsewhere they too are guided by many and different considerations in the search for moral truth. Therefore, as is the case with the Catholic moral tradition, traditional African moral reasoning is partly deontological, partly teleological, and partly everything else, depending on the issue at stake, the view of God the individual has, and the understanding of the human good in question which needs to be preserved, articulated, or enhanced.

FAITH HAS CONSEQUENCES

The story of the killing of Ikemefuna shows in part the failure of palaver and even the limitation of natural law as means for determining moral truths or preserving the human good. As we have noted, palaver is open to being hijacked by the demagogue or distorted by bias. It is obvious from the narrative that some members of the Umuofia community who objected to the plan to kill Ikemefuna had been overridden by "stronger" voices in the assembly, which explains why some of Okonkwo's friends would want to talk privately with their friend to try to dissuade him from joining in what they considered to be evil. The limitation of the natural law here may be inferred from the fact that some in that assembly at Umuofia felt honestly that they were doing the right thing and could not be convinced otherwise. Perhaps it is not right to blame the natural law for their failure to do what is right. However, natural law is implicated here because, as in the case of palaver, its conclusions can sometimes be distorted by sin, laziness, bias, or lack of knowledge. This is why Catholic moral theology does not rely exclusively on natural law in the search for moral truths, important as that may be. Important and useful as it is, natural law needs the light of revelation both for its completion and to bring out the truth that it sometimes reveals only dimly.

Christian ethics in the Catholic tradition is therefore not simply an ethics of natural law. It is also, and especially, an ethics that is drawn from the revealed word of God in the Bible. At the center of this ethics of course is Jesus, his life and his teaching. Considerable time has been spent recently in Catholic theology on the question of the distinctiveness of moral norms. This search for distinctive moral norms—that is, for norms that are completely original to the Christian mind and which no one else has thought of or lived up to—is in many ways a wrongheaded exercise. For what drove Christian discussions about norms in the New Testament and the early church was not the desire to be original for its own sake, but to be in conformity with "the mind of Christ" (Phil. 2:5). Christians were and have always been products of their various milieus and circumstances. The New Testament, for example, "did not build castles in the air, constructing ideal but unfulfillable demands."[27] Instead, the various New Testament communities confronted specific situations and were concerned with finding answers to the problems their various particular contexts were throwing at them. Various ancient traditions were "not only critically received but also repeatedly modified and rejected, not for the sake of originality in Christian conduct but for its substantial adequacy."[28] The test for the adequacy of any moral insights from these various traditions was the teaching and example of Jesus. In his book on the moral teaching of the New Testament, Rudolf Schnackenburg points out that although Jesus' message was primarily religious, it was from this message that his moral demands originated: "Nowhere in the New Testament is it possible to break the unity between religion and morality."[29] Jesus does not elaborate a moral theology. His teaching often started from questions put to him by this person or that, and his answers called for immediate decisions. Even so, Jesus was neither a casuist nor a teacher of "situation ethics." "He uncovered the fundamental principles involved in each special case put to him. His moral teaching is concrete, yet gives authoritative precepts."[30] Therefore, even though the New Testament does not develop a systematic ethics, it would be wrong to picture the conduct of the early Christians too atomistically and the ethics of the New Testament too situationally. For, the variety of specific types of behavior notwithstanding, earliest Christianity "displays constant guidelines and standards of conduct that forbid relativism."[31]

At the center of New Testament ethics and therefore of Christian ethics is love. Christian ethics is a human rational response to the love of God made manifest in Christ. Here is how Pope Benedict XVI puts the matter in his encyclical *Deus Caritas Est*:

> True, no one has ever seen God as he is. And yet God is not totally invisible to us; he does not remain completely inaccessible. God loved us first, says the *Letter of John* (cf. 4:10), and this love of God has appeared in our midst. He has become visible in as much as he "has sent his only Son into the world, so that we might live through him" (1 Jn. 4:9). God has made himself visible: in Jesus we are able to see the Father (cf. Jn. 14:9). Indeed, God is visible in a number of ways. In the love-story recounted by the Bible, he comes towards us, he seeks to win our hearts, all the way to the Last Supper, to the piercing of his heart on the Cross, to his appearances after the Resurrection and to the great deeds by which, through the activity of the Apostles, he guided the nascent Church along its path. Nor has the Lord been absent from subsequent Church history: he encounters us ever anew, in the men and women who reflect his presence, in his word, in the sacraments, and especially in the Eucharist. In the Church's Liturgy,

in her prayer, in the living community of believers, we experience the love of God, we perceive his presence and we thus learn to recognize that presence in our daily lives. He has loved us first and he continues to do so; we too, then, can respond with love. God does not demand of us a feeling which we ourselves are incapable of producing. He loves us, he makes us see and experience his love, and since he has "loved us first," love can also blossom as a response within us.[32]

In other words, neither the desire to catch up with the spirit of the age nor the urge to be in conformity with the agenda of the day constituted the criteria for New Testament ethics or for the ethics of the early Christian communities any more than established customs and conventional pragmatic norms. Today many people are asking Christianity and Christian ethics to do no more than conform to the spirit of the age. Thus, to be relevant, Christian ethics must sanction abortion on demand, same-sex marriage, contraception, and so on. What is sometimes forgotten is that Christian ethics has from the beginning stood up to these tendencies and moral situations. The church was born into a situation where homosexuality was not frowned on in some parts of the Roman Empire, prostitution was tolerated in some areas, child abandonment was rampant, divorce and remarriage were accepted as normal, and abortion for the most part was allowed in many places. In this context, relying at times on the direct teaching of its Lord and Master or sometimes drawing inspiration from the spirit of his teaching, the church challenged many of these practices and was able to formulate norms that captured the essence of the moral teaching of the church in these and other areas. The discussion on norms in Christian theology must therefore draw attention to these two sources of Christian moral norms: the direct words of Jesus, and the teaching of the church drawn from these words down through the ages. Norms derived from either of these are equally binding.

The community of Jesus that has kept the Master's memory alive all these years is empowered by Jesus himself to teach in his name (Matt. 28:19; John 20:22–23). Although this community has the authority to teach in the name of Christ it can teach only what Christ taught or what Christ would have taught had the question arisen or been brought before him. Of course this calls for constant moral discernment that takes both the teaching of the Lord and the new situations and experiences of humankind into consideration as it seeks to formulate norms that capture and preserve the value at stake. For the Christian involved in this process in whatever time or culture the teaching of Jesus takes precedence over any other insights or cultural and historical considerations. Part of the task of Christian ethics today should be to emphasize its awkward and difficult aspects and to resist the temptation to adapt itself to and to conform to the thoughts and practices of the world which are clearly against its founding inspiration in Jesus Christ. This is as true elsewhere as it is in Africa.

The New Testament is certainly concerned that Christians should be "the salt of the earth" and the "light of the world" (Matt. 5:13–14; cf. Phil. 2:15) and maintain their distinctiveness even in their "good works." "Matthew 5:46–47 states that what tax collectors and pagans do is not enough. Without the corrective of the 'extraordinary' Christianity would in fact simply be drowned in the world, and it has reason today to be less fearful of sectarianism than of conformity to the world."[33] What Pope John Paul II stated in *Veritatis Splendor* a few years ago is very much the case today: "All around us we encounter contempt for human life after conception and before birth; the ongoing violation of basic rights of the person; the unjust destruction of goods minimally necessary for a human life. Indeed, something more serious has happened: man is no longer convinced that only in the truth can he find salvation. The saving power of the truth is contested, and freedom alone, uprooted from any objectivity, is left to decide by itself what is good and what is evil" (VS 84). However, as the pope also notes, "it is in the crucified Christ that the church finds the answer to the question troubling so many people today" (VS 107). In other words, "the basis and goal of Christian conduct are God's sovereignty and Jesus' cross and resurrection."[34]

Faith and Moral Norms in African Christian Ethics

Two of the main characters of Achebe's *Things Fall Apart* and *Arrow* are deeply religious men. In *Things Fall Apart* Achebe portrays Okonkwo as someone taking scrupulous care to obey the gods and to attend to their needs. The same is the case with Ezeulu, whose raison d'être as priest of Ulu is to attend with care to the wishes of the god vis-à-vis his people. Two aspects of both men's religiosity, however, also rule their moral lives and eventually lead them to ruin. For Okonkwo the issue is fear. In the story of the killing of Ikemefuna one of the factors leading Okonkwo to kill the boy was fear of reprisal from the gods. This fear controlled and in fact clouded his moral instincts. As for Ezeulu, the problem was that he came to a point where he felt that the god to whom he had given his allegiance all along was no longer trustworthy. Ulu could no longer be trusted to be on the side of his people; in fact he had turned his priest into an arrow with which to shoot his people by forcing Ezeulu to refuse to declare the arrival of the new moon and in this way wasting the people's entire livelihood and means of sustenance.

The lives of these two men illustrate quite clearly the connection between faith and moral norms or morality in general. What we believe about God, the world, the human person, and life in general has direct repercussions on how we reason about right and wrong and how we make moral judgments and decisions. To be more specific, religious belief has a direct and significant impact on our moral dispositions, perspectives, and intentions and on the moral norms we decide to live by. By disposition is meant "the readiness to act in a particular way."[35] As a person acts in a certain way over a period of time, a certain quality is formed in the person which then disposes this person "to act on subsequent occasions in a similar way, or in a way that the quality of which has formed is expressed in those actions."[36] Thus, one could, on account of what one believes, act consistently in a morally upright way (virtue) or in a morally wrong way (vice). We have already noted Saint Thomas Aquinas's definition of virtue as "a good quality of the mind, by which we live righteously, of which no one can make bad use, which God brings about in us, without us."[37]

Every society has its own particular understandings of virtue and of the definition of a virtuous person and of what makes one so. For example, in Okonkwo's Umuofia, industriousness and hard work are traits that are highly prized, as are wisdom and oratorical skills. While some societies may regard justice as the linchpin of the ethical life, others might consider love to be so. The Christian tradition even includes in its list of virtues such qualities as humility and meekness — virtues that were unknown or not highly regarded by Aristotle or his compatriots, and which a person like Okonkwo would regard as effeminate. I am not saying that the sort of person one becomes is completely dependent on being brought up in a particular moral and religious community. I am simply affirming what we have already established in chapter 2, that tradition has a tremendous effect on shaping one's moral dispositions, the stable tendencies that mark the character of the person as a moral agent. With regard to the way Africans reason morally, I next would like to focus on four basic assumptions derived from the Christian faith that have made or can make a difference. These ideas are mentioned throughout this work, but it is worthwhile to comment briefly on them here: the idea of the universality of the God of Jesus Christ and of his love; faith in the reliability of God's creation and in the intention of God; hope borne out of faith in the life, death, and resurrection of Jesus.

Faith provides the believer with an angle of vision—that is, with a posture or perspective on life. In this sense faith is like a camera. Consider how a camera functions. The camera as an instrument of photography provides focus. It enlarges certain objects and brings them into sharp relief, while cutting out others and making them fade into the background or even become "nonexistent." Faith is like that. In chapter 6 we examined briefly some of the aspects of life to which Jesus, by his teaching and life, draws the attention of his listeners and disciples: God, forgiveness, reconciliation, equality of all persons before God, and so on. An African moral theology that begins by focusing Christians' attention on the teaching of Jesus on God would have the additional effect of drawing their attention to interethnic forgiveness and reconciliation as essential elements in the construction of humane and livable societies. An African moral theology that insists on the equality of all persons before God, irrespective of history or geography, would be able to help with the renewal that is so badly needed in Africa today.

The life of Jesus as a whole represents a gold mine from which his disciples and the church, as well as others, have continued to dig up precious insights and truths about life in this world, how to organize it in a humane way, and what actions and type of life lead to or away from God. For example, "God is good!" is a common and oft-repeated phrase among many Christians around the world, including Africa. It contains deep theological insights about life and about reality in general. It expresses "confidence in God, in the goodness of the ultimate power and source of life, and in the power of good-ness."[38] One of the most enduring problems of all time is the problem of evil. This involves what appears to be a contradiction between our belief in God, who is good and all powerful, and the reality of evil among us—sickness, disease, hunger, poverty, natural disasters of all sorts, and ultimately death. The religions of the world have offered three basic answers to this phenomenon. One is from the Vedanta teachings of Hinduism to the effect that evil is illusory. But is that true? How can I convince a young couple who have just lost their lovely one-year-old child in a freak accident that the pain they feel is illu-sory? A second answer comes from the Manicheans and other Gnos-tic groups, who speak of opposing deities, two forces of evil and of good. This view presupposes a dualism in the deity, for one deity is re-sponsible for good, the other for evil. Christian and Jewish theologies supply the third answer, which insists that God is good and blames the evil of the world not on God but on something else. But here arises the dilemma: If God is all good, and all powerful, he should be able to prevent evil. But evil exists. Does that mean then that God is neither all good nor all powerful?

The response by Augustine of Hippo to the problem of theodicy has become the basis for much of the answer to this question in Christian thought.[39] Augustine's answer to the dilemma of theodicy is couched in a number of moves in his response to the Manicheans on evil. In the first move Augustine rejects Manichean dualism. There is only one God who is the sole maker of heaven and earth. God is a being who exists absolutely. He is being in the truest sense of the word. He subsists in himself and "is altogether changeless. There is no nature contrary to God."[40] In the second move, Augustine asserts that God is absolutely good. God is not the author of evil. "For how can He who is the cause of the being of all things be at the same time the cause of their not being—that is, of their falling away from being and tending to non-being."[41] The two questions remain: What is evil,[42] and where does evil come from? In his third move, Augustine presents evil as a privation, a negation, a non-being. In this way, he contradicts the Manichean view of evil as an independent reality and power that is coeternal with God. In the *Enchiridion*, Augustine puts the matter this way: "Now what is the so-called evil but a privation of the good? In the bodies of animals affliction with diseases and wounds is nothing other than the privation of health. For, when a cure is worked, it does not mean that these evils which are present, that is, the diseases and the wounds, recede thence and are elsewhere, they simply are not. For a wound or a disease is not substance, but a vice of the fleshy substance, the substance, surely something good, is flesh itself, its accidents being the aforementioned evils, that is, privations of that good which is called health."[43] For Augustine being is goodness. In this case, God, who is the highest, richest, and most intensely real being, is Goodness himself. God is, and everything made by God, is ipso facto good. Therefore, the corruption, which we call evil, can never be complete. For "if a thing becomes so vitiated in nature that it ceases to exist, the evil which is like a parasite on this creature must cease to exist. Hence, there can be no wholly evil creature."[44] On the other hand, "all natural beings are good, since the Creator of every one of them is supremely good; but because, unlike their creator, they are not supremely and unchangeably good, their good is capable of diminution and increase. But the diminution of good is an evil, even though, howsoever it be diminished, somewhat of good must necessarily remain, to be the source of its being, if its being is to continue. For, of whatever kind or however small, that good which gives it being cannot be destroyed unless the being itself be destroyed."[45]

The next question is how God's good creation came to be spoiled. In the *City of God*, Augustine confronts this question head on. He ends chapter 5 of Book XII this way: "Now God supremely exists, and therefore he is the author of every existence which does not exist in this supreme degree. No existence which came from nothing can claim to be equal to him; nothing could exist in any way, if it had not been created by him. Therefore God is not to be blamed for any fault or defect which offends us; he is to be praised, when we contemplate everything that exists in nature."[46] Augustine's answer to what caused the spoiling of God's work is that evil has entered into the world through the culpable volition of free creatures: angels and human beings. "When we ask the cause of evil angels' misery, we find that it is the just result of their turning away from him who supremely is, and their turning towards themselves, who do not exist in that supreme degree. What other name is there for this fault than pride?" Later on in the same chapter Augustine states that "when the will leaves the higher and turns to the lower, it becomes bad not because the thing to which it turns is bad, but because the turning is itself perverse. It follows that it is not the inferior thing which causes the evil choice; it is the will itself, because it is created, that desires the inferior thing in a perverted and inordinate manner."[47]

In his life and teaching, Jesus bore testimony to the truth of God's goodness and love for all human beings. God cares. God intends the salvation of all humankind. God is so merciful that he allows his rain and his sunshine to fall on both the good and the bad (Matt. 5:45). In his book on Jesus of Nazareth, Pope Benedict XVI points out that for both the Jew and the Christian, God is personal. The *shema*, the "Hear, O Israel" from Deuteronomy 6:4–9 was and still is the real core of the believer's identity, not only for Israel but also for Christianity. The believing Jew dies reciting this profession; the Jewish martyrs breathed their last declaring it and gave their lives for it: "Hear, O Israel, He is our God. He is one."[48]

There is so much suffering and evil in Africa today, a fact that does not bear repeating anymore. What needs to be noted quite vigorously, however, is how this situation is driving many Africans to become prey to various cults, diviners, and faith healers. This is what Pope Benedict XVI was alluding to when stating that "various syncretistic movements and sects have sprung up in Africa in recent decades. . . . These many sects take advantage of an incomplete social infrastructure, the erosion of traditional family solidarity and inadequate catechesis in order to exploit people's credulity, and they offer a religious veneer to a variety of heterodox, non-Christian beliefs."[49] The pope singles out witchcraft for special mention in another passage: "Witchcraft, which is based on the traditional religions, is currently experiencing a certain revival" as a result of widespread "anxiety over health, well-being, children, the climate, and protection from evil spirits."[50] In many parts of Africa today there is also a deficit of hope. Given the facts of the situation many Africans live in a constant state of despair. This is evident in most cities on the continent, with the number of young people who cannot find jobs and are forced into lives of crime and violence. African Christian ethics must inspire people in Africa to faith in the goodness of God and to hope that God will have the last word, not evil. But this hope must not be utopian; it must be followed by a deep commitment to help reform society and to get rid of the death-dealing situations that prevail over the entire continent.

Augustine's view has sometimes been criticized for underestimating the power of evil. But for the African imagination, in which evil is certainly alive and well, this view is certainly what is needed. Evil *is not* ultimately a metaphysical independent positive force; it has no ultimate purchase on reality, on being. It has no coherence but rather the centrifugal tendency toward incoherence and fragmentation— it is nothing ultimately to be afraid of. To put it more theologically, for Augustine Christ has triumphed over evil, over the temptation to stare at incoherence and the tendency to fragmentation as though they were ultimate. In Christ, God has relativized even death. God, and God alone, can put evil—useless by definition, as a privation and corruption of the good—to a good use, and in faith in Christ we all therefore can—as the martyrs do with death. We can participate in the victory over evil through our faith in Christ, our configuration to his sacrifice in the Eucharist. It is a eucharistically configured victory, proleptic of the final Wedding Supper of the Lamb.[51]

Forged in the crucible of both Christian teaching and elements from African traditional ethics, African Christian morality can help to open the eyes of Africans to the truly good and can therefore enable them to desire it with all their hearts and minds. In this way the African Christian can both see what is morally good and be able to do it. This is to say that African Christianity thus conceived should have an educative effect. "It should be hard to escape this effect if one takes seriously what one professes and celebrates about the care, fidelity, love and forgiveness of God and the self-emptying of Christ. . . . Christianity makes for moral seriousness and encourages moral carefulness." Furthermore, it also "contributes a whole range of reason to the moral effort" since the Christian has a whole range of religious and moral reasons for doing good.[52] As Vincent MacNamara puts it, for the Christian "there is a religious hope in doing things and a religious perseverance in well-doing. There is a belief in the purposefulness of things. There is a confidence that the best of our moral endeavors will not end in the grave but will be found again. These relationships between what is inherent to morality and what is inherent to Christian religious experience must find expression in any full consideration of the identity of Christian morality,"[53] in Africa as in every other place.

Aru (Abomination) as a Moral Category

We examined in some detail the issue of homicide/murder in an African society and what considerations go into the moral evaluation in our discussion of the Okonkwo/Ikemefuna story in Achebe's *Things Fall Apart*. As we have seen, both the Catholic tradition and the African one consider some actions to be intrinsically evil based on certain criteria. In some of these instances in Africa the phrase *intrinsic evil* does not adequately convey the reaction of Africans when violations of these norms occur. Elsewhere I have discussed in detail an incestuous/adulterous relationship between a man and his cousin's wife in a particular Igbo community.[54] The process of atonement/reconciliation—*igba oriko*—among members of this community when the sin became public knowledge speaks to the gravity of this issue. When such a thing occurs all relationships are contaminated until expiation is made. Tension also arises in certain African societies between Catholicism and African Traditional Religion on the issue of reconciliation. Simply put, followers of African Traditional Religion cringe at the thought that all sins are a private affair or that private sacramental absolution would be enough in all cases of wrongdoing. The idea is that certain sins so injure relationships and are so disruptive of communion that they demand public penance and a public process of reconciliation. These moral wrongdoings belong to the category referred to as *aru* in Igbo, which can be loosely translated as "abomination" in English. For example, it would be *aru* to have sexual intercourse with one's brother or sister or to commit adultery with a brother's or sister's spouse. Viewed superficially, these wrongdoings could be classified as fornication or adultery. But many African societies realize that this classification does not do justice to the enormity of the disruption caused to the community or to familial harmony. These are just two examples. When African theologians talk about community building or preserving aspects of African ethics, this is what they mean. Christian ethics in the Western churches has largely lost this dimension of some kinds of wrongdoing, but this is something African traditional ethics has to help the church recover. For example, the current spate of cases of sexual abuse of minors by some priests and by some church personnel cannot continue to be treated as a private legal affair between some dioceses and some individuals. A way has to be found for the acknowledgment of *the complicity of the whole church* in this matter—laity, priests, and bishops. Presently, there is a certain segment of the church which, with a holier-than-thou kind of attitude, points fingers at bishops and some church dignitaries as the "sinners" in this case. The fact is that because our members have sinned in such a big way, we are all implicated, either because we were in charge and did nothing when we should have, or because we are simply members of the same body. The nature of the matter is such that this situation has deeply sundered communion among Christ's faithful. What has happened is *aru*. Therefore, we should borrow from African Traditional Religion and deal with it through carefully worked out communal processes of atonement and reconciliation.

More recently there has been a worldwide uproar concerning the strict legislation in some African countries or the attempts in these countries to legislate against same-sex marriages. Even the Nigerian House of Assembly has passed a bill, quickly assented to by the president of Nigeria, Goodluck Jonathan, condemning the practice and the attempt by some Western-backed groups to force this issue in Nigeria. It is interesting to note some of the value terms employed by opponents of this practice to indicate their disagreement with the matter both in the Nigerian society and in the Senate. Some referred to it as "unnatural"; some others spoke of it as going against "our moral values"; yet others called it "abominable." Some foreign governments, like those of the United Kingdom and the United States, threatened to withdraw or withhold foreign aid from all countries in Africa that are trying to or who have passed such legislation, seeing this issue as one of human and civil rights. The Nigerian government and those of other African nations, and in fact most of the people in these countries, called their bluff and asked these governments to keep their aid, for they would rather be poor than go against their core beliefs. Again, at issue in the discussion from the African perspective is the notion of *aru*.

The general rejection of same-sex marriage among Africans brings to the fore another reason African communities would consider an issue as *aru*. Among the Igbo, for example, to classify a thing as an abomination (*aru*) is to say that it is absolutely nonnegotiable because to attempt such an act would incur the wrath not only of human beings but that of the gods as well. Thus, it would be *aru* for a Yoruba man or an Igbo man (or any other African, for that matter) to take home another man and introduce him to his family and friends as his "wife," just as it is *aru* to spill a kinsman's blood knowingly or unknowingly. What makes an act *aru* is not always easy to explain but is, as it were, part of the moral genotype of those who are born in those societies. One is reminded here of David Aiken's position concerning the evocative/expressive level of moral reasoning, at which people react to things from a stock of moral insights that have gone into making them the type of moral agents they have become. By exposure to certain truths and tendencies about life from all sorts of sources, one is shaped to respond morally and spontaneously in certain ways and on certain matters. This reaction, although it might appear illogical sometimes, is never irrational. It comes from that place within the human person where syllogistic logic is not the only or even the predominant form of logic there is. Here, people "see" with more than just one "eye"—including their faith, their emotions, and their experience as human beings.

The Same-Sex Marriage Debate: A Very Brief Discussion

Like all societies everywhere built on a world of a common and shared ethos that formed the basis for agreement on a number of issues, including the meaning and significance of human sexuality and marriage, African societies today are witnessing a certain pluralism that is questioning the once-certain moral outlook that previously characterized them, as the debate on same-sex marriage, sporadic and insignificant as it may currently be in many African countries, shows. The fragmentation in the foundational ethos of African societies provides both a test and an opportunity for Christianity. The test for Christianity is whether and in what ways it can supply an ethos, a compelling and persuasive narrative that would help foster and grow a community able to support moral agreement at a fundamental level in African societies, as African Traditional Religion had done up until recently. The opportunity is for African Christian moral discourse to restate clearly and without ambiguity the theological basis for the moral assertions it makes, both on the continent and everywhere else. African moral theology must lead the way on this issue. It has an important ally on this matter in African traditional ethics.

Like the Thomistic theory of natural law, African traditional ethics has identified certain "morally significant constants in human nature,"[55] in matters relating to sexual ethics at least. In an encounter
I had with an Igbo elder on the question of same-sex marriage I saw
proof of what I have since come to understand to be a widespread
opinion among the Igbo—that biological nature has moral significance. When asked what he thought about the debate on same-sex
marriage, the old man simply said to me that growing up in this part
of the world he had never doubted that his mother was not his father
or that there is a difference biologically, anatomically, and sexually between him and his wife. He said he did not think that these facts were
morally insignificant, as some people were trying to make them out
to be. He believed that any attempt at marriage between two men
was, in his words, "mere mimicry of the real thing." I think what this
old man was saying is clear, for, as Jean Porter puts it, "We can arrive
at moral judgments from within our own particular contexts of beliefs and practices, while hoping that these might prove persuasive to
others in quite different cultural contexts." Porter goes on to argue
that no one can provide universally compelling moral judgments to all
persons of goodwill or even "judgments that all persons would en-
dorse under ideal circumstances." Even so we cannot foreclose the possibility that we might actually be able here and now to persuade others
of the soundness of our moral positions. Since various circumstances
can lead people of goodwill to arrive at different conclusions when
faced with practical dilemmas, Porter determines that what we need
in such a situation is to show that "a given arrangement is defensible
here and now in terms that all parties can accept as reasonable, all
things considered."[56] But what if the parties cannot accept the reasonableness of the arrangement in question, as is the case in the current
debate over certain aspects of sexual morality in contemporary Western
societies, or with regard to the moral evaluation of clitoridectomy by
the Egyptian and American families of the young woman whose case
we considered in chapter 2?

There is perhaps no greater example of the disjointed quality of
moral argumentation in the West today than the disagreement over
the nature and meaning of human sexuality. To put it another way, the
question of sex and sexuality points to the deep fragmentation and the
extent of incommensurability in various ethical starting-points and

standpoints in Western moral discourse. In the last decade or so, the debate over homosexuality has moved from the question of the immorality or otherwise of homosexual acts—that is, from the simpler question of whether homosexual persons could be said to be fornicating (as would be the case with heterosexual persons)—to whether such persons can also morally, legally, and really "marry" like heterosexual individuals. Same-sex marriage has not only moved into public consciousness but has been recognized as legitimate in many countries of the West and in South Africa (at least by law). This is a remarkable feat considering that (as far as I know) no other societies in human history have accorded the status of marriage to the relationship between persons of the same sex, even though the reality of homosexuality was known and lived in many societies all along. What happened? How did we get here so quickly?

It is certainly beyond the scope of this book to answer these questions fully. However, it must be noted that the situation where same-sex marriage became an acceptable option, even for many people who still harbor deep disapproval of homosexuality itself, did not just happen. The ground had been readied by the so-called sexual revolution, which has characterized Western society for a while now. The idea of free love, which Vatican II spoke of (*Gaudium et Spes* 52–54), and the contraceptive mentality that has characterized the West since then are very much part of the issue. What these two trends did was to sunder the unitive from the procreative aspects of human sexuality. With sex losing its connection to procreation, the way was opened not only to massive pornography but to all other relationships in which people believed one should "just do it," as the Nike ad puts it, with whomever one feels like. It was therefore a very logical step to the day when, in President Barack Obama's words, "people should feel free to marry whomever they are in love with." The point here is that the current same-sex debate is indicative of the various traditions of moral discourse in contemporary society. On one hand are those like the old man mentioned earlier who believe that sexual difference is morally important and "is relevant for marriage to exist and actually be a marriage."[57] On the other hand are those who emphasize autonomy, love, and acceptance, as Obama does in his speeches on this matter. In this view anyone who seems not to accept the logic of this latter position is considered as "closed-minded," homophobic, noninclusive, and intolerant.

The same-sex marriage debate thus reveals two or more worlds of meaning about the goal of human sexuality and of marriage itself. More importantly, it reveals the various views of reasonableness that are characteristic of our world today. In the West there is deep disagreement over the meaning of marriage, sexuality, and even the human body. In this situation, it must be clear, as I have repeatedly stated, following Paul Ricoeur, that no one speaks from nowhere; people come to this debate laden with presuppositions that inform the positions they take. The sometimes disturbing situation where defenders of same-sex marriage and such views of human sexuality ask others speaking from a religious point of view on this matter to be quiet and to refrain from "imposing" their morality on everyone else smacks of a sort of "totalitarianism." What this amounts to is asking religious persons to vacate the public square and let it be filled with other points of view on the construal of reality. But the reality is that both the religiously affiliated persons who insist that marriage is something between a heterosexual couple, and the proponent of same-sex marriage who comes at this issue without the warrants of religious dogmas have the right in our so-called liberal democratic arrangement to insist on getting a hearing for their points of view. The task before the church, as Christopher Roberts puts it, is to continue to articulate more clearly the explicit reasons why sexual difference should be considered significant enough and why sexual difference should be the basis for marriage, even when it means asking those persons who are inclined to a homosexual lifestyle to accept a limitation on or even to curtail their sexual desire.

African Christian ethics and African traditional ethics share common grounds on the question of same-sex marriage. First, they agree, as the old man told me, that sexual difference matters. When he asserts that his mother is not his father, that is what he means. No one can explain this away who is not frivolous but sincerely searching for answers to this question, which has vexed society in recent times. The assertion of this significance is one reason the same-sex marriage trend has not yet caught on in Africa. Even in South Africa, where the postapartheid government of Nelson Mandela quickly rammed the legislation legalizing same-sex marriage through parliament, the trend has not caught on, partly for this reason. African Christian ethics of marriage must find a way to reinforce this belief.

Secondly, on a related issue, African Christian ethics and Christian ethics share a belief in the connection between the unitive and the procreative aspects of human sexuality. One of the most insidious effects of globalization on Africa comes from the spread of all sorts of ideologies that are harmful to faith and morals by groups that are very well funded by outside organizations with very deep pockets and longstanding animosity to the church. Some of these groups, like Planned Parenthood and the Gates Foundation, have come to Africa in the guise of working for the health and advancement of women. As Jennifer Hartline points out, however,

> Planned Parenthood is not a network of health care clinics serving women out of the goodness of their hearts. It is the world's largest abortion mill. They exist to perform abortions, period. If tomorrow they could no longer kill babies, then tomorrow they would close their doors. Does anyone seriously believe otherwise? There are no million dollar profits in adoption referrals, or Pap smears, or manual breast exams, or STD testing, or condom distribution. But there are billions of dollars to be made from terminating babies. Planned Parenthood does not now, nor have they ever provided a single woman with a mammogram. There's not one PP clinic in the country that can give a woman a mammogram.[58]

And yet, this organization has been packaged to look like the answer to every problem affecting African women. The Bill and Melinda Gates Foundation, which has funded many good programs around the world, including Africa, has recently announced a program to provide contraceptives to women in sixty-nine poor countries around the world, most of whom are in Africa. In a reaction to the Melinda Gates proposal, Obianuju Ekeocha, a Nigerian woman living in England, has this to say: "I see this $4.6 billion buying us misery. I see it buying us unfaithful husbands. I see it buying us streets devoid of the innocent chatter of children. I see it buying us disease and untimely death. I see it buying us a retirement without the tender loving care of our children. Please Melinda, listen to the heart-felt cry of an African woman and mercifully channel your funds to pay for what we *really* need."[59] African churches must look for the resources—moral, financial, theological, political and otherwise—to face the challenges coming from this well-funded and well-organized lobby. The most important re-source, though, is fidelity to the gospel of Jesus Christ.

Finally, the Western threat to withhold aid if antifamily laws are not put in place in Africa is a missionary, dogmatic imperialism. Accept our "religion" or we won't help you. Wouldn't it be an anti-imperialist attitude to be open to the idea that the strong family cul-ture in Africa can give perspective on a culture that has lost perspec-tive on itself and is bent on the imperialism of culture as part of that decadence? At the same time, one must also condemn strongly such African excesses with regard to the same-sex issue as the death pen-alty for sodomy in Uganda and Zambia. Christian values are equally offended by such laws.

Chapter Nine

MORAL THEOLOGY CHRISTIAN AND AFRICAN

The Ecclesial Dimension

Earlier in this book we discussed Bénézet Bujo's position on memory in African ethics: Bujo insists on anamnesis as an important characteristic of African ethics, for Africans keep alive the memory of the words and deeds of their ancestors and in that way ensure continuity between the past and the future of the peoples of the continent. In my initial response to Bujo I argued that African Christian ethics must be anamnetic in a more inclusive way. It must be an ethic that begins with remembering Jesus, his teaching and his deeds. Further, this ethic must also take seriously the teaching of Jesus' disciples and of those other members of the community of Jesus who through the centuries in every part of the world have kept the memory of Jesus alive. In other words, for the Christian, anamnesis is primarily an ecclesial affair; Christian ethics is anamnetic but in an ecclesial way.

The church is the place in which the memory of Jesus has been kept alive all these centuries. As Edward Schillebeeckx points out, what the historical Jesus left us was not a résumé or bits and pieces "about God's approaching dominion," or even "a kerygma or string of *verba et facta ipsissima*, that is, a pure record of precisely what he

did as a historical individual or a number of directives and wise sayings that can certainly be picked out from the gospels." Rather, "what
he did leave—only through what he was, did and said, simply through
his activities . . . was a movement, a living fellowship of believers who
had become conscious of being the new people of God, the eschatological 'gathering' of God—not 'sacred remnant' but the firstborn
of the gathering together of all Israel, and eventually of all humankind: an eschatological liberation movement for bringing together all
people, bringing them together in unity, Universal Shalom."[1] Without
the church, the story of Jesus would perhaps have been no more than
a historical footnote. The Second Vatican Council was indeed correct
when it referred to the church as sacrament of Christ in the world.
This means that the church is the place where "salvation from God
is made a theme or put into words, confessed explicitly, proclaimed
prophetically and celebrated liturgically."[2] For Christians, there is no
Jesus without the church's confession of Christ, "just as there is no
Church confession without the liberating appearance of the historical
Jesus of Nazareth."[3] The first result of the good news of Jesus Christ is
the calling into being of the Christian community, a community that
finds ultimate meaning in the person and teaching of Jesus Christ.
Even though the first act of Christians has always been faith—that is,
belief in the absolute lordship of Jesus—Christian faith has never been
merely a notional assent to a set of propositional truths. It has always
been an assent to a person, Jesus, the Christ of God; it has always issued in, and been nourished by, worship and expressed in charity or
ethical commitment to and in the world.[4] As Pope Benedict XVI states,
"The Church's deepest nature is expressed in her three-fold responsibility: of proclaiming the word of God (*Kerygma-martyria*), celebrating the sacraments (*leitourgia*), and exercising the ministry of charity
(*diakonia*). These duties presuppose each other and are inseparable."[5]
In other words, the church keeps the memory of Jesus alive through
its proclamation—mission and evangelization—through its worship,
and through its ethical commitment in and to the world. In this chapter we will focus on this last aspect of the trilogy which implies that
the church is a community that "deploys" what it remembers of Jesus
as a guide in its moral deliberations and instructions.

All this is to say that there is no abstract encounter of the gospel
with culture or between Jesus and the culture. Rather Jesus is encoun-

tered in the ecclesial communion defined by his sacrifice—that is, by his love. As the *Catechism of the Catholic Church* puts it, "The Church is born primarily of Christ's total self-giving for our salvation, anticipated in the institution of the Eucharist and fulfilled on the cross" (no. 766). We encounter the risen Lord in the love that forms the church into his body. It is in this encounter through the body of Christ that the human person is renewed and recapitulated in Christ the head. In other words, there is a close connection between ecclesiology and moral theology. I am not thinking here primarily in terms of an authoritative church making authoritative statements about authoritative moral codes, but in terms of a renewed and renewing sense of Christian identity as the basis for ethics and for reimagining the relationship between African cultures and Christianity as between cultures everywhere and Christianity. A share in the risen life of Christ is participation in the sacrifice that is the Eucharist and that makes the church a place or context where forgiveness can be imagined, and the renewal of what personhood is can be filled out with this possibility, which is really the renewal of all in Christ, in hope, in the wedding feast of the Lamb who was slain but now lives. As the catechism puts it, "The Eucharist makes the Church. Those who receive the Eucharist are united more closely to Christ. Through it Christ unites them to all the faithful in one body—the Church" (no. 1396).

This chapter is a case study of the African church as a community of moral discourse—that is, as a community that deliberates on and teaches about what should be done or left undone in Africa and by African Christians in light of the teaching, deeds, and life of Jesus. The intention here is twofold and follows from my assertion above that there is a close connection between ecclesiology and moral theology. I want to show how a fully inculturated moral theology works. For here, in the synods that will be discussed, the church is trying, like the early church gathered in the Acts of the Apostles (Acts 15), to grapple with ways to make the faith real and lived on the continent. This is an exercise in inculturation fully and truly. I also want to show what I mean when I say that the encounter between gospel and culture must necessarily pass by way of the church—that is, the church as "the real, incarnate body of Christ, the Church as it is with all its blemish, and not the abstract, idealized church in our minds," or the church that we sometimes might wish existed, "but the concrete visible communion of 'hierarchic and charismatic gifts,' at once holy and always in need of purification, in which each bishop represents his own diocese and all of [the bishops] together with the Pope represent the whole Church."[6] I will focus exclusively on the moral teaching of the two African synods, in 1994 and 2009, especially on the latter.

A VENERABLE SYNODAL TRADITION

The church has a very long and venerable tradition of meeting in councils and synods. From the first council of Jerusalem which was reported in Acts 15 to the Second Vatican Council, these councils have provided the church with the settings and opportunities for either resolving particular issues of doctrine or morality or charting pastoral courses for more effective governance of the church or for the evangelization of peoples. The present synodal process in the church is, however, the direct result of a *motu proprio*, *Apostolica Sollicitudo*, issued by Pope Paul VI on September 15, 1965.[7] In this text Paul VI called for the establishment of "a permanent council of bishops for the universal Church, to be directly and immediately subject to our power. Its proper name will be the Synod of Bishops." The aims of the synod of bishops, as stated in *Apostolica Sollicitudo*, are "to promote a closer union and greater cooperation between the Supreme Pontiff and the bishops of the whole world; to see to it that accurate and direct information is supplied on matters and situations that bear upon the internal life of the Church and upon the kind of action that should be carrying on in today's world; to facilitate agreement, at least on some essential matters of doctrine and on the course of action to be taken in the life of the Church." The final text of the conciliar decree of the Second Vatican Council on the office of bishops in the church, which was approved on October 28, 1965, also has a passage on the synod of bishops: "Bishops chosen from different parts of the world . . . will give more effective and helpful service to the supreme pastor of the church by meeting in a council which will be called the *synod of bishops*. Acting on behalf of the whole catholic episcopate, it will show that all the bishops in hierarchical communion participate in the care of the whole church."[8]

A number of points should be noted here. First, the synod of bishops is intended to be "a participation in the 'solicitude for the Universal Church' proper to the bishop of Rome." It is a means by which the bishop of Rome as chief shepherd exercises more effectively his ministry of leading "the people of God to eternal pastures," in closer collaboration with the bishops of the whole church "whom the Spirit has placed . . . to rule the Church of God."[9] The second point, which follows from the first, is that the synod of bishops held in Rome in October 2009 is an exercise of the universal church and is not just an African event; hence its proper title: The Second Special Assembly for Africa of the Synod of Bishops. This is an important point to make, since for some people what happened in Rome from October 5 to 25, 2009, was a synod of Africa, a gathering of African bishops, albeit under the watchful eyes of the ecclesiastical authorities in Rome, to deliberate on the African church. Thus, for such people, this was one more piece of evidence of African dependence on or subjugation by Rome. This is not correct. The truth is that since the end of Vatican II the synod of bishops has met at intervals to deliberate on one aspect of the church's life or another.[10] Thus synods have been dedicated to particular regions of the world: Africa, America, Europe, Oceania, Asia, and the Middle East. Africa is not unique in this postconciliar era since it is not the only region that has had two synods devoted to it; Europe at least has had the same number, and if one were to add the special assembly on the Netherlands, then there have been at least three synods on Europe. A third noteworthy point is that the synods that took place in Rome were the culmination of a long process in which the entire church—lay, ordained, and religious—in Africa participated in one way or another.

Even so, when Pope John Paul II, toward the end of his life on November 13, 2004, declared his intention to convoke a second Special Assembly for Africa of the Synod of Bishops, the question on the minds of many was why? Why do we need to have another such synod after only a fifteen-year interval? What happened to all the good ideas voiced at the first synod, which took place in 1994? Had that synod run its course?

The *Instrumentum Laboris* of the synod (the working paper for the synod), which was presented to Africa by Pope Benedict XVI on his trip to Cameroon on March 19, 2009, justifies a second synod for Africa in these words: "Since the last synodal assembly, held in 1994, African society has undergone a significant change. Generally speaking, some basic, human problems exist. However, there are signs which call for a thorough examination of questions highlighted 15 years ago, in the religious, political, economic and cultural spheres."[11] The *Instrumentum Laboris* provides further justification for the second synod in another passage: "The pastors in Africa, in union with the Bishop of Rome, who presides over the universal communion in charity, feel that further discussion needs to be done on the problems already treated at the preceding Special Assembly for Africa of the Synod of Bishops and taken up in the post synodal exhortation *Ecclesia in Africa*. The present synod then is to be considered in continuing the dynamic of the preceding one. This is also the case with not only the subjects to be discussed collegially but the Christian perspective required."[12] These two passages suggest both continuity and discontinuity between the second and first synods. Although the second synod is not just a continuation of the first (or, as a friend of mine would say, "first synod of Africa light," as in Coca-Cola or Pepsi light, implying a less dense or less toxic version of the main product), it presupposes many of the issues and discussions from the first synod. In many ways, the Africa of 1994 and that of 2009 were still the same: poor, badly governed for the most part, riddled with corruption, wracked by so many seemingly unending wars, violent conflicts, and ethnic strife. In other ways, however, the Africa of 2009 was new and full of new opportunities and challenges for the church. The challenge before the bishops and participants in the second synod was how to be better stewards of the African reality by helping the continent, through the gospel, put behind it some of the negative tendencies, both acquired and structural, that are pulling it down, while helping Africa chart a course for true faith, peace, and prosperity in this new millennium; hence the central theme of the synod: The church in Africa in service to reconciliation, justice, and peace; "You are the salt of the earth . . . You are the light of the world" (Matt. 5:13, 14). The *Instrumentum Laboris* also explains the process of preparation for the synod:

> The Special Council for Africa of the General Secretariat of the Synod of Bishops . . . oversaw the preparation of the Lineamenta,

a presentation on the synod topic which was made public 27 June 2006. Subsequently, the same Council drafted this Instrumentum Laboris, the working document of the Synod of Bishops which is a summary of the responses to the questions in the Lineamenta, submitted by the 36 episcopal conferences and the 2 Eastern Catholic Churches sui iuris on the African continent, as well as those of the 25 Departments of the Roman Curia and the union of Superiors General. Its content also includes observations from various ecclesial institutions and Christ's faithful, responsible for evangelization and human promotion in Africa.[13]

What is evident here is that there was an attempt to ascertain the *sensus fidelium*—that is, the sense of the faith of the faithful on the matters pertinent to the theme of the synod. In fact, there was more to this consultation than the above quotation indicates. Catholics all over Africa were given the chance at the level either of the parish or of the base Christian communities, where applicable, to discuss the *Lineamenta* and to offer input into the questions submitted to the diocesan leaders and eventually to the national episcopal conferences for the *Lineamenta*. When the synod participants were determined, it was clear that efforts had been made to include as many voices and experiences as possible in the actual deliberations of the synod. All this goes to show the inclusive sense of church that was evident in the whole synodal process.

THE SECOND AFRICAN SYNOD: MAIN THEMES

The First African Synod was focused on one priority: mission. Thus there were discussions on various aspects of mission, such as proclamation, dialogue, justice and peace, communication, inculturation. Borrowing from *Gaudium et Spes* the synod saw the church in Africa as the family of God in Africa; a family made so by one faith, one baptism, one Lord, and sharing a bond on the basis of the blood of Christ into whom we are all baptized into this family. There was a concerted attempt at this synod to stress the unity of Christians, and to show that, as the late Archbishop Albert Obiefuna of Onitsha at the time quipped, "The waters of baptism are thicker than the blood of ethnicity." *So what?*

Reading through the apostolic exhortation (*Ecclesia in Africa*) is-sued by Pope John Paul II after this synod, one is struck by the sense of optimism that characterized the synod. Two remarkable passages from *Ecclesia in Africa* illustrate this point. In number 6 of this text we hear the pope exhorting the African church to embark on its mis-sion with optimism: "It seems that the 'hour of Africa' has come, a favorable time which urgently invites Christ's messengers to launch out into the deep and to cast their nets for the catch. . . . Today, the Church of Africa, joyful and grateful for having received the faith, must pursue its evangelizing mission" (EA 6). In another striking pas-sage the pope talks of the first synod as one of resurrection and hope:

> This was indeed a Synod of Resurrection and Hope, as the Synod Fathers joyfully and enthusiastically declared in the opening words of their *Message* to the People of God. They are words which I willingly make my own: "Like Mary Magdalene on the morning of the Resurrection, like the disciples at Emmaus with burning hearts and enlightened minds, the Special Synod for Africa, Madagascar and the Islands proclaims: *Christ, our Hope, is risen. He has met us, has walked along with us.* He has explained the Scriptures to us. Here is what he said to us: 'I am the First and the Last, I am the Living One; I was dead, and behold, I am alive for ever and ever and I hold the keys of death and of the abode of the dead' (Rev. 1:17–18). . . . And as Saint John at Patmos during par-ticularly difficult times received prophecies of hope for the People of God, we also announce a message of hope. At this time when so much fratricidal hate inspired by political interests is tearing our peoples apart, when the burden of the international debt and currency devaluation is crushing them, we, the Bishops of Africa, together with all the participants in this holy Synod, united with the Holy Father and with all our Brothers in the Episcopate who elected us, we want to say a word of hope and encouragement to you, Family of God in Africa, to you, the Family of God all over the world: *Christ our Hope is alive; we shall live!*" (EA 11)

Remarkably, these passages were authored right after the Rwan-dan genocides of 1994! Although these events cast a long shadow on the mood of the synod, they did not seem to have dimmed the faith of the synod fathers in the possibility of what then-president Thabo Mbeki of South Africa would later dub the "African Renaissance." The synod fathers knew that all was not yet well with Africa, and if they needed any reminder they did not have far to look: many African countries were then under military dictatorship, Rwanda was witnessing great carnage, Liberia was unstable. Nevertheless, they could look around and see the African church and civic societies everywhere stirring to take control of their destiny and their continent. After all, they had recent examples in various countries of Eastern Europe to draw from. There was hope. God is alive, and a church with firm hope in the resurrection could provide the impetus for a true African renaissance in which cultures would be transformed and made more Christian and more humane through the project of inculturation; peace would be achievable through dialogue with all aspects of society and with Islam; and the mission of the church to bring salvation to the entire continent could be achieved through effective use of modern means of communication, such as the radio, television, and so on.

The second synod of Africa had a tone remarkably different from that of the first. The tone is somber. Consider, for example, this line from the "Message" (*Nuntius*) that the synod issued at the end of its gathering: "We live in a world full of contradictions and deep crisis. . . . In all this, Africa is the most hit. Rich in human and natural resources many of our people are still left to wallow in poverty and misery, wars and conflicts, crisis and chaos. These are very rarely caused by natural disasters. They are largely due to human decisions and activities by people who have no regard for the common good and this often through a tragic complicity and criminal conspiracy of local leaders and foreign interests."[14] This subdued quality is even more evident in the homily the pope gave at the opening Mass of the synod in which he warned that the "deep sense of God" that makes the continent "the repository of an inestimable treasure for the whole world" is itself under attack from at least two dangerous pathologies: (1) a practical materialism, combined with relativist and nihilist thinking; and (2) a "religious fundamentalism, mixed with political and economic interests by which groups who follow various religious creeds are spreading throughout the continent of Africa: they do so in God's name, but follow a logic that is opposed to divine logic, that is, teaching and practicing not love and respect for freedom, but intolerance and violence."

This homily was a warning to all that Africa is in danger on various fronts; at stake is the very survival of the continent as a distinct cultural, religious, and political entity.

In his postsynodal exhortation the pope continues on this somber note, writing of the "various socio-political, ethnic, economic and ecological situations that Africans face daily and that cannot be ignored."[15] Among these are "fratricidal conflicts between ethnic groups," and rivalries and "new forms of enslavement and colonization which leave a painful scar on Africa's memory."[16] Like the rest of the world, Africa is experiencing a culture shock that strikes at the age-old foundations and social life, sometimes making it hard to come to terms with modernity (*Africae Munus* 11). All these problems are creating an "anthropological crisis" in Africa. The only way out is through dialogue "among the members of Africa's constituent religious, social, political, economic, cultural and scientific communities." Such dialogue would help Africa "to rediscover and promote a concept of the person and his or her relationship with reality that is a fruit of the profound spiritual renewal" (AM 11). For *Africae Munus* then the path to reconciliation in Africa must begin with conversion that is ongoing and deep (AM 32). Reconciliation, together with justice, adds to the essential premise of peace, which to some extent also defines its nature (AM 17). Because reconciliation is a prepolitical concept and reality, it is of the greatest importance for politics itself, for "unless the power of reconciliation is created in people's hearts, political commitment to peace lacks its inner premise" (AM 19).

Reconciliation springs from the grace and love of God made manifest in the Lord Jesus Christ. It is God himself who initiates the restoration of the relationship with him that has been damaged or even broken by human sinfulness. In Christ, God offers us reconciliation on two levels: through communion with God himself, and by making the reconciled community ambassadors of reconciliation among humanity. "Reconciliation then, is not limited to God's plan to draw estranged and sinful humanity to himself in Christ through the forgiveness of sins and out of love. It is also the restoration of relationships between people through the settlement of differences and the removal of obstacles to their relationships and their experience of God's love."[17] To be effective, reconciliation in Africa has to be accompanied by "a courageous and honest act: the pursuit of those responsible for the many conflicts on the continent, those who commissioned crimes and those who are involved in trafficking of all kinds and the determination of their responsibility." This is important in order to secure justice for the victims who have had their right to truth and justice taken from them, and to ensure the use of memory in Africa as a way "to build a better society where such tragedies are no longer repeated."

The second leg of the tripod holding up the theme of the Second African Synod is justice. In this regard, the pope indicates as being of primary concern "the plundering of the goods of the earth by a minority to the detriment of entire peoples." This, the pope insists, is unacceptable, because it is immoral. The question here is that of rendering justice to whole peoples in Africa and of giving each person on the continent his or her due. The pope insists that, considering its vast natural and mineral resources, "Africa is capable of providing every individual and every nation on the continent with the basic conditions which would enable them to share in development" (AM 24). For this to happen, the practice of the virtues of solidarity and subsidiarity must take hold on the continent. This means that "the abundance of some compensates for the want of others," and that neither the state nor any larger society "should substitute itself for the initiative and responsibility of individuals and intermediary bodies" (AM 26).

It is an important task of the church to form upright consciences that are "receptive to the demands of justice so as to produce men and women willing to build a just order by their responsible conduct" (AM 26). Even so, the mission of the church is not in the political arena. Rather, it is "to open the world to the religious sense by proclaiming Christ." The church is called therefore "to be a sign and safeguard of the human person's transcendence. She must also enable people to seek the supreme truth regarding their deepest identity and their questions, so that just solutions can be found to their problems" (AM 23). The ultimate aim of the church therefore is to establish a just Christian order in the spirit of the Beatitudes. For the Beatitudes, which are built on a revolution of love, "provide a new horizon of justice, inaugurated in the Paschal mystery through which we can become just and build a better world" (AM 26). The spirit of the Beatitudes invites everyone to give preferential attention to the poor, the hungry, the sick, the stranger, the immigrant, the refugee, and all other poor of the community.

In choosing the famous Pauline passage on reconciliation from 2 Corinthians 5:17–20 as its theme for the synod, the African church was acknowledging the need for healing many relationships in Africa, both vertically and horizontally. Many peoples and institutions are at odds with each other, and there is much lack of justice on the continent, hence the lack of peace and progress. This Corinthian passage, taken together with that in Matthew 5:13 and 14, implies a certain self-understanding of the church as a community with a mission of reconciliation to Africa. The church was thus inviting itself to rise up to its duty as ambassador of reconciliation through peace and justice in the entire continent.

Ecclesiology

The Second African Synod was therefore very much an ecclesiological synod. Although it did not set out to elaborate a new ecclesiology, the synod spent a lot of time discussing the nature, mission, and spirituality of ecclesial communion in Africa. The African church at this second synod was searching openly and sincerely for ways to understand its nature as a church and its mission in relation to the world around it and in service to the world around it. The emerging picture thus resembles those of the church in *Lumen Gentium* and *Gaudium et Spes* rolled into one. As in *Lumen Gentium* this church, the family of God in Africa, during this synod took a good look at its various constitutive elements to see how they relate or can relate to each other in service of reconciliation, justice, and peace on the continent. There were two broad parts to this search. The first concerned the internal life of the church. In this regard, there was a lot of discussion on the need for ongoing conversion at all levels in the church; the need to find ways to live justly in the church and among all entities in the church; the need to find ways to ensure effective involvement of all the members of the church in the church; the need to find ways not only to bring more people into the church in Africa, but also to keep them there as fully active and participating members; and the need to respect the various competences of the constitutive elements. Hence, there were discussions on the role of bishops, priests, laity, deacons, consecrated persons, catechists, and others as agents of reconciliation, justice, and peace and in the work of evangelization.

Pope Benedict XVI devotes considerable space in his postsynodal exhortation to the role of these various constitutive parts of the church in promoting peace, justice, and reconciliation in Africa.[18] Proposition 3[19] maintains that to be effective as an agent of reconciliation the church as such must preserve communion within and among all its constituent entities. Ecclesial communion must be evident "in the Bishops' effective and affective collegiality in their Ecclesiastical Provinces and at the national, regional, continental and international levels."[20] Pope Benedict XVI reinforced the thesis of this proposition when he insisted that the mission of the church in Africa as identified by the synod "will only become a reality if the Church acts, on the one hand, under the guidance of the Holy Spirit, and on the other, as a single body, to use the image of St. Paul, who presents these two conditions in an integrated way" (AM 97). In numbers 106 and 107, the pope builds on the widespread concern, already captured in proposition 3, for more effective regional bodies like SECAM (the Symposium of Episcopal Conferences of Africa and Madagascar) and COMSAM (Confederation of the Conferences of Major Superiors of Africa and Madagascar). He then directs that these continental and regional groupings try to cooperate more closely in the work of evangelization, reconciliation, and peace in Africa "in order to ensure greater visibility, coherence and effectiveness to the Church's pastoral activity" on the continent (AM 106). The pope and the synod were aware that, as Pope Paul VI put it long ago, preaching alone does not move people anymore; rather, the world is moved by those who live what they preach. Speaking in the same vein, an earlier synod counseled that "everyone who ventures to speak to people about justice must first be just in their eyes."[21] The church in Africa cannot be an effective and credible agent of reconciliation, justice, and peace if it is lacking in these qualities and virtues within itself.

Conversion for the effective ministry of reconciliation is not just a structural issue. There are two aspects to the question of conversion: personal and communal. Since people make up the church, the most important conversion is that of the heart of the individual member of the church. An essential means for reconciliation is through the sacrament of penance, and there was considerable discussion on the synod floor of the need to help believers find their way back to this very important sacrament. Propositions 8 and 9 not only stress this need, but

also, very significantly, call for Africa-wide days or even a year of reconciliation during which private and communal acts of reconciliation
would be undertaken and Christians would "ask God for special par-
don for all hurts and wounds inflicted upon each other." Although
Pope Benedict XVI stopped short of calling for a continental day or
year of penance, he recommended "a serious study of traditional African reconciliation ceremonies in order to evaluate their positive aspects
and limitations" (AM 33). Although these traditional forms cannot
take the place of the sacrament of reconciliation, they might contain
pedagogical insights that could be usefully employed to help Christians
on the continent to "open themselves more deeply and more truly to
Christ, the one great Mediator, and to receive the grace of the sacrament of Penance" (AM 33).

In reflecting on the need for a church that is united and at peace in
its various constitutive parts in and for Africa, the pope believes that
the church is a sentinel called to make the voice of Christ heard. In response to its mission, the church "feels the duty to be present wherever
human suffering exists and to make heard the silent cry of the innocent
who suffer persecution, or of peoples whose governments mortgage
the present and future for personal interests" (AM 30). The blood of
Christ shed for us "becomes through Baptism, the principle of a new
fraternity." This fraternity is brought and held together in communion
through the Eucharist. The church, as a communion and community
of individuals in whose veins there circulates "the very blood of Christ
who makes us children of God, [and] members of God's family, is the
very antitheses of division, tribalism, racism and ethnocentrism (cf.
Gal. 3:26–28)" (AM 41). In Africa, which is torn by all sorts of division, the church "must clearly point out the path towards Christ. She
must show how to live, in total fidelity to Christ" (AM 97). God has
endowed the church with different gifts in all its members. The various
members of the church should therefore put these various gifts to use
for the common good. "The gifts given by the Lord to each — bishops,
priests, deacons and religious, catechists and lay people — must all
contribute to harmony, communion and peace in the Church herself
and in the society" (AM 97).

In *Lumen Gentium*, and in some other documents of that council, the Second Vatican Council employs several descriptive terms to
put across its understandings of the church. The church is sometimes

described as a servant, a hierarchical community, a communion, the new Israel of God, the people of God, an eschatological community, and so forth. One of these metaphors is always more operative in a given church at any given time than the others. The self-understanding of any particular church determines to a large extent what kind of church there is in a given place in a particular era. It may be recalled that the theme's subtitle for the Second African Synod is "You are the salt of the earth . . . You are the light of the world" (Matt. 5:13, 14). What happened at this synod was the unfolding of a church that is beginning to appreciate itself as a leaven: the church of the Second African Synod was seriously looking for ways to be effectively salt and light to the African continent. Like the Jerusalem church, the church of the Second African Synod was taking the project of inculturation seriously by searching out conditions that would make the faith a living and life-giving experience for Africans. In addition to individual conversion and holiness was the need to put in place structures, or strengthen existing mechanisms, for the task of promoting evangelization, peace, and reconciliation.

The ecclesiology of the Second African Synod is in some ways also akin to that of *Gaudium et Spes*. Two aspects merit mentioning here. First, as in *Gaudium et Spes*, the African church at this synod understood itself to be intimately linked with humanity (especially in Africa) and its history (GS 1), even though "it has a saving and eschatological purpose that can only be attained in the future world." The second point follows from the first. Thus, "although the role of the Church is primarily a religious one, from this religious mission comes 'a light and energy which can serve to structure and consolidate the human community according to the divine law'" (GS 42).[22] The church's religious ministry is to be fulfilled in a way "that protects human dignity, fosters human rights and contributes to the unity of the human family."[23] This aspect of the understanding of the church is evident in the extensive discussion on politics and good governance (pp. 23, 24; AM 81, 82), elections (p. 25), African intergovernmental and diplomatic activity, the arms trade, peace, and the role the church must play either by itself or through joint action with others to bring about a "just order" that would become "a major instrument at the service of reconciliation, justice and peace" (AM 81). In order to bring about such an order, "the Church in Africa must help to build up society in cooperation with government authorities and public and private institutions that are engaged in building up the common good" (AM 81, p. 24).

Leadership and Related Issues

Politics, governance, public service, and other such matters received a good deal of attention on the main floor of the synod, in the discussions of the various small groups, and in the reports of the principal officers of the synod. There was recognition at this synod that, as Chinua Achebe wrote in *The Trouble with Nigeria, much of the trouble with Africa is leadership.* The synod spent a lot of time considering what the church can do to help this situation. It was clear that Catholics and other Christian public servants are often no better stewards of the public trust and treasure than others in Africa. Considering that many of these corrupt public officials are members of the various Christian churches in Africa, the synod participants were openly asking, Where have we gone wrong, and what can we do as a church? Aside from exhorting African leaders to play by the rules of democracy, to respect human rights, and to uphold the common good over family, personal, ethnic, political, and sectional interest in their work, the synod also made some concrete proposals as to how the church intends to help reform politics and bring about good governance in Africa. The first was through the conscientization of the citizenry. The synod urged the episcopal conferences "to promote multidimensional programs of civic education; implement programs to foster the formation of a social conscience at all levels; and encourage competent and honest citizens to participate in party politics" (p. 24).

Secondly, and with specific reference to the lay Catholic faithful, the synod stressed the need for intense and ongoing catechesis, which would provide the opportunity "for a conversion of heart." The church would undertake the training of Catholic politicians and those in politics and economic and social leadership positions on the social doctrine of the church, "which can provide them with principles for acting in conformity with the Gospel" (AM 128, p. 36). Priests too would be properly trained not only in the social doctrine of the church; since they often serve as advisers and counselors to the lay faithful who are engaged in the public square, they ought to be conversant with the teaching contained in the texts that provide instructions for their way of life.[24] Third, the church would establish chaplaincies and appoint suitable chaplains for those in public office and at various institutions of higher education on the continent. "The chapel will be, as it were, the heart of those institutions. It will enable students to encounter God and to stand in his sight" (AM 138). Fourth, Catholic universities in Africa are to serve the church "by providing trained personnel, by studying important theological and social questions for the benefit of the church, by developing an African theology, by promoting the work of inculturation, by publishing books and publicizing Catholic truth, by undertaking assignments given by the bishops and by contributing to the scientific study of cultures" (AM 136). Fifth, the synod urged the episcopal conferences at all levels "to establish advocacy bodies to lobby members of parliament, governments and international institutions" as a way the church "can contribute effectively to the formulation of just laws and policies for the people's good" (p. 23). Sixth, the synod urged the groups of bishops to support the African Union's NEPAD[25] peer review mechanism and the review of the Maputo Protocol to ensure that it does not contain anti-life provisions (p. 19).

Dialogue and Collaboration with Other Religions
and Groups of Interest

The search for reconciliation and peace in Africa is a multifaceted concern that involves the church in dialogue with other religions and groups on the continent. In the words of the eleventh proposition from the synod, "Peace in Africa and other parts of the world is very much determined by the relations among religions. . . . Dialogue with other religions, especially Islam and African Traditional Religion, is an integral part of the proclamation of the Gospel and the Church's pastoral activity on behalf of reconciliation and peace." This is a remarkable passage in that it sees reconciliation as integral to the work of evangelization. Peace is necessary. And to sit down to talk to people who do not believe what we believe is not a sign of weakness. Rather, it is a recognition of the plural nature of the African society in which Christians and others live and work. The two religions mentioned

—Perhaps here you could find out these 'six' principals of leadership?

here are not seen as challenges or problems, but as neighbors who are worthy of respect and with whom Christianity could work for peace in Africa. One of the synod fathers acknowledged the progress in Islamic-Christian relations in Africa: "We have made progress in building upon the general sense which Muslims and Christians in Africa have of belonging to the same families, communities and nations. We have learnt to join hands to address common challenges on the basis of commonly shared spiritual and moral values, which, we discover, often with joyful surprise, whenever we open our hearts and minds to one another." This prelate went on to cite the successes Christians and Muslims have had in some joint efforts in Africa: the fight against HIV/AIDS in Uganda, the program to eradicate malaria in Nigeria, and interventions for conflict resolution and peace building in Sierra Leone, Côte d'Ivoire, and Niger.[26]

There are different forms of dialogue. First on the list is ecumenical dialogue, which seeks to direct Christians "towards Christian unity, as we listen assiduously to the word of God, faithful to fraternal communion, the breaking of bread and the prayers." As Pope Benedict XVI points out, a divided Christianity remains a scandal because it contradicts the will of the Divine Master. Even if Christians cannot always agree on the fine points of doctrine, they can at least undertake common works of charity in order to protect Christian religious patrimonies "through which Christ's disciples find the spiritual strength they need for building up the human family" (AM 90). Relations with African Traditional Religion received even greater discussion in this synod. African Christianity has the unique opportunity of having to be in constant dialogue with a primal religion. This opportunity has been lost to European and American Christianity and theologies.[27] The synod fathers were very aware of the gains for Christianity from African Traditional Religion, and the challenges posed by some aspects of the faith and practices of this religion to authentic Christian faith. As a result, they ask for thorough and scientific research on African Traditional Religion in African Catholic universities and in the Catholic universities in Rome where many African Catholic leaders train. Also, they insist that a distinction be made between the culture and the religion in Africa, "especially between the cultural and those *malevolent* programs of sorcery, which cause the break-up and ruin of our families and our societies" (p. 13). The synod asked that action be taken at various levels of the church against those involved in witchcraft and occultism.

Pope Benedict takes up the issue of African Traditional Religion as well in his exhortation. In the one passage in which he deals with inculturation in the African church, he calls for a thorough study of African culture with a view to determining those aspects of the culture that represent an obstacle to "the incarnation of Gospel values, as well as those which promote them" (AM 37). In another passage specifically devoted to African Traditional Religion, the pope calls on Christians to work "to preserve and encourage the spiritual and moral truths found among non-Christians, together with their life and culture" (AM 92).

A third aspect to religious dialogue in Africa involves relations with Islam. In this regard, the synod issued several guidelines on the dialogue with Islam. First, priority must be given to the "dialogue of life and partnership in social matters and reconciliation." The point here is that the dialogue with Islam is not a search for the lowest common denominator of the different faiths. It is not as if Christians were going to that dialogue intent on giving away the central beliefs of their faith, or asking Muslims to do the same, for this is not possible. What is possible is that despite doctrinal differences both faiths can agree on certain points about how to construct a humane and just world where people can live in peace together. Second, the synod directs that efforts be made in the formation programs of priests and religious to provide better knowledge of Islam for these future leaders and teachers of the church. Third, the synod fathers believe that dialogue with Islam, as with other religions in Africa, would provide an opportunity for eradicating or at least minimizing religious intolerance and violence (pp. 11, 12). An important issue that the pope and the synod emphasize is that of religious freedom. In *Africae Munus* the pope issues a direct injunction to Christians on this matter: "I ask the whole Church, through patient dialogue with Muslims, to seek juridical and practical recognition of religious freedom, so that every citizen in Africa may enjoy not only the right to choose his religion freely and to engage in worship, but also the right to freedom of conscience. Religious freedom is the road to peace" (AM 94).

Women

Why is that?

Only one proposition is specially devoted to women in the final list sent to the Holy Father by the synod. A careful study of this proposal reveals an enormous concern about the plight of many African women in church and society. In a very telling passage in his *Relatio Post Disceptationem,* Cardinal Turkson, the relator general of the synod, captured succinctly the feeling of the synod about women in Africa when he asserted that although women are making great strides in some areas in Africa, they remain "underdeveloped resources" in certain countries, "suffering exclusion from social roles, inheritance, education, and decision-making places." They remain "defenseless victims in war zones: victims of polygamous marriages, abused, trafficked for prostitution, etc."[28]

Many women were present at the Second African Synod. Many were auditors, who, like the bishops appointed to the synod, were allowed to make interventions on the synod floor. Some others were invited as experts and made their contribution through working with the relator general and in the small discussion groups that were an essential part of the synod. Women spoke out very clearly and very loudly at this synod. As was widely reported in the media, one of the women speakers at the synod, Sr. Felicia Harry, superior general of Our Lady of Apostles Congregation (O.L.A.), invited the synod fathers to do a two-minute exercise before going to bed and to imagine what a church without women would look like. She argued that there was a need for more collaboration between the ordained and women in the work of evangelizing Africa. "As well as teach catechism to children, decorate parish churches, clean, mend and sew vestments, we the religious in Africa would like to be part of various parish councils. We do not want to remain at the periphery of the main body of the parish, we just want to be equal partners in the Lord's vineyard; we want to share in the Church's responsibility of ensuring reconciliation, peace and justice on our continent."[29] But Sr. Harry's effort was not the most incisive intervention on women. There was a general feeling at this synod that something needs to be done and quickly to enhance the status of African women. Many bishops took the lead in articulating the structural impediments to true emancipation of women in Africa. Hence, there were discussions on marriage customs in Africa

that place undue stress on women, on inheritance rights, and on wid-
owed women and the treatment they receive in some African societies.
With regard to the church there was a lot of soul-searching on how to
bring women on board in those areas of leadership and governance
that are legal in canon law, and there were discussions on providing
theological and other educational opportunities for women. The concerns extended to all categories of women, lay, religious, and single, for
instance. The question of trafficking of women was also raised. Tersely
worded as it is, proposition 47 captures succinctly the widespread concern of the synod and the determination to do something about the
situation of women in Africa. Among other things, the synod proposed
the creation of shelters for abused women; close collaboration between
various episcopal conferences and other entities to stop the trafficking
of women; greater integration of women into church structures and
decision-making processes; setting up of diocesan commissions at various levels of the church in Africa to address women's issues and to
help them carry out their work in church and society; and the setting
up of a study commission on women in the church, within the pontifical council for the family (p. 47).

In *Africae Munus*, the pope states some of the basic assumptions
that lie behind the synod's and indeed the church's teaching on
women. First is the recognition that both men and women are made
in the image and likeness of God and therefore are equal in human
personhood and dignity as human beings. Secondly, "the church has a
duty to contribute to the recognition and liberation of women, following the example of Christ's own esteem for them (cf. Mt. 15:21–28;
Lk. 7:37–50; 8:1–3; 10:38–42; Jn. 4:7–42)." Thus, as the pope argues, giving women opportunities to make their voices heard and to
express their talents freely in whatever way possible "would enable
them to occupy a place in society equal to that of men—without con-
fusing or conflating the specific character of each—since both men
and women are the 'image' of the Creator (cf. Gen. 1:27)" (AM 58). In
Pope Benedict's exhortation, women are not simply passive subjects.
They are also moral agents with responsibilities to themselves, their
families, their church, and their world. Thus, they have the duty to acquire and grow in knowledge, secular and religious; "to engage with
discernment in the various projects involving women"; to defend life at
all its stages; to help young girls through counsel and example "so that

they may approach adult life serenely"; to support one another; to show respect to the elderly in our midst; to help the church create "a human ecology" through their sympathetic love, friendly and thoughtful demeanor; and to instill in their children all the necessary values they need for life in today's world. In this way they will be able to "foster the reconciliation of individuals and communities" (AM 59).

Some Other Pressing Moral Concerns

There is sense in which everything discussed at the Second African Synod was a moral issue. However, for the sake of convenience I have decided to group some particular topics under this heading since they are obviously of normative concern. The first concerns what was referred to at the synod as toxic elements or viruses that were being foisted on Africa from foreign sources. The first indication of this concern came from the widely reported homily of the Holy Father, Pope Benedict XVI, at the opening Mass of the synod. Other participants took up this issue as well. For example, Archbishop Robert Sarah[30] expressed concern in his presentation with what he referred to as a new gender theory being imported into Africa that was intent on doing away with traditional truths about the spousal identity of men and women in marriage, the complementary nature of this relationship between men and women in marriage, the issue of maternity and paternity in the human family, and procreation.[31] This gender ideology also denies the sexual classification into male and female as intrinsic to human biological identity. On the contrary, it posits that the identification of male and female is only a social construct with no intrinsic worth except as an oppressive cultural imposition that does not allow the individual to choose his or her sexual orientation and makes homosexuality an open and culturally acceptable lifestyle. Sarah was concerned that this gender ideology is being imposed on Africans through the manipulation of the legislative process and through privileged access to the media by which information on homosexuality, abortion, and contraception is spread, ostensibly in the name of "reproductive health" for women and in the name of civil rights for homosexual persons. He believes that the gender ideology being peddled by these foreign agencies is contrary to African culture and to the gospel, and is undermining the view of family and married life that Africans have nurtured and preserved intact until the present time, with this new ideology thus destabilizing African societies.

The synod also expressed concerns regarding negative foreign influences on Africa when in the *Nuntius* it denounced "all surreptitious attempts to destroy and undermine the precious African value of family and human life."[32] The synod had particularly harsh words for the Maputo Protocol (technically known as "The Protocol to the African Charter on Human and Peoples' Rights on the Rights of Women in Africa," but called the "Maputo Protocol" because it was adopted during a 2003 summit in the Mozambique capital city).[33] Although the fathers of the synod were in agreement with most of the rights the protocol seeks to secure for women, they rejected outright article 14, which is devoted to health and reproductive rights, asserting a right to abortion "in cases of sexual assault, rape, incest, and where and when the continued pregnancy endangers the mental and physical health of the mother or the life of the mother or the fetus."[34] The *Nuntius* refers to this article as "obnoxious," and the final list of propositions condemned the position of the protocol on abortion while maintaining that the value and dignity of human life must be protected "from the moment of conception to natural death" (p. 20). In his postsynodal exhortation Pope Benedict XVI pointed out that the position of the church on abortion is unambiguous. "The Child in his or her mother's womb is a human life which must be protected. Abortion, which is the destruction of an innocent unborn child, is contrary to God's will, for the value and dignity of human life must be protected from conception to natural death" (AM 70). And although many people and groups reject or oppose the church's view on this matter, the church, the pope insists, must not fear hostility or unpopularity or agree to any compromise that would make it conform to the thinking "of this world" on this matter (AM 71).

Other specifically moral issues of concern to the synod include migration, poverty, the arms trade, drugs and substance abuse, capital punishment, treatment of prisoners, religious liberty, ethnicity, concern for the environment, mineral resources, and land and water resources. The synod was aware that several issues are at the root of the challenges and problems in these areas. These include bad governance, injustice, and, in some cases, negative effects of globalization. In this situation, the synod called for conversion. For, as the *Nuntius* points out, true reconciliation, justice, and peace can come only "from a change of heart, and a change of heart comes from conversion to the Gospel."[35] Conversion is needed in the way Africa treats its prison population (p. 54), disabled persons, the environment, and so on.

External or foreign influence on Africa and the way it seeks to affect or alter the African traditional ethos in some areas, especially in matters relating to sex, sexuality, family, and reproduction, has been a constant concern for African church leaders. These are very controversial matters, and Catholic moral theologians sometimes disagree on how to respond to them without succumbing to relativism or situational ethics or utilitarianism. But the natural moral law has a context. Even though it holds and teaches eternal immutable truths, these truths cannot be discerned in a vacuum. Should Africans have no access to the Internet or television or travel? Are Africans incapable of deciding for themselves what is authentic and true in relation to their traditions and cultural memory? Have Africans escaped "secularism" and "secularization" altogether? Many contemporary Africans navigate between the West (whether London or New York or Boston or Chicago or Paris or Dublin or Madrid or Munich) and their respective countries and home villages and cultural demands (e.g., initiation or covenant rites) with ease and thoroughgoing sophistication. As I indicated in chapter 1, the subjects of inculturation today are today's Africans in their contemporary contexts, and not an imaginary set of Africans who do not exist anymore or live in contexts that are nonexistent. Ethical reasoning is difficult work for all of us human beings—no matter our cultures, traditions, religious practices, countries, and diverse backgrounds and personal, familial, and work experiences. To reason well ethically, we require direction, guidance, and encouragement, appropriate to the various stages of our human and personal development. Formation of conscience is a delicate and necessary task. Thus, beyond bemoaning these external influences, the African church at its different levels ought to make every effort to catechize the faithful, at their various levels, in their varying degrees of sophistication, and in their differing living conditions and situations.

Finally, what has been presented so far does not even begin to do justice to the enormity and scope of work undertaken by the Second African Synod, nor has it exhausted the pope's teaching in his postsynodal exhortation. For example, nothing has been mentioned about the discussions on the economy, HIV/AIDS, the family, youth, malaria, the media, and education. All these topics were significantly mentioned by the pope and the synod and would need a whole book to digest. The discussion so far is simply meant to show the extent of the concern the second synod and the entire church have for the present and the future of Africa. Here is how I put it in a letter I sent to some friends from Rome during the synod:

> Over these past three weeks I have seen a church which is aware of the great gifts which it has been given by God. I have seen a Church which is aware that it has something to offer to Africa and to the world. I have seen a Church which has grown in greater understanding of its role as leaven or catalyst. I heard in that hall a great cry of disappointment for the Church's failure so far to live up to its promise in Africa, for Africa and for the whole world. I heard a Church leadership which is determined as ever to be light and leaven and to seek cooperation in doing so with other African and international entities. There is a great sense of urgency here for people to go home and begin the work of the "new Pentecost," as this synod has been variously described.
>
> During a press conference at the end of the disputed elections which brought George W. Bush to power in 2000 a reporter said to President Clinton, in these or similar words: "Mr. President, the American people have spoken!" Clinton responded quickly, "Yes, but we have yet to figure out what they said!" Every synod as an ecclesial event is packed with meaning. Although the Spirit has spoken, it will take ages and a lot of hard work to understand more clearly what the Spirit said through this synod to the churches of Africa and to bring its ideas to fruition.

A Final Word

The African synods are indeed theologically interesting and significant, apart from the challenges they present for moral theology. What they show is that despite its obvious flaws and growing pains, the church is the one international organization that actually listens to Africa and accepts it and is allowing a center of gravity shift to take place, however slowly. These two synods are the enactment of a real solidarity, a real communion formed on real ideals. And because of these ideals the Catholic Church is one of the only truly credible worldwide institutions in Africa, credible locally, as local church, not as a global conglomerate. More than any other organization with Western roots the church seems to have kicked the imperialist addiction in favor of communion. And it is important to remember that in this case, the worldwide and long-term stature of the church offers one way for Africa actually to be connected, transpolitically and across time, to the wider world. It is the church, which, after all, proclaims herself provisional, in the sense that she is "on pilgrimage" to an eschatological fulfillment, which explicitly refuses to absolutize herself. She is "sacrament," the Kingdom present in "mystery," and not fulfillment and clarity of beatific vision. That is why she is so beautiful, and a true locus of renewal, both potential and actual, in Africa and for Africans, even for those who are not Christian. She is witness, sign, and sacrament of their transcendent dignity too.

GO AND DO LIKEWISE

Some essential features of a moral theology that is both Christian and African have emerged from our discussion so far in this book: as ethics, African Christian ethics pays attention to the rigors and rules of morality as do all other types of ethics; as Christian ethics it is built on firm Christian foundations concerning God, the human person, and reality in general and on the teachings and example of the Lord Jesus. As Christian ethics done from a Catholic perspective, moral theology in the African context takes the church in all its aspects into account in deliberating on matters concerning ethical conduct, moral reasoning, and moral judgments. Finally, because African moral theology is Christian ethics done in the African setting, it takes into account the lived experiences and realities of the peoples of Africa. In this regard, then, African Christian ethics is dialogical and an ethics with big ears.[36] It is in dialogue with African tradition and with the Christian tradition all at once. I have tried so far to show the terms on which the dialogue between African tradition and the Christian tradition has gone or the lines along which it can proceed. I have also contended that the African ethical tradition has more to learn about the foundations of a

Christian theological ethic that is truly African than the Christian tradition properly so-called. Even though in this book I have given pride of place to what African ethics can learn from Christian ethical traditions, I have tried as well to stress the fact that Christian ethical tradition acknowledges whatever is good among various peoples, including and especially in African traditional moral reasoning. This is why I have taken issue with those African theologians who insist that natural law reasoning is not an aspect of African Christian ethics because, in their view, it is a Western imposition. I have argued that, to the contrary, natural law is a human mode of reasoning that is at home in all cultures and traditions where people have an innate sense of right and wrong, what is good and bad, what is sensible and what is nonsensical. I have shown repeatedly the terms on which the dialogue between African traditional ethics and Christian theological ethics has proceeded. There is therefore no further need for elaboration on this matter. All that needs to be emphasized once again is that African Traditional Religion as the main interlocutor with African Christian ethics in Africa is both a blessing for and in some instances a restriction on African theological ethics. Some of the blessings include the following: an ever-present sense of the divine which ensures that theological ethics in Africa remains theological and grounded on firm metaphysical and transcendental foundations; fundamental dispositions about life and therefore about ethics as a search for what constitutes the good life or what enhances life; the sacredness of the human person and of all reality in general. All these make it possible for the African theologian to do his or her work as a Christian ethicist without having to reinvent the wheel, so to speak, or being distracted by extreme secularist concerns. On the other hand, the restricting marks of African religions on African Christian ethics are also obvious. These include a limited notion of God, which, although it may have been adequate for another time or for other purposes, can no longer adequately express the Christian view of reality; the operative understanding of the notion of the human person in African Traditional Religion, which, as has been shown in this book, also can no longer fully carry the weight of Christian ethical reasoning because it is based on a limited anthropology.

Since the human person is also the way of the church, the church everywhere, and particularly in our case, Africa, we must be aware of the situation of the human person in all of his or her aspects. The church must be aware of the threats to the human person—those things that conspire to negate life or to make it less human. The church must, as *Gaudium et Spes* puts it, identify with the joys, the anguish, and aspirations of the human person in every age and place. The church in Africa has shown a deep awareness of her mission in this regard, as we have seen in this chapter. For its part, African Christian ethics, in collaboration with the rest of the church, must be at the forefront of the search for remedies and solutions to the threats to life in Africa. To play such a role effectively African Christian ethics can no longer rely on the limited assumptions about the human person which have characterized its discourse so far. These assumptions, which come largely from African Traditional Religion and African traditions, are largely sound. The only problem, however, and a major one, is that they are severely limited and can no longer adequately handle the expectations and understandings of the human person which arise from Christian faith and convictions and from the realities of life informed both by this faith and by life in the world today. Pope Benedict XVI is therefore right on the mark when in his postsynodal exhortation he calls on Africa to rediscover and promote a new concept of the human person. As he notes, again accurately, African renewal must begin with a renewal of anthropology on the continent. It has been my contention in this book, at least from a Christian point of view, that this renewal is possible only when we take into consideration the expanded meaning and horizon of the human person which Christian anthropology offers.

The African as subject and agent of morality is today being affected by much more than African Traditional Religion. Therefore, the latter alone can no longer assume or retain the pride of place earlier generations of Christian theologians and ethicists have tended to give it. This is not to say that its role as an essential interlocutor must be or can be taken by another. This is not possible, given the reality of African Traditional Religion not only as a living religion that is in constant interaction with Christianity in Africa, but also because it is still in many respects intertwined with the tradition and cultures of African societies and peoples. To a large extent, its influence is salutary and indicative of a possible alternative to the dry and secular reading of reality prompted by the continuing influence of the Enlightenment on Western Christian theological ethics. Much more than African Traditional Religion, African Christian ethics is being affected by a whole host of other realities that it must pay attention to, learn from, challenge, or be challenged by, if it is to stay relevant to the church of Africa and to the Christian theological world in general. The phenomenon generally referred to as globalization is forcing the movement of peoples and ideas around the world at a dizzying rate. The reality of the world as "a single place" which this phenomenon entails means that African populations are no longer listening just to religions, Christian or traditional, for guidance for their lives; there are many other voices with competing claims. The question then is how ethics can be done in an Africa that has become very plural in its religious affiliations, more open to secular forces and influences, increasingly urban—an Africa where a significant proportion of the citizenry is largely unchurched or scarcely touched by any religions, despite the obvious boom in religious sentiments, affiliations, and attendance on the continent. The point is that even though dialogue with ATR remains a sine qua non for any Christian theological ethics in Africa, it can no longer claim the complete attention of African moral theologians as it once did. In this view of the expanded horizon for the operation of African theological ethics, the latter must participate in the solutions to problems that arise today on the African continent as a result of the plural nature of life on the continent.

As has already been noted, the Second African Synod drew attention to some of the moral and social issues of concern to the African church as well as to the generality of Africans today: migration; the flawed use and exercise of political power; economic mismanagement and abuse of funds at all levels of public life; the debt burden; the importation of "lifestyles and values, attitudes, values, etc. which destabilize" Africa; and new trends that attack traditional family systems, threatening their stability and very existence by increasingly proposing alternative unions and relationships "devoid of the concept of lasting commitments, non-heterosexual in character and without the aim of procreation."[37] Other moral challenges include drugs and arms trafficking, environmental degradation, and war. The reality of life in Africa thus portrayed widens the scope of interest for Christian ethics today. In addition to the initial question of how the gospel can be related to African culture, one can include the following: How can moral theology contribute to the search for more humane living in densely populated cities of Africa? How can moral theology contribute to finding solutions to the miserable and poverty-stricken situation in Africa's cities? How can Christian ethics contribute positively to the lives of desperate and unemployed youth in Africa's cities? How can moral theology that is truly Christian help provide healing to the ethnically divided populations of Africa's nations? How can Christian ethics supply insights for answers to the endemic violence in many African situations? How can Christian ethics help Africans live and work in the very religiously plural situations of African societies? The questions are legion.

At the end of his parable about the Good Samaritan Jesus asks the lawyer who had initially asked him to explain who the neighbor was, which of the characters in the story had proved himself a neighbor to the man who had fallen into the hands of the robbers. The response was "the one who had shown him mercy. Jesus said to him, 'Go and do likewise'" (Luke 10:37). Christian ethics is a response ethics. It is a response to God's loving initiative in Jesus. In this sense then Christian ethics is an ethics of discipleship. To be a disciple of Jesus "is to take seriously what Jesus took seriously."[38] And what did Jesus take seriously? From our analysis of the parables and of his teaching and praxis, we can see that Jesus took God seriously; he took the human person seriously, especially as poor, vulnerable, sinner, outcast; he took women seriously as daughters and creatures of God; and he took reconciliation seriously. African ethics must in this way also be an ethics of discipleship. Finally, Catholic moral theology in Africa "must be a collaborative venture, a critical enterprise, and a discipline with big ears that are attuned to the movement of ideas within all parts of the worldwide church and the global community."[39] As a critical inquiry, it must not allow itself "simply to validate cultural patterns," since all cultures "because they are human creations, bear the imprint of their makers," for good or for ill. As a discipline with big ears it must be open to good insights from as many sources as possible, even though it must eventually test their soundness by exposing them to the gospel and the tradition of the church. As a collaborative venture, African moral theology must be prepared to enter into relationships of friendship with other forms of ethical discourse and with all other entities who are genuinely seeking the good of the human person integrally and adequately considered in Africa.

NOTES

Introduction

1. Walbert Bühlmann, *The Coming of the Third Church: An Analysis of the Present and Future of the Church* (Slough, UK: St. Paul Publications, 1976), p. 20.

2. Andrew F. Walls, *The Missionary Movement in Christian History: Studies in the Transmission of Faith* (Maryknoll, NY: Orbis Books; Edinburgh: T & T Clark, 1996), p. 149.

3. Ibid., p. 146.

Chapter 1. African Christian Theology

1. Desmond Tutu, "Whither African Theology?," in *Christianity in Independent Africa,* ed. Edward Fasholé-Luke, Richard Gray, Adrian Hastings, and Godwin Tasie (Bloomington: Indiana University Press, 1979), p. 368.

2. Edward W. Fasholé-Luke, "The Quest for an African Christian Theology," *Ecumenical Review* 27:3 (July 1975): p. 263.

3. Tutu, "Whither African Theology?," p. 368.

4. Bernard Lonergan, "Theology in Its New Context," in *A Second Collection: Papers by Bernard J. F. Lonergan, S.J.,* ed. William F. J. Ryan and Bernard J. Tyrell (London: Darton, Longman and Todd, 1970), p. 58.

5. Edward Schillebeeckx, *Christ: The Experience of Jesus as Lord* (New York: Seabury Press, 1980), p. 650.

6. Robert Schreiter, *Constructing Local Theologies* (Maryknoll, NY: Orbis Books, 1985), p. 4.

7. Ibid., p. 3.

8. Ibid., pp. 22 ff.

9. Onuorah Nzekwu, *Blade among the Boys* (London: Heinemann, 1972), p. 139.

10. Peter Sarpong, "Christianity Should Be Africanized, Not Africa Christianized," *AFER* (1975): p. 22.

11. Kwame Bediako, *Theology and Identity: The Impact of Culture upon Christian Thought in the Second Century and in Modern Africa* (1992; Cumbria, UK: Regnum Books, 1999), p. 237.

12. Tutu, "Whither African Theology?," p. 366.

13. Andrew Walls, "Africa and Christian Identity," *Mission Focus* 6:7 (1978): p. 13.

14. Justin Ukpong, *African Theologies Now: A Profile* (Eldoret, Kenya: Gaba Publications, 1984), p. 9.

15. Anselm of Canterbury, *The Proslogion*, http://www.fordham.edu/halsall/basis/anselm-proslogium.asp.

16. John Macquarie, *Thinking about God* (London: SCM Press, 1975), p. 7.

17. Ibid., p. 8.

18. James C. Okoye, "African Theology," in *Dictionary of Mission: Theology, History, Perspectives*, ed. Karl Müller, Theo Sundermeier, Stephen B. Bevans, and Richard H. Bliese (Maryknoll, NY: Orbis Books, 1997), p. 1.

19. See William O'Neil, "African Moral Theology," *Theological Studies* 62 (2001): pp. 122–39.

20. Adrian Hastings, *African Christianity* (New York: Seabury Press, 1976), pp. 50–51.

21. Bediako, *Theology and Identity*, p. 1.

22. We cannot go into too much detail on these subjects here, nor can we cover all epochs and all segments of African history in these introductory remarks. To be comprehensive in our treatment we would have to extend our discussion to the periods before Christianity and the relationship of Africa with the whole known world. This would include the role of Egypt in world history and the interaction of all North Africa with other civilizations such as the Persian Empire and the Roman Empire. With regard to Rome, for example, we know of the continued interaction between Rome and North Africa up until the birth of Christianity and subsequently Islam. So, I will limit the discussion to the history of Africa from about the seventh century up until now to buttress my assertion that Africans have long had to live with the clash of various traditions on the African continent and with the results of these various encounters. I am also interested mostly in Africa south of the Sahara, and will isolate three well-known historical markers on the African continent for discussion.

23. Ali Mazrui, *The Africans: A Triple Heritage* (London: BBC Publications, 1986), p. 12.

24. See Basil Davidson, *Africa in History: Themes and Outlines* (Frogmore, UK: Paladin Books, 1974), pp. 194–96.

25. Sir Frederick D. Lugard, *The Dual Mandate in British Tropical Africa* (Edinburgh and London: William Blackwood and Sons, 1923), p. 613.

26. Mazrui, *The Triple Heritage*, p. 13.

27. Ogbu Kalu, *African Pentecostalism: An Introduction* (Oxford: Oxford University Press, 2008), p. viii.

28. Allan H. Anderson, *African Reformation: African Initiated Christianity in the 20th Century* (Trenton, NJ, and Asmara, Eritrea: Africa World Press, 2001), p. 5.

29. I have taken the liberty of reproducing this long passage from the Nigerian scholar Mathew Kukah to show the origins and the depth of some of the ethnically charged situations that continue to bedevil the Great Lakes region of Africa. See Hassan Mathew Kukah, *The Fractured Microcosm: The African Condition and the Search for Moral Balance in the New World Order*, Faculty of Social Sciences Guest Series, no. 1 (Lagos, Nigeria: Lagos State University Press, 1998), pp. 14–15.

30. See James Chukwuma Okoye, *Scripture in the Church: The Synod on the Word of God* (Collegeville, MN: Liturgical Press, 2011), pp. 25–27.

31. Fasholé-Luke, "The Quest for an African Christian Theology," p. 263.

32. Hastings, *African Christianity*, pp. 50–51.

33. Edward Fasholé-Luke, Introduction, *Christianity in Independent Africa* (London: R. Collings; Bloomington: Indiana University Press, 1978), p. 357.

34. Fasholé-Luke, "The Quest for an African Theology," p. 265.

35. Emmanuel Katongole, *A Future for Africa: Critical Essays in Christian Social Imagination* (Scranton, PA: University of Scranton Press, 2005), p. 154.

36. Ibid., p. 156.

37. Aylward Shorter, *African Christian Spirituality* (London: Geoffrey Chapman, 1978), p. 21.

38. Kwame Bediako, "Understanding the African Theology in the 20th Century," *Themelios* 20 (1994): p. 17.

39. Kwame Bediako, *Christianity and Africa: The Renewal of a Non-Christian Religion* (Maryknoll, NY: Orbis Books, 1995), p. 4.

40. Katongole, *A Future for Africa*, pp. 162–63.

41. Léonard Santedi Kinkupu, et al., *Des prêtres noirs s'interrogent: Cinquante ans après* (Paris: Editions Karthala, 1956).

42. The Holy Ghost Fathers (Spiritans) who evangelized southern Nigeria, the Middle Belt, and parts of the northeast of Nigeria made extensive use

of catechists for passing on the faith to the new converts and to the younger generations. Since many of these missionaries could not read or speak Igbo or the other local languages in use in the areas of their mission, it often fell to the catechists who were themselves bilingual actually to interpret the faith to the people. Another factor at play was that there were very few priests in relation to the vast area and population in the mission field. The missionaries created many mission "outstations," which they visited at sometimes very lengthy intervals, depending on the size of the area in question. The catechists had the responsibility of teaching the faith and holding religious services, such as daily prayers, Sunday services, and Christian burials, until the next visit of the parish priest. Even when the priest came, these visits lasted two to three hours at the most. The catechists were often the interpreters of the priest's homily where the priest in question could not speak the local language, which was most of the time. Some of the catechists were indeed very famous men, because of their longevity of service or having moved from one locality to another, or because they were trusted and visible partners of the priests. Catechist Modebelu was from Onitsha but had followed the priests to various parts of Igboland on mission. Maduforkwa was from Uzoakwa Ihiala but had worked in various places around Ihiala and in Orlu. The same goes for Nwabugwu. Nna anyi Mathew Onwuzuruike was from Umuzu, Amucha, from Saint Paschal's Church. He was never formally employed as a catechist but played a very crucial role in part of Amagigbo parish, including Amucha, Nkume, and Umuowa. He was always present for morning Masses, and on Sundays would always show up early for Sunday instructions to the people before the parish priest arrived for Mass. There were many others like these men. Their stories in the evangelization of the church in Nigeria and other parts of Africa have yet to receive the attention they deserve.

43. The *Igbo Hymn Book* was for many years the main source of hymns for liturgical worship among the Igbo. It contained hymns for Sunday worship, for the various high feasts of the church, and for the various important mysteries and dogmas of the faith. For most Igbo Christians the hymns in this book were a veritable source of theological insights into very important truths of the church: about God, Jesus, the Holy Spirit, Mary, the church, salvation, and other things. *Mary Nne Jesu* is a short treatise on Mary, the Mother of Jesus. Many Igbo Catholics of the missionary era up until Vatican II were instructed on this text, as on Igbo Catechism, a compendium of the teachings of the church. These texts reflected the mode and theological stress and spirit of the period from Trent up until Vatican II. Bishop Joseph Shanahan, C.S.Sp., the great pioneer missionary and evangelizer of southern Nigeria, was very insistent on teaching the catechism to the young. Here is an instruction he issues to his priests on this matter: "The priest who would neglect

every other instruction and teach the catechism to the children of his youth would have done a great deal. The priest who would discharge every other duty and neglect this would have done nothing. The one will be preparing for his successor a generation of believing Christians, the other, a generation of baptized pagans" (quoted in Charles A. Ebelebe, *Africa and the New Face of Mission: A Critical Assessment of the Legacy of the Irish Spiritans among the Igbo of Southern Nigeria* [Lanham, MD: University Press of America, 2009], p. 106). Ebelebe also points out that "with the number of catechumens ever on the increase and the later missionaries' rudimentary grasp of the Igbo language, they had neither the time nor the tools to effectively implement" Shanahan's directive. It was left "to the catechists to do the teaching and examining" of candidates for the sacraments (Ebelebe, *Africa and the New Face of Mission*, p. 115, no. 32).

44. Paulinus I. Odozor, *Moral Theology in an Age of Renewal: A Study of the Catholic Tradition since Vatican II* (Notre Dame, IN: University of Notre Dame Press, 2003), p. 18.

45. Ibid., p. 18.

46. Pope John XXIII, opening address at the Second Vatican Council, Oct. 11, 1962, http://www.catholic-forum.com/saints/pope0261i.htm.

47. Hastings, *African Christianity*, pp. 50–51.

48. Kwame Bediako, *Jesus and the Gospel in Africa: History and Experience* (Maryknoll, NY: Orbis Books, 2004), p. 53.

49. Pope John Paul II, *Ecclesia in Africa*, no. 59, http://www.vatican.va /holy_father/john_paul_ii/apost_exhortations/documents/hf_jp-ii_exh _14091995_ecclesia-in-africa_en.html.

50. Laurenti Magesa, *African Religion: The Moral Traditions of Abundant Life* (Maryknoll, NY: Orbis Books, 1997), p. 5.

51. See Kinkupu, *Des prêtres noirs s interrogent.*

52. James C. Okoye, "Inculturation and Theology in Africa," *Mission Studies* 14:1 & 2, 27 & 28 (1997): p. 67.

53. Bolaji Idowu, *Towards an Indigenous Church* (London: Oxford University Press, 1965).

54. Ibid., pp. 1–2.

55. Ibid.

56. Ibid., p. 8.

57. Ibid., p. 11.

58. Ibid., p. 12.

59. Ibid., pp. 24–25.

60. Ibid.

61. Ibid., p. 26.

62. Ibid., p. 13.

63. Ibid., p. 15.

64. Ibid., p. 45.

65. Luke Mbefo, *The True African: Impulses for Self-Affirmation* (Enugu, Nigeria: SNAAP Press, 2001), p. 46.

66. Ibid., p. 47.

67. Pope John Paul II, *Redemptoris Missio: Encyclical Letter of the Supreme Pontiff John Paul II on the Permanent Validity of the Church's Missionary Mandate*, no. 33.2, in *The Encyclicals of John Paul II*, ed. J. Michael Miller (Huntington, IN: Our Sunday Visitor, 1996), p. 456.

68. See Laurenti Magesa, *Anatomy of Inculturation: Transforming the Church in Africa* (Maryknoll, NY: Orbis Books, 2004), pp. 5–6; Aylward Shorter, *Toward a Theology of Inculturation* (Maryknoll, NY: Orbis Books, 1988), p. 11.

69. Peter Schineller, *A Handbook on Inculturation* (New York: Paulist Press, 1990), p. 1.

70. Pedro Arrupe, "Letter to the Whole Society on Inculturation," in *Other Apostolates Today, Selected Letters and Addresses 3*, ed. Jerome Aixala (St. Louis: Institute of Jesuit Sources, 1981), p. 172.

71. Vatican Council II, "Pastoral Constitution on the Church in the World of Today," no. 36, in *Decrees of the Ecumenical Councils*, vol. 2, *Trent to Vatican II*, ed. Norman P. Tanner (Washington, DC: Georgetown University Press, 1990), p. 1090.

72. Shorter, *Toward a Theology of Inculturation*, p. 11.

73. Ibid., p. 12.

74. Luke Mbefo, *The True African*, p. 45.

75. Pope John Paul II, *Redemptoris Missio*, no. 52.3–4, pp. 470–71.

76. Ibid., no. 37.14, p. 461.

77. Ibid., no. 52.2, p. 470.

78. See, for example, T. Frank Kennedy, ed., *Inculturation and the Church in North America* (New York: Crossroad, 2006).

79. Bénézet Bujo, *Foundations of African Christian Ethics beyond the Universal Claims of Western Morality* (New York: Crossroad, 2001), p. 8.

80. See Elochukwu Uzukwu, *Worship as Body Language. Introduction to Christian Worship: An African Orientation* (Collegeville, MN: Liturgical Press, 1997).

81. Joseph Cardinal Cordeiro, *Vatican II Revisited: By Those Who Were There*, ed. Dom Alberic Stacpoole (Minneapolis, MN: Winston Press, 1986), p. 188.

82. Vatican II, *Optatam Totius*, 16, in *Vatican II Constitutions, Decrees, Declarations (A Completely Revised Translation in Inclusive Language)*, ed. Austin Flannery (Northport, NY: Costello, 1996).

83. Justin Ukpong, "Developments in Biblical Interpretation in Africa: Historical and Hermeneutical Directions," in *The Bible in Africa: Transactions, Trajectories and Trends*, ed. Gerald O. West and Musa W. Dube (Leiden: Brill, 2000), pp. 11–28.

84. Ibid., p. 14.

85. This is true of the entire continent of Africa. I am not in a position to enumerate all these great composers and liturgical musicians; I do not know them all. Suffice it here to mention a few of the veterans I know from southeastern Nigeria. The first is Fr. Raymond Arazu, C.S.Sp. Arazu has managed to translate and render all one hundred and fifty Psalms into Igbo music. The impact of these compositions is felt in the whole area of eastern Nigeria. His compositions have given rise to Abuoma (Psalms) societies in villages and hamlets across the land. His psalms (Abuoma) have been turned into dance music by many local men's and women's organizations in the area. Fr. Ify Ezenduka of Awka diocese is another great composer of liturgical music based on the Psalms and on biblical passages. Also of note in this regard is Fr. Marcel Izu Onyeocha, C. M. F., and the late Fr. Ambrose (Jim) Madu. There is a crop of promising younger composers who have started to make significant contributions in this area.

86. See *Program of Studies* (Enugu, Nigeria: Spiritan International School of Theology, 1998).

87. See Facultés Catholiques de Kinshasa (DRC), Secrétariat Général Académique: *Programmes d'études: Années académiques, 2007–2006 et 2008–2009*.

88. Tangaza College is a constituent college of the Catholic University of Eastern Africa in Nairobi, Kenya. The references here are from the college's *Academic Handbook, 2005–2006*.

89. Paulinus Odozor, "Christian (Catholic) Theological Ethics in Africa: In Search of Firm Foundations," in *In the Service of Charity and Truth: Essays in Honor of Lucius Ugorji*, ed. Uzochukwu J. Njoku and Simon O. Anyanwu (New York: Peter Lang, 2012), pp. 35–52.

90. I reproduce a large portion of the papal injunction here to show the extent of the pope's thinking on this matter: "The expression, that is, the language and mode of manifesting this one Faith, may be manifold; hence, it may be original, suited to the tongue, the style, the character, the genius, and the culture, of the one who professes this one Faith. From this point of view, a certain pluralism is not only legitimate, but desirable. An adaptation of the Christian life in the fields of pastoral, ritual, didactic and spiritual activities is not only possible, it is even favored by the Church. The liturgical renewal is a living example of this. And in this sense you may, and you must, have an African Christianity. Indeed, you possess human values and characteristic

forms of culture which can rise up to perfection such as to find in Christianity, and for Christianity, a true superior fullness, and prove to be capable of a richness of expression all its own, and genuinely African. This may take time. It will require that your African soul become imbued to its depths with the secret charisms of Christianity, so that these charisms may then overflow freely, in beauty and wisdom, in the true African manner. It will require from your culture that it should not refuse, but rather eagerly desire, to draw, from the patrimony of the patristic, exegetical, and theological tradition of the Catholic Church, those treasures of wisdom which can rightly be considered universal, above all, those which can be most easily assimilated by the African mind. The Church of the West did not hesitate to make use of the resources of African writers, such as Tertullian, Optatus of Milevis, Origen, Cyprian and Augustine (cf. *Optatam Totius*, no. 16). Such an exchange of the highest expressions of Christian thought nourishes, without altering the originality, of any particular culture. It will require an incubation of the Christian 'mystery' in the genius of your people in order that its native voice, more clearly and frankly, may then be raised harmoniously in the chorus of the other voices in the Universal Church. Do we need to remind you, in this regard, how useful it will be for the African Church to possess centers of contemplative and monastic life, centers of religious studies, centers of pastoral training? If you are able to avoid the possible dangers of religious pluralism, the danger of making your Christian profession into a kind of local folklore, or into exclusivist racism, or into egoistic tribalism or arbitrary separatism, then you will be able to remain sincerely African even in your own interpretation of the Christian life; you will be able to formulate Catholicism in terms congenial to your own culture; you will be capable of bringing to the Catholic Church the precious and original contribution of 'negritude,' which she needs particularly in this historic hour." Pope Paul VI, "Concluding Remarks at the Eucharistic Celebration in Kampala (Uganda) at the Conclusion of the Symposium of Bishops of Africa," http://www.catholicnewsagency.com/document.php?n=490.

91. See, for example, Agbonkhiameghe E. Orobator, *From Crisis to Kairos: The Mission of the Church in the Time of HIV/AIDS, Refugees and Poverty* (Nairobi: Paulines Publications Africa, 2005).

92. See Bede Ukwuije, *Trinité et inculturation* (Paris: Desclée de Brouwer, 2008).

93. Bonaventure Ikenna Ugwu, *The Holy Spirit as Present and Active in the Cosmic Turmoil and Human Suffering: A Dialogue between Pierre Teilhard de Chardin and Jürgen Moltmann* (Rome: Editrice Pontifical Università Gregoriana, 2004); *Holy Spirit: Fire from Above* (Enugu, Nigeria: Sans Press, 2008).

94. Mary Sylvia Chinyere Nwachukwu, *Creation-Covenant Scheme of Justification by Faith: A Canonical Study of the God-Human Drama in the Pentateuch and the Letter to the Romans* (Rome: Editrice Pontifical Università Gregoriana, 2002).

95. Ernest M. Ezeogu, "The African Origin of Jesus: An Afrocentric Reading of Matthew's Infancy Narrative (Matthew 1–2)," in *Postcolonial Perspectives in African Biblical Interpretations*, ed. Musa W. Dube, Andrew M. Mbuvi, and Dora Mbuwayesango (Atlanta: Society of Biblical Literature, 2012), pp. 259–82.

96. Anthony A. Akinwale, "The Theology of the Passion of Christ in St. Thomas Aquinas and Its Possible Relevance to Liberation Theology" (Ph.D. diss., Boston College, 1996).

97. Francis Anekwe Oborji, *Towards a Christian Theology of African Religion: Issues of Interpretation and Mission* (Eldoret, Kenya: AMECEA Gaba Publications, 2005).

98. Patrick C. Chibuko, *Igbo Christian Rite of Marriage: A Proposed Rite for Study and Celebration* (Frankfurt am Main: Peter Lang, 1999); *Paschal Mystery of Christ: Foundation for Liturgical Inculturation in Africa* (Frankfurt am Main: Peter Lang, 1999); Patrick C. Chibuko, "Liturgy and Social Justice According to the Roman Missal of Paul VI, *Excerptum ex Dissertatione ad Doctoratum Sacrae Liturgiae Assequendum in Pontificio Istituto Liturgico, S. Anselmo, Romae, Thesis ad Lauream*" (doctoral thesis, nr. 161, N. Domenici Pecheux, Rome, 1991).

99. Léonard Santedi Kinkupu, *Dogme et Inculturation: Perspective d'une théologie de l'invention* (Paris: Editions Karthala, 1999).

100. See, for example, Anne Nasimiyu-Wasike, "Christology and an African Woman's Experience," in *Faces of Jesus in Africa*, ed. Robert Schreiter (Maryknoll, NY: Orbis Books, 1991); "Christianity and African Rituals of Birth and Naming," in *The Will to Anise: Women, Tradition and the Church in Africa*, ed. Mercy Amba Oduyoye and M. R. A. Kanyoro (Maryknoll, NY: Orbis Books, 1992).

101. See for example, T. M. Hinga, "Women, Power and Liberation in an African Church: A Theological Case Study of the Legio Maria Church in Kenya" (Ph.D. diss., Department of Religious Studies, University of Lancaster, 1990). Also, "Between Colonialism and Inculturation: Feminist Theologies in Africa," in *Feminist Theologies in Different Contexts*, ed. Elizabeth Schüssler Fiorenza and M. S. Copeland (London: SCM Press, 1996).

102. James Henry Owino Kombo, *The Doctrine of God in African Christian Thought: The Holy Trinity, Theological Hermeneutics and the African Intellectual Culture* (Leiden: Brill, 2007).

103. Thankfully, Elochukwu Uzukwu has now directed his considerable erudition and knowledge to this issue in his latest book, *God, Spirit, and Human Wholeness: Appropriating Faith and Culture in West African Style* (Eugene, OR: Pickwick Publications, 2012).

104. Joseph Ratzinger, *Principles of Catholic Theology* (San Francisco: Ignatius Press, 1987), p. 378.

105. Barry Hallen, "African Ethics?," in *The Blackwell Companion to Religious Ethics*, ed. William Schweiker (Oxford: Blackwell, 2005), p. 412.

106. Kwame Gyekye, "African Ethics," in http://plato.stanford.edu/entries/african-ethics/.

107. John Mbiti, *African Religions and Philosophy* (Garden City, NY: Doubleday, 1970), p. 269.

108. K. Wiredu and K. Gyekye, eds., *Person and Community: Ghanaian Philosophical Studies* 1 (Washington, DC: Council for Research in Values and Philosophy and UNESCO, 1992), p. 194.

109. Gyekye, "African Ethics," p. 4.

110. Ibid.

111. Hallen, "African Ethics?," p. 406.

112. John P. Reeder, Jr., "Religious Ethics as a Field and Discipline," *Journal of Religious Ethics* 6:1 (Spring 1978): p. 34.

113. Ibid.

114. Cf. the work of Laurenti Magesa, whom we will discuss later.

115. Jeffrey Stout, "Commitments and Traditions in the Study of Religious Ethics," *Journal of Religious Ethics* 25:3, 25th anniversary supplement (1997): p. 24.

Chapter 2. Tradition, Rationality, and Morality

1. George H. Tavard, "Tradition," in *The New Dictionary of Theology*, ed. Joseph A. Komonchak, Mary Collins, and Dermot A. Lane (Collegeville, MN: Liturgical Press, 1987), p. 1037.

2. See Majid Khadduri and Herbert J. Liebesny, eds., *Law in the Middle East*, vol. 1, *Origin and Development of Islamic Law* (New York: AMS Press, 1984). See especially pp. 85–112. Also see W. Montgomery Watt, *What Is Islam?*, 2nd ed. (1968; London/New York: Longman and Librarie du Liban,1979), esp. pp. 205–8.

3. Edward Shils, *Tradition* (London: Faber, 1981), p. 14.

4. Yves Congar, *The Meaning of Tradition*, trans. A. N. Woodraw (New York: Hawthorn Books, 1964), p. 8.

5. David Tracy, *The Analogical Imagination: Christian Theology and the Culture of Pluralism* (New York: Crossroad, 1989), p. 101.

6. Alan Keightley, *Wittgenstein, Grammar and God* (London: Epworth Press, 1970), p. 29.

7. H. O. Mounce, "Understanding a Primitive Society," *Philosophy* 48 (1973): p. 349.

8. Cf. John Hick, "Sceptics and Believers," in *Faith and the Philosophers*, ed. John Hick (London: Macmillan, 1964), pp. 239–40.

9. D. Z. Phillips, *Belief, Change, and Forms of Life* (Atlantic Highlands, NJ: Humanities Press International, 1986), p. 10.

10. Ibid., p. 20.

11. Hilary Putnam, *Realism and Reason: Philosophical Papers*, vol. 3 (Cambridge: Cambridge University Press, 1985), p. 230.

12. Kai Nielsen, *Contemporary Critique of Religion* (London: Macmillan, 1971), p. 96.

13. Alasdair MacIntyre, *After Virtue: A Study in Moral Theory*, 2nd ed., (London: Gerald Duckworth, 1985), p. 218.

14. Ibid., p. 208.

15. Ibid., p. 222.

16. Alasdair MacIntyre, *Whose Justice? Which Rationality?* (Notre Dame, IN: University of Notre Dame Press, 1988), p. 350.

17. Ibid., p. 370.

18. Bernard F. Lonergan, "Theology in Its New Context," in *A Second Collection: Papers by Bernard J. F. Lonergan, S.J.*, ed. William F. J. Ryan and Bernard J. Tyrell (London: Darton, Longman and Todd, 1970), p. 58.

19. Paulinus I. Odozor, *Richard A. McCormick and the Renewal of Moral Theology* (Notre Dame, IN: University of Notre Dame Press, 1995), p. xii.

20. Robert Schreiter, *Constructing Local Theologies* (Maryknoll, NY: Orbis Books, 1985), pp. 102–4.

21. Paulinus I. Odozor, *Moral Theology in an Age of Renewal: A Study of the Catholic Tradition since Vatican II* (Notre Dame, IN: University of Notre Dame Press, 2003), p. 103.

22. Henry David Aiken, "Levels of Moral Discourse," in *Reason and Conduct: New Bearings in Moral Philosophy* (Westport, CT: Greenwood, 1978), pp. 65–87.

23. Ibid., p. 67.

24. Ibid., p. 70.

25. Ibid., p. 73.

26. Ronald M. Green, "Morality and Religion," in *The Encyclopaedia of Religion*, ed. Mircea Eliade (New York: Macmillan; London: Collier Macmillan, 1987), p. 100.

27. Aiken, "Levels of Moral Discourse," p. 75.

28. Ibid., p. 77.

29. Judaism, Christianity, and Islam emphasize God's grace and the recurrent possibility of repentance. "Pauline Christianity takes this teaching to the extreme conclusion that salvation comes not by works of the moral and religious law, but through God's free, necessitated love. Similar conceptions are found in the devotional (*bhakti*) tradition of Hindu thought, but in the Indian-derived traditions the retributive order is more commonly qualified differently: ultimate redemption requires one to attain the consciousness that liberated *moksa* (*nirvana*) is open to those who transcend attachment to *samusara*, the karmic realm of merit and demerit" (Green, "Morality and Religion," p. 104).

30. Richard A. McCormick, "The Judeo-Christian Tradition and Bio-ethical Codes," in *How Brave a New World?: Dilemmas in Bioethics* (Garden City, NY: Doubleday, 1981), p. 6.

31. Cf. James M. Gustafson, *Christ and the Moral Life* (Chicago: University of Chicago Press, 1968), p. 240.

32. See Geoffrey Stout, *Ethics after Babel: The Languages of Morals and Their Discontents* (Boston: Beacon Books, 1988), p. 186.

33. John Cavadini, "Open Letter to the University Community," http://www.ndsmcobserver.co/2.2756/open-letter-to-the-university-community-1.265347.

34. Odozor, *Richard A. McCormick*, p. 155.

35. Obioma Nnaemeka, "The Challenge of Border-Crossing: African Women and Transnational Feminisms," in *Female Circumcision and the Politics of Knowledge: African Women in Imperialist Discourses*, ed. Obioma Nnaemeka (Westport, CT: Praeger, 2005), p. 4.

36. Ibid., p. 11.

37. Sondra Hale, "Colonial Discourse and Ethnographic Residuals: The 'Female Circumcision' Debate and the Politics of Knowledge," in Nnaemeka, *Female Circumcision and the Politics of Knowledge*, p. 212.

38. Ibid., pp. 212–13.

39. Ibid., p. 212.

40. Ibid., p. 215.

41. Gavin Kitchling, "Why I Gave up African Studies," http://www.arts.uwa.edu.au/MotsPluriels/MP1600gk.html.

42. Chielozona Eze, *Postcolonial Imagination and Moral Representations in African Literature and Culture* (Lanham, MD: Lexington Books, 2011), p. x.

43. F. Abiola Irele, *The African Imagination: Literature in Africa and the Black Diaspora* (Oxford: Oxford University Press, 2001), p. 7.

44. Kwame Bediako, *Jesus and the Gospel in Africa: History and Experience* (Maryknoll, NY: Orbis Books, 2004), p. 58.

45. A. G. Leonard, *The Lower Niger and Its Tribes* (London: Macmillan, 1906; London: Frank Cass, 1968), p. 429.

46. Laurenti Magesa, *African Religion: The Moral Traditions of Abundant Life* (Maryknoll, NY: Orbis Books, 1997), p. 35.

47. See E. B. Idowu, *Olódùmarè: God in Yoruba Belief* (London: Longman, 1962; New York: Frederick A. Praeger, 1963). Idowu explores the idea of the Supreme God among the Yoruba of Nigeria, and most of the anthropomorphic attributes he gives to Olódùmarè are similar to those we apply in the description of the Christian God.

48. Magesa, *African Religion*, p. 40.

49. Ibid., pp. 41–44.

50. Regina N. Igwemezie, *Widowhood: A Harrowing Experience* (Enugu, Nigeria: privately published, 2005).

51. Without minimizing the indignities she went through, I must also note that in most Igbo communities, men who lose their wives are also required, along with the children of the deceased, to shave their heads at the start of the mourning period. The difference is that whereas this is required of most women as an obligation, it is optional for men. The practice is changing rapidly, though. When one of my younger sisters, Eunice, lost her husband in a tragic car crash in February 2013, her husband's family told her not to cut her hair. They left it optional to her to find other ways of mourning the loss of her husband. This liberal attitude, however, is not yet a universal practice in this part of Nigeria.

52. Igwemezie, *Widowhood*, p. 24.

53. Ifi Amadiume, *Daughters of the Goddess, Daughters of Imperialism: African Women Struggle for Culture, Power and Democracy* (London: Zed Books, 2000), p. 110.

54. Mercy Amba Oduyoye, *Daughters of Anowa: African Women and Patriarchy* (Maryknoll, NY: Orbis Books, 1995), p. 35.

55. Ibid., p. 9.

56. Ibid., p. 23.

57. Ibid., pp. 19–29.

58. Ibid., pp. 28–29.

59. Ibid., p. 31.

60. Ibid., p. 30.

61. Ibid., p. 31.

62. Ibid., p. 32.

63. Ibid., p. 33.

64. "How God Withdrew from the World," a Malozi (Zambian) creation story, in *The Origins of Life and Death: African Creation Myths*, ed. Ulli Beier (London: Heinemann, 1966), p. 12.

65. Ibid., p. 13.

66. See, respectively, J. P. Clark-Bekederemo, ed., *The Ozidi Saga* (Ibadan, Nigeria: Ibadan University Press, 1977), and J. P. Clark, *Ozidi: A Play* (London: Oxford University Press, 1966).

67. Joseph-Therese Agbasiere, *Women in Igbo Life and Thought* (London: Routledge, 2000), p. 40.

68. Ibid., p. 41.

69. Romeo Igwebuike Okeke, *The Osu Concept in Igboland: A Study of the Types of Slavery in Igbo Speaking Areas of Nigeria* (Enugu, Nigeria: SNAAP Press, 1986), p. 9.

70. Ibid.

71. Irele, *The African Imagination*, p. 146.

Chapter 3. African Theological Evaluations of African Religion

1. Segun Gbadegesin, "The Origins of African Ethics," in *The Blackwell Companion to Religious Ethics*, ed. William Schweiker (Oxford: Blackwell, 2005), p. 416.

2. Ibid., p. 417.

3. Andrew F. Walls, "The Gospel as the Prisoner and Liberator of Culture," *Faith and Thought* 108:1–2 (1981): p. 49. Quoted in Kwame Bediako, *Theology and Identity: The Impact of Culture upon Christian Thought in the Second Century and in Modern Africa* (1992; Cumbria, UK: Regnum Books, 1999), p. 4.

4. Mbonu Ojike, "Christianity in Africa," in *Christianity in Africa: As Seen by the Africans*, ed. Ram Desai (Denver: Allan Swallow, 1962), p. 63. This essay is excerpted from Ojike's book *My Africa* (New York: John Day, 1946).

5. This term comes from the word *omenani* or *Omenana* in some parts of Igboland. The word could be translated as tradition/custom/culture. Here, Ojike is using this unique coinage to refer to adherents of African Traditional Religion.

6. Ojike, "Christianity in Africa," p. 63.

7. Ibid.

8. Arnold Toynbee, *Christianity among the Religions of the World* (New York: Scribner, 1957), pp. 111–12.

9. Ibid.

10. Cyril C. Okorocha, *The Meaning of Religious Conversion in Africa: The Case of the Igbo of Nigeria* (Aldershot, UK: Avebury, 1987), p. 5.

11. Ulu is the name of the deity of this local community, Umuaro, in the novel. Ezeulu is the chief priest of Ulu, and in his capacity as spiritual leader he offers his counsel against going to war with Okperi.

12. Chinua Achebe, *Arrow of God* (New York: Anchor Books, 1969), p. 27.

13. Tinyiko Sam Maluleke, "Half a Century of African Christian Theologies: Elements of the Emerging Agenda for the Twenty First Century," *Journal of Theology for Southern Africa* 99 (1997): p. 13.

14. Gabriel Setiloane, "Where Are We in African Theology?," in *African Theology en Route*, ed. Kofi Appiah-Kubi and Sergio Torres (Maryknoll, NY: Orbis Books, 1979), p. 64.

15. Edward Fasholé-Luke, "The Quest for an African Christian Theology," *Ecumenical Review* 27:3 (July 1975): p. 265.

16. John Mbiti, *Introduction to African Religion*, 2nd ed. (Portsmouth, NH: Heinemann Educational, 1991), p. 36.

17. Ibid., p. 41.

18. Ibid.

19. Ibid.

20. John Mbiti, *African Religions and Philosophy*, 2nd ed. (Portsmouth, NH: Heinemann, 1990), p. 197.

21. Ibid., p. 200.

22. Ibid., p. 208.

23. Ibid.

24. See Paulinus Odozor, "Liturgy and Life: A Discussion from an African Christian Theological Perspective," *Worship* 82:5 (Sept. 2008): pp. 413–33.

25. See Laurenti Magesa, *African Religion: The Moral Traditions of Abundant Life* (Maryknoll, NY: Orbis Books, 1997).

26. Ronald M. Green, "Religion and Morality in the African Traditional Setting," *Journal of Religion in Africa* 14:1 (1983): pp. 1–23.

27. Ibid., p. 1.

28. Ibid.

29. Ibid., p. 3.

30. Ibid., pp. 3–4.

31. Ibid., p. 5.

32. Ibid., p. 4.

33. Ibid.

34. Mbiti, *African Religions and Philosophy*, p. 205.

35. Green, "Religion and Morality in the African Traditional Setting," p. 5.

36. Peter Fry, *Spirits of Protest* (Cambridge: Cambridge University Press, 1976), p. 21.

37. Green. "Religion and Morality in the African Traditional Setting," p. 8.

38. Ibid., p. 11.

39. Ibid., p. 20.

40. Magesa, *African Religion*, p. 13.

41. Ibid., p. 35.

42. Ibid., p. 36.

43. Ibid., p. 39.

44. Ibid., p. 79.

45. Ibid., p. 47.

46. Ibid.

47. Ibid., p. 49.

48. Ibid., p. 50.

49. Ibid., p. 51.

50. Ibid.

51. Kwame Bediako, *Jesus and the Gospel in Africa: History and Experience* (Maryknoll, NY: Orbis Books, 2004), p. 59.

52. Bediako, *Theology and Identity*, p. 1.

53. Fasholé-Luke, "The Quest for an African Christian Theology," p. 267.

54. Bolaji Idowu, *Towards an Indigenous Church* (London: Oxford University Press, 1965), p. 12.

55. Ibid., p. 25.

56. Fasholé-Luke, "The Quest for an African Christian Theology," p. 267.

57. Idowu, *Towards an Indigenous Church*, p. 11.

58. Ibid., p. 12.

59. Harold Turner, *Religious Innovation in Africa* (Boston: G. K. Hall, 1979), p. 92.

60. J. D. Y. Peel, *Aladura: A Religious Movement among the Yoruba* (London: Oxford University Press, 1968), p. 153. Quoted in Nathaniel Ndiokwere, *Prophecy and Revolution: The Role of Prophets in the Independent Churches and in Biblical Tradition* (London: SPCK, 1981), p. 235.

61. Ndiokwere, *Prophecy and Revolution*, p. 235.

62. Ibid., p. 244.

63. Allan H. Anderson, *African Reformation: African Initiated Christianity in the 20th Century* (Trenton, NJ: Africa World Press, 2001), p. 5.

64. Bediako, *Theology and Identity*, pp. 4–5.

65. Ibid., p. 10.

66. Ezra Chitando, "The (Mis) Appropriation of the African Traditional Religion in African Theology," in *Inculturation and Post-Colonial Discourse in African Theology*, ed. Edward P. Antonio (New York: Peter Lang, 2006), p. 100.

67. Birgit Meyer, "Make a Complete Break with the Past: Memory and Post-Colonial Modernity in Ghanaian Pentecostalist Discourse," *Journal of Religion in Africa* 28:3 (1998): p. 317.

68. Ogbu Kalu, *African Pentecostalism: An Introduction* (Oxford: Oxford University Press, 2008), p. 174.

69. Kenneth Enang, *The Nigerian Catholics and the Independent Churches: A Call to Authentic Faith* (Nairobi: Paulines Publications Africa, 2012), p. 175.

70. Ibid., p. 259.

71. Mercy Amba Oduyoye, "The Value of African Religious Beliefs and Practices for Christian Theology," in *African Theology en Route*, ed. Kofi Appiah-Kubi and Sergio Torres (Maryknoll, NY: Orbis Books, 1979), pp. 110–11.

Chapter 4. Issues in the Theology of Non-Christian Religions

1. Eugene Hillman, "Evangelism in a Wider Ecumenism: Theological Grounds for Dialogue with Other Religions," *Journal of Ecumenical Studies* 12 (Winter 1975), p. 4.

2. Justin Martyr, *Apologia*, 1, 10, 46, quoted in Otto Karrer, *The Kingdom of God Today*, trans. Rosaleen Ockenden (New York: Herder and Herder, 1964), p. 11.

3. Walbert Bühlman, *The Chosen Peoples*, trans. Robert R. Darr (Middle Green, Slough: St. Paul's Publications, 1982), p. 95.

4. Pope Boniface VIII, *Unam Sanctam*, in *Documents of the Christian Church*, ed. Henry Bettenson (Oxford: Oxford University Press, 1979), pp. 115–16.

5. Hans Küng, *On Being a Christian* (Glasgow: Collins Fount, 1974), p. 97. See also Hans Küng, *The Church* (London: Search Press, 1978), p. 313.

6. Pope Pius XII, *Mystici Corporis* (London: Catholic Truth Society, 1943), p. 59.

7. I am deliberately stressing this point here in view of a widespread approach in mission studies and in African theology today which tends generally to cast European missionaries to Africa more or less as villains. By doing so, I am not saying that there are no villains among missionaries to Africa, nor am I saying that certain attitudes to African cultures and religious institutions

were not downright racist, arrogant, ignorant, wrongheaded, or misguided. I am simply saying that considering how we all tend to be wiser in hindsight we must judge people's motivations and actions from the historical past with a certain measure of detachment and generosity. Africa is littered with graves and graveyards of young men and women who in their effort to bring the good news to Africans paid the supreme price. These were not always agents of imperialism and colonialists (although some were), and their aim was not necessarily to colonize (although some may have gone to Africa arm in arm with colonial agents and powers). Generally, though, these many men and women acted from the theology they knew then and out of concern for the eternal well-being of Africans. They should also be praised for that.

8. Walbert Bühlman, *All Have the Same God* (Middle Green, Slough: St. Paul's Publications, 1979), p. 27.

9. Pope Pius XI, *Rerum Ecclesiae*, in *The Papal Encyclicals 1903–1939*, trans. Claudia Carlen (Raleigh, NC: McGrath, 1981), p. 285.

10. Pope Pius XII, *Fidei Donum*, in *The Papal Encyclicals 1939–1958*, trans. Claudia Carlen (Raleigh, NC: McGrath, 1981), p. 324. See also Bühlman, *All Have the Same God*, p. 27.

11. Vatican Council II, *Lumen Gentium*, no. 14, in *Vatican Council II: The Conciliar and Postconciliar Documents*, ed. Austin Flannery (Dublin: Dominican Publications, 1981), pp. 365–66.

12. Küng, On *Being a Christian*, p. 104.

13. Heinz Robert Schlette, *Towards a Theology of Religions*, trans. W. J. O'Hara (New York: Herder and Herder, 1966), p. 16.

14. Ibid., pp. 67–68.

15. Ibid., p. 67.

16. Ibid., p. 70.

17. Note Schlette's use of the word *covenant* for the relation of the one living God to the whole of mankind.

18. Ibid., p. 73.

19. Ibid., p. 77.

20. Ibid., p. 79.

21. Ibid., p. 86.

22. Ibid., p. 89.

23. Ibid., p. 90.

24. Ibid.

25. Ibid., p. 93.

26. Ibid., p. 97.

27. Paul Knitter, "European Protestant and Catholic Approaches to the World Religions: Complements and Contrasts," *Journal of Ecumenical Studies* 12 (Winter 1975): p. 20.

28. Karl Barth, *Church Dogmatics*, vol. 1, pt. 2, *The Doctrine of the Word of God: The Prolegomena to Church Dogmatics*, trans. G. T. Thompson and H. Knight (1956; Edinburgh: T & T Clark, 1978), p. 71.

29. Ibid., p. 83.

30. Ibid., p. 102.

31. Ibid., p. 103.

32. Ibid., p. 119.

33. Ibid., p. 282.

34. Ibid.

35. Ibid., p. 293.

36. Ibid., p. 294.

37. Ibid., pp. 299–300.

38. Ibid., p. 302.

39. Ibid., p. 309.

40. Ibid., p. 337.

41. Ibid., p. 338.

42. Ibid., p. 339.

43. Paul Tillich, *Systematic Theology*, vol. 1, *Reason and Revelation, Being and God* (Chicago: University of Chicago Press, 1951), p. 108.

44. Ibid., p. 118.

45. Ibid., p. 120.

46. Tillich described miracle as an event that is "astonishing, unusual, without contradicting the rational structure of reality . . . it is an event which points to the mystery of being, expressing its relation to us in a definite way . . . it is an occurrence which is received as a sign event in an ecstatic experience." Only if all these are present can an event be considered genuinely miraculous, strictly speaking, Tillich says. Ecstasy and miracle mean the same thing: while one is "the miracle of the mind," the other is the "ecstasy of reality." Tillich, *Systematic Theology*, vol. 1, p. 108.

47. Ibid., p. 121.

48. Ibid., p. 139.

49. Ibid., p. 141.

50. Ibid., pp. 141–42.

51. Paul Tillich, *Christianity and the Encounter of the World Religions* (New York: Columbia University Press, 1964), p. 4.

52. Paul Tillich, *Systematic Theology*, vol. 3, *Life and the Spirit, History and the Kingdom of God* (Chicago: University of Chicago Press, 1963), p. 366.

53. Tillich, *Systematic Theology*, vol. 1, p. 133.

54. Ibid.

55. Ibid., p. 134.

56. Ibid.

57. Tillich, *Systematic Theology*, vol. 3, p. 144.

58. Ibid., p. 146.

59. Ibid., p. 140.

60. Tillich, *Systematic Theology*, vol. 1, p. 146.

61. Paul Tillich, *Systematic Theology,* vol. 2, *Existence and the Christ* (Chicago: University of Chicago Press, 1957), p. 167.

62. Ibid., p. 168.

63. Paul Tillich, "The Significance of the History of Religions for the Systematic Theologian," in *The Future of Religions*, ed. Jerald C. Bauer (New York: Harper & Row, 1966), pp. 81, 89.

64. Knitter, "European Protestant and Catholic Approaches," p. 24.

65. Paul Knitter, "Christianity as Religion: True and Absolute? A Roman Catholic Perspective," in *What Is Religion? An Enquiry for Christian Theology*, ed. Mircea Eliade and David Tracy (Edinburgh: T & T Clark, 1980).

66. Ibid., p. 17.

67. Ibid., p. 18.

68. Ibid., p. 19.

69. John Hick, "Jesus and the World Religions," in *The Myth of God Incarnate*, ed. John Hick (London: SCM Press, 1977), p. 180.

70. Ibid., p. 171.

71. Ibid., p. 170.

72. John Hick, *God and the Universe of Faiths*, rev. ed. (Glasgow: Collins Fount, 1977), p. 130.

73. Ibid., p. 135.

74. Ibid., p. 156.

75. Ibid., p. 146.

76. Ibid., p. 146.

77. Knitter, "Christianity as Religion," p. 18.

78. Congregation for the Doctrine of the Faith, "'*Dominus Jesus*': On the Unicity and Salvific Universality of Jesus Christ and the Church," in *Sic et Non: Encountering Dominus Jesus*, ed. Stephen Pope and Charles Hefling (Maryknoll, NY: Orbis Books, 2002), no. 5, p. 6.

79. Edward Schillebeeckx, *Jesus: An Experiment in Christology*, trans. Hubert Haskins (London: Collins, 1979), pp. 47–48.

80. Jost Eckert, "The Gospel for Israel and the Nations: The Problem of the Absoluteness of Christianity in the New Testament," in *True and False Universality of Christianity*, ed. Claude Geffre and Jean-Pierre Jossua (Edinburgh: T & T Clark, 1980), p. 138.

81. Schillebeeckx, *Jesus: An Experiment in Christology*, p. 602.

82. Karl Rahner, *Foundations of Christian Faith: An Introduction to the Idea of Christianity*, trans. William V. Dych (New York: Seabury Press, 1978), p. 233.

83. Ibid., p. 205.

84. See Schillebeeckx, *Jesus: An Experiment in Christology*, p. 588.

85. Hick, *The Myth of God Incarnate*, p. 180.

86. See Schillebeeckx, *Jesus: An Experiment in Christology*, p. 586.

87. Congregation for the Doctrine of the Faith, *Dominus Jesus*, no. 1.

Chapter 5. African Moral Theology and the Challenge of Inculturation

1. This work has appeared in published form as *Moralautonomie und Normenfindung bei Thomas von Aquin: Unter Einbeziehung der neutestamentlischen Kommentare*, Veröffentlischungen des Grabmann-Institutes zur Erforschung der Mittelalterlichen Theologie und Philosophie, n.s. 29 (Paderborn: Schöningh, 1979).

2. For more biographical detail about Bujo, see Juvénal Ilunga Muya, "Bénézet Bujo: The Awakening of a Systematic and Authentically African Thought," in *African Theology in the 21st Century*, vol. 1, *The Contribution of the Pioneers*, ed. Bénézet Bujo and Juvénal Ilunga Muya (Nairobi: Paulines Publications Africa, 2003).

3. For a comprehensive listing of Bujo's publications, see Muya, "Bénézet Bujo."

4. Bénézet Bujo, *The Ethical Dimension of Community: The African Model and the Dialogue between North and South* (Nairobi: Paulines Publications Africa, 1998); *Foundations of an African Ethic: Beyond the Universal Claims of Western Morality* (New York: Crossroad, 2001); and "Differentiations in African Ethics," in *The Blackwell Companion to Religious Ethics*, ed. William Schweiker (Malden, MA: Blackwell, 2005), pp. 423–37.

5. Bujo, *Foundations of an African Ethic*, p. xii.

6. Ibid., p. xiv.

7. Dividing the work of any scholar into periods is always risky since it could imply a neat demarcation between the periods under discussion. Rarely is such demarcation very neat. I use this method, however, merely to get a handle on aspects of Bujo's work pertinent to my discussion. For indeed, the influence of his early formation as theologian and Catholic priest is still evident in his most recent works.

8. Muya, "Bénézet Bujo," p. 109.

9. Ibid.

10. Bénézet Bujo, *Le diaire d'un théologien Africain*, Spiritualité du Tiers-monde 1 (Kinshasa: Éditions de l'église d'en bas, 1987), p. 24; quoted in Muya, "Bénézet Bujo," p. 110n10.

11. Vincent McNamara, *Faith and Ethics: Recent Roman Catholicism* (Dublin: Gill and Macmillan; Washington, DC: Georgetown University Press, 1985).

12. Ibid., p. 10.

13. Gérard Gilleman, *The Primacy of Charity in Moral Theology*, trans. William P. Ryan, S.J., and André Vachon, S.J. (Westminster, MD: Newman, 1959).

14. For an extensive discussion on the various approaches and answers to this issue, see Paulinus I. Odozor, *Moral Theology in an Age of Renewal: A Study of the Catholic Tradition since Vatican II* (Notre Dame, IN: University of Notre Dame Press, 2003), pp. 101–33.

15. See McNamara, *Faith and Ethics*, p. 44.

16. Bujo, *Foundations of an African Ethic*, p. 12.

17. See, for example, ibid., p. 11.

18. Ibid., p. 5.

19. Ibid., pp. 5–6.

20. See Bénézet Bujo, *African Christian Morality at the Age of Inculturation* (1990; Nairobi: Paulines Publications Africa, 1998), p. 40.

21. Bujo, "Differentiations in African Ethics," p. 427.

22. Muya, "Bénézet Bujo," p. 143.

23. For a more complete discussion of palaver in Bujo's work, see his *Foundations of an African Ethic*, pp. 45–63.

24. For an extensive discussion of the differences among discourse ethics, North American communitarian ethics, and African palaver ethics, see ibid., pp. 63–71.

25. Bujo, "Differentiations in African Ethics," p. 424.

26. Bujo, *Foundations of an African Ethic*, p. 33.

27. Ibid., p. 8.

28. See, for example, Laurenti Magesa, *African Religion: The Moral Traditions of Abundant Life* (Maryknoll, NY: Orbis Books, 1997), esp. pp. 14–18. See also Emefie Ikenga Metuh, *Comparative Studies of African Traditional Religions* (Onitsha: IMCO, 1987), pp. 5–10.

29. Bujo, *Foundations of an African Ethic*, pp. 5–6.

30. We will return to this issue in a later chapter.

31. Pope John Paul II, *Evangelium Vitae*, no. 20, in *The Encyclicals of John Paul II*, ed. J. Michael Miller (Huntington, IN: Our Sunday Visitor, 1996), p. 2809.

32. Bujo, *Foundations of an African Christian Ethic*, p. 12.

33. Martin Rhonheimer, *Natural Law and Practical Reason: A Thomist View of Moral Autonomy*, trans. Gerald Malsbary (New York: Fordham University Press, 2000), p. 309.

34. Vatican Council II, "Pastoral Constitution on the Church in the Modern World," no. 16, in *Vatican Council II: The Basic Sixteen Documents: Constitutions, Decrees, Declarations*, ed. Austin Flannery (Northport, NY: Costello, 1996), p. 178.

35. Joseph Boyle, "Natural Law," in *The New Dictionary of Theology*, ed. Joseph A. Komonchack, Mary Collins, and Dermot A. Lane (Collegeville, MN: Liturgical Press, 1987), p. 704.

36. Ibid., p. 705.

37. Bujo, "Differentiations in African Ethics," p. 433.

38. Ibid.

39. Chinweizu, *The West and the Rest of Us: White Predators, Black Slavers, and the African Elite* (New York: Random House, 1975), p. 54.

40. I will develop this issue further in the last chapter.

41. Richard A. McCormick, *The Critical Calling: Reflections on Moral Dilemmas since Vatican II* (Washington, DC: Georgetown University Press, 1989), p. 196.

42. Joseph Sittler, *The Structure of Christian Ethics* (Louisville: Westminster John Knox Press, 1980), p. 87.

43. Richard A. McCormick, "Theology and Bioethics: Christian Foundations," in *Theology and Bioethics: Exploring the Foundations and Frontiers*, ed. Earl E. Shelp (Boston: Reidel, 1985), pp. 101–2.

44. Ibid., p. 97.

45. Paulinus I. Odozor, *Richard A. McCormick and the Renewal of Moral Theology* (Notre Dame, IN: University of Notre Dame Press, 1995), p. 167.

46. McCormick, *Critical Calling*, p. 203.

47. See, for example, David Tuesday Adamo, "The Use of Psalms in African Indigenous Churches in Nigeria," in *The Bible in Africa: Transactions, Trajectories, and Trends*, ed. Gerald O. West and Musa W. Dube (Boston: Brill Academic, 2001), pp. 336–49; Musa W. Dube, "Readings of Semoya: Botswana Women's Interpretations of Matt. 15:21–28," *Semeia* 73 (1966): pp. 111–29.

48. Bujo, *Ethical Dimension of Community*, p. 25.

49. Ibid.

50. Pope John Paul II, *Redemptoris Missio*, no. 54.1, in Miller, *Encyclicals of John Paul II*, p. 540.

51. Odozor, *Richard A. McCormick*, p. 8.

52. Walter J. Burghardt, "The Role of the Scholar in the Catholic Church," in *Moral Theology: Challenges for the Future: Essays in Honor of Richard A. McCormick*, ed. Charles E. Curran (New York: Paulist Press, 1990), p. 27.

53. Pope John Paul II, *Redemptoris Missio*, no. 37.14, in Miller, *Encyclicals of John Paul II*, p. 526.

54. Bujo, *Ethical Dimension of Community*, p. 19.

55. Odozor, *Richard A. McCormick*, p. 150.

56. Richard A. McCormick, "Genetic Technology and Our Common Future," *America* 152.6 (April 27, 1985): p. 341.

Chapter 6. God and Morality in African Theology

1. James M. Gustafson, *Ethics from a Theocentric Perspective*, vol. 2, *Ethics and Theology* (Chicago: University of Chicago Press, 1984), p. 98.

2. Stephen J. Pope, "Overview of the Ethics of Thomas Aquinas," in *The Ethics of Aquinas*, ed. Stephen J. Pope (Washington, DC: Georgetown University Press, 2002), p. 31.

3. M. D. Chenu, "The Plan of St. Thomas' Summa Theologiae," *Cross Currents* 2 (1952): pp. 70–71.

4. Gerald McCool, *Catholic Theology in the Nineteenth Century* (New York: Seabury Press, 1987), p. 196.

5. Herwi Rikhof, "Trinity," in *The Theology of Thomas Aquinas*, ed. Rik Van Nieuwenhove and Joseph Wawrykow (Notre Dame, IN: University of Notre Dame Press, 2005), p. 41.

6. Saint Thomas Aquinas, *Summa Theologica*, I-I, q. 32, art. 1, trans. the Fathers of the English Dominican Province (New York: Benziger Brothers, 1941; Notre Dame, IN: Ave Maria Press, 1981).

7. Rikhof, "Trinity," p. 41.

8. Jean Porter, "Right Reason and the Love of God: The Parameters of Aquinas' Moral Theology," in Nieuwenhove and Wawrykow, *Theology of Aquinas*, p. 171.

9. Paulinus I. Odozor, *Richard A. McCormick and the Renewal of Moral Theology* (Notre Dame, IN: University of Notre Dame Press, 1995), p. 9.

10. James Gustafson, *Ethics from a Theocentric Perspective*, vol. 1, *Theology and Ethics* (Chicago: University of Chicago Press, 1981); *Ethics from a Theocentric Perspective*, vol. 2, *Ethics and Theology* (Chicago: University of Chicago Press, 1984).

11. Gustafson, *Ethics from a Theocentric Perspective*, vol. 1, p. 308.

12. Gustafson, *Ethics from a Theocentric Perspective*, vol. 2, p. 293; Gustafson, *Ethics from a Theocentric Perspective*, vol. 1, p. 264.

13. Gustafson, *Ethics from a Theocentric Perspective*, vol. 1, p. 257.

14. Ibid., p. 267.

15. Ibid., p. 268.

16. Gustafson, *Ethics from a Theocentric Perspective*, vol. 2, p. 28.

17. Stephen Toulmin, "Nature and Nature's God," *Journal of Religious Ethics* 13:1 (Spring 1985): p. 38.

18. Gustafson, *Ethics from a Theocentric Perspective*, vol. 1, p. 61.

19. Ibid., p. 201.

20. Ibid., p. 202.

21. Richard A. McCormick, "Gustafson's God: Who? What? Where? (ETC)," *Journal of Religious Ethics* 13:1 (Spring 1985): p. 61.

22. Anthony J. Blasi, *Moral Conflict and Christian Religion* (New York: Peter Lang, 1988), p. 4.

23. Lisa S. Cahill, "Consent in Time of Affliction: The Ethics of a Circumspect Theist," *Journal of Religious Ethics* 13:1 (Spring 1985): p. 32.

24. James M. Gustafson, "A Response to Critics," *Journal of Religious Ethics* 13:2 (Fall 1985): pp. 192–93.

25. Gustafson, *Ethics from a Theocentric Perspective*, vol. 1, p. 196.

26. Ibid., p. 83.

27. Ibid., p. 111.

28. Ibid., vol. 2, p. 145.

29. Ibid., pp. 1–22.

30. Ibid., p. 8.

31. Ibid., vol. 1, p. 293; vol. 2, p. 8.

32. Ibid., vol. 1, p. 293; vol. 2, pp. 12–17.

33. Ibid., vol. 2, p. 19.

34. Ibid., p. 19.

35. Ibid., p. 21.

36. Ibid., vol. 1, p. 327.

37. Ibid., p. 315.

38. Ibid., pp. 333 ff.

39. Ibid., vol. 2, p. 315.

40. Ibid., vol. 1, pp. 316–17.

41. Ibid., vol. 2, p. 112.

42. Stanley Hauerwas, "Time and History in Theological Ethics: The Work of James Gustafson," *Journal of Religious Ethics* 13:1 (Spring 1985): p. 3.

43. Joseph Ratzinger (Pope Benedict XVI), *Introduction to Christianity*, trans. J. R. Foster (San Francisco: Ignatius Press, 1990), p. 21.

44. James Henry Owino Kombo, *The Doctrine of God in African Christian Thought: The Holy Trinity, Theological Hermeneutics and the African Intellectual Culture* (Leiden: Brill, 2007), p. 12.

45. Anthony Akinwale, "A Timely Reaffirmation and Clarification of Vatican II," in *Sic et Non: Encountering Dominus Jesus*, ed. Stephen J. Pope and Charles Hefling (Maryknoll, NY: Orbis Books, 2002), p. 171.

46. Kombo, *The Doctrine of God in African Christian Thought*, p. 260.

47. Ibid., p. 277.

48. E. Bolaji Idowu, *Towards an Indigenous Church* (London: Oxford University Press, 1965), pp. 24–25.

49. Kombo, *The Doctrine of God in African Christian Thought*, p. 14.

50. See http://www.zenit.org/article-27046?l=english.

51. Pope Benedict XVI, *Jesus of Nazareth*, trans. Adrian J. Walker (New York: Doubleday, 2007), p. 44.

52. Ratzinger, *Introduction to Christianity*, p. 116.

53. Ibid., p. 117.

54. Ibid., p. 123.

55. Ibid., p. 128.

56. Ibid., p. 23.

57. Ibid., p. 25.

58. Ibid., p. 22.

59. Pope Benedict XVI, *Jesus of Nazareth*, pp. 116–17.

60. Ibid., p. 119.

61. Arland J. Hultgren, *The Parables of Jesus: A Commentary* (Grand Rapids, MI: Eerdmans, 2000), p. 2.

62. Klyne R. Snodgrass, *Stories with Intent: A Comprehensive Guide to the Parables of Jesus* (Grand Rapids, MI: Eerdmans, 2008), p. 2.

63. Hultgren, *The Parables of Jesus*, p. 3.

64. Joachim Jeremias, *The Parables of Jesus* (London: SCM Press, 1981), p. 13.

65. Sean Freyne, *Jesus: A Jewish Galilean*, quoted in Andrew Greeley, *Jesus: A Meditation on His Stories and His Relationships with Women* (New York: Tom Doherty, 2007), p. 107.

66. Edward Schillebeeckx, *Jesus: An Experiment in Christology*, trans. Hubert Haskins (London: Collins, 1979), p. 156.

67. Hultgren, *The Parables of Jesus*, p. 6.

68. Schillebeeckx, *Jesus: An Experiment in Christology*, p. 159.

69. See Jeremias, *The Parables of Jesus*, pp. 114–227.

70. Greeley, *Jesus: A Meditation on His Stories*, p. 108.

71. Snodgrass, *Stories with Intent*, p. 175.

72. Greeley, *Jesus: A Meditation on His Stories*, p. 111.

73. Hultgren, *The Parables of Jesus*, p. 41.

74. Jeremias, *The Parables of Jesus*, p. 38.

75. Greeley, *Jesus: A Meditation on His Stories*, p. 117.

76. Hultgren, *The Parables of Jesus: A Commentary*, p. 43.

77. Greeley, *Jesus: A Meditation on His Stories*, p. 130.

78. Ibid., p. 131.

79. Pope Benedict XVI, *Jesus of Nazareth*, p. 55.

80. Ibid.

81. Ibid., pp. 60–61.

82. Sandra Schneiders, *The Revelatory Text: Interpreting the New Testament as Sacred Scripture*, 2nd ed. (Collegeville, MN: Liturgical Press, 1999), p. 189.

83. Elizabeth Schüssler Fiorenza, *In Memory of Her: A Feminist Theological Reconstruction of Christian Origins* (New York: Crossroad, 1983), p. 121.

84. Greeley, *Jesus: A Meditation on His Stories*, p. 135.

85. Pope Benedict XVI, *Africae Munus: Post-Synodal Exhortation on the Church in Africa in Service to Reconciliation, Justice and Peace* (Vatican City: Libreria Editrice Vaticana, 2011), no. 7.

86. Cf. Emefie Ikenga Metuh, *God and Man in African Religion* (London: Chapman, 1981), pp. 38–39. Metuh acknowledges that there is ground in African mythology for a theory of an absent God who has little contact with human beings. However, he believes that the African myths that suggest this idea have largely been misunderstood. The fact is, though, as most African scholars have reported on this matter, that African Traditional Religionists are in awe of the supreme being, and consequently the reality that interaction between human beings and the divine is really an issue between the lower divinities in African Traditional Religion and human beings.

87. Ronald Green, "Religion and Morality in the African Traditional Setting," *Journal of Religion in Africa* 14:1 (1983): p. 2.

88. Ibid., pp. 2–3.

89. Ibid., p. 3.

90. Pope Benedict XVI, *Jesus of Nazareth*, pp. 200–201.

Chapter 7. Anthropology in African Theological Ethics

1. I-IIae, prologue.

2. Klaus Demmer, *Shaping the Moral Life: An Approach to Moral Theology*, trans. Roberto Dell'Oro (Washington, DC: Georgetown University Press, 2000), p. 4.

3. E. Bolaji Idowu, *Olódùmarè: God in Yoruba Belief* (New York: Praeger, 1963), p. 18.

4. Ulli Beier, ed., "The Revolt against God (A Fang Story)," in *The Origin of Life and Death: African Creation Myths*, ed. Ulli Beier (London: Heinemann, 1966), p. 18.

5. Ibid., p. 19.

6. Ibid., p. 21.

7. Ibid., p. viii.

8. Ibid., p. vii.

9. Josef Thérèse Agbasiere, *Women in Igbo Life and Thought* (London: Routledge, 2000), p. 65.

10. Raymond Arazu, "A Cultural Model for Christian Prayer," in *African Christian Spirituality*, ed. Aylward Shorter (London: Geoffrey Chapman, 1978), p. 114.

11. Iochukwu Uzukwu, *A Listening Church: Autonomy and Communion in African Churches* (Maryknoll, NY: Orbis Books, 1996), pp. 36–37.

12. Chinua Achebe, "Chi in Igbo Cosmology," in *African Philosophy: An Anthology*, ed. Emmanuel Chukwudi Eze (Oxford: Blackwell, 1998), p. 67.

13. Leopold Sedor Senghor, *African Socialism*, trans. Mercer Cook (New York: Praeger, 1964), pp. 93–94.

14. Uzukwu, *A Listening Church*, pp. 36–37.

15. Placide Tempels, *Bantu-Philosophie: Ontologie und Ethik* (Paris: Présence africaine, 1959), p. 33; quoted in Bénézet Bujo, *Foundations of an African Ethic: Beyond the Universal Claims of Western Morality* (New York: Crossroad, 2001), p. 86.

16. Kwame Gyekye, "Person and Community in African Thought," in *The African Philosophy Reader*, 2nd ed., ed. P. H. Coetzee and A. P. J. Roux (London: Routledge, 2003), p. 299.

17. Ibid.

18. Uzukwu, *A Listening Church*, p. 38.

19. Bujo, *Foundations of an African Ethic*, p. 6.

20. Peter Paris, *The Spirituality of African Peoples: The Search for a Common Moral Discourse* (Minneapolis: Fortress Press, 1995), p. 61.

21. Paulinus I. Odozor, "Truly African, *and* Wealthy! What Africa Can Learn from Catholic Social Teaching about Sustainable Economic Prosperity," in *The True Wealth of Nations: Catholic Social Thought and Economic Life*, ed. Daniel K. Finn (Oxford: Oxford University Press, 2010), p. 276.

22. It must be added here that the African version of communitarianism is hardly the only one suffering from these limitations; most other communi-

tarian theories in ethics do so as well. The focus in this book is on Africa, hence the stress on the African reality.

23. Pope Benedict XVI, *Africae Munus: Post-Synodal Exhortation on the Church in Africa in Service to Reconciliation, Justice and Peace*, no. 11 (Vatican City: Libreria Editrice Vaticana, 2011).

24. Uzukwu, *A Listening Church*, p. 43.

25. Ibid.

26. *The Catechism of the Catholic Church*, no. 356.

27. Karl Rahner, "Anthropology," in *Theological Dictionary*, ed. Karl Rahner and Herbert Vorgrimler (New York: Seabury Press, 1973), p. 26.

28. Barry L. Whitney, *What Are They Saying about God and Evil?* (New York: Paulist Press, 1989), p. 5.

29. Josef Fuchs, "The 'Sin of the World' and Normative Morality," in *Personal Responsibility and Christian Morality* (Washington, DC: Georgetown University Press; Dublin: Gill and Macmillan, 1983), p. 154.

30. Mark O'Keefe, *What Are They Saying about Social Sin?* (New York: Paulist Press, 1990), pp. 10–11.

31. See John Mahoney, *The Making of Moral Theology: A Study of the Roman Catholic Tradition* (Oxford: Clarendon Press, 1987).

32. O'Keefe, *What Are They Saying about Social Sin?*, p. 8.

33. See Council of Trent, *Doctrina de Sanctissimis Poenitentiae et Extremae Unctionis Sacramentis*, chap. 8, "*De Satisfactionis Necessitate et Fructu,*" in *Decrees of the Ecumenical Councils*, vol. 2, *Trent to Vatican II*, ed. Norman Tanner (London: Sheed and Ward; Washington, DC: Georgetown University Press, 1990), p. 709.

34. Gregory Baum, *Religion and Alienation: A Theological Reading of Sociology* (New York: Paulist Press, 1975), p. 201.

35. Ibid., pp. 201–2.

36. Ibid., p. 202.

37. Ibid.

38. Fuchs, "The 'Sin of the World' and Normative Morality," p. 160.

39. Pope John Paul II, *Sollicitudo Rei Socialis*, in *The Encyclicals of John Paul II*, ed. J. Michael Miller (Huntington, IN: Our Sunday Visitor, 1996), no. 36, p. 459.

40. Ibid.

41. Ibid., no. 37, p. 461.

42. Bernard Lonergan, *Method in Theology* (Minneapolis: Seabury Press, 1972), p. 130. See also Paulinus I. Odozor, C.S.Sp., *Richard A. McCormick and the Renewal of Moral Theology* (Notre Dame, IN: University of Notre Dame Press, 1995), p. xii.

43. Pope Benedict XVI, *Africae Munus: The Post-Synodal Exhortation on the Church in Africa in Service to Reconciliation, Justice and Peace* (Vatican City: Libreria Editrice Vaticana, 2011), no. 24.

44. Ibid., no. 22.

45. Josef Fuchs, "Basic Freedom and Morality," in *Introduction to Christian Ethics: A Reader*, ed. Ronald P. Hamel and Kenneth R. Himes (Mahwah, NJ: Paulist Press, 1989), p. 189.

46. Karl Rahner, *Foundations of Christian Faith: An Introduction to the Idea of Christianity*, trans. William V. Dych (New York: Seabury Press, 1978), p. 94.

47. Ibid., pp. 98–99.

48. Fuchs, "Basic Freedom and Morality," p. 188.

49. Ibid.

50. Ibid.

51. Avery Dulles, "The Truth about Freedom: A Theme from John Paul II," in *Veritatis Splendor and the Renewal of Moral Theology*, ed. J. A. DiNoia and Romanus Cessario (Huntington, IN: Our Sunday Visitor, 1999), p. 129.

52. Ibid., p. 133.

53. *Veritatis Splendor*, no. 92, in *The Encyclicals of John Paul II*, ed. J. Michael Miller (Huntington, IN: Our Sunday Visitor, 1996), pp. 674–771.

54. Dulles, "The Truth about Freedom," pp. 133–34.

55. See Paulinus I. Odozor, *Moral Theology in an Age of Renewal: A Study of the Catholic Tradition since Vatican II* (Notre Dame, IN: University of Notre Dame Press, 2003), esp. pp. 92–96.

56. Odozor, *Richard A. McCormick*, p. 12.

57. Ibid., p. 87.

58. Ibid., p. 88.

59. Richard A. McCormick, "Moral Theology since Vatican II: Clarity or Chaos?," in *The Critical Calling: Moral Dilemmas since Vatican II* (Washington, DC: Georgetown University Press, 1989), p. 21.

60. "Christian Family Life and Marriage in Africa Today," a working paper, in *Acts of the 6th Plenary Assembly of the Symposium of Episcopal Conferences of Africa and Madagascar (SECAM)*, Yaoundé, Cameroon, 1981, p. 92; henceforth referred to as SECAM document.

61. Ifi Amadiume, *Male Daughters, Female Husbands: Gender and Sex in an African Society* (London: Zed Books, 1987), p. 71.

62. G. T. Basden, *Niger Ibos* (London: Frank Cass, 1966), p. 214.

63. Lisa Cahill, "Marriage: Institution, Relationship, Sacrament," in *One Hundred Years of Catholic Social Thought: Celebration and Challenge*, ed. John A. Coleman (Maryknoll, NY: Orbis Books, 1991), p. 116.

64. Ibid., p. 114.

65. Ibid., p. 116.

66. André Guindon, *The Sexual Creators: An Ethical Proposal for Concerned Christians* (Lanham, MD: University Press of America, 1986), p. 23.

67. Gregory Baum, quoted in James B. Nelson, "Sexual Salvation: Grace and the Resurrection of the Body," in *Sexuality, Marriage and Family: Readings in the Catholic Tradition*, ed. Paulinus I. Odozor (Notre Dame, IN: University of Notre Dame Press, 2001), p. 18.

68. See George Weigel, *Witness to Hope: The Biography of Pope John Paul II* (New York: Cliff Street Books/HarperCollins, 1999), p. 288.

69. Pope John Paul II, *Crossing the Threshold of Hope* (New York: Random House Digital, 1995).

70. Pope John Paul II, *Redemptor Hominis*, no. 10, in *The Encyclicals of John Paul II*, ed. J. Michael Miller (Huntington, IN: Our Sunday Visitor, 1996).

71. Cf. Joseph Wawrykow, "Grace," in *The Theology of Thomas Aquinas*, ed. Rik Van Nieuwenhove and Joseph Wawrykow (Notre Dame, IN: University of Notre Dame Press, 2005), pp. 193–96.

72. Ibid., p. 194.

73. Thomas O'Meara, "Aquinas in Africa," *America* (Feb. 6, 2006): p. 15.

74. M. D. Chenu, "The Plan of St. Thomas' *Summa Theologiae*," *Cross Currents* 2 (1952): p. 75.

75. Romanus Cessario, *The Moral Virtues and Theological Ethics* (Notre Dame, IN: University of Notre Dame Press, 1991), pp. 1–2.

76. John S. Mbiti, *African Religions and Philosophy*, 2nd ed. (Portsmouth, NH: Heinemann, 1990), p. 102.

77. Carolyn Osiek, "The Family in Early Christianity: 'Family Values' Revisited," in Odozor, *Sexuality, Marriage and Family*, p. 220.

78. Ibid.

79. Ibid., p. 227.

80. Vatican II, *Gaudium et Spes*, no. 22, in *Vatican II: Constitutions, Decrees, Declarations*, ed. Austin Flannery (Northport, NY: Costello, 1996), pp. 185, 186.

Chapter 8. Moral Reasoning in African Theological Ethics

1. Bénézet Bujo, *Foundations of an African Christian Ethic: Beyond the Universal Claims of Western Morality* (New York: Crossroad, 2001).

2. Ibid., p. 12.

3. Ibid., pp. 12–14. See *Summa Theologica*, I, q. 1.1a; II-IIae, q. 2, q. 4.

4. Bujo, *Foundations of an African Christian Ethic*, pp. 7 ff.

5. Ibid., p. 15. There appear to be two senses to the term *communitarianism* and its cognate *communitarian* in Bujo's usage. In the first sense, the term applies to the involvement of the community in determining moral norms, or to the rightness or wrongness of moral action or norms through the process of palaver. In other instances Bujo uses the term when referring to the consequences or outcomes of moral action—that is, in determining whether they promote or are destructive of community and community relationships.

6. Ibid., p. 22.

7. Paulinus I. Odozor, *Moral Theology in an Age of Renewal: A Study of the Catholic Tradition since Vatican II* (Notre Dame, IN: University of Notre Dame Press, 2003), p. 91.

8. Joseph Boyle, "Natural Law," in *The New Dictionary of Theology*, ed. Joseph A. Komonchak, Mary Collins, and Dermot A. Lane (Collegeville, MN: Liturgical Press, 1991), p. 705.

9. See Paulinus Odozor, "An African Moral Theology of Inculturation: Methodological Considerations," *Theological Studies* 69:3 (Sept. 2008): pp. 583–609.

10. International Theological Commission, "The Search for Universal Ethics: A New Look at Natural Law," trans. Joseph Bolin, March 25, 2010, in http://www.pathsoflove.com/universal-ethics-natural-law.html, no. 52.

11. Ibid.

12. Chinua Achebe, *Things Fall Apart* (New York: Anchor Books, 1994), p. 57.

13. See, for example, David Hoegberg, "The Logic of Cultural Violence in Achebe's *Things Fall Apart*," *College Literature* 26:1 (Winter 1999): pp. 69–79; Jonathan Greenberg, "Okonkwo and the Storyteller: Death, Accident and Meaning in Chinua Achebe and Walter Benjamin," *Contemporary Literature* 48:3 (Fall 2007): pp. 423–50; Emeka Nwabueze, "Theoretical Construction and Constructive Theorizing on the Execution of Ikemefuna in Achebe's *Things Fall Apart*: A Study in Critical Dualism," *Research in African Literatures* 31:2 (Summer 2000): pp. 163–73; Damian U. Opata, "Eternal Sacred Order versus Conventional Wisdom: A Consideration of Moral Culpability in the Killing of Ikemefuna in *Things Fall Apart*," *Research in African Literatures* 18:1 (Spring 1987): pp. 71–79; Neil Ten Kortenaar, "Becoming African and the Death of Ikemefuna," *University of Toronto Quarterly* 73:2 (Spring 2004): pp. 773–94.

14. The earth goddess (Ala or Ani) oversees morality in Igbo religion.

15. Achebe, *Things Fall Apart*, pp. 66–67.

16. Plato, "Euthyphro," in *Five Great Dialogues of Plato: Euthyphro, Apology, Crito, Meno, Phaedo*, trans. Benjamin Jowett (Claremont, CA: Coyote Canyon Press, 2009), p. 10.

17. Louis P. Pojman, *Ethics: Discovering Right and Wrong*, 4th ed. (Belmont, CA: Wadsworth Thompson Learning, 2002), p. 17.

18. William K. Frankena, *Ethics*, 2nd ed. (Englewood Cliffs, NJ: Prentice-Hall, 1973), p. 14.

19. Pojman, *Ethics*, p. 11.

20. Frankena, *Ethics*, p. 15.

21. Glen G. Graber, "Divine Command Morality," in *The Westminster Dictionary of Christian Ethics*, ed. James F. Childress and John Macquarie (Philadelphia: Westminster Press, 1986), pp. 159–61.

22. Immanuel Kant, *The Critique of Practical Reason*, in *The Philosophy of Kant*, ed. Carl J. Friedrich (New York: Modern Library, 1949), p. 109. All references to Kant are to the translations of his works in this collection.

23. Ibid., p. 211.

24. Pojman, *Ethics*, pp. 10–11.

25. Pope John Paul II, *Veritatis Splendor*, no. 80, in *The Encyclicals of John Paul II*, ed. J. Michael Miller (Huntington, IN: Our Sunday Visitor, 1996), p. 740.

26. Bruno Schüller, "Various Types of Grounding for Ethical Norms," in *Readings in Moral Theology*, vol. 1, *Moral Norms and Catholic Tradition*, ed. Charles E. Curran and Richard A. McCormick (New York: Paulist Press, 1979), p. 186.

27. Wolfgang Schrage, *The Ethics of the New Testament*, trans. David Green (Philadelphia: Fortress Press, 1988), p. 5.

28. Ibid., p. 8.

29. Rudolf Schnackenburg, *The Moral Teaching of the New Testament* (London: Burns and Oates, 1965), p. 13.

30. Ibid., pp. 13–14.

31. Schrage, *The Ethics of the New Testament*, p. 7.

32. Pope Benedict XVI, *Deus Caritas Est: Encyclical Letter of the Supreme Pontiff on Christian Love* (Vatican City: Editrice Vaticana, 2006), no. 17.

33. Schrage, *The Ethics of the New Testament*, p. 11.

34. Ibid., p. 10.

35. James M. Gustafson, *Can Ethics Be Christian?* (Chicago: University of Chicago Press, 1975), p. 40.

36. James M. Gustafson, *Christ and the Moral Life* (Chicago: University of Chicago Press, 1968), p. 141.

37. Saint Thomas Aquinas, *Summa Theologica*, I-II, 554.4.

38. Gustafson, *Christ and the Moral Life*, p. 243.

39. See John Hick, "Evil, the Problem of," in *The Encyclopedia of Philosophy*, vols. 3 and 4, ed. Paul Edwards (1967; New York: Macmillan, 1972), pp. 136–41.

40. Augustine of Hippo, "The Way of the Manicheans," in *The Fathers of the Church: A New Translation*, vol. 56 (Washington, DC: Catholic University of America Press, 1966), p. 65.

41. Ibid., pp. 66–67.

42. We must note the different senses of the notion of evil. In one sense the word refers to physical evil: the physical sensation of pain, mental anguish, or suffering that is a result either of human action, intended or unintended, or of natural causes. We also speak of moral evil. This is evil that occurs when human beings intentionally will, bring about, or let happen (for no just cause) the instance of physical evil.

43. Augustine of Hippo, *The Enchiridion on Faith, Hope and Love*, ed. Thomas S. Hibbs (Washington, DC: Regnery Gateway, 1996), chap. 3. See also chaps. 4, 5, and 6.

44. Hick, "Evil," p. 137.

45. Augustine, *Enchiridion*, chap. 4.

46. Augustine of Hippo, *City of God*, trans. Henry Bettenson (Harmondsworth, UK: Penguin, 1972), p. 477.

47. Ibid., bk. 12, chap. 6.

48. Joseph Ratzinger, *Introduction to Christianity*, trans. J. R. Foster (1990; San Francisco: Ignatius Press, Communion Books, 2004), p. 27.

49. Pope Benedict XVI, *Africae Munus: Post-Synodal Exhortation of His Holiness Pope Benedict XVI on the Church in Africa in Service to Reconciliation, Justice and Peace* (Vatican City: Editrice Vaticana, 2011), no. 91.

50. Ibid., no. 93.

51. See John C. Cavadini, "Ambrose and Augustine: *De Bono Mortis*," in *The Limits of Ancient Christianity: Essays on Late Antique Thought and Culture in Honor of R. A. Markus*, ed. William E. Klingshirn and Mark Vessey (Ann Arbor: University of Michigan Press, 1999), pp. 232–49.

52. Vincent MacNamara, *Faith and Ethics: Recent Roman Catholicism* (Dublin: Gill and Macmillan; Washington, DC: Georgetown University Press, 1985), pp. 199–200.

53. Ibid., p. 200.

54. See Paulinus Odozor, "Liturgy and Life: A Discussion from an African Christian Theological Perspective," *Worship* 82:5 (Sept. 2008): pp. 413–33.

55. Jean Porter, *Nature as Reason: A Thomistic Theory of the Natural Law* (Grand Rapids, MI: Eerdmans, 2005), p. 340.

56. Ibid.

57. Christopher C. Roberts, *Creation and Covenant: The Significance of Sexual Difference in the Moral Theology of Marriage* (London: T&T Clark International, 2007), p. 2.

58. Jennifer Hartline, "Obama and Cecile Richard's Caricature of the American Woman," http://www.catholic.org/national/national_story.php?id=48127.

59. Obianuju Ekeocha, "Nigerian Woman Writes to Melinda Gates: 'We Don't Need Your Contraception,'" http://www.catholic.org/national/national_story.php?id=47264.

Chapter 9. Moral Theology Christian and African

1. Edward Schillebeeckx, *Jesus: An Experiment in Christology*, trans. Hubert Haskins (London: Collins, 1979), pp. 47–48.

2. Edward Schillebeeckx, *On Christian Faith: The Spiritual, Ethical and Political Dimensions* (New York: Crossroad, 1987), p. 32.

3. Ibid., p. 36.

4. See C. Plini Caecili Secundi, *Epistolarum Libri Decem*, ed. R. A. B. Mynors (Oxford: Clarendon Press, 1963). Gaius Plinius Caecilius Secundus, also known as Pliny the Younger, was imperial legate to Bithynia et Pontus (c. AD 110–13) when Trajan was emperor in Rome. Like many Roman officials of his day, Pliny found the Christians in one way insufferable, and in another quaint. The more Pliny tried to deal with the "Christian problem" the more it seemed to grow. Pliny felt compelled to investigate this group further in order to be in a position to give a more comprehensive report to his imperial masters in Rome. In a portion of his letter Pliny pinpoints the central issue in the Christian religion. In the course of his investigation he had discovered, he said, that Christians gathered on a fixed day, before dawn, and together recited a hymn "to Christ as to a god, alternating back and forth [*carmenque Christo quasi dicere secum invicem*]," and committing themselves not to anything criminal, but to avoiding theft, robbery, and adultery, to not breaking their word, and to not refusing to deliver up a deposit when summoned to do so. After that, they would disband, and come together again to have a meal, but with ordinary and harmless food. See Franz Jozef van Beeck, *God Encountered: A Contemporary Catholic Systematic Theology*, vol. 1, *Understanding the Christian Faith* (New York: Harper & Row, 1989), p. 146.

5. Pope Benedict XVI, *Deus Caritas Est: Encyclical Letter of the Supreme Pontiff on Christian Love* (Vatican City: Editrice Vaticana, 2006), no. 25a.

6. John C. Cavadini, "Open Letter to the University Community," in http://www.ndsmcobserver.com/2.2756/open-letter-to-the-university-community-1.265347.

7. See http://www.vatican.va/holy_father/paul_vi/motu_proprio/documents/hf_p-vi_motu-proprio_19650915_apostolica-sollicitudo_en.html.

8. Vatican Council II, *De Episcoporum Munere* [On the Office of Bishops], also known as *Christus Dominus*, in the *Decrees of the Ecumenical Councils*, vol. 2, *Trent to Vatican II*, ed. Norman P. Tanner (London: Sheed and Ward; Washington, DC: Georgetown University Press, 1990), p. 922.

9. Cf. *Apostolica Sollicitudo*, http://www.vatican.va/holy_father/paul_vi/motu_proprio/documents/hf_p-vi_motu-proprio_19650915_apostolica-sollicitudo_en.html.

10. A full listing of all the synods to date is available from the following Vatican source: http://www.vatican.va/roman_curia/synod/documents/rc_synod 20050309_documentation profile_en.html#C._ordo synodi_Episcoporum_the _order_of_the_synod_of_Bishops.

11. Synod of Bishops, 2nd Special Assembly for Africa, in *Instrumentum Laboris* (Vatican City: Editrice Vaticana, 2009), no. 6, p. 3.

12. Ibid., no. 15.

13. Ibid., p. iii.

14. Synod of Bishops, 2nd Special Assembly for Africa, *Nuntius* (Vatican City: Editrice Vaticana, 2009), nos. 4, 5, p. 2.

15. Pope Benedict XVI, *Africae Munus: Post-Synodal Apostolic Exhortation of His Holiness Pope Benedict XVI on the Church in Africa in Service to Reconciliation, Justice and Peace* (Vatican City: Editrice Vaticana, 2011), no. 4.

16. Ibid., no. 9.

17. Ibid., no. 20. See also *Relatio ante Disceptationem*, no. 11a. http://www.vatican.va/roman_curia/synod/documents/rc_synod_doc_20091005 _rel-ante-disceptationem_en.html.

18. Pope Benedict XVI, *Africae Munus*, nos. 97–102.

19. At the end of the synod, the synod fathers drew up a list of fifty-four "propositions," which were meant to capture the essence of the discussions and agreements throughout the course of the synod. These propositions were debated and voted on and subsequently sent to the pope to help him and his collaborators put together the postsynodal exhortation, *Africae Munus*. These propositions (henceforth referred to as "p." in the text) can be found in http://www.vatican.va/roman_curia/synod/documents/rc_synod_doc_20091023_ elenco-prop-finali_en.html.

20. Cf. Synod of Bishops, "2nd Special Assembly for Africa," *Elenchus Finalis Propositionum*, p. 3.

21. Synod of Bishops, "Justice in the World" (1971), in *Catholic Social Thought: The Documentary Heritage*, ed. David J. O'Brien and Thomas A. Shannon (Maryknoll, NY: Orbis Books, 1998), p. 287.

22. Paulinus Odozor, *Moral Theology in an Age of Renewal: A Study of the Catholic Tradition since Vatican II* (Notre Dame, IN: University of Notre Dame Press, 2003), p. 25. See also Pope Benedict XVI, *Africae Munus*, no. 22.

23. J. Bryan Hehir, "The Social Role of the Church: Leo XIII, Vatican II and John Paul II," in *Catholic Social Thought and the New World Order: Building on One Hundred Years*, ed. Oliver F. Williams and John W. Houch (Notre Dame, IN: University of Notre Dame Press, 1993), p. 38.

24. Here the pope provides a reading list for African priests: "In the context of the ongoing formation of clergy, I consider it important to reread and meditate on such documents as the conciliar Decree on the Ministry and Life of Priests *Presbyterorum Ordinis*, the 1992 Post-Synodal Apostolic Exhortation *Pastores Dabo Vobis*, the 1994 *Directory on the Ministry and Life of Priests* and the 2002 Instruction *The Priest, Pastor and Guide of the Parish Community.*" See *Africae Munus*, no. 110.

25. NEPAD stands for *New Economic Partnership for African Development*. The peer review mechanism is the process by which governments are assessed for their performance, particularly with the set objectives of NEPAD such as democratic governance and sound economic stewardship.

26. Archbishop John O. Onaiyekan, "Islam and the Church Family of God in Africa: Beyond Dialogue to Collaboration: In the Service of Reconciliation, Justice and Peace," http://www.vatican.va/news_services/press /sinodo/documents/bollettino_23_ii_speciale-africa-2009/02_inglese/b10 _02.html.

27. Cf. Kwame Bediako, *Jesus and the Gospel in Africa: History and Experience* (Maryknoll, NY: Orbis Books, 2004), p. 59.

28. Peter Kodwo Appiah Cardinal Turkson, *Relatio post Disceptationem* (Vatican City: Synod of Bishops, 2nd Special Assembly for Africa, 2009), p. 6.

29. "Religious Women in the Church in Africa," intervention by Sr. Felicia Harry, N. S. A. (O. L. A.), Superior General of the Sisters of Our Lady of Apostles, Ghana, http://www.catholicnews.com/data/stories/cns/0904518.htm.

30. Archbishop (now Cardinal) Sarah is the emeritus archbishop of Conakry, Guinea, and now president of the Pontifical Council, "Cor Unum," at the Vatican.

31. "La théorie du genre est une idéologie sociologisante occidentale des relations hommes-femmes, qui s'attaque à l'identit sponsale de la personne humaine, à la complémentarité anthropologique entre l'homme et la

femme, au mariage, à la maternité et la paternité, à la famille et à la procréation. Elle est contraire à la culture africaine et aux vérités humaines éclairées par la Révélation divine en Jésus Christ." This quotation is taken from the synodal intervention of Archbishop Sarah entitled "L'église et la théorie du genre en Afrique." http://www.zenit.org/en/articles/interventions-from-synod -s-5th-congregationhttp://www.zenit.org/en/articles/interventions-from -synod-s-5th-congregation.

32. Synod of Bishops, 2nd Special Assembly for Africa, *Nuntius*, p. 11.

33. As John Allen points out in the *National Catholic Reporter*, the Maputo Protocol "is an adjunct to a charter of the African Union on human rights. Elaborated in twenty-five articles, it guarantees a host of rights to Africa's women, such as social and political equality, voting rights, and an end to genital mutilation. The protocol legally came into force on November 25, 2005, after having been ratified by the required fifteen member states of the African Union." See "Ghost of Maputo Protocol Hangs over African Synod," Oct. 11, 2009, http://ncronline.org/blogs/ncr-today/ghost-maputo-protocol -hangs-over-african-synod.

34. See "Protocol to the African Charter on Human and Peoples' Rights on the Rights of Women in Africa," art. 14, p. 16, http://www.africa-union.org /root/au/Documents/Treaties/Text/Protocol on the Rights of Women.pdf.

35. *Nuntius*, p. 5.

36. To borrow a phrase made popular by Elochukwu Uzukwu in his book *A Listening Church: Autonomy and Communion in African Churches* (Maryknoll, NY: Orbis Books, 1996).

37. Peter Kodwo Appiah Cardinal Turkson, *Relatio ante Disceptationem* (Vatican City: Synod of Bishops, 2nd Special Assembly for Africa, 2009), pp. 12–13.

38. William Spohn, "Jesus and Ethics," *CTSA Proceedings* 51 (1994): p. 51.

39. Paulinus Ikechukwu Odozor, "Classical Moral Theology and the World Church: Some Suggestions on How to Move Forward," *Louvain Studies* 30 (2005): p. 289.

BIBLIOGRAPHY

Achebe, Chinua. *Arrow of God*. New York: Anchor Books, 1969.

———. "Chi in Igbo Cosmology." In *African Philosophy: An Anthology*, edited by Emmanuel Chukwudi Eze, pp. 67–72. Oxford: Blackwell, 1998.

———. *Things Fall Apart*. New York: Anchor Books, 1994.

Adamo, David Tuesday. "The Use of Psalms in African Indigenous Churches in Nigeria." In *The Bible in Africa: Transactions, Trajectories, and Trends*, edited by Gerald O. West and Musa W. Dube, pp. 336–49. Boston: Brill Academic, 2001.

Agbasiere, Josef Thérèse. *Women in Igbo Life and Thought*. London: Routledge, 2000.

Aiken, Henry David. "Levels of Moral Discourse." In *Reason and Conduct: New Bearings in Moral Philosophy*, pp. 65–87. Westport, CT: Greenwood, 1978.

Akinwale, Anthony A. "The Theology of the Passion of Christ in St. Thomas Aquinas and Its Possible Relevance to Liberation Theology." PhD diss., Boston College, 1996.

———. "A Timely Reaffirmation and Clarification of Vatican II." In *Sic et Non: Encountering Dominus Jesus*, edited by Stephen J. Pope and Charles Hefling. Maryknoll, NY: Orbis Books, 2002.

Amadiume, Ifi. *Daughters of the Goddess, Daughters of Imperialism: African Women Struggle for Culture, Power and Democracy*. London: Zed Books, 2000.

———. *Male Daughters, Female Husbands: Gender and Sex in an African Society*. London: Zed Books, 1987.

Anderson, Allan H. *African Reformation: African Initiated Christianity in the 20th Century*. Trenton, NJ: Africa World Press, 2001.

Anselm of Canterbury, Saint. *The Proslogion*. http://www.fordham.edu/halsall/basis/anselm-proslogion.asp.

Arazu, Raymond. "A Cultural Model for Christian Prayer." In *African Christian Spirituality*, edited by Aylward Shorter, pp. 112–16. London: Geoffrey Chapman, 1978.

Arrupe, Pedro. "Letter to the Whole Society on Inculturation." In *Other Apostolates Today, Selected Letters and Addresses 3*, edited by Jerome Aixala. St. Louis: Institute of Jesuit Sources, 1981.

Augustine of Hippo. *City of God*. Translated by Henry Bettenson. Harmondsworth, UK: Penguin Books, 1972.

———. *The Enchiridion on Faith, Hope and Love*. Edited by Thomas S. Hibbs. Washington, DC: Regnery Gateway, 1996.

———. *The Manichean Debate*. Edited by Boniface Ramsey. Hyde Park, NY: New City Press, 2006.

———. "The Way of the Manicheans." In *The Fathers of the Church: A New Translation*, vol. 56. Washington, DC: Catholic University of America Press, 1966.

Barth, Karl. *The Doctrine of the Word of God: The Prolegomena to Church Dogmatics*. Vol. 1. Translated by G. T. Thompson and H. Knight. 1956; Edinburgh: T & T Clark, 1978.

Baum, Gregory. *Religion and Alienation: A Theological Reading of Sociology*. New York: Paulist Press, 1975.

Bediako, Kwame. *Christianity and Africa: The Renewal of a Non-Christian Religion*. Maryknoll, NY: Orbis Books, 1995.

———. *Jesus and the Gospel in Africa: History and Experience*. Maryknoll, NY: Orbis Books, 2004.

———. *Theology and Identity: The Impact of Culture upon Christian Thought in the Second Century and in Modern Africa*. 1992; Cumbria, UK: Regnum Books, 1999.

———. "Understanding the African Theology in the 20th Century." *Themelios* 20 (1994).

Beier, Ulli, ed. *The Origin of Life and Death: African Creation Myths*. London: Heinemann, 1966.

Benedict XVI, Pope. *Africae Munus: Post-Synodal Exhortation of His Holiness Pope Benedict XVI on the Church in Africa in Service to Reconciliation, Justice and Peace*. Vatican City: Editrice Vaticana, 2011.

———. *Deus Caritas Est: Encyclical Letter of the Supreme Pontiff on Christian Love*. Vatican City: Editrice Vaticana, 2006.

———. *Introduction to Christianity*. Translated by J. R. Foster. 1990; San Francisco: Ignatius Press and Communio Books, 2004.

———. *Jesus of Nazareth*. Translated by Adrian J. Walker. New York: Doubleday, 2007.

Blasi, Anthony J. *Moral Conflict and Christian Religion.* New York: Peter Lang, 1988.

Boniface VIII, Pope. *Unam Sanctam.* In *Documents of the Christian Church*, edited by Henry Bettenson. Oxford: Oxford University Press, 1979.

Bühlmann, Walbert. *All Have the Same God.* Middle Green, Slough, UK: St. Paul's Publications, 1979.

———. *The Chosen Peoples.* Translated by Robert R. Darr. Middle Green, Slough, UK: St. Paul's Publications, 1982.

———. *The Coming of the Third Church: An Analysis of the Present and Future of the Church.* Middle Green, Slough, UK: St. Paul's Publications, 1976.

Bujo, Bénézet. *African Christian Morality at the Age of Inculturation.* 1990; Nairobi: Paulines Publications Africa, 1998.

———. *Le diaire d'un théologien Africain.* Spiritualité du Tiers-monde 1. Kinshasa: Éditions de l'église d'en bas, 1987.

———. "Differentiations in African Ethics." In *The Blackwell Companion to Religious Ethics*, edited by William Schweiker, pp. 423–38. Malden, MA: Blackwell, 2005.

———. *The Ethical Dimension of Community: The African Model and the Dialogue between North and South.* Nairobi: Paulines Publications Africa, 1998.

———. *Foundations of an African Ethic: Beyond the Universal Claims of Western Morality.* New York: Crossroad, 2001.

———. *Moralautonomie und Normenfindung bei Thomas von Aquin: Unter Einbeziehung der neutestamentlischen Kommentare.* Veröffentlischungen des Grabman-Institutes zur Erforschung der Mittelalterlichen Theologie und Philosophie n.s. 29. Paderborn: Schöningh, 1979.

Burghardt, Walter J. "The Role of the Scholar in the Catholic Church." In *Moral Theology: Challenges for the Future: Essays in Honor of Richard A. McCormick*, edited by Charles E. Curran, pp. 15–31. New York: Paulist Press, 1990.

Cahill, Lisa S. "Consent in Time of Affliction: The Ethics of a Circumspect Theist." *Journal of Religious Ethics* 13:1 (Spring 1985): pp. 28–36.

Cavadini, John C. "Ambrose and Augustine: *De Bono Mortis.*" In *The Limits of Ancient Christianity: Essays on Late Antique Thought and Culture in Honor of R. A. Markus*, edited by William E. Klingshirn and Mark Vessey, pp. 232–49. Ann Arbor: University of Michigan Press, 1999.

Cavadini, John. "Open Letter to the University Community." http://www.ndsmcobserver.com/2.2756/open-letter-to-the-university-community-1.26347.

Cessario, Romanus. *The Moral Virtues and Theological Ethics*. Notre Dame, IN: University of Notre Dame Press, 1991.

Chenu, M. D. "The Plan of St. Thomas' *Summa Theologiae*." *Cross Currents* 2 (1952): pp. 67–79.

Chinweizu. *The West and the Rest of Us: White Predators, Black Slavers, and the African Elite*. New York: Random House, 1975.

Chitando, Ezra. "The (Mis)Appropriation of the African Traditional Religion in African Theology." In *Inculturation and Post-Colonial Discourse in African Theology*, edited by Edward P. Antonio, pp. 97–114. New York: Peter Lang, 2006.

Congar, Yves. *The Meaning of Tradition*. Translated by A. N. Woodraw. New York: Hawthorn Books, 1964.

Cordeiro, Joseph Cardinal. *Vatican II Revisited: By Those Who Were There*. Minneapolis: Winston Press, 1986.

Council of Trent. *Doctrina de Sanctissimis Poenitentiae et Extremae Unctionis Sacramentis*. In *Decrees of the Ecumenical Councils*, vol. 2, *Trent to Vatican II*, edited by Norman Tanner. London: Sheed and Ward; Washington, DC: Georgetown University Press, 1990.

Davidson, Basil. *Africa in History: Themes and Outlines*. Frogmore, UK: Paladin Books, 1974.

Demmer, Klaus. *Shaping the Moral Life: An Approach to Moral Theology*. Translated by Roberto Dell'Oro. Washington, DC: Georgetown University Press, 2000.

Dube, Musa W. "Readings of Semoya: Botswana Women's Interpretations of Matt. 15:21–28." *Semeia* 73 (1966): pp. 111–29.

Dulles, Avery. "The Truth about Freedom: A Theme from John Paul II." In *Veritatis Splendor and the Renewal of Moral Theology*, edited by J. A. DiNoia and Romanus Cessario, pp. 129–42. Huntington, IN: Our Sunday Visitor, 1999.

Ebelebe, Charles A. *Africa and the New Face of Mission: A Critical Assessment of the Legacy of the Irish Spiritans among the Igbo of Southern Nigeria*. Lanham, MD: University Press of America, 2009.

Eckert, Jost. "The Gospel for Israel and the Nations: The Problem of the Absoluteness of Christianity in the New Testament." In *True and False Universality of Christianity*, edited by Claude Geffre and Jean-Pierre Jossua. Edinburgh: T&T Clark, 1980.

Ekeocha, Obianuju. "Nigerian Woman Writes to Melinda Gates: 'We Don't Need Your Contraception.'" http://www.catholic.org/national/national _story.php?id=47264.

Enang, Kenneth. *The Nigerian Catholics and the Independent Churches: A Call to Authentic Faith*. Nairobi: Paulines Publications Africa, 2012.

Eze, Chielozona. *Postcolonial Imagination and Moral Representations in African Literature and Culture.* Lanham, MD: Lexington Books, 2011.

Eze, Emmanuel Chukwudi, ed. *African Philosophy: An Anthology.* Oxford: Blackwell, 1998.

Ezeogu, Ernest M. "The African Origin of Jesus: An Afrocentric Reading of Matthew's Infancy Narrative (Matthew 1–2)." In *Postcolonial Perspectives in African Biblical Interpretations,* edited by Musa W. Dube, Andrew M. Mbuvi, and Dora Mbuwayesango, pp. 259–82. Atlanta: Society of Biblical Literature, 2012.

Facultés Catholiques de Kinshasa. *Programmes d'études: Années Academiques 2006–2007 et 2008–2009.* Kinshasa: Secrétariat Général Académique, 2006, 2008.

Fasholé-Luke, Edward. Introduction, *Christianity in Independent Africa.* London: R. Collings; Bloomington: Indiana University Press, 1978.

———. "The Quest for an African Christian Theology." *Ecumenical Review* 27:3 (July 1975): pp. 259–69.

Frankena, William K. *Ethics.* 2nd ed. Englewood Cliffs, NJ: Prentice-Hall, 1973.

Freyne, Sean. *Jesus: A Jewish Galilean.* New York: Continuum, 2004.

Fry, Peter. *Spirits of Protest.* Cambridge: Cambridge University Press, 1976.

Fuchs, Josef. "Basic Freedom and Morality." In *Introduction to Christian Ethics: A Reader,* edited by Ronald P. Hamel and Kenneth R. Himes, pp. 187–98. Mahwah, NJ: Paulist Press, 1989.

———. "The 'Sin of the World' and Normative Morality." In *Personal Responsibility and Christian Morality,* pp. 153–75. Washington, DC: Georgetown University Press; Dublin: Gill and Macmillan, 1983.

Gbadegesin, Segun. "The Origins of African Ethics." In *The Blackwell Companion to Religious Ethics,* edited by William Schweiker, pp. 413–22. Oxford: Blackwell, 2005.

Gilleman, Gérard. *The Primacy of Charity in Moral Theology.* Translated by William P. Ryan, S.J., and André Vachon, S.J. Westminster, MD: Newman, 1959.

Graber, Glen G. "Divine Command Morality." In *The Westminster Dictionary of Christian Ethics,* edited by James F. Childress and John Macquarie, pp. 159–61. Philadelphia: Westminster Press, 1986.

Greeley, Andrew. *Jesus: A Meditation on His Stories and His Relationships with Women.* New York: Tom Doherty Associates, 2007.

Green, Robert M. "Morality and Religion." In *The Encyclopaedia of Religion,* edited by Mircea Eliade, p. 100. New York: Macmillan; London: Collier Macmillan, 1987.

———. "Religion and Morality in the African Traditional Setting." *Journal of Religion in Africa* 14:1 (1983): pp. 1–23.

Greenberg, Jonathan. "Okonkwo and the Storyteller: Death, Accident and Meaning in Chinua Achebe and Walter Benjamin." *Contemporary Literature* 48:3 (Fall 2007): pp. 423–50.

Guindon, André. *The Sexual Creators: An Ethical Proposal for Concerned Christians*. Lanham, MD: University Press of America, 1986.

Gustafson, James M. *Can Ethics Be Christian?* Chicago: University of Chicago Press, 1975.

———. *Christ and the Moral Life*. Chicago: University of Chicago Press, 1968.

———. *Ethics from a Theocentric Perspective*. 2 vols. Chicago: University of Chicago Press, 1981, 1984.

———. "A Response to Critics." *Journal of Religious Ethics* 13:2 (Fall 1985): pp. 192–93.

Gyekye, K., and K. Wiredu, eds. *Person and Community: Ghanaian Philosophical Studies* 1. Washington, DC: Council for Research in Values and Philosophy and UNESCO, 1992.

Gyekye, Kwame. "African Ethics." http://plato.stanford.edu/entries/african-ethics/.

———. "Person and Community in African Thought." In *The African Philosophy Reader*, 2nd ed., edited by P. H. Coetzee and A. P. J. Roux, pp. 287–313. London: Routledge, 2003.

Hale, Sondra. "Colonial Discourse and Ethnographic Residuals: The 'Female Circumcision' Debate and the Politics of Knowledge." In *Female Circumcision and the Politics of Knowledge: African Women in Imperialist Discourses*, edited by Obioma Nnaemeka, pp. 211–18. Westport, CT: Praeger, 2005.

Hallen, Barry. "African Ethics?" In *The Blackwell Companion to Religious Ethics*, edited by William Schweiker, pp. 406–12. Oxford: Blackwell, 2005.

Hartline, Jennifer. "Obama and Cecile Richard's Caricature of the American Woman." http://www.catholic.org/national/national_story.php?id=48127.

Hastings, Adrian. *African Christianity*. New York: Seabury Press, 1976.

Hauerwas, Stanley. "Time and History in Theological Ethics: The Work of James Gustafson." *Journal of Religious Ethics* 13:1 (Spring 1995): pp. 3–21.

Hehir, J. Bryan. "The Social Role of the Church: Leo XIII, Vatican II and John Paul II." In *Catholic Social Thought and the New World Order: Building on One Hundred Years*, edited by Oliver F. Williams and John W. Houch, p. 38. Notre Dame, IN: University of Notre Dame Press, 1993.

Hick, John. "Evil, the Problem of." In *The Encyclopedia of Philosophy*, vols. 3–4, edited by Paul Edwards, pp. 136–41. 1967; New York: Macmillan, 1972.

———. *God and the Universe of Faiths*. Glasgow: Collins Fount, 1977.

———, ed. *The Myth of God Incarnate*. London: SCM Press, 1977.

———. "Sceptics and Believers." In *Faith and the Philosophers*, edited by John Hick, pp. 239–40. London: Macmillan, 1964.

Hillman, Eugene. "Evangelism in a Wider Ecumenism: Theological Grounds for Dialogue with Other Religions." *Journal of Ecumenical Studies* 12 (Winter 1975).

Hoegberg, David. "The Logic of Cultural Violence in Achebe's *Things Fall Apart*." *College Literature* 26:1 (Winter 1999): pp. 69–79.

Hultgren, Arland J. *The Parables of Jesus: A Commentary*. Grand Rapids, MI: Eerdmans, 2000.

Idowu, Bolaji. *Olódùmarè: God in Yoruba Belief*. New York: Praeger, 1963.

———. *Towards an Indigenous Church*. London: Oxford University Press, 1965.

Igwemezie, Regina N. *Widowhood: A Harrowing Experience*. Enugu, Nigeria: privately published, 2005.

Ikenga Metuh, Emefie. *Comparative Studies of African Traditional Religions*. Onitsha, Nigeria: IMCO, 1987.

———. *God and Man in African Religion*. London: Chapman, 1981.

International Theological Commission. "The Search for Universal Ethics: A New Look at Natural Law." Translated by Joseph Bolin. March 25, 2010. http://www.pathsoflove.com/universal-ethics-natural-law.html.

Irele, Abiola. *The African Imagination: Literature in Africa and the Black Diaspora*. New York: Oxford University Press, 2001.

Jeremias, Joachim. *The Parables of Jesus*. London: SCM Press, 1981.

John Paul II, Pope. *Crossing the Threshold of Hope*. New York: Random House Digital, 1995.

———. *Ecclesia in Africa: The Post Synodal Exhortation of His Holiness Pope John Paul II on the Church in Africa and Its Evangelizing Mission Towards the Year 2000*. Vatican City: Editrice Vaticana, 1995.

———. *Evangelium Vitae*. In Miller, *The Encyclicals of John Paul II*.

———. *Redemptor Hominis: Encyclical Letter of John Paul II at the Beginning of His Papal Ministry*. In Miller, *The Encyclicals of John Paul II*.

———. *Redemptoris Missio: Encyclical Letter of the Supreme Pontiff John Paul II on the Permanent Validity of the Church's Missionary Mandate*. In Miller, *The Encyclicals of John Paul II*.

_____. *Veritatis Splendor: Encyclical Letter of the Supreme Pontiff Regarding Certain Fundamental Questions of the Church's Moral Teaching*. In Miller, *The Encyclicals of John Paul II*.

Kalu, Ogbu. *African Pentecostalism: An Introduction*. Oxford: Oxford University Press, 2008.

Kant, Immanuel. *The Critique of Practical Reason*. In *The Philosophy of Kant*, edited by Carl J. Friedrich. New York: Modern Library, 1949.

Karrer, Otto. *The Kingdom of God Today*. Translated by Rosaleen Ockenden. New York: Herder and Herder, 1964.

Katongole, Emmanuel. *A Future for Africa: Critical Essays in Christian Social Imagination*. Scranton, PA: University of Scranton Press, 2005.

Keightley, Alan. *Wittgenstein, Grammar and God*. London: Epworth Press, 1970.

Kennedy, Frank, ed. *Inculturation and the Church in North America*. New York: Crossroad, 2006.

Khadduri, Majid, and Herbert J. Liebesnyeds. *Law in the Middle East*. Vol. 1, *Origin and Development of Islamic Law*. New York: AMS Press, 1984.

Kinkupu, Léonard Santedi. *Des prêtres noirs s'interrogent: Cinquante ans après*. Paris: Karthala, 1956.

Kitchling, Gavin. "Why I Gave up African Studies." http://www.arts.uwa.edu .au/MotsPluriels/MP1600gk.html.

Knitter, Paul. "Christianity as Religion: True and Absolute? A Roman Catholic Perspective." In *What Is Religion? An Enquiry for Christian Theology*, edited by Mircea Eliade and David Tracy. Edinburgh: T & T Clark, 1980.

———. "European Protestant and Catholic Approaches to the World Religions: Complements and Contrasts." *Journal of Ecumenical Studies* 12 (Winter 1975): pp. 20–24.

Kombo, James Henry Owino. *The Doctrine of God in African Christian Thought: The Holy Trinity, Theological Hermeneutics and the African Intellectual Culture*. Leiden: Brill, 2007.

Kortenaar, Neil ten. "Becoming African and the Death of Ikemefuna." *University of Toronto Quarterly* 73:2 (Spring 2004): pp. 773–94.

Kukah, Hassan Mathew. *The Fractured Microcosm: The African Condition and the Search for Moral Balance in the New World Order*. Lagos State University Guest Series, no. 1. Lagos, Nigeria: Lagos State University, Faculty of Social Sciences, 1998.

Küng, Hans. *The Church*. London: Search Press, 1978.

———. *On Being a Christian*. Glasgow: Collins Fount, 1974.

Leonard, A. G. *The Lower Niger and Its Tribes*. London: Macmillan, 1906; London: Frank Cass, 1968.

Lonergan, Bernard. *Method in Theology*. Minneapolis: Seabury Press, 1972.

———. "Theology in Its New Context." In *A Second Collection: Papers by Bernard J. F. Lonergan, S.J.*, edited by William F. J. Ryan and Bernard J. Tyrell. London: Darton, Longman and Todd, 1970.

Lugard, Sir Frederick D. *The Dual Mandate in British Tropical Africa*. Edinburgh and London: William Blackwood and Sons, 1923.

MacIntyre, Alasdair. *After Virtue: A Study in Moral Theory*. 2nd ed. London: Gerald Duckworth, 1985.

———. "Epistemological Crises, Narrative and Philosophy of Science." In *Why Narrative: Readings in Narrative Theology*, edited by Stanley Hauerwas and L. Gregory Jones. Grand Rapids, MI: Eerdmans, 1989.

———. *Whose Justice? Which Rationality?* Notre Dame, IN: University of Notre Dame Press, 1988.

MacNamara, Vincent. *Faith and Ethics: Recent Roman Catholicism*. Dublin: Gill and Macmillan; Washington, DC: Georgetown University Press, 1985.

Macquarie, John. *Thinking about God*. London: SCM Press, 1975.

Magesa, Laurenti. *African Religion: The Moral Traditions of Abundant Life*. Maryknoll, NY: Orbis Books, 1997.

———. *Anatomy of Inculturation: Transforming the Church in Africa*. Maryknoll, NY: Orbis Books, 2004.

Mahoney, John. *The Making of Moral Theology: A Study of the Roman Catholic Tradition*. Oxford: Clarendon Press, 1987.

Maluleke, Tinyiko Sam. "Half a Century of African Christian Theologies: Elements of the Emerging Agenda for the Twenty First Century." *Journal of Theology for Southern Africa* 99 (1997): pp. 4–23.

Mazrui, Ali. *The Africans: A Triple Heritage*. London: BBC Publications, 1986.

Mbefo, Luke. *The True African: Impulses for Self-Affirmation*. Enugu, Nigeria: SNAAP Press, 2001.

Mbiti, John S. *African Religions and Philosophy*. 2nd ed. Oxford, Portsmouth, NH: Heinemann, 1990.

———. *Introduction to African Religion*. 2nd ed. Portsmouth, NH: Heinemann, 1991.

McCool, Gerald. *Catholic Theology in the Nineteenth Century*. New York: Seabury Press, 1987.

McCormick, Richard A. *The Critical Calling: Reflections on Moral Dilemmas since Vatican II*. Washington, DC: Georgetown University Press, 1989.

———. "Genetic Technology and Our Common Future." *America* 152:6 (April 27, 1985).

———. "Gustafson's God: Who? What? Where? (ETC)." *Journal of Religious Ethics* 13:1 (Spring 1985): pp. 53–70.

————. "The Judeo-Christian Tradition and Bioethical Codes." In *How Brave a New World? Dilemmas in Bioethics*. Garden City, NY: Doubleday, 1981.

————. "Theology and Bioethics: Christian Foundations." In *Theology and Bioethics: Exploring the Foundations and Frontiers*, edited by Earl E. Shelp. Boston: Reidel, 1985.

Meyer, Birgit. "Make a Complete Break with the Past: Memory and Post-Colonial Modernity in Ghanaian Pentecostalist Discourse." *Journal of Religion in Africa* 28:3 (1998): pp. 316–49.

Miller, J. Michael, ed. *The Encyclicals of John Paul II*. Huntington, IN: Our Sunday Visitor, 1996.

Mounce, H. O. "Understanding a Primitive Society." *Philosophy* 48 (1973).

Muya, Juvénal Ilunga. "Bénézet Bujo: The Awakening of a Systematic and Authentically African Thought." In *African Theology in the 21st Century*. Vol. 1, *The Contribution of the Pioneers*, edited by Bénézet Bujo and Juvénal Ilunga Muya. Nairobi: Paulines Publications Africa, 2003.

Ndiokwere, Nathaniel. *Prophecy and Revolution: The Role of Prophets in the Independent Churches and in Biblical Tradition*. London: SPCK, 1981.

Nelson, James B. "Sexual Salvation: Grace and the Resurrection of the Body." In Odozor, *Sexuality, Marriage and Family: Readings in the Catholic Tradition*.

Nielsen, Kai. *Contemporary Critique of Religion*. London: Macmillan, 1971.

Nnaemeka, Obioma. "The Challenge of Border-Crossing: African Women and Transnational Feminisms." In *Female Circumcision and the Politics of Knowledge: African Women in Imperialist Discourses*, edited by Obioma Nnaemeka. Westport, CT: Praeger, 2005.

Nwabueze, Emeka. "Theoretical Construction and Constructive Theorizing on the Execution of Ikemefuna in Achebe's *Things Fall Apart*: A Study in Critical Dualism." *Research in African Literatures* 31:2 (Summer 2000): pp. 163–73.

Nwachukwu, Mary Sylvia Chinyere. *Creation-Covenant Scheme and Justification by Faith: A Canonical Study of the God-Human Drama in the Pentateuch and the Letter to the Romans*. Rome: Editrice Pontificia Università Gregoriana, 2002.

Nzekwu, Onuorah. *Blade among the Boys*. London: Heinemann, 1972.

Oborji, Francis Anekwe. *Towards a Christian Theology of African Religion: Issues of Interpretation and Mission*. Eldoret, Kenya: AMECEA Gaba Publications, 2005.

Odozor, Paulinus I. "An African Moral Theology of Inculturation: Methodological Considerations." *Theological Studies* 69:3 (Sept. 2008): pp. 583–609.

———. "Classical Moral Theology and the World Church: Some Suggestions on How to Move Forward." *Louvain Studies* 30 (2005): pp. 276–98.

———. "Liturgy and Life: A Discussion from an African Christian Theological Perspective." *Worship* 82:5 (Sept. 2008): pp. 413–33.

———. *Moral Theology in an Age of Renewal: A Study of the Catholic Tradition since Vatican II*. Notre Dame, IN: University of Notre Dame Press, 2003.

———. *Richard A. McCormick and the Renewal of Moral Theology*. Notre Dame, IN: University of Notre Dame Press, 1995.

———, ed. *Sexuality, Marriage and Family: Readings in the Catholic Tradition*. Notre Dame, IN: University of Notre Dame Press, 2001.

———. "Truly African, *and* Wealthy! What Africa Can Learn from Catholic Social Teaching about Sustainable Economic Prosperity." In *The True Wealth of Nations: Catholic Social Thought and Economic Life*, edited by Daniel K. Finn, pp. 267–87. Oxford: Oxford University Press, 2010.

Oduyoye, Mercy Amba. *Daughters of Anowa: African Women and Patriarchy*. Maryknoll, NY: Orbis Books, 1995.

———. "The Value of African Religious Beliefs and Practices for Christian Theology." In *African Theology en Route*, edited by Kofi Appiah-Kubi and Sergio Torres, pp. 109–16. Maryknoll, NY: Orbis Books, 1979.

Ojike, Mbonu. "Christianity in Africa." In *Christianity in Africa: As Seen by the Africans*, edited by Ram Desai, pp. 60–68. Denver, CO: Allan Swallow, 1962. Excerpted from Ojike, Mbonu. *My Africa*. New York: John Day, 1946.

O'Keefe, Mark. *What Are They Saying about Social Sin?* Mahwah, NJ: Paulist Press, 1990.

Okeke, Romeo Igwebuike. *The Osu Concept in Igboland: A Study of the Types of Slavery in Igbo Speaking Areas of Nigeria*. Enugu, Nigeria: SNAAP Press, 1986.

Okorocha, Cyril C. *The Meaning of Religious Conversion in Africa: The Case of the Igbo of Nigeria*. Aldershot, UK: Avebury, 1987.

Okoye, James C. "African Theology." In *Dictionary of Mission: Theology, History, Perspectives*, edited by Karl Müller, Theo Sundermeier, Stephen B. Bevans, and Richard H. Bliese. Maryknoll, NY: Orbis Books, 1997.

———. "Inculturation and Theology in Africa." *Mission Studies* 14:1 & 2, 27 & 28 (1997): pp. 64–83.

Okoye, James Chukwuma. *Scripture in the Church: The Synod on the Word of God*. Collegeville, MN: Liturgical Press, 2011.

O'Meara, Thomas. "Aquinas in Africa." *America* (Feb. 6, 2006): pp. 14–17.

Onaiyekan, John O. "Islam and the Church Family of God in Africa: Beyond Dialogue to Collaboration in the Service of Reconciliation, Justice and

Peace." http://www.vatican.va/news_services/press/sinodo/documents
/bollettino_23_ii_speciale-africa-2009/02_inglese/b10_02.html.

O'Neil, William, "African Moral Theology." *Theological Studies* 62 (2001): pp. 122–39.

Opata, Damian U. "Eternal Sacred Order versus Conventional Wisdom: A Consideration of Moral Culpability in the Killing of Ikemefuna in *Things Fall Apart.*" *Research in African Literatures* 18:1 (Spring 1987): pp. 71–79.

Orobator, Agbonkhiameghe E. *From Crisis to Kairos: The Mission of the Church in the Time of HIV/AIDS, Refugees and Poverty.* Nairobi: Paulines Publications Africa, 2005.

Osiek, Carolyn. "The Family in Early Christianity: 'Family Values' Revisited." In Odozor, *Sexuality, Marriage and Family.*

Paris, Peter. *The Spirituality of African Peoples: The Search for a Common Moral Discourse.* Minneapolis: Fortress Press, 1995.

Peel, J. D. Y. *Aladura: A Religious Movement among the Yoruba.* London: Oxford University Press, 1968.

Phillips, D. Z. *Belief, Change and Forms of Life.* Atlantic Highlands, NJ: Humanities Press International, 1986.

Pius XI, Pope. *Rerum Ecclesiae.* In *The Papal Encyclicals 1903–1939*, translated by Claudia Carlen. Raleigh, NC: McGrath, 1981.

Pius XII, Pope. *Fidei Donum.* In *The Papal Encyclicals 1903–1939*, translated by Claudia Carlen. Raleigh, NC: McGrath, 1981.

———. *Mystici Corporis.* London: Catholic Truth Society, 1943.

Plato. "Euthyphro." In *Five Great Dialogues of Plato: Euthyphro, Apology, Crito, Meno, Phaedo*, translated by Benjamin Jowett. Claremont, CA: Coyote Canyon Press, 2009.

Pojman, Louis P. *Ethics: Discovering Right and Wrong.* 4th ed. Belmont, CA: Wadsworth Thompson Learning, 2002.

Pope, Stephen J. "Overview of the Ethics of Thomas Aquinas." In *The Ethics of Aquinas*, edited by Stephen J. Pope, pp. 30–53. Washington, DC: Georgetown University Press, 2002.

Porter, Jean. *Nature as Reason: A Thomistic Theory of the Natural Law.* Grand Rapids, MI: Eerdmans, 2005.

———. "Right Reason and the Love of God: The Parameters of Aquinas' Moral Theology." In *The Theology of Thomas Aquinas*, edited by Rik Van Nieuwenhove and Joseph Wawrykow, pp. 167–91. Notre Dame, IN: University of Notre Dame Press, 2005.

Putnam, Hilary. *Realism and Reason: Philosophical Papers.* Vol. 3. Cambridge: Cambridge University Press, 1985.

Rahner, Karl. "Anthropology." In *Theological Dictionary*, edited by Karl Rahner and Herbert Vorgrimler, pp. 25–28. New York: Seabury Press, 1973.

———. *Foundations of Christian Faith: An Introduction to the Idea of Christianity*. Translated by William V. Dych. New York: Seabury Press, 1978.

Ratzinger, Joseph. *Introduction to Christianity*. Translated by J. R. Foster. San Francisco: Ignatius Press, 1990; San Francisco: Communion Books, 2004.

———. *Principles of Catholic Theology*. San Francisco: Ignatius Press, 1987.

Reeder, John P., Jr. "Religious Ethics as a Field and Discipline." *Journal of Religious Ethics* 6:1 (Spring 1978): pp. 32–53.

———. "What Is a Religious Ethics?" *Journal of Religious Ethics* 25:3, 25th Anniversary Supplement (1997): pp. 157–81.

Rhonheimer, Martin. *Natural Law and Practical Reason: A Thomist View of Moral Autonomy*. Translated by Gerald Malsbary. New York: Fordham University Press, 2000.

Rikhof, Herwi. "Trinity." In *The Theology of Thomas Aquinas*, edited by Rik Van Nieuwenhove and Joseph Wawrykow, pp. 36–57. Notre Dame, IN: University of Notre Dame Press, 2005.

Roberts, Christopher C. *Creation and Covenant: The Significance of Sexual Difference in the Moral Theology of Marriage*. London: T & T Clark International, 2007.

Sarpong, Peter. "Christianity Should Be Africanized, Not Africa Christianized." *AFER* (1975).

Schillebeeckx, Edward. *Christ: The Experience of Jesus as Lord*. New York: Seabury Press, 1980.

———. *Jesus: An Experiment in Christology*. Translated by Hubert Haskins. London: Collins, 1979.

———. *On Christian Faith: The Spiritual, Ethical and Political Dimensions*. New York: Crossroad, 1987.

Schineller, Peter. *A Handbook on Inculturation*. New York: Paulist Press, 1990.

Schlette, Heinz Robert. *Towards a Theology of Religions*. Translated by W. J. O'Hara. New York: Herder and Herder, 1966.

Schnackenburg, Rudolf. *The Moral Teaching of the New Testament*. London: Burns and Oates, 1965.

Schneiders, Sandra. *The Revelatory Text: Interpreting the New Testament as Sacred Scripture*. 2nd ed. Collegeville, MN: Liturgical Press, 1999.

Schrage, Wolfgang. *The Ethics of the New Testament*. Translated by David Green. Philadelphia: Fortress Press, 1988.

Schreiter, Robert. *Constructing Local Theologies*. Maryknoll, NY: Orbis Books, 1985.

Schüller, Bruno. "Various Types of Grounding for Ethical Norms." In *Readings in Moral Theology*. Vol. 1, *Moral Norms and Catholic Tradition*, edited by Charles E. Curran and Richard A. McCormick. New York: Paulist Press, 1979.

Schüssler Fiorenza, Elisabeth. *In Memory of Her: A Feminist Theological Reconstruction of Christian Origins*. New York: Crossroad, 1983.

Secundi, C. Plini Cacili. *Epistolarum Libri Decem*. Edited by R. A. B. Mynors. Oxford: Clarendon Press, 1963.

Senghor, Leopold Sedor. *African Socialism*. Translated by Mercer Cook. New York: Praeger, 1964.

Setiloane, Gabriel. "Where Are We in African Theology?" In *African Theology en Route*, edited by Kofi Appiah-Kubi and Sergio Torres. Maryknoll, NY: Orbis Books, 1979.

Shils, Edward. *Tradition*. London: Faber, 1981.

Shorter, Aylward. *African Christian Spirituality*. London: Geoffrey Chapman, 1978.

———. *Toward a Theology of Inculturation*. Maryknoll, NY: Orbis Books, 1988.

Sittler, Joseph. *The Structure of Christian Ethics*. Louisville: Westminster John Knox Press, 1980.

Snodgrass, Klyne R. *Stories with Intent: A Comprehensive Guide to the Parables of Jesus*. Grand Rapids, MI: Eerdmans, 2008.

Spiritan International School of Theology. *Program of Studies*. Enugu, Nigeria: Spiritan International School of Theology, 1998.

Spohn, William. "Jesus and Ethics." *CTSA Proceedings* 51 (1994): pp. 40–57.

Stout, Geoffrey. *Ethics after Babel: The Languages of Morals and Their Discontents*. Boston: Beacon Press, 1988.

Stout, Jeffrey. "Commitments and Traditions in the Study of Religious Ethics." *Journal of Religious Ethics* 25:3, 25th Anniversary Supplement (1997): pp. 23–56.

Synod of Bishops. "Justice in the World." In *Catholic Social Thought: The Documentary Heritage*, edited by David J. O'Brien and Thomas A. Shannon, pp. 288–300. Maryknoll, NY: Orbis Books, 1998.

———. "2nd Special Assembly for Africa." In *Instrumentum Laboris*. Vatican City: Editrice Vaticana, 2009.

Tavard, Gerorge H. "Tradition." In *The New Dictionary of Theology*, edited by Joseph A. Komonchak, Mary Collins, and Dermot A. Lane, pp. 1037–41. Collegeville, MN: Liturgical Press, 1987.

Tempels, Placide. *Bantu-Philosophie: Ontologie und Ethik*. Paris: Présence africaine, 1959.

Thomas Aquinas, Saint. *Summa Theologica.* Translated by the Fathers of the English Dominican Province. New York: Benziger Brothers, 1941; Notre Dame, IN: Ave Maria Press, 1981.

Tillich, Paul. *Christianity and the Encounter of the World Religions.* New York: Columbia University Press, 1964.

———. "The Significance of the History of Religions for the Systematic Theologian." In *The Future of Religions,* edited by Jerald C. Bauer, pp. 80–94. New York: Harper & Row, 1966.

———. *Systematic Theology.* 3 vols. Chicago: University of Chicago Press, 1951–63.

Toulmin, Stephen. "Nature and Nature's God." *Journal of Religious Ethics* 13:1 (Spring 1985): pp. 37–52.

Toynbee, Arnold. *Christianity among the Religions of the World.* New York: Scribner, 1957.

Tracy, David. *The Analogical Imagination: Christian Theology and the Culture of Pluralism.* New York: Crossroad, 1989.

Turner, Harold. *Religious Innovation in Africa.* Boston: G. K. Hall, 1979.

Tutu, Desmond. "Whither African Theology?" In *Christianity in Independent Africa,* edited by Edward Fasholé-Luke, Richard Gray, Adrian Hastings, and Godwin Tasie, p. 368. Bloomington: Indiana University Press, 1979.

Ugwu, Bonaventure Ikenna. *The Holy Spirit as Present and Active in the Cosmic Turmoil and Human Suffering: A Dialogue between Pierre Teilhard de Chardin and Jürgen Moltmann.* Rome: Editrice Pontificia Università Gregoriana, Facultas Theologiae, 2004.

———. *Holy Spirit: Fire from Above.* Enugu, Nigeria: Sans Press, 2008.

Ukpong, Justin. *African Theologies Now: A Profile.* Eldoret, Kenya: Gaba Publications, 1984.

———. "Developments in Biblical Interpretation in Africa: Historical and Hermeneutical Directions." In *The Bible in Africa: Transactions, Trajectories and Trends,* edited by Gerald O. West and Musa W. Dube, pp. 11–28. Leiden: Brill, 2000.

Ukwuije, Bede. *Trinité et Inculturation.* Paris: Desclée de Brouwer, 2008.

Uzukwu, Elochukwu. *A Listening Church: Autonomy and Communion in African Churches.* Maryknoll, NY: Orbis Books, 1996.

———. *Worship as Body Language. Introduction to Christian Worship: An African Orientation.* Collegeville, MN: Liturgical Press, 1997.

Uzukwu, Elochukwu E. *God, Spirit, and Human Wholeness: Appropriating Faith and Culture in West African Style.* Eugene, OR: Pickwick Publications, 2012.

van Beeck, Franz Jozef. *God Encountered: A Contemporary Catholic Systematic Theology.* Vol. 1, *Understanding the Christian Faith.* San Francisco: Harper & Row, 1989.

Vatican Council II. *Decrees of the Ecumenical Councils.* Vol. 2, *Trent to Vatican II.* Edited by Norman P. Tanner. London: Sheed and Ward; Washington, DC: Georgetown University Press, 1990.

———. *Vatican Council II: The Basic Sixteen Documents: Constitutions, Decrees, Declarations.* Edited by Austin Flannery. Northport, NY: Costello, 1996.

———. *Vatican Council II: The Conciliar and Postconciliar Documents.* Edited by Austin Flannery. Dublin: Dominican Publications, 1981.

Walls, Andrew. "Africa and Christian Identity." *Mission Focus* 6:7 (1978): pp. 11–13.

———. "The Gospel as the Prisoner and Liberator of Culture." *Faith and Thought* 108:1–2 (1981): pp. 39–52.

———. *The Missionary Movement in Christian History: Studies in the Transmission of Faith.* Maryknoll, NY: Orbis Books; Edinburgh: T & T Clark, 1996.

Watt, W. Montgomery. *What Is Islam?* 2nd ed. London: Longman; New York: Praeger, 1979.

Wawrykow, Joseph. "Grace." In *The Theology of Thomas Aquinas*, edited by Rik Van Nieuwenhove and Joseph Wawrykow, pp. 192–221. Notre Dame, IN: University of Notre Dame Press, 2005.

Weigel, George. *Witness to Hope: The Biography of Pope John Paul II.* New York: Cliff Street Books/HarperCollins, 1999.

Whitney, Barry L. *What Are They Saying about God and Evil?* New York: Paulist Press, 1989.

INDEX

abomination (*aru*), 261–63
abortion, 253, 267, 291
Achebe, Chinua. *See also Things Fall
Apart*
    Arrow of God, 96, 254
    on *chi*, 209–10
    No Longer at Ease, 84–85
    The Trouble with Nigeria, 284
administrative palaver, 157
adultery, 199–200
Africa
    art of, 38
    colonialism in, 15–16, 18–20, 22,
        32, 91, 167
    communitarianism in, 210–13,
        226–28, 238, 250, 326n22
    concept of, 76
    historical consciousness of, 20–21
    historical context of, 14–16,
        300n22
    intellectuals in, 90–92, 106
    internecine conflicts in, 18–20
    issues in, 3
    leadership in, 284–85
    missionaries from, 1
    moral actors in, 158, 160–61
    moral reasoning in context of,
        240–50
    pessimism about, 235–36
    renewal of, 235–36
    "savages" in, 11

    seminaries in, 1, 41–44
    slavery and, 18, 159–60, 165, 212
    social stratification in, 18
    as spiritual lung, 190
    Western culture destroying, 153,
        204, 291–92
Africae Munus (Benedict XVI)
    Second African Synod and, 201,
        222, 278–79, 281–87, 289–91,
        334n19
    on women, 289–90
African Catholic Church
    growth of, 1
    Igbo, 26
    inherited Christian tradition of, 22
    social questions in, 14
African Christianity
    African intellectual challenge to,
        90–92, 106
    AICs in, 17–18, 38, 108–10
    anthropology of, 233–36
    authentic, 31–32
    changes caused by, 86
    continuity and, 107–10
    growth of, 16–17, 77
    history of, 16
    introduction of, 11, 86
    Judaism and, 109–10
    liturgical music in, 38, 305n85
    moral beliefs of, 52–53
    morality in, 52–53, 176–205

Paulinus Ikechukwu Odozor, C.S.Sp.
is associate professor of moral theology, the theology of world church, and
Africana studies at the University of Notre Dame. He is the author of *Moral
Theology in an Age of Renewal: A Study of the Catholic Tradition since
Vatican II* and *Richard McCormick and the Renewal of Moral Theology,*
and editor of *Sexuality, Marriage, and Family,* all published by the University
of Notre Dame Press.

"This is an ambitious book, a big book. The scholarship is sound and the author engages a range of authors and their views. Odozor takes seriously the critical and moral demands of Christian theology as well as those of African indigenous religions and their cultures. There is perhaps nothing so thoroughgoing on this topic since Bénézet Bujo's *Foundations of an African Ethic: Beyond the Universal Claims of Western Morality*."

—*M. Shawn Copeland, Boston College*

"There are very few in theological ethics who can draw people into conversation through their combination of insightful argument and their gracious welcome to those in other academic fields. In *Morality Truly Christian, Truly African*, Paulinus Odozor succeeds on both counts, speaking boldly but charitably across ecclesial, cultural, and academic divides. By articulating an ethical methodology drawn from the moral reasoning of the African Christian churches, taking seriously the challenges of cultural particularity but also moral realism, and also giving the reader a sense of the complex pursuit of the truth about God and the human in history, Odozor has dared (and delivered) what few would attempt but many need—a genuinely comparative theological ethics."

—*David A. Clairmont, Tisch Family Associate Professor of Theology, University of Notre Dame*

"This work is truly astounding in its breadth and depth, and is bound to become a standard textbook in African moral theology. New is the accent on received Christian tradition as a principal source of such moral theology. Odozor engages in dialogue with various moral theologians (Karl Barth, Paul Tillich, Paul Knitter, and James Gustafson) and theologians of African morality (John Mbiti, Laurenti Magesa, and Elochukwu Uzukwu). The seven guidelines for theological inculturation in Africa are particularly illuminating and may be a good entry point into this work for the nonspecialist."

—*James Chukwuma Okoye, C.S.Sp., Duquesne University*

"Odozor has produced a definitive study that will determine the future of theological conversations about the place of African moral theology in world Christianity. His triple dialogue with African Christian theologies, Catholic fundamental moral theologies, and African traditional religious ethics is comprehensive in scope, rich in depth, systematic in analysis, and encyclopedic in presentation. This is Odozor at his best as he displays the traits of an ethical reasoning which is both Christian and African, addresses contextual questions without being parochial, and engages with moral issues which will help navigate the shifting landscape of World Catholicism."

—*Stan Chu Ilo, DePaul University*